‘skil

AF

M

ent

the understanding of Australia’s involvement in the Great War.’
Chief of Air Force Reading List, 2015

‘significant conclusions, supported by detailed analysis . . .
Molkentin deserves much praise for producing a
scholarly and accessible study; highly recommended.’
James Pugh, *Journal of the Society of Army Historical Research*

‘All aficionados of WWI will wish to read this book.’
Christian Busby, *Aerospace*

Michael Molkentin is a teacher and historian with a particular interest in aviation and air power. He has a PhD in History from the University of New South Wales and in 2014 the Australian War Memorial awarded his doctoral research the Bryan Gandevia Prize for Military-Medical History. Michael's first book, *Fire in the Sky: The Australian Flying Corps in the First World War* was published by Allen & Unwin in 2010 and Highly Commended in the Fellowship of Australian Writers Sid Harta Literature Award for Non-fiction. His second book, *Flying the Southern Cross: Aviators Charles Ulm and Charles Kingsford Smith* was published by the National Library of Australia in 2012. Oxford University Press published his third book, *Australia and the War in the Air*, in 2014 as part of its Centenary History of Australia and the Great War series.

ANZAC & AVIATOR

THE REMARKABLE STORY OF SIR ROSS SMITH AND THE 1919 ENGLAND TO AUSTRALIA AIR RACE

MICHAEL MOLKENTIN

ALLEN&UNWIN
SYDNEY • MELBOURNE • AUCKLAND • LONDON

Program

Seven Nights
and
Six Matinees
At 2.30 and 8 p.m.

TOWN HALL
MELBOURNE
COMMENCING
Saturday Night
July 3rd, 1920

MONDAY	-	JULY 5
TUESDAY	-	JULY 6
WEDNESDAY	-	JULY 7
THURSDAY	-	JULY 8
FRIDAY	-	JULY 9
SATURDAY	-	JULY 10

UNION THEATRES LTD
Present

The ROSS SMITH FLIGHT

from England to Australia

Personally related to you, in conjunction with the epoch-making Motion Pictures, by

SIR ROSS SMITH, HIMSELF

After a triumphant season in Sydney, and prior to his departure for England.

First published in 2019

Allen & Unwin
83 Alexander Street
Crows Nest NSW 2065
Australia
Phone: (61 2) 8425 0100
Email: info@allenandunwin.com
Web: www.allenandunwin.com

A catalogue record for this book is available from the National Library of Australia

ISBN 978 1 74237 919 7

Internal design by Lisa White
Maps by Julia Eim and Keith Mitchell
Page v image: 'The Ross Smith flight from England to Australia' (brochure), 1920, SLVIC, H13093.
Set in 11/17.5 pt Minion by Post Pre-press Group, Australia
Printed and bound in Australia by Griffin Press, part of Ovato

10 9 8 7 6 5 4 3 2 1

MIX
Paper from responsible sources
FSC® C009448
www.fsc.org

The paper in this book is FSC® certified. FSC® promotes environmentally responsible, socially beneficial and economically viable management of the world's forests.

For Harriet and Edmund: my animal vet and aviator aspirant.

FOREWORD

He was courageous. He was ambitious. He was skilled. He was visionary. He could be ruthless. He was someone born of a new nation. But he was of a time now long past. And yet in the language of a later generation it could be said he had the 'right stuff'.

The story of Ross Macpherson Smith is usually of his winning the 1919 Great Air Race, showing that England to Australia flight was possible, in theory at least. Yet even that impressive achievement has been largely lost in the mists of history. But it is his background in the years leading up to the race that defined him, a background forged in the horrors of the conflict in Gallipoli, and in the dangerous new form of warfare, aerial combat.

Ross Smith grew up in the last years of the pre-war British Empire, deep in the South Australian outback, as far from the seat of that imperial power as could be imagined. He learned how to survive in harsh conditions, how to hunt and shoot. He learned to be resourceful. Survival depended upon it. He also learned what it meant to be a member of the empire, and that meant defending it. But that obligation was not mandated, rather it was seen as an expected and natural part of any young man's development. So when the call of war came, for many like Ross, enlisting was a step to be taken without questioning the merits or otherwise of the decision.

Serving in the infantry took him, with so many of that youthful and optimistic generation, to that lonely peninsula called Gallipoli. It was a name about to be brutally carved into the legacy of too many Australian families. My own maternal grandfather was wounded there. At Gallipoli they learned just how ghastly modern warfare was. Miraculously Ross Smith survived and certainly fought with distinction. But with the death of a younger brother in France, it left him bitter toward the enemy. And when he saw what flying machines could do it was not surprising that he would be drawn to the new form of fighting that enemy, perhaps seeing it as more surgical and more controlled than the bloody chaos and carnage of trench warfare.

It was the subsequent aerial combat experiences that groomed Ross Smith to be the winner of the 1919 Great Air Race. Although the race took 28 days to fly, his success ultimately came down to meticulous planning based on his years of flying and his years of outback life learning to survive and to be resourceful. This story is a unique part of the Australian character and Michael Molkentin captures it brilliantly in this book. It is a very well researched summary of the steps Ross Smith took in his long and sometimes frightening journey to worldwide fame, ending tragically in an untimely death at an early age.

Ross Smith and his generation emerged just a few years after Australia was established as a nation, and they helped define that new nation. His winning the race particularly lifted the new nation in spirit after four weary years of a horrible war. It was also a hugely significant event in the annals of aviation and, judging by the press reports of the day, was applauded the same way as the moon landing that took place a mere 50 years later. My maternal grandfather who served at Gallipoli at the same time as Ross Smith lived to witness both events. What an extraordinary time to live through.

But the race, the war and people like Ross Smith are of a time long past. When I flew my first space flight in 1996, I chose to honour the memory of him and his flight by carrying his pilot wings into space with me. One wonders what he would have made of that and the speed and comfort that the England–Australia flight can be flown in today.

Andy Thomas
NASA Astronaut (Retired)
Houston, Texas
February 2019

CONTENTS

PART FOUR: '14,000 MILES THROUGH THE AIR' 1918–1919

PART FIVE: 'THE FOREMOST LIVING AVIATOR' 1919–1922

PREFACE

I first became acquainted with Ross Smith while researching the airmen of the Australian Flying Corps for my first book, *Fire in the Sky*, and the PhD thesis (and later second book) that I subsequently wrote about Australia's aerial involvement in the Great War. One of my thesis supervisors at UNSW Canberra, Professor Peter Stanley, had come across Ross Smith's papers at the State Library of South Australia while researching his book, *Digger Smith and Australia's Great War*. He suggested I have a look at them.

I knew Ross Smith to be one of Australia's most successful pilots in the Great War and one of the world's first great pioneering aviators. I knew his victory in the 1919 England-to-Australia Air Race had contributed to bringing the air age to Australia. I knew that he had died soon after the race in an accident while preparing to circumnavigate the globe by air.

Reading Ross's letters and his diaries, though, I realised that there was much more to his life than the flight from England to Australia in 1919 which made him world famous. He had, it turned out, an atypical upbringing—one that transcended city and bush as well as social class and, indeed, which had little about it that suggested a renowned pioneer aviator in the making. At the same time, in his youth we perceive the germ of the towering ideals that once gave many lives a unifying sense of purpose and instilled them with a cohesive worldview—one built upon the cornerstones of nation, empire, race, civilisation and God.

During days spent in the quiet stillness of the State Library of South Australia's reading room, I discovered that Ross Smith's wartime experiences extended beyond his service as an aviator in the Australian Flying Corps. Before that, he fought in the Australian light horse—first at Gallipoli, where he endured the worst of that campaign's depravities, and later in the Sinai Desert, where he led a section of machine guns at the pivotal battle of Romani. Ross's letters and diary confronted me with an experience of combat at odds with the popular assumption that those in his generation were helpless victims of a futile war. Combat—and indeed killing—thrilled Ross; he perceived the war as being fought for worthwhile causes even after suffering the loss of friends and a brother. War stoked Ross's ambitions to better his station in life and provided the circumstances to do so. A tragedy of global and personal dimensions, the Great War nevertheless provided Ross Smith with opportunities he could not have hoped for in his pre-war job as a warehouseman.

Besides the air race in 1919, the Smith family papers also document Ross's earlier and little-known involvement in a Royal Air Force mission to survey an air route across the Middle East and Asia. And whereas the Ross Smith story I knew concluded with his successful landing in Darwin in December 1919 to claim the government's £10,000 prize, the archival record reveals a final—albeit brief—chapter in his life, one characterised by the relentless pressure of celebrity and the restless pursuit of a next great adventure. Ross Smith's efforts to exceed his earlier achievement of flying an aeroplane halfway around the globe would end in the tragedy of a life cut short.

To paraphrase John Lewis Gaddis, history is not the past—it is, much as a map is to a landscape, a representation of the past: a compressed, finite and simplified textual depiction of an infinitely complex reality. Like maps, all histories have their specific purposes and audiences—and their limitations. In this book, I have attempted to map Ross Smith's life and to position it in the contexts that shaped and defined it. As much as I felt that Ross's life would make for an absorbing and compelling story in itself, I also selected him because I wanted to explore how individual lives and the historical contexts that contain them interact. How was Ross Smith shaped by his circumstances—by his family, his education, his friends, his wartime experiences, his formative and then subsequent experiences of aviation and the other technological innovations of his day? And how did Ross make history? Did he, among the millions of individuals who fought the Great War, make a difference—indeed, could anybody? How did his flying contribute to the evolution of aviation during and immediately after the Great War? Perhaps most pertinently, what can we learn about the extraordinary period straddled by Ross's short life—an era of political, social, cultural and technological change, not to mention unprecedented carnage, through his eyes and through his experiences?

While not always leading to conclusive answers, these questions have nevertheless guided me: they acted as my compass as I explored the contours of Ross Smith's life and the extraordinary years in which he lived in and interacted with the world. I hope that, through this book, you discover a man as fascinating and a life as deeply absorbing as I did, and that you come away with a better understanding of a past world that resounds with such clamour in our own.

MAPS

TEXT NOTES

Military acronyms and abbreviations

AFC – Australian Flying corps

AIF – Australian Imperial Force

ANZAC – Australian and New Zealand Army Corps

CO – Commanding Officer

DFC – Distinguished Flying Cross

MC – Military Cross

NCO – Non-commissioned officer

RFC – Royal Flying Corps

RAF – Royal Air Force

RAAF – Royal Australian Air Force

Australian Flying Corps squadron nomenclature

The squadrons of the Australian Flying Corps had a confusing variety of titles during the war. This reflects their ambiguous status as units raised, administered and paid by the Australian government but under the operational command of the British Royal Flying Corps (and, after its formation in April 1918, the Royal Air Force). For the sake of clarity, Ross's squadron is referred to as No. 1 Squadron throughout the text, as it was eventually officially titled in 1918.

Military organisation

The basic unit of the Australian light horse during the Great War was the regiment, three of which made up a light horse brigade. Regiments were usually commanded by a lieutenant colonel and, at full strength, comprised

25 officers and 400 men. Light horse regiments were divided into three squadrons (A, B and C Squadrons) and these were, in turn, each organised into four troops. Each troop comprised ten sections of four men. At the beginning of the war each light horse regiment had a section of machine guns. In mid-1916 the regimental machine gun sections were grouped into brigade-level machine gun squadrons.

The basic unit of the Australian Flying Corps was the squadron. It typically comprised around 180 men and two dozen officers; by the middle of the war squadrons operated 18 aircraft. Each squadron consisted of a headquarters and three flights: A, B and C Flights. A major commanded a squadron while captains commanded each of the flights. In the AFC pilots and observers were practically always commissioned officers (lieutenants). Two or more squadrons served together in a wing; multiple wings made up a brigade. Because of the small size of the AFC (only four operational squadrons during the war; three on the Western Front and one in the Middle East) Australian squadrons always operated in British wings and brigades, alongside British squadrons and under the operational command of British officers.

PROLOGUE

BROOKLANDS AERODROME, WEYBRIDGE, ENGLAND

1 August 1910

A large crowd has come out from London on the train to pass a hot and bright Bank Holiday Monday. They want to see for themselves what the papers have been reporting: stories of men in flying machines, taking off from the grassy field at the centre of the great oval race track and flying—*flying!* Machines have allowed humans to defy nature and become like the birds.

There are three boys in the crowd: Australian army cadets visiting Britain as part of a tour around the world. One of them is Ross Smith; he is seventeen years old and aspires to a career of soldiering on behalf of the empire. But even as he looks forward, imagining his future, young Ross also looks back: to the 'deeds that won the empire'—to wars fought by Clive and Wellington, Gordon and Roberts during the past two centuries.

Today, though, the spectacle of seeing men fly might prompt him to think of warfare differently—perhaps even to conceive of a different future altogether. For the time is not far off when these frail, ungainly contraptions putting across the grass and circling slowly overhead will change everything for Ross Smith, for his friends and for the world.

11 November 1919

There is a break in the storm and Ross Smith is determined to start.

At his word, the giant, twin-engine biplane bomber is wheeled out of its hangar and prepared for flight. Conceived to bomb Berlin in the recently concluded Great War, tomorrow, from nearby Hounslow aerodrome, this aeroplane, a Vickers Vimy, will begin a journey halfway around the globe—a journey intended to show the world that aeroplanes, conceived in peacetime but brought to maturity in the terrible crucible of war, can now revolutionise international travel.

With his brother, Keith, and their mechanics, Jim Bennett and Wally Shiers, Ross has accepted the Australian government's challenge: £10,000 for the first airmen to fly from England to Australia. But they will need to do it within 30 days.

Of all the competitors attracted by the huge cash prize, Ross and his crew have an enormous advantage. Besides his standing as one of Australia's most successful wartime aviators—a reputation earned during nearly 800 hours of flying in the Middle East and acknowledged through half a dozen decorations for skill and courage—Ross is one of the only people in the world who has personally surveyed the air route to Australia. Earlier in 1919, as part of a Royal Air Force mission, Ross flew to India and then sailed through Southeast Asia, identifying places where a pilot might land during a flight to Australia.

The engines start and Ross and his crew climb aboard. The Vimy taxies out across Brooklands' grass airfield and turns into the wind. Ross and Keith exchange a glance, throttle levers are pushed forward. An epic journey has begun.

13 April 1922

Keith Smith is frustrated. Of all the days he could be running late, why did it have to be this one?

He has just arrived at the factory of Vickers Limited at Brooklands—one of hundreds who have gathered to see Ross and him test the Viking IV, a new amphibious aeroplane that Vickers has given them for their next great adventure. The brothers plan to become the first to circumnavigate the globe by air. It has taken two years for Ross and Keith to convince the company to back this audacious proposition, but the worldwide renown they gained in 1919, on being the first airmen to fly from England to Australia, has helped their case. If anyone can do it, it will be Ross and Keith Smith.

Just as Keith arrives at Brooklands, the Viking—which truly does resemble a boat with biplane wings attached—is taking off. Ross has decided to start without him.

The crowd cheers as the Viking lifts off, with Ross waving from the cockpit. It climbs steeply. It is his first time flying the aircraft, but Ross seems keen to put it through its paces.

Climbing to 1500 feet, Ross flies a circuit, following the motor racing track that surrounds the airfield. He is above the southern boundary when he banks the Viking onto its wing-tips and turns back towards the airfield. Is he preparing to land? Is he 'stunting'?

Part-way through the manoeuvre, the Viking's nose drops and the aeroplane tumbles into a spin. In an instant, the machine is spiralling towards the ground.

Panic grips Keith. The crowd gasps. The Viking spins out of control.

PART ONE

'A DETERMINED BOY'

1892–1914

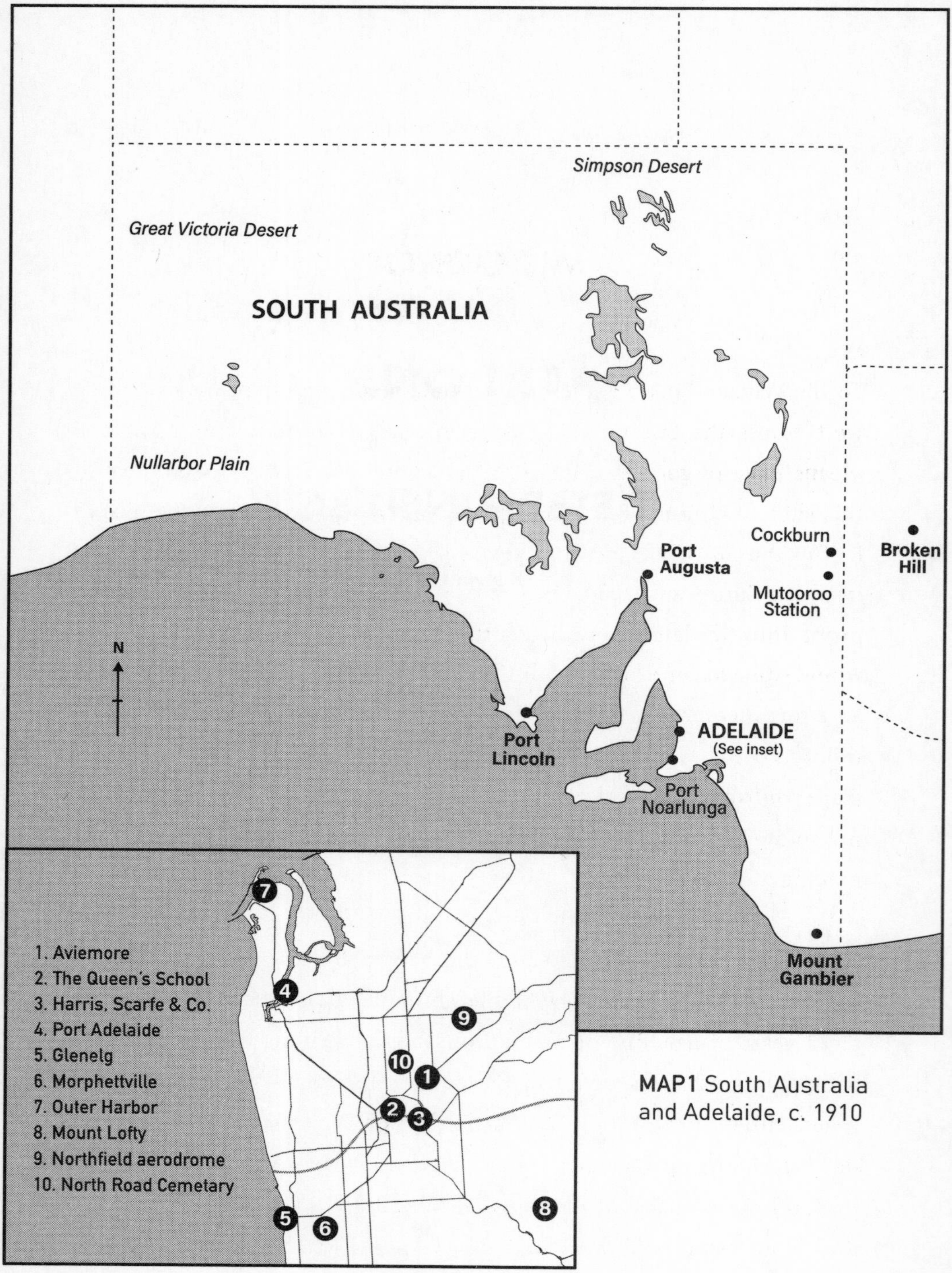

MAP1 South Australia and Adelaide, c. 1910

1

MUTOOROO

To the Wiljakali people, the original inhabitants of the plains extending west across the South Australian border from Broken Hill, *Mutooroo* means 'place of good food'.[1] For the white men who dispossessed them of this land and 'improved' it into sheep grazing stations during the second half of the nineteenth century, it was a vast and unforgiving space—one in which Europeans faced a perennial struggle to survive, let alone turn a profit. Into this landscape, during the latter part of the 1800s, the settlers would come to confront the daunting prospect of bending it to their will—an effort measured in tens of thousands of work hours and sustained by millions of yards of fencing wire. The desolate emptiness with which this place confronted the white families who tried to transform it in their own image drained the life from some; yet, paradoxically, it proved to be the making of others.

In early 1888, a Scottish migrant named Andrew Smith arrived on Mutooroo's sun-parched plains with his new bride, Jessie Macpherson. The son of a ploughman, Andrew had left humble circumstances in Scotland at 22 years of age, one of many thousands of Britons who dispersed—willingly or otherwise—out to the empire's colonial fringes during the nineteenth century. Arriving in Australia in 1875, Andrew spent four years in Western Australia, working in its burgeoning pastoral industry. Moving to South Australia in 1879, he found work on Paratoo station, one of the colony's first long-term, large-scale pastoral leases. The leaseholders, Sir Thomas Elder and Peter Waite (both Scottish migrants themselves), had divided the 1.7 million acres (688,000 hectares) they held into two neighbouring properties, Paratoo and Mutooroo; together, they extended 175 kilometres into South Australia from the New South Wales border. For the next eight years, Andrew toiled as part of an enormous effort by Elder and Waite to transform Paratoo from 'waste lands of the Crown', as the colonial government officially designated it, into fenced paddocks sustained by wells and dams to supplement the region's intermittent and generally small amount of rain.[2] When Elder and Waite's lease on Paratoo expired in 1888, the two pastoralists switched the focus of their business to the neighbouring property, Mutooroo. Impressed with Andrew Smith's work on their former station, they appointed him the station manager and charged him with developing its 620,000 acres of scrub and grass plains into another profitable wool venture.

Andrew had met Jessie Macpherson while working in Western Australia, but—as he later admitted—it took him three years to convince her to marry him.[3] It may have been, as one family member explained, that Jessie's father did not approve of Andrew, 'so he left, but returned and married her, and took her back to Mutooroo'.[4]

Although both Scots, Andrew and Jessie's father, Donald Macpherson, hailed from opposite ends of colonial society. A highlander from Kingussie, Macpherson had been one of the first white men to settle on the Victoria Plains after arriving in Western Australia in 1845. During the next four decades, he transformed his property, Glentromie, into one of the colony's most successful grazing stations. Indeed, by the time Donald Macpherson died in August 1887—perhaps not coincidentally around the time Jessie consented to marry Andrew—Glentromie's 150,000 acres supported 8000 sheep and a thoroughbred breeding venture that produced successful racehorses.[5] In the same week that Andrew and Jessie married, in February 1888, Glentromie sold at auction for £11,000.[6] Typical of the time, in his will Donald allocated most of the estate to his sons; Jessie received £200—about the average salary of a female teacher in those days.[7] It was a start, but she and her new husband would begin their lives together in South

Australia with little apart from their own determination to improve their circumstances.

Arriving at Mutooroo in early 1888, Andrew and Jessie moved into the general manager's house, a stone-walled structure surrounded by a verandah, onto which all its rooms opened. Less than a couple of hundred metres from the house, a creek crossed the homestead on its course south from Cockburn, the closest town at nearly 40 kilometres away. Broad and shallow, and divided in half by a sandy bar from which sugar gums grew in a line, the creek was, for most of the year, as dry as the landscape through which it ran. Across the yard from the Smiths' home, work had commenced on the new station's work buildings: offices, sheds, a blacksmith's workshop and quarters for both the permanent staff and the seasonal shearers who Andrew would hire each year. In every direction beyond the station, the terrain, rising gently here and there, stretched off to the horizon. A dull, red-brown that contrasted brilliantly with the deep blue sky, the landscape of Mutooroo was, for a few months each year, transformed into a verdant carpet of green. A friend of the Smiths described how, 'motoring' across the station, 'one passes through bluebush country and plains with bastard black oak to dense scrub where one might easily be lost . . . you see a few sheep at the trough, an occasional fox, a few rabbits here and there, a couple of emus, or a kangaroo'.[8] The remoteness, immensity and unforgiving harshness of the country to which Andrew Smith had brought his wife is perhaps best illustrated by the instance in which he discovered on the station the corpse of a drifter who, as it turned out, had been dead for three months.[9]

When Andrew Smith started at Mutooroo in the baking summer heat of early 1888, he faced a formidable task. Besides its inaccessibility, and the wild dogs and rabbits that inundated its plains and scrublands, the property possessed just four wells to supplement the 200 millimetres average annual rainfall. Drawing on his experience at Paratoo, Andrew adopted the 'big dams and small paddocks' approach that had been so successful on that station.[10] In the following decade, he oversaw the establishment of dozens of new paddocks sustained by reservoirs and pipe systems to move water around the property, the longest extending 50 kilometres. In one instance, Andrew had 20 tonnes of galvanised steel pipe delivered by rail to Cockburn and then pulled 40 kilometres by mule trains out to the station.[11] A journalist who visited Mutooroo remarked on the optimism and 'great grit and determination' that Andrew Smith possessed. He had 'that never-say-die characteristic of the true Scot. He was always buoyed up in the face of the greatest difficulties by an eternal hopefulness which eventually carried him to successes'.[12]

Indeed, Andrew Smith's efforts transformed Mutooroo's landscape. And while his achievements may not quite live up to the verses a poet wrote in tribute at the end of his life ('In desert wastes appeared bright running streams: he made a garden of a wilderness'), they were considerable enough.[13] By 1898, when the Elder and Waite venture became incorporated as the Mutooroo Pastoral Company, the station had become capable of sustaining 139,000 sheep. The following year, its wool grossed over £28,000 at auction.[14] At the station's peak, Andrew managed a hundred station hands and 50 seasonal shearers.[15] Recognising his role in their venture's success, in 1898 the company's directors appointed Andrew as the station's general manager. He and Jessie continued to live at Mutooroo, overseeing the station's operations, but his new responsibilities included visits to Adelaide to advise the company's board of directors. In this role, Andrew continued to impress his employers. Peter Waite would later describe Andrew Smith's work as among the most important in South Australia's history.[16]

It was during these pioneering years at Mutooroo that Ross Smith was born, the third of Andrew and Jessie's four children. The first, Janet, died a month after her birth in September 1889. Jessie became pregnant again early the following year and gave birth to a son, Keith, in December 1890. Ross followed two years later, on 4 December 1892, and a third son, Colin, was born in April 1895. As she had done for Keith, and would later for Colin, Jessie gave her second son her birth name, christening him Ross Macpherson Smith.

Ross spent the first decade of his life on the station at Mutooroo. He had a bush upbringing surrounded by hard work and the hard men his father employed. Horses played a prominent role in his childhood; Ross learned to ride as a young boy, developing a great affection for the animals and becoming skilled at handling them. With his brothers, he spent entire days in the saddle, ranging far from the homestead and returning with the kangaroos and rabbits they had shot. It was a toss-up as to who had the better eye. By their father's assessment, Colin may have been the best marksman, but Ross and Keith were still 'jolly good shots'. This upbringing instilled in Ross a sense of independence, resourcefulness and initiative. 'He was always a determined boy,' recalled his father. 'When he made up his mind to do a thing, he invariably succeeded.'[17]

Despite their isolation, Andrew and Jessie ensured that Ross and his brothers had an education. The boys learned to read and write on the station under the tutelage of Mutooroo's bookkeeper and in 1902, shortly after Ross's ninth birthday, he and Keith started school in Adelaide as boarders. For their sons, Jessie and Andrew chose the Queen's School, a privately run preparatory school situated among North Adelaide's 'gracious houses, macadamised streets and attractive squares and parklands'.[18] For young Ross, it would have been difficult to imagine a setting more different from the dusty, desolate plains on which he had spent his first decade.

2

FROGGY

In an area considerably smaller than Mutooroo, 160,000 people called Adelaide home in the first years of the twentieth century. Most of them lived in suburbs clustered around the city's compact centre, with a handful of smaller settlements stretching out along the railway lines toward Port Adelaide and Glenelg. The construction of many of Adelaide's impressive public buildings had by then been finished, as had the carefully manicured parklands that surrounded the city, and the magnificently exotic botanical gardens.

Coming to North Adelaide, with its palatial homes and yards of semi-tropical flowers and trees, must have made Ross aware of a level of wealth, comfort and sophistication that he could never have encountered among the shearers and boundary riders who his father employed at Mutooroo. Had young Ross eavesdropped on the conversations between his teachers and boarding masters, he might have discovered that the otherwise comfortable city's dusty, unsealed roads were one of the few persistent local gripes. Another was its continued use of horse-drawn trams at a time when other cities had invested in electric models. There had been some progress, though: the neighbourhood in which Ross started school in 1902 had recently been illuminated by electric lights.[1]

Established a decade earlier, the Queen's School represented another new and unfamiliar realm for Ross. The school's prospectus claimed that it existed to emulate, as closely as possible, 'the lines of an English public school'. The 'thorough grounding in all elementary subjects' it offered was underpinned by the pillars of Victorian public (non-government) school education: an imperial worldview, self-discipline, sport ('games') and Protestant Christianity.[2] Although Queen's was not a 'church school', Ross's school days nevertheless opened and closed with prayer and he studied scripture twice each week. Boarders like Ross and Keith were also expected to attend church on Sunday—a weekly ritual they had perhaps not had at Mutooroo. Military-style drill promoted the school's exacting standards of discipline and, where this proved inadequate, Queen's headmaster and owner, Mr R.G. Jacomb Hood, employed a ruthless ('sadistic', claims one account) form of corporal punishment.[3] 'A strict disciplinarian who gave a cut of the cane for every spelling error' is how one of Ross's peers remembered him.[4] Another recalled Hood as being 'very English in his manner' and condescending to native-born Australians like Ross: he referred to hats carelessly left on the floor as being hung on 'the colonial hat peg'.[5]

The style of education that Andrew and Jessie had chosen for Ross catered to Adelaide's burgeoning community of professionals, many of whom had been raised and educated in Britain and wanted something similar for their boys. Ross thus entered an institution that existed to produce young men destined for secondary school and university, followed by professions in law, medicine or business.

At the time Ross started at Queen's in 1902, the school had about 50 boys enrolled, most ranging from ten to sixteen years of age. With his older brother, Ross lived in the Queen's boarding house, a nondescript nineteenth-century style villa next to the school on Barton Terrace, typical of residences in the area but renovated to accommodate 25 boys. Arriving there at just nine years of age, and despite all his bush-bred independence apparently missing his mother, Ross formed an especially close bond with the motherly boarding house mistress, Miss Benda, with whom he would continue corresponding into his adult years.[6]

Visiting home involved a fourteen-hour rail journey, so Ross and Keith only returned to Mutooroo during the holidays, each time having their bags packed in eager anticipation a week before travelling. Keith would later recall, 'I think we spent the whole of a term waiting for the holidays to skip back to the station, where we had a lot of riding and shooting.'[7] On weekends the two brothers visited the homes of school friends who lived in Adelaide. One of them, Archibald Grenfell Price, became 'very attached to the Smiths who used to come to the house, which my mother rented for winter use, and join in sing-songs around our piano'.[8]

The Victorian preoccupation with sport, and the perception that it developed moral as well as physical qualities, played a significant part in Ross's education at Queen's. The school emphasised both physical activity and competitive sport, and engaged in an active schedule of carnivals and fixtures against other private schools in Adelaide and from the surrounding districts. At speech day in 1904, Ross and his parents heard the headmaster urge 'the importance of every boy joining in the school games' and argue that academic success and effort on the sporting field 'went hand in hand'. As evidence, he drew a comparison between that year's impressive university entrance results and Queen's victories on the cricket pitch.[9]

Ross excelled on the sporting field. He won both the junior and senior athletics championships and, at an unconventionally young age, worked his way into the Queen's Australian Rules football and cricket teams. During his final year of school, in 1908, Ross captained both—an experience that no doubt began to both reflect and develop in him some bearing as a leader. Ross's success on the sporting field was, it seems, due as much to his affable yet quiet and unassuming nature as it was to his physical abilities.[10] In their recollections of him, two close friends, Grenfell Price and Jack Howard, used the expression 'universally popular' to describe Ross, whom they nicknamed 'Froggy' for reasons nobody could later recall.[11] Ross's ability to mix well and to get along with those from a more urbane background perhaps owed something to his upbringing at Mutooroo, surrounded by adults from many walks of life, ranging from his father's wealthy employers to rough and ready seasonal shearers. This allowed him to begin integrating into the sphere of aspiration and influence that Queen's represented.

Jessie Smith recalled of her son, 'He was one of the most modest of boys, never one who looked for praise or comment upon what he might do.' Yet Ross was also emerging as a focused and self-disciplined young man, who from an early age demonstrated a tendency to doggedly pursue activities to the point of mastery. Again, as his mother recollected, 'If he had an object to achieve he went straight away at it, and its successful completion was all he desired or thought of.'[12] These characteristics, stemming from his father's example on the station and cultivated in Ross during his years at Queen's, would come to define him as he grew into adulthood: they would make him universally well-liked in whatever social setting he found himself, embarrassed by attention and perennially, but quietly, driven to learn, to achieve—to prevail.

In early 1906, Andrew and Jessie took Ross and his two brothers to Scotland. Jessie and the boys remained there for two years. They spent time in the village of Moffatt, in the Southern Uplands, where Andrew had been born. Ross, Keith and Colin attended the Warriston School, a small private prep school for boys. Andrew Smith was pleased with the progress his sons made at Warriston, believing their two years there 'made the boys—the school was a really good one'.[13] Andrew, a highly practical man himself, also valued the educational opportunities that travel around the United Kingdom presented Ross and his brothers. The Smiths hired a yacht to tour the coast of Scotland. In June 1906 they attended the launch of the ill-fated RMS *Lusitania* at Clydebank and, at a Royal Navy exercise off Plymouth, witnessed the tremendous firepower of the battleship HMS *Triumph* in action.[14] They also explored the Scottish Highlands, from which Jessie's family originated and where, she recalled, the thirteen-year-old Ross demonstrated an enthusiasm for heights: 'His great ambition always was to climb to the tops of the highest hills and mountains he could find. He had a love for high places and I have heard him give expression to feelings of envy at the facility of the flight of an eagle hawk.'[15] Years later, Ross would look back on the two years that he spent in the United Kingdom and conclude that they had been formative ones—especially the time he spent at Warriston. They had, he believed, 'made all the difference in the world to me in every way.'[16]

The family returned to Adelaide in February 1908. Keith left school to work for the pastoral company Elder, Smith and Co. while Ross returned to Queen's to complete his primary examination—a preliminary to progressing onto the two-year secondary school course required to matriculate and attend university. Tradition has it that although Ross excelled on the sporting field, he was not particularly bright.[17] Jessie apparently fumed when the headmaster at Queen's reported that Ross would 'never set the Thames on fire'.[18] As it happened, Ross qualified for his primary certificate, passing the two compulsory subjects (English grammar, composition and dictation; and arithmetic) and four supplementary subjects: English history, Latin, French and Algebra (he need only have passed two of these). Ross was one of 548 South Australian students to pass the primary examination in 1908—nearly as many candidates failed.[19]

Ross had finished with study, though: he apparently had no aspirations to go to university, so did not bother with high school. He spent the summer of 1908–09 at Mutooroo before taking a job as a warehouseman for Harris, Scarfe & Co., a wholesaler in Adelaide that traded in hardware, homewares, sporting goods and agricultural machinery. Ross intended, according to his father, to 'gain commercial experience'—although to exactly what end remains as uncertain to us today as it perhaps did to him then.[20]

Looking back on his childhood from the middle of his twenties, Ross would realise that he and his brothers had been 'lucky kids'. Andrew and Jessie had provided a childhood in which they had been both nurtured and challenged, and one that broadened their horizons considerably beyond what might have been expected given their rural upbringing. 'I don't think I have a single unhappy or unpleasant memory of my childhood or boyhood to look back upon,' he claimed.[21]

3

A LITTLE MORE *ÉCLAT*

A year in the warehouse at Harris Scarfe had Ross contemplating a career in the army. In 1910, at seventeen years of age, he joined the Commonwealth Military Cadet Corps, an organisation for adolescent boys that represented a precursor to service, as an adult, in Australia's part-time volunteer militia or the professional 'permanent' army.

At the time, cadets was a popular activity for Australian boys; nearly 24,000 served in the corps when Ross joined. The adults in Ross's world valued the military training that the Cadet Corps provided through weekly parades, rifle competitions, ceremonial turnouts and annual camps; as well as the physical conditioning involved, they believed it inculcated the discipline and values which pundits feared were degenerating in the nation's young men.[1]

Ross elected to join Adelaide's mounted cadet squadron—a unit restricted to boys who were not only able to meet the corps' physical standards, but could also provide their own horse and saddlery. As one journalist observed at the time, the mounted cadets attracted lads who sought 'a little more *éclat*, and perhaps not so much fag [hard, tedious work] . . . as is entailed upon the infantryman'.[2] Perhaps also attracting Ross to the corps' cavalry regiment were its plans to undertake a round-the-world expedition that year. Ross applied for a place and was accepted, along with five other cadets from the regiment's Adelaide unit. Having worked for just a year in the modestly paid position of warehouseman, Ross probably had to borrow much of the £130 fare from his parents.

Twenty-two cadets joined the tour from all around Australia; they were commanded by two subalterns and the expedition's organiser, Captain Alexander Rushall, a prominent and well-connected soldier in the Victorian cadet movement. Rushall conceived the expedition and only secured the begrudging support of Australia's military authorities after the influential parents of some of its young participants lobbied the Defence Minister.[3] His plan was for the cadets to inspect military establishments and armaments factories across Europe and North America, to prepare them for military careers and to promote the mounted cadet movement throughout the empire. 'The lads will carry with them only their uniforms and one tourist suit,' reported the foreign correspondent of Washington DC's *Evening Standard*, even before they had left Australia. 'They will study military matters at all the leading centres they visit and will be kept in training from start to finish. The entire expedition will be subject to military discipline.'[4]

Ross left Adelaide with his fellow cadets on 20 May 1910. They crossed the Indian Ocean, docking briefly at Colombo and Port Said. During the voyage, Ross made friends with another seventeen-year-old cadet named Clifford Harding Browne; the unit's trumpeter, Browne hailed from a prominent Melbourne family and kept a detailed diary of the trip. He described how, by travelling in third class, he and the other boys saw 'a great deal more of life than we would otherwise'. The stopovers in Ceylon and Egypt provided further new—and perhaps confronting—experiences. Browne thought Colombo's native quarter 'dirty and evil smelling' and noted in his diary how four cadets spent a few hours in prison following a fight with a fruit vendor. At Port Said, the smell compelled Ross and his friends to go about with their handkerchiefs at their noses.[5]

A month after leaving Australia, Ross disembarked in Naples and began a fortnight-long tour across Italy, Switzerland and France. The boys had a wonderful time: 'They treated us first class. It was just the thing,' reported Quarter-master Sergeant Pitt. 'You ought to see Lake Como,' added Sergeant Waring from Melbourne, who had never before been as far as Sydney. 'It's beautiful. And did we have a good time in Switzerland. We saw all the military colleges and all the mountains and the lakes. It's something beautiful.'[6] Barracks and military academies received the cadets as guests; Ross had tours of some of Europe's principal arms manufacturers and saw examples of the latest weapons, which the continent's great powers were then competing to produce. In Paris he visited the plant of Clement Buyard, a motorcar manufacturer that had recently started producing dirigible airships for the French Army. Between scheduled, formal receptions Ross and his friends hired tour guides to show them the sights; they explored Pompeii and the Roman Forum, sailed the Venetian canals and climbed the Eiffel Tower.

Ross arrived in London—his second time there—on 1 July 1910, and for six weeks he and the other cadets used the Kensington Barracks as a base from which to tour the United Kingdom. With a letter of recommendation from the Defence Minister, Captain Rushall secured the party an endorsement from the Australian High Commissioner, which in turn allowed the cadets to see the inner workings of the British Army. Several regimental barracks between London and Edinburgh received the boys as guests; Ross spent a day at Aldershot, then home to 30,000 British troops, and a few days at the Olympia, where he witnessed the British Army stage an awe-inspiring military pageant titled 'Britannia's Muster'. The cadets toured the 800-acre (324-hectare) Woolwich arsenal, where 14,000 employees manufactured munitions, and the Birmingham Small Arms Company, where 3000 Lee Enfield rifles came off the production line each week. At Portsmouth, Ross and the other boys saw the Dreadnought HMS *Orion* under construction and went aboard a submarine.

As word of the cadet squadron's visit (and the cadets' good behaviour) spread, they received some prestigious invitations. Field Marshal Earl Roberts, famed throughout the empire for his heroism during campaigns in India, Afghanistan and South Africa, had the boys at his home in Ascot for tea. 'Now boys, look here,' he told them, 'if war should break out you will have to come and help.'[7] In later years, Ross would recall meeting this imperial hero as one of the formative experiences of his youth.[8] The King inspected the cadets at Marlborough House; although he was 'pretty busy so he couldn't stay long', as one of Ross's fellow cadets explained, 'we had a grand time'.[9] The boys also enjoyed the hospitality of Sir George Reid, the Australian High Commissioner, Lady Reid and their daughter, Thelma, who Ross's friend Clifford Browne thought 'really good looking' and who 'seemed to be in her element with 22 boys around her'.[10]

The most important experience for Ross may have been a visit to Brooklands motor racing track on 1 August 1910. With Browne and two other friends, he took the train from Waterloo to Weybridge, 30 kilometres outside London. Opened for automobile racing three years earlier, Brooklands had soon attracted pioneer aviators with their rudimentary flying machines. From a makeshift aerodrome in the middle of the ovoid-shaped track, in October 1909 Frenchman Louis Paulhan had given a series of public flying demonstrations watched by 20,000 spectators. Ten months later, when Ross and his three friends visited, Brooklands had become the epicentre of Britain's nascent aviation scene.

Ross left no written impressions of his experiences that day, but according to Clifford Browne, it was a wondrous experience, none of them ever having seen an aeroplane before. From the aerodrome's edge, they watched the French aviator Gustave Blondeau prepare his Farman biplane for take-off:

> After starting the engine several men hold the plane from moving until the engine is well worked up. Suddenly all hold is released from the plane, and it shoots along the ground on its wheels. It runs in this manner for several hundred yards, and then the driver, by tilting the tail, sends it into the air at a gentle angle.[11]

The aircraft reminded Browne, who as yet lacked the terminology to describe what he was seeing, of 'some tremendous bird'. Blondeau made fifteen circuits, remaining airborne for nearly 37 minutes. Among a crowd of hundreds who had come out from London to spend the Bank Holiday marvelling at the spectacle of men flying, Ross and his friends stayed at Brooklands until dusk. Robert Cordonnier, another amateur French pilot, attempted to take off in his Hanriot monoplane but careered off the end of the aerodrome into the River Wey. Fortunately, members of the 1st Weybridge Scouts were on hand to pull the aviator from the water.[12] What an astonishing thing for Ross Smith—born just over a decade before the first powered flight by the American Wright Brothers in 1903, and who had probably only ridden in a motorcar on a handful of occasions—to have witnessed!

A fortnight after visiting Brooklands, Ross and his fellow cadets sailed across the Atlantic, landing in Quebec after six days at sea. From there they travelled across North America, making stops in Montreal, New York, Philadelphia, Washington DC and Vancouver. Culturally, Canada and the United States were a revelation for the Australian boys—even for Ross, who had travelled overseas before. There they enjoyed ice-cream 'sundaes' for the first time—a true novelty; there was nothing like it in Adelaide, which must have appeared so provincial in comparison to the wonders of a city like New York. During a day of sightseeing in Manhattan, they viewed the city from the top of the Metropolitan Life Insurance Building—then the world's tallest at 50 floors. Ross and Clifford Browne didn't have to climb the stairs; they found many buildings fitted with escalators, 'stair-ways . . . running in the same manner as a machine belt,' marvelled Ross's friend in his diary: 'You stand on one of the steps and in a few seconds you are deposited on the next floor.' American department stores also provided a spectacle. Ross had probably heard about them, but they still surprised, including the custom of women eating counter lunches at a tea bar, just as a man would do back in an Adelaide pub.[13]

Between sightseeing trips, the cadets visited more barracks and academies, including West Point, and while they did not have the same status in North America as they had enjoyed in London, they did become the subject of reports in the American press and had a chance meeting with ex-President Theodore Roosevelt on the platform at Grand Central Station. While crossing to the Pacific coast, the party visited Niagara Falls, where

Ross contracted mumps, an illness which had been through much of the squadron by this stage.

From Vancouver, the cadets embarked on a three-week voyage home across the Pacific, stopping in Hawaii and Fiji. They disembarked in Sydney and took the train to Melbourne, where they were greeted the following day with a lavish reception at Prahran Town Hall, attended by the State Governor and diplomatic personnel from the countries visited on the tour. Ross and the other South Australian boys then returned to Adelaide by rail, arriving home after almost five months away.

4

AVIEMORE

Ross returned from the world tour to his old job in the warehouse at Harris, Scarfe & Co. Handling stock, filling orders, taking inventory—it must all have seemed mundane after travelling the world in the uniform of the Australian Mounted Cadets. He kept up with the cadets though, and two months after returning he turned eighteen and joined the local part-time militia unit, the 10th Australian Infantry Regiment—known around town as the 'Adelaide Rifles'.

In early 1912, though, after a year of Saturday afternoon drills and the part-time army's annual four-day Easter camp, Ross left the regiment. His reasons for resigning are unrecorded; perhaps citizen soldiering was taking too much time from his other great passions, sport and socialising. Maybe, like many other volunteers in the militia, Ross did not like serving alongside younger and less enthusiastic conscripts who were forced into the militia under the government's new compulsory military training scheme. By mid-1913, half of the volunteers in the Commonwealth's new Citizen Military Forces had resigned.[1]

For five years (1910–14), Ross remained at Harris Scarfe. Practically nothing exists in the family's written records about his time there, perhaps suggesting that it was mostly uneventful. An exception occurred in May 1911, when Ross and two colleagues volunteered to break an industrial strike by unloading a shipment of barbed wire at Port Adelaide. They were confronted by the strikers and things turned ugly; someone flung a piece of road metal, striking Ross in the head. According to a newspaper report, 'the missile made a deep cut in his head and a considerable quantity of blood flowed'.[2] The wound required stitches and would likely have been worse—perhaps even fatal—had Ross's hat not deflected some of the blow. Despite a £50 reward offered by the Adelaide Rope, Nail and Barb-Wire Manufacturing Company, police failed to apprehend the perpetrator.

When not working, Ross spent his time during these years—from the ages of nineteen to 21—enjoying a vibrant social life. He continued to play sport, both with the Hardware Assistants' Athletics Association and the Glenferrie Football Club. He also joined the Adelaide Rowing Club—although, as his friend Jack Howard suggested, he was more interested in the club's dances than the rowing.[3] Dancing, indeed, emerged as one of Ross's favourite pastimes. The social columns of Adelaide's newspapers regularly mentioned his name among those in attendance at the debutant balls, 'smoke socials' and charity fundraisers that filled the calendars of Adelaide's wealthy and influential families.

Ross had matured into a handsome young man. He had fair hair and blue eyes that one contemporary described as 'fearless and penetrating, but kindly and above all frank and honest'.[4] Many who knew him mentioned his broad smile; from a young age, it left prominent crow's feet at the corners of his eyes. Lean and athletic, Ross weighed around 70 kilograms and stood at 175 centimetres—a little taller than most Australian men at the time. Assuming that habits from later in his life started at this point, as a young man he was inevitably well groomed and dressed. At some point he had a 'butterfly crest' tattooed on his left arm.[5] The design's significance is unknown, but tattoos were at this time becoming fashionable among young men and women in Australia.[6] Like most Australian men, Ross smoked prolifically. At one stage, he tried to quit but only lasted three months before lapsing. His time without tobacco made him 'very bad tempered'.[7]

By the 1910s, the Smiths could count themselves as part of Adelaide society. Andrew Smith's success in transforming Mutooroo into one of the state's most successful pastoral holdings had brought the family both status and a degree of financial security that his modest beginnings in the colony 30 years earlier could not have predicted. In November 1911, Andrew moved Jessie and the boys into a spacious home in the congenial suburb of Gilberton in Adelaide's north. They dubbed the house Aviemore, after the village in the Scottish Highlands from which Jessie's family had originated.

Andrew Smith's frequent absences at Mutooroo perhaps encouraged Ross to see himself as the man of the house. He was close to his mother and very protective of her. The letters they would later write to each other suggest warmth and openness, even a comfortable frankness; they could tell each other anything. Jessie apparently knew her middle son well. She trusted him, treated him as a grown-up and seems to have taken pride in the young man he was becoming.[8] Ross was likewise 'deeply attached' to Colin, and played the role of older brother well, readily offering advice and taking pride in the youngest Smith's achievements on the sporting field. Ross and Keith shared a particularly close bond, their dependence on each other having been fashioned in Mutooroo's remoteness and their years at boarding school. As young men, they continued to be drawn together by a shared circle of friends and love of sport. Though Ross was two years younger than Keith, friends observed that, of the three boys, it was Ross who often took the lead.[9]

Beyond the family, Ross had a group of friends whose orbit he had first entered through the Queen's School. They included the children of some of South Australia's most prominent families, representing both the traditional landed and political gentry and those, like the Smiths, who had more recently established a name through commercial success. Among those with whom Ross danced, dined and spent weekends in the Adelaide Hills, were the Schomburgk sisters, Pauline and Molly, granddaughters of the founder of Adelaide's botanic gardens and great-nieces of a South Australian premier; their cousins, Jean and Bobbie Warren, daughters of a notable Adelaide businessman; Jean's future husband and mayor of Adelaide, John Lavington Bonython; and fellow Queen's boys Matt Woodley, whose parents were part of the British expatriate community in Japan, and Lyndsay Sandford, whose father owned the large South Australian import enterprise A.W. Sandford.

Ross and Keith remained particularly close to two school friends, Jack and Roy Howard. The four frequented Kindermann's Café on Rundle Street, where they enjoyed this establishment's famous coffee and cakes, and met for lunch each week in one of its private rooms. They also spent weekends at the Howards' place in the Adelaide Hills, where Roy and Jack's eccentric father experimented with the steam-powered automobile he owned (occasionally, they actually saw it work). When Jack and Roy bought Triumph motorcycles, Ross and his brother did too—though, according to Jack, Ross proved to be a 'hopeless rider and never became proficient. He had no judgement in manoeuvring his machine and was also a bad judge of pace and distance.' He also knew nothing about mechanics, being incapable of making 'the simplest repair'. These were curious deficiencies, thought Jack in hindsight, for one who would later excel at the controls of an aeroplane.[10]

Typical of the events Ross frequented was the Adelaide Kindergarten Union's fundraising ball at the Training College on East Terrace in April 1914. Strung with Chinese lanterns, the college's hall provided a vibrant backdrop to an entertaining evening. Young women garbed as mob-capped and aproned housemaids welcomed Ross and his friends and invited them to enjoy their selection of sweets, ices, cool drinks, tea and coffee, cigarettes and cigars. The entertainment program included music for dancing and a fortune teller who attracted a long line of inquirers wanting to discover the hidden mysteries of their future. The evening took an unexpectedly exciting turn when some of the lanterns caught fire.[11]

The *Mail*'s social columnist, Ethelwyn Robin, writing under the pen name 'Cousin Kate', recalled a weekend spent with Ross at Port Noarlunga in 1912. Ross and Matt Woodley cycled 30 kilometres from the city to join 'Kate' and another female friend. 'That week-end was a joyous time,' she remembered. 'We explored the beach for miles every day, went in for a swim at frequent intervals, and fed on cream and honey and other delectable things at the farmhouse where we all stayed'.[12] That 'Kate' was eighteen years Ross's senior again suggests the ease and confidence with which he mixed and socialised.

On the subject of whether Ross had a romantic relationship with 'Kate' or her friend—or anyone else—before the war, the records remain silent.

The ease with which Ross and his friends enjoyed their early days of adulthood began to disintegrate in the winter of 1914. On Saturday, 4 July, as Ross danced and 'sat out' at an Adelaide Rowing Club ball, a funeral took place in Austria for the heir to the Austro-Hungarian Empire's throne, the Archduke Franz Ferdinand, and his wife Sophie. A Serbian Yugoslav nationalist had assassinated them in Sarajevo in protest against Austro-Hungarian expansion into the Balkans. In the weeks that followed, Ross—who had a keen appetite for newsprint—would have followed the dramatic repercussions through Adelaide's newspapers. Their reports revealed how the conflict between Serbia and Austria-Hungary began to draw in other European powers through a complex system of alliances and treaties. Before the end of July, all of Europe's major powers and the colonies that made up their global empires appeared to be on the cusp of war. Making his way to work at Harris Scarfe's warehouse on Wednesday, 5 August, Ross would have learned, along with the rest of Adelaide, that on behalf of all its colonies and dominions, the British Government had declared war on Germany. Pre-empting this, Australia's federal government had already committed to raise a 20,000 men-strong expeditionary force to fight overseas on the empire's behalf.

That Saturday night, Ross attended an annual ball at the St Peters Town Hall. He arrived to find the proscenium hung with the Union Jack, and Australian and French flags, and many of the women swirling about the dancefloor in frocks of matching red, white and blue. Talk about the war undoubtedly replaced the usual society gossip. Ross, Keith and the Howards spent the evening discussing their futures, and by the time the rousing sounds of 'God Save the King', lustily sung by all, ended the evening, they had made a decision: together, they would join the expeditionary force and go to war.[13]

We don't know exactly why Ross decided to enlist. He had no explicit obligation to do so, as the government had announced that the force would only take volunteers. Was he caught up in the patriotic fervour of the evening? Did he recall Field Marshal Lord Roberts' entreaty four years earlier, during the cadet tour, that if war broke out he and his friends would have to come to Britain's aid? Was joining Britain's defence, for him—the son of a Scot who had spent two years at 'home' in the United Kingdom—simply the 'right' thing to do? Did Ross yearn for something more exciting than the warehouse at Harris Scarfe could offer? Looking back on his motivations for enlisting, even he was not entirely sure. 'Perhaps it's a bit of the old Highlands in me,' he explained to his mother, 'because since I went away with the Cadets I've made up my mind that if I ever had the chance I would go to War.'[14]

What is clear is that, in August 1914, the outbreak of war changed the trajectory of Ross's life dramatically—just as it did for millions of others, all around the globe. But whereas for many it would prove to be an unmitigated catastrophe, for Ross Macpherson Smith, it would be his making in ways he could not possibly have imagined.

PART TWO

'A BRITISHER WITH HIS BACK TO THE WALL'

1914–1916

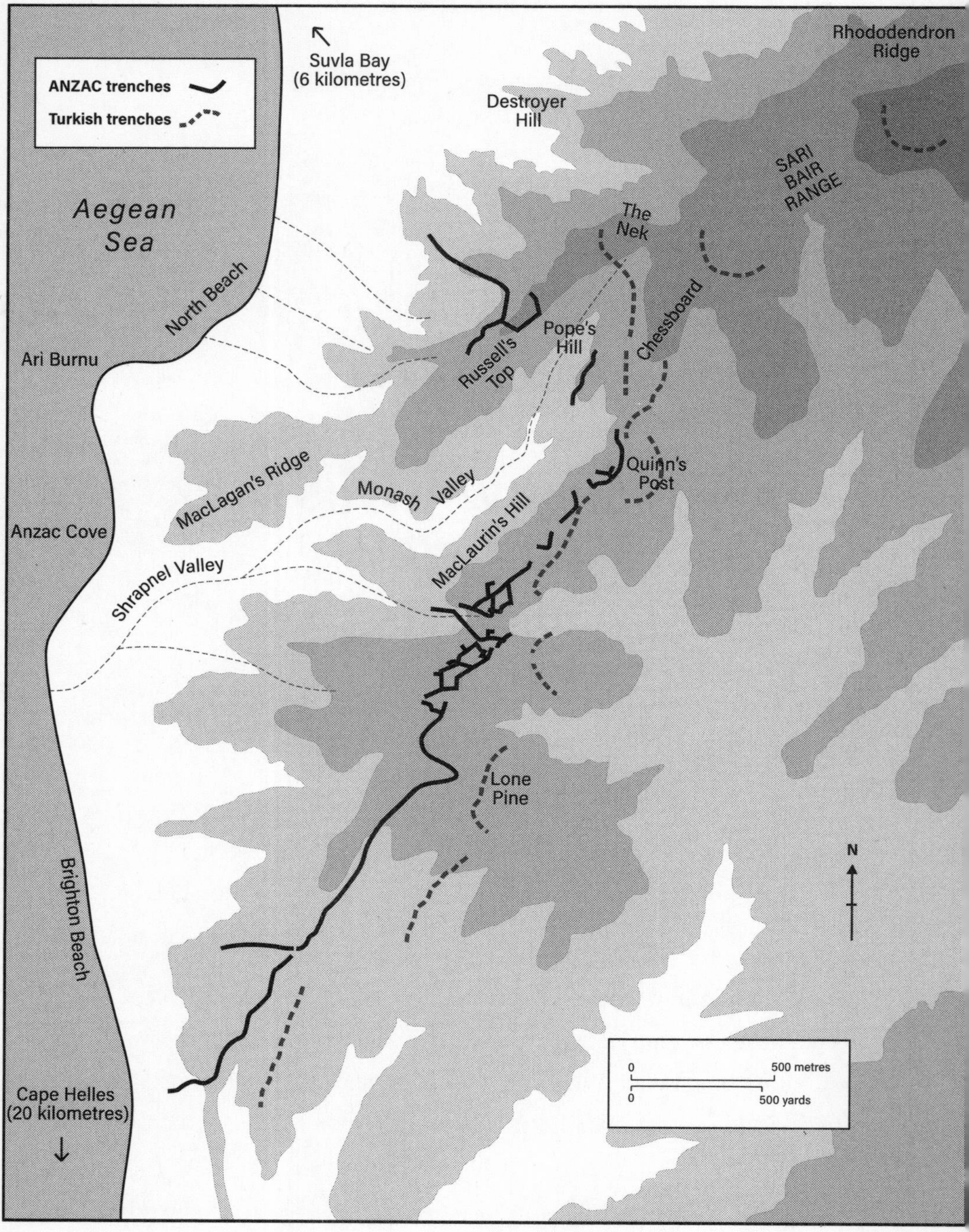

MAP2 Anzac, Gallipoli, May 1915

5

THE GREAT WAR

Ross presented himself to enlist a week after the dance at St Peters Town Hall. Arriving at a recruitment office at the Morphettville horse racing track for what newspapers were now describing as the 'Australian Imperial Force' (AIF), Ross found himself among hundreds of other South Australian men eager to volunteer for overseas service.

The enthusiastic response to the federal government's call for 20,000 volunteers made getting into the AIF competitive. Indeed, by the time Ross turned up for a medical examination on 17 August 1914, the camp had already accepted over a thousand of the 1700 volunteers that South Australia's contingent required.[1] The recruiters at Morphettville nevertheless enlisted Ross right away, his athletic physique, fitness and experience in the cadets and Citizen Forces distinguishing him. They turned Jack and Roy Howard down on their first attempt but accepted them when they tried again later in the month. Keith did not end up enlisting with his brother and friends. According to Jack Howard, Ross ('who always dominated') convinced his older brother to stay home and look after their mother.[2] Their father later explained that Keith did, in fact, try to enlist but that the AIF's recruiters turned him down on medical grounds.[3] Colin, who was taking his compulsory service in the Citizen Military Forces quite seriously, might have wanted to join the AIF with Ross but was still too young. At nineteen, he would have needed written permission from Andrew and Jessie, which he apparently could not convince them to provide.

Along with Jack and Roy Howard, Ross joined the 3rd Australian Light Horse Regiment—a combined Tasmanian and South Australian unit that would, with two other mounted regiments raised in New South Wales and Queensland, form the AIF's 1st Light Horse Brigade. Joining as a private, Ross was appointed to the 3rd Regiment's B Squadron. Within a week, positions in the unit's two South Australian squadrons (the third was being raised in Tasmania) were filled and they had established a camp at Morphettville, 9 kilometres south-west of Adelaide, to equip and undertake some much-needed training before embarking overseas.

Like Ross, roughly a quarter of the regiment's new recruits had been part-time soldiers in the Citizen Military Forces; most were unmarried and aged in their twenties. Some of the older men had fought in South Africa during the Boer War. The majority, however, had no military experience and hailed from all parts of South Australian society, with farmers, labourers, miners and stockmen the most common recruits.[4] Even among the regiment's officers, few had a professional military background. The commanding officer (CO), Lieutenant Colonel Frank Milton Rowell, who Ross probably knew from his time in the cadets and the Adelaide Rifles, had sixteen years' experience as a part-time militia officer and had fought in South Africa. Such circumstances meant that any military experience equipped a man for rapid promotion. Within a fortnight, with just eighteen months of part-time military experience, Ross was appointed as one of B Squadron's nine sergeants, skipping the intermediate ranks of lance-corporal and corporal and doubling his pay in the process.

As a non-commissioned officer (NCO), Ross suddenly became a manager of men—some much older and more worldly than him—and responsible for seeing that they carried out orders issued by the lieutenant of his troop and maintaining appropriate standards of discipline.[5] Periodically rostered as orderly sergeant, Ross also had to run morning parades and inspect the tents and equipment of the 32 light horsemen in his troop. Although glad of the extra pay and prospects the promotion secured, Ross quickly came to appreciate the difficult task that his elevated rank presented. Most of the work of handling the men rested with the NCOs, he explained to his mother, and some of those placed under his charge were tough characters, neither accustomed nor inclined to do what they were told.[6]

Although he may have felt the weight of this responsibility, Ross's upbringing had actually provided him with a number of experiences from which he might have drawn inspiration. He could have looked to the example of the disciplinarian teachers who taught drill twice each week at the Queen's School, or that of the NCOs with whom he served in the cadets and the Adelaide Rifles. Perhaps Ross's leadership on the sporting field had some practical application too; then there was the uncompromisingly firm, but fair, example of how his father handled the shearers he employed each year at Mutooroo. Andrew provided each with a decent wage, relatively cheap rations and free accommodation, but strictly banned the bringing of any 'intoxicating liquor' onto the station and the use of 'profane or obscene language' and songs in the shearing shed.[7]

For the first few weeks in camp, Ross and his fellow NCOs acquired equipment for their men and instructed them in how to handle it—frequently after a crash course in using it themselves. Like AIF units being raised all around the country in August 1914, the leaders of South Australia's light horse regiment struggled with both the inexperience of their recruits and a shortage of military equipment. To begin with, Ross and his comrades had to share personal kit and make do with 'fairly rough' conditions in camp.[8] They slept on the ground, with a dozen men sleeping shoulder to shoulder in round bell tents—an experience that would have been far less comfortable than what Ross had grown accustomed to in his mother's house in Gilberton.

As usual in cavalry regiments throughout the British Empire, Ross's unit received a pair of guns to establish a regimental machine gun section—but they turned out to be antiquated pieces, the paperwork accompanying them revealing a service history that stretched back two decades to campaigns in Malta and South Africa.[9] Local defence authorities also struggled to provide Ross and his comrades with quality horses. The country was then in the midst of a severe drought and, as one journalist predicted, many of the state's farmers would sooner send a son to war than one of their prized mounts. By 10 September, the 3rd Light Horse Regiment had nevertheless managed to acquire its full establishment of 435 horses—although, as *The Register*'s military correspondent noted, they were of 'an uneven quality'. His concern about what overseas observers might make of the calibre of Australian horseflesh reflects a widely felt apprehension that Australians felt in 1914 as their troops prepared to establish their nation's reputation on the world's stage.[10] The expectations on Ross and his comrades of the AIF's first contingent were high indeed.

For the first few weeks, Ross's training focused on the fundamentals of soldiering, with which he would have had some familiarity from his days in the cadets and militia: dismounted drill, marching, the handling of a rifle and—of special importance for a light horseman—care of his mount. Once equipped with horses and saddlery, in mid-September Ross's troop commenced mounted drill and shortly afterwards began venturing out into Adelaide's sparsely populated coastal region on military exercises. Unless on night manoeuvres or sentry duty, men could secure evening leave until 11 p.m. Ross perhaps took this opportunity to catch the tram back into town to see his mother and escape the reportedly miserable food in camp.

One night Ross secured leave to attend a 'complimentary smoke social' hosted by the Adelaide Rowing Club to honour him and fifteen fellow members who had volunteered to 'fight for the Honour of the British Empire'.[11] Ross found the club's familiar boathouse decked in bunting representing the flags of Britain and her allies and he enjoyed an evening of stirringly patriotic songs like 'Britannia, the Pride of the Ocean', 'Let Me Like a Soldier Fall' and 'Mandalay'. The club used the occasion to issue awards for the summer's rowing and swimming champions, and many of them, observed a journalist from Adelaide's *Chronicle*, had volunteered for the AIF. He predicted that they 'should do equally well on the battlefield' as they had on the sporting field. The club's contribution to the empire's war effort impressed another local reporter who claimed that Ross and his fellow rowers represented 'a fine type of manhood in every way' and anticipated that they would 'be a credit to the British Empire wherever they may go'.[12] Such analogies and sentiments would have made perfect sense to Ross and his friends, for they had been reared in a culture that conditioned them to see military service as a civic duty and war as part of an inexorable historical process—part of the natural order of things—that forged nations and empires.

After four weeks in camp, it appeared to Ross that the regiment's embarkation was imminent. On 21 September, the 3rd Light Horse Regiment led the AIF's 1800-strong South Australian contingent on a parade through the streets of Adelaide. Attended by thousands, the march reflected both the ebullience of South Australians regarding the embarkation of their men to fight and the AIF's thoroughly provincial and amateur character. As one of Adelaide's journalists described the occasion, 'It was in many respects an intimate kind of farewell.'

> There was someone in the crowd looking for Pte Smith, and someone else looking for Cpl Robinson. And so above the cheering there were personal notes like this—'Good luck, Jack!'—'Here you are, Harry; good-bye, old man,' 'Shoot the Kaiser, Bill,' and so on. The soldiers waved to their friends as they passed and laughed along. They were very happy about it all, and wore little flags and bunches of wattle. One merry fellow nursed a great bulldog, an appropriate emblem of Britain's tenacity . . . In the transport carts and wagons it was also noticeable that many of the regimental pets were carried, including several kangaroos and dogs.[13]

Somewhere among the fervent crowds lining Pulteney, Rundle, King William or Grote Streets—perhaps opposite the steps of parliament house where the Governor received the force's salute—must have been Jessie, Keith and Colin and, if he were in town on business from Mutooroo, Andrew Smith. Besides them we can assume that, as Ross rode through the streets of his town, he would have scanned the crowd for friends' faces: old boys from

Queen's, colleagues from Harris Scarfe, team-mates from the rowing and football clubs and the rest of the merrymaking social set with whom he had whiled away his first years of adulthood. Who knew when—and whether—he would see them again at the conclusion of this great adventure on which he was about to embark?

As things turned out, Ross and the rest of South Australia's volunteers had to wait another month before leaving Australia's shores. Nervous about the suspected presence of German cruisers in the Indian Ocean, the Australian government postponed the AIF's embarkation until the British Admiralty could supply the troopships with an escort. The delay would have frustrated the men, although it did provide the regiment with time to undertake some of the additional training it sorely needed. In early October, Ross's troop joined B Squadron's three other troops and began training as a complete unit, 160-men strong. On exercises in the countryside between Henley Beach and Glenelg, Ross and his comrades simulated the classic cavalry roles of reconnaissance, providing a defensive screen for other arms and charging an 'enemy' position.[14] In some instances, Ross's squadron went on overnight patrols up into the Adelaide Hills, bivouacking there and returning to camp at Morphettville the following morning.[15]

The 3rd Light Horse Regiment finally broke camp on 21 October 1914 and sailed from Adelaide's Outer Harbor aboard the HMAT *Port Lincoln* the following day. Friends and family gathered there to see Ross off, giving him sweets for the voyage. Jessie presented her son with some new pyjamas—they were light, ideal for tropical nights, though neither she nor her son knew the regiment's destination. Before leaving, Ross allocated a quarter of his weekly pay to Keith and purchased £500 of life insurance. In his absence, he was trusting Keith to take care of Jessie.[16] Ross's closeness to his mother and brothers must have made the parting a sad one. Desperate to see his older brother one last time, Colin persuaded a soldier guarding the gangway to let him aboard to see Ross.[17] The gesture was one Ross would remember in the difficult years ahead—a time that would turn out to be far longer than he or anyone else had anticipated.

6

SIX-BOB-A-DAY TOURISTS

From Adelaide, the *Port Lincoln* sailed west across the Great Australian Bight. Heavy seas made many of the men ill and two horses died on the voyage. Having apparently gained his sea legs during two previous overseas journeys, Ross remained well and cared for the sick men in his troop by sharing his private supply of Bovril.

At Albany, in Western Australia, the *Port Lincoln* joined 36 other ships that had assembled to carry the first contingent of Australian and New Zealand forces—soon to be known as the Australian and New Zealand Army Corps (ANZAC)—overseas to the war. Ross wrote while anchored off Albany: 'It is a wonderful sight—all the transports and out further, the fleet.' While on guard duty that night, Ross used semaphore flags to converse with one of his friends from Adelaide on a neighbouring vessel.[1]

The convoy sailed from Albany on 1 November 1914 and set a north-westerly course across the Indian Ocean. For the voyage, the 3rd Light Horse Regiment's officers rostered their men to alternate between stable work (cleaning, grooming and exercising the horses), sentry duty and training—mainly lectures and physical drill. After hours, the men gambled (Ross doubled his money during the voyage), boxed and enjoyed performances by the regimental band. Each man could purchase one pint of beer a day. Reflecting his keen sense of humour, Ross enjoyed a satirical newspaper produced on board in which, he reported, everyone—including the horses—'gets "slung off" at'.[2] As they approached the equator, Ross and the other sergeants took to sleeping on deck; they had 'one of those raised portions' to themselves, he described to Jessie, 'so we get away from the crowd a bit'. Among the crowd of privates confined below decks were several of Ross's friends from home, including Roy and Jack Howard. Ross checked on them and found that although they were 'getting on alright . . . they get a good bit more hard work than I do now [as an NCO]'. He anticipated that might change when they went into battle.[3]

The most exciting moment of the voyage occurred nine days out from Albany, when one of the convoy's escorts, HMAS *Sydney*, engaged and destroyed the German light cruiser SMS *Emden*. Ross happened to be up on deck when the *Sydney* received a distress message from a wireless station on the nearby Cocos Islands, reporting that it was under attack from the German raider. Ross watched as the *Sydney* suddenly went to full speed, its four funnels belching smoke, and passed close by the *Port Lincoln*. 'It was all very thrilling,' thought Ross, despite not knowing what was happening. 'She was out of sight in no time, and we heard nothing for eight hours, when news came through.'[4] The two ships had exchanged fire for over 90 minutes until the *Emden*, badly damaged, was wrecked on North Keeling Island.

After stopping for coal at Colombo and Aiden, the convoy sailed up the Suez Canal and arrived at Port Said. For a day, they waited in the harbour: it was crowded with warships and transports and nobody was sure of what was happening. Like most of his comrades, Ross still expected a brief stopover in Egypt before continuing the journey to Britain. While at Port Said, the men saw one of several French 'hydroplanes' take off from the water and circle the harbour before landing again.[5] Shortly before the war, Egypt's supposedly ideal flying conditions had attracted a number of Europe's burgeoning aviation community.

The next day, the *Port Lincoln* sailed into the harbour at Alexandria and anchored to wait its turn to berth. To help pass the time, Ross volunteered to operate the transport's rowboat to ferry the officers ashore and chase away locals who sailed out in their hundreds to sell cigarettes, fruit and alcohol to the men aboard the troopships. On 4 December 1914, Ross celebrated his 22nd birthday with a small group of friends and 'a quantity of beer, and a big cake for tea, and later on two big bottles of champagne'. Huddled around a lantern, the party shared the 'fizz' from the single cup at hand, 'with a few cases of onions for a background'.[6]

The *Port Lincoln* finally docked at Alexandria on 8 December. The 3rd Light Horse Regiment disembarked with its horses and unloaded 16,000 bags of fodder, a process that took all day. The unit boarded the evening train to Cairo and then marched in the rain, the men leading their horses, out to a camp at Maadi on the city's southern fringe. They arrived at 3 a.m. 'Ye Gods! Will I ever forget it?' complained Ross: 'Seven weeks of idleness, and then a 12 mile [19 kilometre] walk in full marching order.'[7] Arriving ahead of their camp equipment, the men spent their first night at Maadi in the open: Ross slept in the sand and woke the following morning soaked through. The realisation that they were staying in Egypt surprised and disappointed Ross and many of his comrades. At least Maadi was the pick of the AIF's two camps in that country. Unlike the infantry, camped at Mena on the western side of the Nile, the light horsemen were both closer to Cairo and situated right alongside one of the city's comfortable expatriate suburbs. The two-storey villas, with their lush lawns and colourful gardens, would provide Ross with an oasis of familiar culture in a land filled with uncomfortably strange sights, sounds and smells. One English gentleman opened part of his house for the light horsemen to use as a recreation room and other residents soon extended the same hospitality.[8] Part-way through their stay in Egypt, at the end of January 1915, the regiment's good fortune with accommodation would continue when it moved camps to Heliopolis, another salubrious European community, just a short tram ride from the centre of Cairo.

Joined at Maadi by C Squadron from Tasmania, the 3rd Light Horse became a complete unit and, after giving the horses a fortnight to let them acclimatise, recommenced training. The regiment fought mock battles against imaginary objectives, which Ross found great fun:

> In the mornings we go out mounted and attack different hills, and all sorts of other work. It's great sport because we always tear up to our position for

> the last 400 yards [366 metres] at a good gallop, and then fall off our horses, and hand them over to the horse-holders, and shoot at imaginary Turks till we are satisfied they are all done in. Sometimes the scheme is that we are getting the worst of it, and we have to clear out, so we cut back to our horses and fall back on the position we have just captured and left.[9]

Although Ross would occasionally write about training in his letters home, he described the sightseeing that he did in much greater detail. Like many who joined the AIF, he went overseas armed with both a rifle and a camera: a soldier tourist. Indeed, he even ironically applied to himself the title that some sceptics in the Australian press had labelled the soldiers of the AIF: 'six-bob-a-day tourists' (a reference to the relatively high six shillings Australian privates received each day).[10] While in Egypt. Ross made the most of opportunities to get away from camp. He cruised the Nile and shopped for souvenirs in Cairo, patronised the stylish cafés of Maadi and Heliopolis, and dined with hospitable expatriate families. On longer leave passes, Ross and his mates immersed themselves in Egypt's compelling history; they visited famous ancient sites including the Giza pyramids, Luxor's temple complex and the tombs of Sakkhara ('we explored them by candlelight').[11] Ross marvelled at the age and splendour of such places and enjoyed luxuries restricted to officers of the British Army but that he, as a comparatively well-paid Australian NCO, could afford. Indeed, it amused him to see cashed-up Australian corporals and sergeants dining off tablecloths and having waiters light their cigarettes alongside British officers at the world-famous Shepheard's Hotel in Cairo. 'You'll find me spoiled beyond redemption when I get home,' he warned his mother.[12]

At the same time, however, and despite being unusually well travelled for his age, like most Australians of his generation Ross's innate sense of racial and cultural superiority made many aspects of Egyptian society confronting and hard to tolerate. He wrote unreservedly of the antipathy that he and other Australians developed towards the locals ('The niggers are dirty beggars') during their time in Egypt and the bad behaviour that this encouraged among the troops.[13] Just a fortnight after arriving in Egypt, Ross described what fun it was to harass the proprietors of local businesses:

> Sometimes you will see a mob of Territorials or Australians rush into a shop and take charge for a time. They grab everything and serve the customers, but it all ends peacefully after a lot of arguing by the niggers.[14]

Except that it did not always end peacefully. Ross's letters to his mother also frankly describe violent and destructive behaviour by Antipodean troops in Cairo, including the so-called 'battle of the Wazzir'. Late in the afternoon of Good Friday, 2 April 1915, Ross and his friend, Geoff Wells, returned from a cruise on the Nile to find a 'big riot' in progress. Its cause has been disputed ever since but, by Ross's account, a Māori soldier had been stabbed, prompting a mob of Australians and New Zealanders to rampage through Cairo's brothel quarter and 'clear it out properly'. Over two thousand soldiers joined in, ransacking brothels and starting fires. Ross did not take part, but nor did he censure the perpetrators: 'These chaps here are holy terrors when they get on a job like that, and, if we don't get out of [Egypt] soon, there will be more trouble.'[15] There was: just two nights later, Ross received orders to take two sections of his troop into Heliopolis to help quell another disturbance caused by drunken Australians.

Leading mounted patrols through Cairo's streets at night to maintain order would thereafter become one of his regular responsibilities. All the while, he also faced the challenges of maintaining discipline within his own troop (No. 2 Troop, B Squadron), which he described to his mother as 'the toughest lot and hardest to manage in the whole regiment'.[16] During the early months of 1915, Ross routinely had to administer discipline, 'becoming fairly proficient in handling drunks', and he appeared as a witness for the prosecution at a number of courts-martial.[17] Things improved as the AIF's justice system weeded out the most persistent offenders. Ross was relieved to report in mid-January 1915 that a number of them had been sent home, while 'the worst man I had is now doing 3 months' penal servitude prior to his discharge and since he's been away things have been much better'.[18] The man in question, a 29-year-old boilermaker named John Barnett, had gone absent without leave, threatened to shoot A Squadron's sergeant-major who apprehended him, then tried to escape custody.[19]

Nevertheless, Ross did not feel that such men represented the force as a whole. Along with many others in the AIF, he was incensed when an article by the official war correspondent Charles Bean appeared in Australian newspapers in January 1915 reporting the bad conduct of Australians in Egypt. 'That --- correspondent Bean,' Ross thundered in a letter to Jessie. 'He is a --- liar . . . we have not blighted the fair name of Australia, as he asserts.' Besides a few Australians 'running amok', explained Ross, it was the New Zealanders who were the real troublemakers in Egypt.[20] New Zealand soldiers, unsurprisingly, reported precisely the opposite in their letters home.[21]

In any case, Ross himself wasn't above breaking the rules when it suited him. Apparently, like many of the men in his troop, he was yet to entirely surrender his youthful civilian individuality to the expectations of military discipline and conformity. On Christmas Eve, Ross and his two closest friends, who had only secured leave for the early evening, went into Cairo for dinner at Shepheard's. They returned to camp in time for curfew and then snuck back into town. 'All the shows and cafes were going by then,' he candidly explained to his mother, 'and we wandered about from one place to the other.' Struggling to find a taxi for the return journey to Maadi, they made it back to camp just before dawn.[22] Evidence that such behaviour reflected a broader spirit of amateurism among the regiment's NCOs is found in Ross's frank admission, when witness at the court-martial of one of his fellow sergeants, that it was typical for NCOs to break standing orders and neglect to report their comings and goings from camp.[23]

Although Ross knew many men from Adelaide in the regiment, the two with whom he stole out to Cairo that Christmas Eve became his closest friends during the months of training in Egypt. Corporal Gordon 'Timmy' Timbrell was his 'best pal'; a year older than Ross, 'Timmy' also had Scottish parentage and before the war had lived in North Adelaide. He had been in the Adelaide Rowing Club with Ross and they shared the same circle of friends. 'We always do things together,' wrote Ross.[24] The other man, Private Oscar Senhouse, 'a blasé sort of Englishman', had migrated to Australia and worked on one of South Australia's other large grazing stations, Bungaree, before the war. Sergeant Geoff Wells, who had been in Cairo with Ross on the day of the Wazir riot, also became a firm friend. Like Ross, he was a talented sportsman and ex-cadet. When the war started, he travelled 200 kilometres to Adelaide from his farm at Georgetown to enlist in the 3rd Light Horse.

Despite the differences in their rank, Ross maintained his friendship with Jack and Roy Howard, who both remained privates—although he saw them less frequently on account of their posting to A Squadron. When Ross ended up in hospital with influenza in February, he found Jack—who had been admitted with pneumonia—in a very serious condition. 'Ross saved my life that day,' claimed Howard; the 1st Australian General Hospital had only recently arrived in Egypt and still lacked the basics to care for its patients. 'There were no beds, no doctors, no food, no nothing,' recalled Howard, whose temperature spiked at 40°C that night. 'Ross made me up a bunk, kept me supplied with drinks without which I most surely would not have survived.'[25] Ross recovered in a few days, but Jack would remain in hospital for weeks to come.

Although he faced some challenges in dealing with the indiscipline of some of his men, Ross's experience as an NCO while training in Egypt stoked his ambition. In January, when B Squadron's senior NCO, its sergeant major, injured himself in a riding accident, Ross became his temporarily appointed replacement. The promotion pleased Ross and, despite being frustrated by his new responsibility for overseeing the horses behind the firing line when the squadron dismounted to fight, he developed aspirations to secure an officer's commission. While in Egypt, Ross continually sought opportunities to develop his skills as a soldier: he spent hours tinkering with new equipment, studied 'military books' and volunteered to lead extra patrols. 'Getting that patrol job on Monday, and doing well at it, has made me twice as keen on learning more,' he wrote to Jessie from the Heliopolis camp in March. 'I won't be satisfied until I can wear a [lieutenant's] star on my shoulder, but that won't be until some of the other poor beggars get shot.'[26]

Impatient for promotion, in March Ross considered applying for a commission in a British regiment along with his friend Oscar Senhouse, who left the AIF to accept a commission in the Coldstream Guards. Ross changed his mind, however, when rumours began circulating that the AIF would shortly go into action. Indeed, it was by this stage no secret that the British Army planned to invade Ottoman Turkey and that the Australians in Egypt would support the campaign. Back in Adelaide, the newspapers reported on British preparations and claimed, with increasing confidence, that the Australians were bound for Constantinople.[27] Although anxious to get into action, the prospect of fighting the Turks disappointed Ross, who had been influenced by the British press to see Germany as the principal enemy. 'The Germans are the ones we want to fight, and not the Turks,' he explained to his mother, asking her whether she had read reports of German U-boats attacking passenger liners and shelling coastal towns in Britain. 'I can't find an expression strong enough for the beasts.'[28] By the end of March, Ross and his comrades had grown sick of training; inaction was now undermining morale. 'We sit in our tents and swear at the country, and each other, and the Government who won't send us to the front,' wrote Ross.[29]

Ross's keenness for getting involved in the fighting did not result from naivety regarding the true nature of the war. From its early stages, Ross seems to have grasped the scale and destructiveness of the conflict in which he had volunteered to fight. In a letter he sent home in December 1914, he suggested to his mother that, as the British professional army had been all but wiped out in the opening battles on the Western Front, it would be up to the 'second army, training now' to either win or be annihilated too, leaving it up to a third army to prevail: 'It's going to be a long scrap, and the survival of the fittest.'[30]

In these comments we perceive the martial and imperial worldview with which Ross had been raised. A private school education, sport, British-born parents and relatives, the cadets and militia had all conditioned Ross to see war as part of the natural order of things: a Darwinian struggle between nations in which the strongest flourished and the weak crumbled. Further, like most Australians of his generation, Ross perceived himself as part of Britain's global empire: he was as much a Briton as an Australian, with no apparent tension between these two complementary identities. Ross venerated the British Army's leadership and wrote a glowing account of its retreat from the Belgian town of Mons in August 1914, based on his conversations with British troops in Egypt and some official despatches he had read. 'It's the British musketry that does it,' enthused Ross, 'and they say their shooting is absolutely the finest in the world.'[31] Few could explain what had started the war, he admitted, 'but it's that wonderful British fighting spirit in them that is crying out for Adventure and Danger more than anything else'.[32]

In early April 1915, as the Australian light horse regiments continued to train, the infantry battalions left their camp at Mena and embarked for Gallipoli. News of the landing at Anzac Cove on 25 April aggravated the sense of injustice that Ross and the other light horsemen felt at not being sent to fight. It disappointed them to hear that they would not be joining the invasion force for some time when the regiment's officers revealed that they needed to wait until shelters could be built for the horses at Gallipoli. Among the excitement and irritation that news of the landing provoked came sadness too. Ross learned that 'big Tom White', a fellow Adelaide rower, had died after being shot in his landing boat and that two other club members, Frank Crowhurst and Keith Green, had also been killed.[33]

In the following days, Ross heard of more men whom he knew—men about his age with whom he had worked and played in Adelaide—who had been killed or wounded at Gallipoli. The news confirmed his grim predictions about the violent intensity of the war, but also prompted him to consider its implications for him personally. Ross remained upbeat in his letters to his mother but to Keith he sent a matter-of-fact farewell letter, believing that he would need to be 'extraordinarily lucky' to live to see home again. 'Our fellows are going down like nine-pins,' he explained to his older brother. 'The hospitals [are] full of wounded.' Anticipating that his death would affect their mother 'pretty badly', he asked Keith to do what he could to take care of her. Ross reminded his brother of the life insurance he had and insisted on him giving it to their father to use. He finished by asking Keith to pass the letter onto their younger brother, Colin (but to keep it from their mother), and included a carton of cigarettes for each of them. 'Goodbye, Keith, and my love to Nebs [Colin], and I'll keep my end up all right.'[34]

Anticipating that the force on Gallipoli would urgently require more men and hoping to avoid having their regiments broken up and parcelled out as reinforcements to the infantry, the COs of the Australian and New Zealand mounted brigades in Egypt proposed deploying at Gallipoli without their horses. On 7 May, the regiments of the 1st Australian Light Horse and New Zealand Mounted Rifles Brigades received orders to break camp and move to Alexandria for embarkation to Anzac Cove. Leaving their horses in Cairo, Ross and his comrades made the overnight rail journey to the harbour at Alexandria, 'packed like sardines in terrible old dog boxes of carriages'.[35] As they filed aboard their transport, HMT *Grantully Castle*, they exchanged their leather riding leggings and spurs for infantry puttees. 'I don't feel like a light horseman at all now,' objected Ross.[36]

At dusk on 9 May 1915, with 2000 light horsemen masquerading as infantrymen on board, the *Grantully Castle* steamed out of the harbour and onto the 'beautifully smooth' Mediterranean. Its captain set course for Gallipoli.[37]

7

ANZAC

HMT *Grantully Castle* arrived off Cape Helles shortly after dawn on 12 May 1915. It had been seventeen days since British troops had landed on this southern extremity of the Gallipoli peninsula. Like the landing by Australian and New Zealand troops further north at Anzac Cove, the Helles operation had turned out to be a bloody fiasco: British troops struggled ashore under devastatingly effective Turkish fire and advanced only a few kilometres inland before being forced to dig in, still a long way from their objectives. As at Anzac Cove, the situation at Helles became mired in a stalemate of trench warfare. The precarious Allied position at Gallipoli had, indeed, come to resemble the hopeless situation in France that the invasion of Ottoman Turkey had been conceived to circumvent.

Gun smoke blanketed Helles that morning. Warships and transports of all sizes waited at anchor in the grey sea surrounding the cape. From the decks of the *Grantully Castle*, Ross listened with excitement and trepidation. On shore the artillery rumbled menacingly; closer, the big guns of Royal Navy battleships and cruisers thundered with breathtaking concussion. When the British dreadnought the *Queen Elizabeth* fired its 15-inch guns, the men aboard the troopships could follow the slow, arching trajectory of its 880-kilogram projectiles on their way to the Turkish lines at Cape Helles, where they 'ejaculated huge ugly gouts of clay and bursting scrub'.[1] Confronted with the ominous noise of a battle he could not yet see, the moment proved a sobering one for Ross Smith. It was the first time he 'really realised that there was a war on'.[2]

That afternoon, the *Grantully Castle* sailed up the Gallipoli coast to Ari Burnu, the point around which troops of the Australian and New Zealand Army Corps (ANZAC) had landed on 25 April. Despite facing only a handful of Turkish defenders, the Australian and New Zealand landing force struggled to make headway in rugged and confusing terrain. They failed to secure their objectives inland and, in a series of well-conducted Turkish counter-attacks, were driven back into a line of entrenched outposts that in most places overlooked the shore. The Australian and New Zealand mounted brigades had come to Ari Burnu (soon known generally as 'Anzac Cove', or simply 'Anzac') to help shore up the precarious foothold to which the invasion force clung. The entire beachhead extended along the coast for a distance of about 1800 metres and, at its farthest point, penetrated inland just over a kilometre. The Australian and New Zealand troops held trenches that they had dug along the inland perimeter of this roughly triangular position. They were effectively under siege from the Ottoman forces that encircled the ANZAC position—a situation that would remain more or less unchanged for the next eight months.

Shortly after sunset, the light horsemen boarded 'little pinnaces and barges' to transport them ashore under the cover of darkness. As they approached Anzac Cove, Ross became fixated on the 'rattle and roar of musketry' and listened as bullets whizzed close by 'plonking in the water'. Struggling with a tremendously heavy kit, he hauled himself up the pebbly beach to find it 'teeming with life and work, men carrying tins of biscuits, others loading mules, and others again unloading and stacking cases and cases of every sort of thing that goes to supply an army'.[3]

After assembling on the beach, the men of the 3rd Light Horse Regiment followed their guide inland into a dark and disorientating landscape. After climbing a knoll known as Maclagan's Ridge, the light horsemen filed down into the darkness of Shrapnel Valley, the main thoroughfare that connected the beach with the front line. Ross could see nothing, but the peculiar sounds that would come to characterise Anzac in the coming weeks were immediately apparent: the perpetual 'knock knock' of rifles from up on the ridge, punctuated periodically by bursts of machine gun fire and the thud of bombs lobbed across the narrow strip of no-man's land that separated the opposing front lines. The noises blended together and, in the dark, Ross 'had not the least idea where it was all coming from'.[4] Periodically throughout the night, this strange, demented symphony of trench warfare would rise and reach a crescendo before dying away again—only to be revived again later by a nervous sentry opening fire at a phantom enemy in no-man's land and thus setting his comrades and their enemies off again. Then there was the overpowering olfactory sensation of the place—a reek produced by wood fires and thousands of bodies unwashed or unburied; by latrines—open pits used by ten thousand men occupying the besieged beachhead—and by the acrid smell of cordite and gunpowder from the Turkish shrapnel shells that intermittently whined and burst overhead.

Ross spent his first night in this strange and disorientating landscape sleeping in the open, in the holly scrub, a short distance behind the front line at MacLaurin's Hill. It was a relatively safe bivouac in the dark, but at dawn it came to the attention of Turkish snipers occupying high ground at the apex of the ANZAC position. At first the unfamiliar 'clipping noise' of bullets passing close by did not alarm the novice light horsemen; five were hit before Ross realised what was happening.[5] With few other places available to camp in the cramped confines of Anzac, Ross and the men of his squadron had to make do; they spent their first day digging dugouts to afford some protection. Before sunset, eleven men had been wounded. Some may have been conveyed to the beach by a stretcher bearer named Simpson who, as some of the men noted in their diaries, used a donkey to carry his patients and seemingly paid no attention to the bullets and shrapnel that flew around him as he worked. They also noticed when he was shot dead by a Turkish sniper the following week.[6]

During their first days at Anzac, Ross and his troop built sandbag barricades along the floor of Monash Valley to provide cover to those moving back and forth between the beach and the front line. Ross described the thoroughfare as 'a veritable death road by day', on which men were 'picked off like flies' by Turkish snipers perched on a hill overlooking the length of the valley. Indeed, while working in Monash Valley during their first week at Gallipoli, four of Ross's comrades were killed and 51 wounded—more casualties than the 3rd Light Horse Regiment would suffer in any other week during its time on the peninsula. It was while moving between sheltered sections of Monash Valley that the AIF's commander, Major General William Throsby Bridges, would receive a fatal gunshot wound on 15 May 1915. Ross had some narrow escapes himself as he sprinted between barricades along the valley with bullets kicking up dust around his feet. Later, making light of the danger, he recalled that, 'I often used to wonder if I ever did my 100 yards faster on the Adelaide Oval than some of my short sprints around corners and across that road.'[7]

Three nights after landing, B Squadron received orders to go up to the front line. Under the cover of darkness, Ross and the other men in the unit moved up Monash Valley, behind and parallel to the front line that ran along the ridge above. Close to the head of the valley, the men climbed a steep slope to reach an isolated redoubt of trenches known as Quinn's Post. Already developing a reputation as the most dangerous spot at Anzac, the position sat sandwiched between the steep slopes dropping into Monash Valley and Turkish trenches that lay within bomb-throwing range. Situated about 1200 metres from the shore, Quinn's Post represented the apex of the roughly triangular beachhead; its loss would jeopardise the entire Anzac position.

B Squadron went to this precarious place on 15 May to reinforce its badly depleted garrison. Clambering up the steep slope behind Quinn's, they found that the post's support line trenches existed only as a series of rough depressions. In the dark, Ross and his troop crawled, shuffled and stooped to move forward into the firing trench.[8] Ross likewise found this only partially dug in places—'very narrow and shallow'—and overlooked by the Turkish front line, only a dozen metres away and up a gentle slope. The trench lay scattered with smashed and discarded equipment and the whole place reeked of putrefying corpses.[9]

From the moment that Ross entered the front line at Quinn's, the position was under attack from bullets and bombs. 'To put one's head up an inch above the parapet was sudden death,' he said. 'There were no loop-holes, and it was just a case of putting your rifle up quickly, firing, and getting it down again.' Some of the men in Ross's squadron had their weapons knocked from their grasp; some were wounded in the hands and arms. One man had four rifles smashed in quick succession.[10]

During the night, Ross was ordered to take eighteen men out to occupy an outpost in no-man's land, established to protect a section of Quinn's that had been only partially dug. He had a harrowing experience out there; the exposed position was under constant fire. Ross handled his men well, though, deploying them to take advantage of the available cover; only one soldier in the section was wounded. At the first sign of dawn, Ross withdrew his men to the main position. The promise that had seen him promoted during training had been justified.

The Turkish bombing intensified at daylight. With none of their own to throw back, the light horsemen could do little besides smothering the Turkish grenades with their coats—something the exhausted infantrymen holding Quinn's had shown them. During the morning, one burst on the parapet just in front of Ross, collapsing the sandbags in on top of him. He felt terrified and suddenly wanted to be at home again. Soon, the intensity of the bombing forced the light horsemen to abandon the firing trench and take cover in the support line. Again demonstrating initiative, Ross remained behind with another man to repair the parapet; as they worked, another Turkish bomb landed, 'a little round ball of cast iron about the size of a cricket ball, sizzling on the bottom of the trench between us'. Ross tossed his overcoat on it moments before it exploded: 'The fumes were awful, and the row knocked me silly for a bit.'[11] When the bombing subsided, the light horsemen reoccupied the post's front line. Those who had left kit and rations behind found them cut to ribbons, the trench's clay wall spattered with bully beef. In one place, the boot of a dead Turk protruded from the parapet into the trench; it had, in the words of one of Ross's comrades, 'sprung a long leak of indescribable matter'.[12]

In letters home, Ross spared Jessie these details. One of the other men in B Squadron, however, candidly articulated the shock and trauma of the seventeen hours the unit spent under fire in Quinn's Post. 'Have just come out of Hell,' he began. 'I don't think a man could put in a worse night than we did. It was something awful.' He described the 'continual stream' of Turkish bombs they had to endure, helplessly: 'We had to crawl into any hole and just wait until we were nearly driven mad with suspense.' This man saw two of B Squadron's troopers 'literally smashed to pieces' by shrapnel. Another man had his 'head blown off' when he glanced above the parapet.[13]

Ross spent a second, comparatively quiet, night with B Squadron in the support line of Quinn's Post before returning to the 3rd Light Horse bivouac in Monash Valley. Another of Ross's comrades noted how utterly exhausted they were. The men 'just sank where they were, in all sorts of positions and fell asleep, taking no notice of the ordinary daily noise of desultory action a hundred feet away.'[14]

8

LIFE IN THE TRENCHES

On 18 May 1915, the day after Ross returned from Quinn's Post, the Turkish artillery opened fire on the Anzac sector to prepare for a major offensive. Having massed 42,000 troops, the Ottoman command intended to overrun the beachhead and push the invaders into the sea. The shells began falling among Ross and his comrades as they huddled around their small campfires, cooking breakfast. The first explosion sent frypans flying and took both legs and an arm off one man. More than 40 of the 9.2-inch projectiles landed among the regiment's dugouts during the morning, their detonations stupefying men and flinging lethal splinters of iron through the air. Men who had shown no sign of fear to date were 'completely unnerved' by the onslaught.[1]

The shelling continued for twenty hours and then the Ottoman infantry attacked. All along the front they charged across no-man's land in densely packed waves. Expecting an attack, the Australians and New Zealanders defended their trenches with an enormous volume of rifle and machine gun fire. Besides making a few brief incursions into the ANZAC lines, the Ottoman infantry captured no ground and suffered 10,000 casualties. Seven hundred Australians and New Zealanders had been killed or wounded.

Ross and the men of the 3rd Light Horse remained in reserve in Monash Valley throughout the fighting on 19 May but early the following morning they received orders to relieve the 1st Light Horse Regiment in the trenches at Pope's Hill.

Situated at the head of Monash Valley, Pope's Hill had been established as an outpost to cover a gap in the Australian trenches between Quinn's Post and Russell's Top. A series of narrow spurs and steep ravines separated Pope's from the Turkish front line, creating a wide no-man's land that neither side had been able to occupy. The Pope's garrison was responsible for ensuring that the Turks did not cross this rugged terrain and gain access to Monash Valley, and hence the area behind the ANZAC front line. In one of the letters he sent Jessie from Pope's Hill, Ross described the outpost as being 'on top of a big hill' from where he could follow shells fired by the ships of the Royal Navy off Anzac Cove to where they burst in the Turkish lines.[2] Compared with Quinn's, thought Ross, Pope's Hill represented 'a fairly easy post'.[3] The trenches were deep and well-constructed, and the broad no-man's land—about 80 metres—made bombing and raiding by Turkish patrols unlikely.

During his first week at Pope's Hill, Ross had a grandstand view of two of the most talked-about incidents of the campaign. On 24 May, the Ottoman and ANZAC commanders agreed to a nine-hour ceasefire to bury the thousands of decaying corpses that lay in no-man's land—the smell had become unbearable. Shortly after daybreak, soldiers from both sides cautiously emerged from their trenches and began to dig burial pits in no-man's land. 'The lack of noise, clamour and clatter in the air was uncanny,' observed one of Ross's comrades. 'The most striking thing about the armistice was this extraordinary silence.'[4] The 3rd Light Horse Regiment remained in the trenches on Pope's Hill, ready at arms in case the Turks broke the ceasefire. From his position, Ross could, for the first time, gaze out on the battlefield. Thousands of dead men—predominantly Turks who had been killed trying to cross no-man's land during their attack on 19 May—carpeted the ground. They lay in great lines and heaps where ANZAC machine guns and rifle fire had mown them down. Their dull khaki uniforms obscured whole sections of the battlefield.[5] 'I watched part of it,' wrote Ross, 'but it was a terrible sight and thousands were buried that day.'[6]

The following day, Ross witnessed the dramatic sinking of the British battleship HMS *Triumph*. It was shelling Ottoman artillery positions onshore when a torpedo, fired by a German U-boat, struck. As he watched the scene unfold, Ross recalled how, in 1906 when he was thirteen years old, he and his family had watched the *Triumph* fire her guns during a naval exercise at Plymouth.[7] Now 'she heeled over very quickly . . . her starboard rail touched the water 8 minutes after the explosion, and she floated bottom up for 22 minutes, and then took her final plunge'.[8] Nearby destroyers rescued most of the *Triumph*'s 800 crew.

With the move to Pope's Hill, Ross's life at Anzac settled down into a relatively predictable routine of stretches in and out of the line. He typically spent a week at a time in the outpost's trenches, alternating in two twelve-hour shifts between the firing and support lines. Ross joined in the effort to suppress sniper fire from the Turkish trenches: 'I would get at a steel loop hole and pick up a man firing fairly constantly, and get a rough sight on the place, and the moment I saw his flash I would fire.' The sniping helped Ross to stay awake during long night watches. Just before dawn each day, the garrison stood to arms and remained at the ready, in full battle kit, for an hour in case the Turks attacked. It was this part of the trench warfare routine that Ross liked least—though the rum issued each morning 'puts new life into a man and does us worlds of good'.[9]

Bombing emerged as the activity Ross enjoyed most. With the opposing trenches at Pope's Hill too far apart to throw bombs, the outpost acquired a Garland Trench Mortar—a crudely improvised weapon designed and manufactured in Egypt for use at Gallipoli. Employing the shared enthusiasm for contraptions that they had demonstrated on motorcycles before the war, Ross and Roy Howard had 'such fun' using it to launch bombs across the valley to the opposing Ottoman trenches.[10] Ross's expertise with the weapon soon saw him appointed to replace the regiment's officer in charge of bombing. 'I'll make a good anarchist after the war,' he quipped in a letter to Keith.[11] As the campaign wore on, Turkish aircraft began appearing over Anzac. Ross enjoyed the 'sport' of shooting at them—it reminded him of 'that man at Mulyungarie who used to lie on his back and shoot eagle hawks'.[12]

In between the standard, week-long tours in the trenches, Ross typically had a week or so in the post's reserve positions, situated in a gully behind

Pope's Hill. There was really no rest for anyone at Anzac; while in reserve, Ross laboured in working parties to build roads, repair defences and carry supplies from the beach up to the front. The men did, however, get more sleep when in reserve than in the trenches, with dugouts built into the side of the hill providing some shelter from the elements, if not shellfire. Ross described his dugout as 'a comfy little place, 18 inches [45 centimetres] deep, and [sand] bagged on the side, and 2 waterproof sheets for a roof'.[13] He had to remove the overhead cover to stand up. Although he usually had this small space to himself, there was one occasion when Ross allowed an old friend from his cadet days, Sophus 'Solly' Vohr, to take shelter with him during a storm. As they lay in the dark reminiscing, the two friends recalled how the last time they had been forced to share a bed had been five years earlier, in Edinburgh during the mounted cadet tour. Back then, Ross had pushed Vohr out to sleep on the floor. Had he done so this time, Ross reasoned, his mate 'would have gone rolling down the hill'.[14]

Whether in the trenches or in reserve, Ross had no illusions that his life was in constant danger. There was nowhere at Anzac where anybody could feel completely safe. During June and July, as his regiment took its turn rotating in and out of the post on Pope's Hill, Ross watched as a slow toll of sickness, wounds and death claimed friends and comrades. Ottoman shells caused some of the casualties as they fell randomly, day and night. To his mother, Ross admitted that the shelling frightened him: 'The nasty time is just before it hits, and you think it has surely got your dugout.' He had a number of close calls but escaped injury; in one instance, a piece of high-explosive shell sheared the heel off his boot and in another, when a shell exploded just a few metres from him, its brass fuse cap thumped him in the leg.[15]

Snipers presented another potentially lethal threat to Ross and the men of the Pope's Hill garrison. The introduction of periscopes and steel loopholes, and a vigorous counter-sniping effort, mitigated the danger to some degree, although Turkish marksmen continued to exact a toll on the unwary and the unlucky. The experience of seeing comrades' lives ended by a sniper's bullet, in a shockingly violent moment of blood and gore, became a relatively common one for Ross.[16] While he appears to have tried to avoid dwelling on the loss of men in his unit, the death of his best friend, Gordon Timbrell, killed by a sniper at Pope's Hill on 1 July 1915, affected Ross severely. 'Timmy' had been 'too careless', recorded Ross, 'and got his head up too high on a nasty corner.' Ross 'fixed' him a grave at the cemetery in Shrapnel Valley the following night and wrote to Timmy's mother, hoping to provide the heartbroken woman with some measure of comfort.[17] 'You don't know how much I miss the poor chap,' he wrote to Jessie.[18] He would spend July, 'a rotten month for me', struggling with grief.[19]

As Ross's attribution of Timmy's death to 'carelessness' suggests, he did not turn to fatalism as a means of coping with his constant exposure to danger. Indeed, Ross's immersion in violence and death produced no religious or otherwise metaphysical response at all in his letters; he remained a pragmatist. Accordingly, after adjusting to the initial shock of his first few weeks on a battlefield, Ross became used to the sight of men mutilated by bombs and bullets.[20] He found another means of coping in humour, explaining in a letter to Keith that 'there is really an awfully lot of fun' to be had on the battlefield: 'Funny little episodes are always happening.' The incidents that Ross and his friends found comical invariably involved a narrow escape from death, such as the evening when a piece of high-explosive shell landed in a pot of soup that Solly Vohr was cooking. 'His surprised look and language were too funny.'[21]

At the same time, Ross tried to ease his mother's anxiety by presenting her with a reassuringly upbeat picture of life at the front. Besides Timmy's death, he rarely mentioned casualties in his letters and, for the time that he was on the peninsula, he tended to keep his narrow escapes from shellfire and snipers' bullets out of his correspondence. 'Have just done a week in the trenches,' began a typical letter dated 30 May 1915. 'We are living very well and get more tucker than we can eat. Fresh meat, ham, bacon and vegetables.'[22]

In reality, privation and discomfort characterised life at Anzac. Although Ross generally had plenty to eat, the food—especially early in the campaign—tended to be monotonous and of poor quality. It often spoiled on its long journey to Gallipoli. 'Bully [corned beef] and biscuits with a bit of rice and jam you could hardly eat,' is how Ross later (and more candidly) recalled the Gallipoli diet. Occasionally he received a ration of bread and could recall, in four months on the peninsula, eating fresh meat just six times.[23] For breakfast, Ross usually made a porridge 'by pounding up biscuits in an old shell'.[24] As the weather heated up during June, Anzac became inundated with flies, attracted by open latrines and rotting corpses. Most men took to eating before dawn and after dusk to avoid the worst of the buzzing black plague.

Relief from rations came inside the parcels Ross received from his family, friends and charitable organisations all over the world. He wrote gratefully of receiving such delicacies as tinned fruit, chocolate and cigarettes, telling Jessie in one instance that 'you've got no idea' how one parcel of such delicacies 'gladdened my eye'. For Ross, the joy of receiving such treats was only enhanced by sharing them with good company, and he accordingly invited Solly Vohr, Roy Howard and Geoff Wells to 'an afternoon' at his dugout.[25] On another occasion, Ross employed his characteristically dry humour to thank his mother for some slippers and hankies that turned up in late August: 'The slippers are far too good for this work, and I am going to cause some jealousy tonight when I appear in them.'[26]

Parcels could take two months to cover the distance from Adelaide to Gallipoli, however, and delays in the mail system (at one stage Ross received nothing for seven weeks) forced him to look elsewhere for small comforts. On the beach at Anzac Cove, he found 'enterprising individuals' from the naval crews, who ferried men and equipment from Egypt, engaged in a 'roaring trade' on the beach. Ross found the prices exorbitant: two shillings for a tin of milk and four for a bottle of lime juice when he received a daily wage of just under twelve shillings. It did not bother Ross, though; his pragmatic outlook again characterised his approach to these beachside merchants: 'money doesn't count for much here, and if a man has a few bob he doesn't mind how he spends it'.[27]

On the beach, Ross also found some relief from the warming summer weather and the lice that inundated everyone at Gallipoli. When the shelling wasn't too severe, he joined the hundreds of men who bathed in the sea 'at every hour of the day'. When the Turkish shrapnel burst above the cove too regularly, Ross prudently stayed out of the water, leaving the swimming to his more daring comrades. He found the 'contempt' that some men showed the shelling 'extraordinary', and was amused when it became too intense and sent naked diggers bounding from the sea to find cover, 'swearing only as an Australian can because he had been disturbed at his bathe'. Otherwise, Ross spent his spare time playing card games, smoking and reading. 'We play cards for cigarettes, and money rarely changes hands,' he told his mother. 'Books are very scarce, and you will see the proud owner of a "Nat Gould" [a popular British novelist] going round the camp, demanding so many cigarettes, or so much tobacco, for the pleasure of reading his literature.'[28] Like many soldiers there, Ross took advantage of the relaxed rules at Anzac concerning photography, and used his folding vest pocket camera to document life at the front and send the pictures home to his family and to the parents of his friends.

As the heat and flies intensified during July, illness swept through the Anzac garrison, debilitating men and depleting units to as little as half their strength. Ross managed to stay well but many of his comrades became sick, with enteric (intestinal) illnesses—spread by flies—among the most persistent diagnoses. In the second half of July alone the 3rd Light Horse lost 58 men sick compared with seven wounded by enemy fire. By the end of the month the unit's strength had declined to a point that garrisoning Pope's Hill required reinforcements from the other regiments of the 1st Light Horse Brigade. Ross's popular CO, Lieutenant Colonel Frank Rowell, was among those evacuated. He died aboard a hospital ship on 8 August 1915, his passing a 'staggering blow' to the 3rd Light Horse Regiment.[29] 'We all felt the loss of Colonel Rowell very much,' wrote Ross. 'If we had a few more men like him we might have been in Constantinople by now.'[30]

9

THE AUGUST OFFENSIVE

As illness claimed more and more men on the Gallipoli peninsula during the summer heat of July, the British general staff planned what would become the largest military operation of the entire campaign. With an offensive launched from Anzac Cove and supported by a British landing at Suvla Bay, 7 kilometres to the north, the British generals sought to end the stalemate at Gallipoli, and ultimately achieve their original objective of forcing Ottoman Turkey out of the war. Scheduled to begin in early August, the ambitious plans would, after the staff's complex calculations regarding logistics, communications and artillery fire plans, rely on the efforts of Ross Smith and around 120,000 other soldiers of the British Empire and its allies.

Although nobody at Pope's Hill knew the details, the influx of reinforcements and stores into the Anzac area during July made it clear that preparations for a major offensive were underway. Besides his usual rotations in and out of the front line, Ross spent the latter part of July carrying out extra fatigue duties to stockpile rations, water and ammunition close behind the front line. For eleven days straight, he had no more than two hours' sleep each night.[1]

The offensive began on the afternoon of 6 August 1915. The first stage involved a series of diversionary operations at various points along the Gallipoli Peninsula to confuse the Turks. At Anzac, the first of these occurred at Lone Pine, where the 1st Australian Infantry Brigade assaulted a well-entrenched part of the Ottoman front line. From Pope's Hill, just a few hundred metres away, Ross watched as the Australian infantry, distinguished in the twilight by white patches sewn onto their tunics, charged across a bare plateau towards the Turkish trenches. Machine guns all along the ANZAC line, including on Pope's Hill, supported them with covering fire. 'The hubbub was indescribable,' recalled one man in Ross's regiment.[2] Following a bloody struggle that lasted throughout the night, the men of the 1st Brigade held the Lone Pine trenches.

Meanwhile, the main British operation began overnight on 6–7 August. Its objective was to capture the peaks of the Sari Bair mountain range, which extended north of the ANZAC sector. The British generals hoped that these positions, which offered commanding views across Gallipoli, would give their forces a significant tactical advantage in subsequent operations to secure the rest of the peninsula. After sunset on 6 August, three columns of Australian, New Zealand, British and Indian infantry left Anzac Cove and marched north along the coast under the cover of darkness. A few kilometres north of the ANZAC sector, they turned inland and began climbing through impossibly rugged terrain towards their objectives.

In order to draw Turkish reinforcements away from the main British attack on the Sari Bair peaks, at dawn on 7 August, Australian units back at Anzac launched further diversionary operations. From Pope's Hill and Quinn's Post, the 1st Light Horse Brigade launched two simultaneous attacks, with the 1st and 2nd Regiments charging while the 3rd remained in reserve. Ross later heard that his unit was chosen to sit out because it was the weakest of the brigade's three regiments.[3] Others believed a rumour that the three COs decided it by tossing coins.[4] Either way, as Ross observed, 'our share was watching the wounded coming down' and listening to the clatter of gunfire on the ridges above. Both of the 1st Light Horse Brigade's charges failed: at Pope's Hill the 1st Regiment briefly made it into the Turkish front line before being forced to withdraw. At Quinn's, most men in the 2nd Regiment's charge did not make it more than a few metres before Turkish machine guns cut them down. The story was the same elsewhere along the ANZAC front line that morning—including at the Nek, which Peter Weir would famously depict in his 1981 film *Gallipoli*.

Shortly after dawn, B Squadron received orders to reinforce the front line on Pope's Hill. Entering the trenches, Ross found the position nearly deserted; only a handful of survivors from the 1st Light Horse Regiment had made it back after their charge. 'We expected a counter attack any minute,' wrote Ross. Taking his position on the left of Pope's Hill, he could see Turks across the valley, boldly standing up in their trenches to fire at the light horsemen who were, at that moment, charging at the Nek. The men in Ross's troop returned fire. 'We had some fine shooting at head and shoulder targets at 300 yards,' he reported. The Royal Navy soon joined in, pummelling the Ottoman front line with high-explosive shells. Although their bombardment fell a hundred metres or more away, the explosions showered Pope's Hill with debris. Ross was soon 'black with dust and dirt'.[5]

For three days, Ross remained on the front line at Pope's Hill while the main battle raged to the north of Anzac on the Sari Bair range and at Suvla Bay. Rumours circulated but nobody knew for certain what was happening. At Pope's, things remained tense: would the Turks launch a counter-attack against the now-weakened and dispersed ANZAC garrison? Ross remained at his post for 72 hours; he did not wash or remove his boots and he ate while peering out into no-man's land through periscopes. Both sides shelled the battlefield relentlessly; for hours at a time, the noise made it impossible for men to speak with one another.[6]

From their trenches on Pope's Hill, the men of the 3rd Light Horse Regiment could see some of their comrades who had survived the charge on 7 August, stranded in no-man's land under the blazing hot sun, without food or water; some of them were wounded. The morning after the attack, Ross spotted an Australian sergeant sheltering in a shallow depression only a few metres from the Turkish front line. Ross attracted the man's attention and they began signalling to each other; using paper, the hapless sergeant communicated his name, 'Shepherd', and asked 'Any hope?' Forbidden by his CO from venturing out into no-man's land himself, Ross signalled to Sergeant Shepherd, instructing him to wait until dark and then roll into a nearby gully where some stretcher bearers could collect him. In the meantime, Ross kept watch, firing at any Turks who rose above their parapet to shoot at Shepherd. 'It meant my staying there nearly all day with a periscope in one hand, and my rifle in the other . . . Every time the Turk put his rifle up I would let him have one. How the bullets whistled round my old nut!!' Thanks to Ross's intervention, Sergeant George Shepherd made it back to the Australian lines that night and would recover from gunshot wounds to his hip and foot.

With characteristic modesty, Ross left this out of his letters home. He only revealed it nine months later when Jessie heard about it from the family of one of his friends and pressed Ross for the details. Even then, Ross reasoned that 'anyone else would have done the same' and pointed out that they had not been able to rescue everyone. To emphasise the point, he related to Jessie the horrible experience of watching another wounded light horseman die slowly out in no-man's land. The memory remained a vivid one: 'I'll never forget those two days, and watching that man die, and not being able to do anything.'[7]

The August offensive had failed. While Ross and his comrades worked to rescue survivors from the battlefield in front of Pope's Hill, the attacks on the peaks of the Sari Bair range and the British advance inland from Suvla Bay both faltered, with neither achieving its objectives. Fighting would continue in the area north of Anzac Cove throughout August, although it would not change the battle's outcome: there was no breakout; British forces on the peninsula remained mired in a trench warfare deadlock. Attempting to break the stalemate had cost Britain and her dominions 45,000 men killed, wounded or missing. But still the fighting at Gallipoli ground on.

10

QUINN'S POST

The routine of trench warfare resumed at Anzac following the failure of the August offensive. Now, though, the garrison had to hold a line that extended north to connect with the new British beachhead at Suvla Bay. To defend this longer front, the ANZAC units were badly depleted and flushed with inexperienced reinforcements. Having come through the battles of early August relatively unscathed, Ross's regiment became responsible for shouldering a larger burden of work on the front line. On 9 August, the 3rd Light Horse Regiment left Pope's Hill, a position it had occupied for three months, and moved across Monash Valley to Quinn's Post. For the next month, Ross and his comrades would hold this dangerous position without relief or reinforcement.

The state of Quinn's surprised Ross. It had become a much more secure position since his first terrifying night there in May. He wrote, 'Now there are nice deep wide trenches, and in places overhead cover, and steel loop holes, and all the way along netting is put up high in front of the trench to stop bombs coming in.' Still, compared with Pope's Hill, Ross considered Quinn's a 'rotten post'. To its immediate rear, steep slopes dropped down into Monash Valley. In front, barely a dozen metres away, the Turks had a heavily defended front line with numerous machine guns trained on Quinn's.[1]

Ross would say little else about his month at Quinn's Post. He apparently sent home only two relatively brief letters during his month there. This uncharacteristic disruption in his correspondence is itself suggestive of the difficult time that he had there during August. The accounts of other men in the 3rd Light Horse confirm that it was a dreadful experience for all of them. 'Here the enemy are less than 15 yards [13.7 metres] away and bombs are thrown into our trenches all day and night long', were the first impressions that one man in Ross's unit had of Quinn's. 'One has to be ever ready for a charge too on account of the very short warning.'[2] Five days later, another of Ross's comrades in B Squadron recorded that 'the smell of our dead in front is something sickening and the flies are nearly driving me silly'.[3] Another added, 'One's food is simply black with flies while the weather is cruelly hot.'[4]

With insufficient men to hold the post using the conventional method of rotating squadrons in and out of the front and reserve positions, practically the entire regiment remained in action without a relief. Two of Ross's comrades recorded in their diaries that they slept for no longer than two hours a night during the month they spent at Quinn's.[5] Adding to the strain Ross experienced would have been his responsibility for the regiment's bomb-throwing section. It was, indeed, the hand-thrown bomb, manufactured in a makeshift 'factory' on the beach from jam tins, which characterised the fighting at Quinn's—something Ross recognised all too well, stating that bombing was 'a dangerous job, perhaps the most. One lives within 5 seconds of sudden death all the time . . .'[6] Several of the casualties sustained by his section during its tour at Quinn's resulted from bombs detonating prematurely in their throwers' hands.

By mid-August, practically every man in the regiment—including Ross—was sick with influenza. The lack of reinforcements, however, permitted the evacuation of only the most serious cases. In his diary, one of the corporals in Ross's unit documented the decrepit state into which the regiment had fallen. 'Everyone is run down and thin & weak so they have nothing to fight against disease,' he wrote on 17 August. A week later he observed how, 'Our numbers are dwindling and there are only a handful of us left.' Then, at the end of the month, 'I am passing a lot of blood but still we have to stick it.'[7] The number of combat casualties paled into insignificance. During its month at Quinn's Post, the 3rd Light Horse Regiment lost a man killed and fourteen wounded, most of them by bombs. In the same period, 139 officers and men—over a quarter of the regiment's nominal strength—were evacuated sick.[8] By 10 September, Ross was one of only 90 men left of the 516 who had landed at Anzac in May. 'Our boys are nearly all absolute wrecks and are being carried away in scores,' recorded one of Ross's comrades.[9]

The constant stream of medical evacuations created the opportunity for promotion to which Ross had aspired all year. When, on 11 August, the unit's regimental sergeant major (RSM) was commissioned to replace a sick lieutenant, Ross took his place as the unit's senior NCO. Then, three weeks later, Ross received a commission himself. Appointed 2nd Lieutenant, he was put in command of No. 3 Troop of the 3rd Light Horse Regiment's A Squadron. In the space of a year, Ross had risen from private to lieutenant—a regimental record, he claimed, when writing to his mother to share the good news.[10] Becoming a commissioned officer represented a considerable increase in his responsibilities. He now had command of about 40 men and, under normal trench warfare conditions, was accountable for the defence of a section of the front line. Being commissioned in the field allowed Ross no opportunity to receive formal training as a leader—although, in his experiences as an NCO, he had seen plenty of examples of both good and bad leadership by the AIF's junior officers. Ross's four months at Anzac also gave him as much combat experience as practically anyone else in the AIF.

The first week of September proved to be a good one for Ross. Besides his commission, orders arrived at Quinn's Post for the 3rd Light Horse Regiment's relief. After 29 days there, Ross and his emaciated, exhausted comrades, struggling to carry their equipment, shuffled back down to Anzac Cove. From the beach, they 'staggered . . . a semi silent and pitiable throng', along a trench that led north from Anzac Cove to the new outposts established during the August offensive.[11] The regiment spent a blessed three days resting and establishing a bivouac in a valley at the end of Rhododendron Ridge before taking over the trenches at the nearby Destroyer Hill. The new assignment pleased Ross; he noted how the more open countryside north of Anzac Cove allowed proper latrines and better supplies. The sector was quiet, with infrequent sniping and bombing. A large mail, the first in weeks, was also waiting at the new post; Ross received comfort parcels from prominent Adelaide women and a supply of tobacco from a charity in South America. The unit ate a ration of mutton—the first they had seen since leaving Egypt. 'After we buried sundry dead Turks, things began to get quite comfortable,' wrote Ross of their new bivouac.[12]

Ross had just a few days to enjoy the comparatively salubrious conditions at Destroyer Hill before he became ill with paratyphoid, an intestinal infection that he had seen claim many friends in recent weeks—some with fatal consequences. The onset of fever, headache and abdominal pain was typical enough among the discomforts of Gallipoli, but the severity of Ross's symptoms warranted a medical evacuation. On 12 September 1915, he left Anzac Cove aboard a minesweeper that had been adapted to carry patients. It was the beginning of a long journey through the British Army's medical system that would see him pass through hospitals on Imbros, Lemnos and Gibraltar before finally arriving in London. Ross's parents and brothers learned of his condition a month after he left Gallipoli, when a telegram arrived at Aviemore, in Adelaide's leafy north, all the way from Gibraltar. Just twelve hours later, to Ross's delight, he had a reply from his mother: she was relieved to know that he was alright and was checking that he had enough money.[13]

Gallipoli had provided a watershed experience for Ross Smith. His first experience of combat, it had exposed him to extensive physical, mental and emotional duress. Despite the largely unrecorded moments of terror and personal self-doubt that he probably endured, the experience had provided him with the opportunity to demonstrate his initiative, his resilience and his ability to handle men under the stress of battle.

Six weeks after leaving the peninsula, Ross wrote his mother a lengthy account of his time at Gallipoli—4500 words that filled in some of the details he had omitted from the letters he wrote from the trenches. It is not particularly reflective in tone or content, but nevertheless offers some clues about how the campaign affected him. First, it is clear that he emerged from the experience of Gallipoli proud of what he perceived to be the outstanding fighting prowess of Australian soldiers—although his nationalism remained firmly fixed in a broader imperial identity. Indeed, Ross did not attribute the success of ANZAC troops to their distinct Antipodean background, but, rather 'the old fighting blood . . . A Britisher with his back to the wall'. Although he suffered both physically and emotionally, and lost good friends, at Gallipoli, there is no sense in Ross's letter that he had become disillusioned with the cause for which he fought. Indeed, from later correspondence it is clear that it remained Ross's conviction that Britain must fight and win this war for the good of civilisation. Of the violence, he noted that he had become used to seeing comrades wounded and killed—and apparently had also become inured to danger himself. 'As far as bullets go,' he told Jessie, perhaps with a touch of bravado intended to reassure, 'one treats them with contempt and never thinks of being hit.' With disappointment, he admitted that he had 'unfortunately' never participated in a bayonet charge.[14]

For three months after Ross left, the situation at Gallipoli remained the same. There were no further major battles and, in increasingly bad weather, both sides prepared for a winter in the trenches. The British authorities intervened, concluding that they had now exhausted all prospects of success at Gallipoli. On 8 December 1915, the last ANZAC forces left the peninsula under a brilliantly conceived and executed evacuation plan. The Turks did not even realise that their adversaries of eight months had gone until the following day. The British evacuated Helles in January 1916, bringing the Gallipoli campaign to a close. The AIF had suffered 28,000 casualties, 8700 of whom died. In the British Army, casualties approached 74,000; for the Turks they exceeded a quarter of a million.

When news of the evacuation reached Ross, by then comfortably ensconced at a convalescent home in rural England, it surprised him. No doubt reflecting on the loss of Timmy and numerous other friends, he wondered what the point of it all had been: 'It's hard to think it was all for nothing.'[15] Mulling it over in the coming weeks as he diligently followed the war's progress in the newspapers, Ross concluded that while the Gallipoli invasion had failed, the campaign had secured some strategic advantages for the Allies. It drew Ottoman resources away from other fronts, allowing the British to secure Egypt and parts of Mesopotamia, he reasoned, and it helped Britain's Russian allies to make gains in the Caucasus. Ross predicted that with a century of hindsight people would come to appreciate this broader assessment of the Gallipoli campaign—much like the way 'we of today look back on Waterloo [1815], where our forefathers died for us'.[16]

What, then, would Ross have made of how the campaign is remembered today, a hundred years later? In one respect, his prediction has proved prescient: in its centenary year, Gallipoli somewhat paradoxically transcended its innate human tragedy to emerge as a celebrated triumph of national character—the defining moment not just in Australia's involvement in the Great War, but in the nation's entire history. Just as Ross and his generation viewed Waterloo in its centenary year of 1915, Australians have cast Gallipoli in their own image: the soldiers there fought for 'us' and established a tradition that we can and should emulate. The importance of the Anzac legend to modern Australia may not have surprised Ross—although the crass commercialisation of commemoration in the centenary year would probably have seemed bizarre and inappropriately ostentatious to him.

At the same time, however, Ross's optimistic assessment of the campaign's strategic value was based on wishful thinking—the product of censorship and propaganda in wartime Britain and his own understandable need to justify the carnage he had witnessed. In the best modern studies of it, the campaign stands as a badly misconceived endeavour that had little to no chance of success and, in the end, achieved nothing for the British cause.[17] A notion too difficult for Ross Smith to countenance in 1915, this might just represent the most utterly tragic aspect of the entire Gallipoli campaign.

11

CUTTING SOME ICE

Ross left Gallipoli on 12 September 1915 aboard a dilapidated minesweeper that the Royal Navy had converted to evacuate sick men from the peninsula. Diagnosing his illness as infectious, the crew isolated Ross from the other patients by putting his stretcher in the vessel's covered-over lifeboat. He made the voyage to the island of Imbros sharing this improvised quarantine ward with another light horseman named Les Sutherland, who was also suffering enteritis, and—of all things—a live pig tied in a bag and squealing incessantly. The resourceful minesweeper's crew planned to keep the swine 'quarantined' until Christmas dinner. Ross and Sutherland struck up a conversation during the voyage but were separated at its conclusion, probably assuming that their paths would never cross again. If so, they would be wrong.

Ross spent a few days at a British field hospital on Imbros, where 'some damned hound' stole his money belt. A hospital ship then conveyed him to Lemnos where, to his relief, he was admitted to the 1st Australian Stationary Hospital and into the care of Australian nurses and a 'ripping chap' of a British doctor.[1] He arrived in a bad way: his temperature spiked to 40°C and one night he nearly died. For three weeks, Ross suffered fevers and subsisted on a diet of soda water and a little milk. His doctor determined that the seriousness of his condition warranted evacuation to Britain for treatment.

On 13 October 1915, Ross wrote to his mother for the first time in nearly a month. He was aboard the TSS *Caledonia*, a converted Atlantic passenger liner, and 'getting near Gibralter [sic]'. Ross described himself as 'a weak and thin, very thin, little boy' with legs that were 'just like sticks' but said that his health was now improving. He also noted his great fortune at being commissioned just a few days before getting sick. As 'an "hofficer" now', as he self-deprecatingly put it, he travelled in a ward that had been established in the ship's first-class music hall. 'You can imagine with what unutterable joy I scan those Menus three times a day,' he wrote to his mother. After five months of Anzac's 'hard tucker' and three weeks of being unable to eat anything, the ship's cuisine almost made him 'weep with joy'. Ross enjoyed the company of the other officers in the ward, most of whom were British ('awfully decent chaps'). One played Chopin on the piano near Ross's bed. 'It's the first decent music I've heard for months, and I love it.'[2]

When the *Caledonia's* patients disembarked at Gibraltar, volunteers from the town's sporting clubs and militia carried those too ill to walk to the colony's army hospital, including Ross. Most of the town turned out to greet these men who Gallipoli had marked with wounds and sickness. Girls handed out cigarettes to the patients as they made their way on stretchers through the township. Although he knew he was bound for Britain, Ross expected a lengthy stay at Gibraltar, having heard that they needed to wait for a properly marked hospital ship to convey them through the U-boat infested waters around the United Kingdom. At Gibraltar's military hospital, a large and very well-equipped establishment, Ross came under the care of some 'very nice' British nurses and an energetic matron who, 'just like a rubber ball . . . bounces from one place to the other'.[3] After a few days there, they encouraged Ross out of bed for the first time in five weeks but his legs could not yet support his weight.

While at Gibraltar, Ross kept in touch with home, sending cables and writing letters. Learning that his twenty-year-old brother, Colin, had left his job at the Union Bank and enlisted in the AIF, Ross wrote to 'the Kid', sharing some advice on army life and suggesting what he should take overseas.[4] In Egypt back in February, when Ross had first heard that his younger brother planned to enlist, he had encouraged it, declaring that it was Colin's duty to join what was bound to be a long and difficult struggle.[5] If Ross's subsequent experiences at Gallipoli led him to have misgivings about his younger brother's enlistment in an infantry battalion, then he did not reveal them in his letters to his mother at this time.

After a fortnight at Gibraltar, Ross embarked for Britain aboard the hospital ship *Braemar Castle.* He had an 'uneventful' voyage and arrived at Southampton on 4 November 1915.[6] Despite improving health, he relapsed shortly after arriving and again needed hospitalisation. With the AIF's medical organisation struggling to cope with the 11,500 other Australian patients who had arrived in Britain by November, Ross found himself admitted to the British Army's 3rd London General Hospital, at Wandsworth. Established in the grounds of a converted orphanage and school, it could accommodate 1800 patients.

Ross's health improved during his first couple of weeks at Wandsworth. Propped up beside a fireplace, he wrote home in mid-November of the 'jolly good' treatment he had received. 'People are awfully good to us, and lots come into the wards and talk.' Some were family connections, but most of them were well-meaning strangers, keen to demonstrate their gratitude to the colonial soldiers who had travelled so far to fight for the empire. One wealthy woman, on whom Ross made a particularly good impression, sent her car to bring him to tea so he could meet her daughter. On another occasion, Ross enjoyed a visit from 'three beauteous damsels' who treated him with sweets and tobacco.[7] 'I'm overwhelmed by people wanting me to go and stay with them,' he wrote. 'Everyone thinks Australians are wonderful.'[8]

By the end of November, Ross was well enough to secure a discharge from hospital. He was still weak and with a befuddled memory, but a medical board granted him two months' leave to recover before returning to the front. Ross spent his first days out of hospital reacquainting himself with London, which he found 'much the same' as he had as a cadet in 1910, except for the restricted drinking hours in hotels and blackout conditions prompted by 'those damned Germans and their dirty Zeppelins'.[9] Ross wasted no time in being fitted for an officer's uniform, which he wore with great satisfaction.

'I keep my leggings and belt and spurs well-polished,' he told his mother. 'The pants are fine and baggy at the sides, so I cut some ice when I go out.'[10] With plenty of pay unclaimed from his time at Gallipoli, Ross enjoyed London's nightlife, including celebrations for his 23rd birthday. He discovered that his lieutenant's pips gave him access to more socially exclusive settings and turned the heads of young women. As he told Jessie, 'Ross Smith of Harris, Scarfe & Co is quite a decent sort of chap but Lieutenant Ross Smith of the 3rd Light Horse seems to attract considerably more attention.'[11]

Ross spent Christmas 1915 at the Dales, a country estate on the Norfolk coast. He went at the invitation of its owner, Margaret King; the daughter of a South Australian pastoralist; she had once spent time at Mutooroo. With her husband away at Gallipoli, Mrs King had transformed their estate into a convalescent home and established a canteen for soldiers on leave. Ross relished his few weeks at the Dales, enjoying the 'lovely gardens and lawns' and 'huge' well-furnished home, and playing games with the Kings' five children. Reminders of the war were never far away, though. Just a mile down the road Ross found trenches, artillery batteries and barbed wire protecting the coast. All the windows in the nearby seaside town of Sheringham had been blacked out and motorists crawled about after dark without their headlights. The wreck of a torpedoed merchant ship lay on a nearby beach.[12]

Ross said goodbye to Mrs King and her children on 10 January, having 'enjoyed every minute' of his stay and believing that he had never experienced better hospitality.[13] He spent a few days with family friends in Warwickshire before returning to London to stay with the relatives of Pauline and Molly Schomburgk, his friends from the prominent Downer family of Adelaide. For a fortnight, Ross socialised with expatriate Australians and their London friends. In a letter home, he mentioned going to dinner with a Miss Lila Hornabrook, daughter of another notable family from Adelaide. The following night Ross accepted an invitation to dine with Miss Hornabrook at her flat. We hear nothing more of that evening or Miss Hornabrook in his letters, only that six months later she sent Ross a carton of cigarettes. If Ross and Lila shared a romance, it was a fleeting one.[14]

Although grateful for the hospitality of the families with whom he stayed, Ross became critical of what he perceived as a 'half-hearted' attitude towards the war among British civilians. He could not believe that the Asquith government had not yet introduced conscription and he dismissed calls for peace from some political factions as 'utter madness'.[15] It especially irked him when women boasted about what their distant relatives were doing at the front—even if, as Ross suspected, they were in relatively safe logistical jobs. 'The women of England are helping a great deal,' he opined, 'but some of them are such silly asses.'[16]

The ignorance that Britons had regarding Australia and Australians surprised and amused Ross. He found himself a constant source of novelty, especially in the countryside, where children stared 'in an astonished sort of way'. In one instance, the curate of a stately home in which he stayed inquired about Aborigines. After Ross shared what he knew, his host asked if there wasn't another type of 'low savage in Australia called "bushmen"'. Ross politely explained that his father was a bushman and that he, indeed, considered himself one too. On another occasion, Ross's hosts admitted to not knowing what to feed him and were surprised when he assured them that Australian 'customs and food were the same as in England'.[17]

A medical board passed Ross fit for active service on 26 January 1916 and posted him to a 'camp of mud' at Weymouth, on the Dorset coast. He again reaped the benefits of his commission, receiving a comfortable room and little work to do.[18] 'This is a jolly lazy life, and we hardly do any work at all, except go for a march in the afternoon,' he wrote to his mother in mid-February. As usual, Ross soon became restless. He passed the time studying Morse code, but became 'sick' of waiting in camp. He looked forward to rejoining his regiment, now stationed back in Egypt, and getting on a horse.[19]

At the beginning of March, Ross received orders to report to a 'fit camp' where, with other recovering troops, he recommenced physical training.[20] Eager to get back to the front and recognising that he was competing for positions in the regiment against newly commissioned officers fresh from

Australia, he signed up for as many training courses as he could, including those in bombing and machine gunnery.[21] He even contemplated a transfer to the Australian infantry, which was then preparing to deploy to the Western Front, where he perceived greater prospects for promotion. 'I am after 3 stars and mean to have them,' he declared to Jessie, referring to the insignia worn by captains.[22]

Ross left Weymouth on 25 March 1916 and began what would be an uncomfortable voyage back to Egypt. The transport, a captured Austrian steamer designed to carry 100 passengers, had over 1700 on board. Heavy seas tossed it 'about like a cork' and kept the decks awash; water poured in, drenching all aboard and their belongings. Ross complained of rotten food and the discomfort of having to wear his life jacket at all times because of the threat posed by German U-boats. He noted that if torpedoed, the ship had lifeboats for only a third of its passengers. As Ross put it, the others would need to 'attempt the long distance swimming record'.[23] It was with great relief that, five months after leaving Anzac, Ross arrived at Alexandria, safe and rested but eager to rejoin his regiment.

12

ONCE MORE OUT IN THE DESERT

Ross's enthusiasm for being back in Egypt lasted four days. By 8 April, he was 'once more out in the desert'—camped north-east of Cairo among hundreds of other Australian soldiers waiting to be posted to a unit. He learned that his own unit—the 3rd Light Horse—had been sent nearly 500 kilometres up the Nile to Girga to do 'frontier work'. Temperatures there were supposed to be 50ºC in the shade.

Promptly deciding 'that sort of job is no good to me', Ross applied to transfer to one of the AIF's new artillery brigades that were preparing to go to France.[1] For three weeks he heard nothing and was shunted about between camps, doing menial jobs and despairing at his prospects for gainful employment—let alone further promotion. 'There are hundreds of us all trying to get a job, and they are hard to get,' he complained.[2] Here and there he ran into people he knew from home. Ross heard reports about his younger brother, Colin, who had been on his way to Gallipoli with the 10th Battalion when he had become ill with typhoid. He was now back home in Australia recovering.[3]

At the end of April, Ross finally received orders to rejoin his regiment and a few days later was on a 'bloomin' train' headed for Girga in upper Egypt. Since December 1915 the regiment had participated in a British campaign against the Senussi, an Islamic sect incited by the Turks to revolt against British and Italian occupation of northern Africa. For the light horsemen, there had been little fighting—mostly they conducted long and uneventful patrols out among the desert oases west of the Nile. Ross had mixed feelings as his train steamed south along the Nile towards Girga. On the one hand, his failure to secure a transfer into the artillery and out of Egypt disappointed him. At the same time, he recognised that he had been selected to rejoin the unit over four other available 3rd Light Horse officers. 'I suppose I should take it as a compliment,' he wrote.[4]

The regiment's CO had, in fact, selected Ross for a specific job. On arrival at Girga, he was appointed to command the 3rd Light Horse Regiment's machine gun section. This put Ross in charge of 28 men and two old Maxim machine guns. Besides a horse for each man in the squadron, the section had a couple of additional mounts to carry the guns (they weighed over 20 kilograms each) and ammunition. Ross knew some of his men, but he noted that many new faces had joined since the Gallipoli evacuation: 'I don't know a quarter of them.'[5]

As he had done previously with motorcycles, rangefinders and trench mortars, Ross became infatuated with the new contraptions he had at his disposal. Three weeks after taking command of the section, he wrote to Jessie, 'I'm more keen on machine guns than anything else I have taken on so far, and they are certainly *the* weapons in this country.'[6] He applied to attend a school to learn about the newer model Vickers gun, which the regiment hoped to acquire shortly, and in the meantime drilled his men on the firing range. He found operating a machine gun an exhilarating experience: 'I love the noise they make, they fairly purr, and the firing of a machine gun gives me one of those delightful lighter-than-air sensations.'[7]

Ross only spent a week amid the black dust and sandflies of Girga before the regiment received orders to return to lower Egypt. Since the Gallipoli evacuation, the British general staff had nervously anticipated a Turkish invasion of the Sinai Peninsula that would threaten British control of the Suez Canal and Egypt. Determining that the best way to protect Egypt was by seizing control of the few east–west routes across the desert, in the spring of 1916 they began establishing a force in the Sinai Peninsula that included the Anzac Mounted Division. At the end of May, Ross arrived with the 3rd Light Horse Regiment at Romani, the main British camp in the northern Sinai.

Situated about 10 kilometres from the coast and only a short distance from the British Army's railhead, Ross found himself camped 'on some high ground' around which extended 'undulating sandy desert'. For as far as he could see, 'soft, sandy ridges covered with low bushes' extended towards the horizon, occasionally towering so high as to warrant their description as 'mountains'. Oases, nestled among date trees, interrupted the desert's desolate monotony and marked the ancient caravan routes that extended from the Nile across the Sinai to Palestine.[8]

Ross had only been at Romani a few days when he came under fire for the first time since leaving Gallipoli. Early on 1 June 1916, a German aeroplane flew over the camp, dropping several bombs. They exploded in the 1st Light Horse Brigade's lines, killing eight men, wounding 22 and causing hundreds of horses to bolt. One of the bombs landed among the tents occupied by Ross's machine gun section, killing one of his men and eleven horses. Ross ordered his men to open fire on the aircraft but the section's clapped-out Maxim guns both jammed. Furious, Ross wrote a report complaining about the deplorable condition of his section's equipment. It found its way up the chain of command to the headquarters of the Anzac Mounted Division, where it seems to have had the desired effect.[9] Ten days after the raid, Ross's section received two new machine guns. 'They are beauties,' he enthused. 'We are very keen to get a suitable target to try them on.'[10]

From Romani, Ross's unit began a weekly rotation of mounted patrols out into the desert, east of the camp. To deny use of the oases to the Turks and provide warning of an invasion force, the light horsemen typically ranged 50 kilometres from Romani, sometimes staying out for three days and spending up to fourteen hours in the saddle at a time. Ross found the enemy frustratingly elusive; when the regiment occasionally did locate a Turkish patrol, they invariably fled before Ross could get his machine guns off their horses and into action.

During a typical patrol, the 3rd Light Horse Regiment acted as 'covering troops' for the rest of the 1st Light Horse Brigade. Ross left Romani on the afternoon of 10 June, his section escorting an 18-pounder field gun of the

Royal Horse Artillery. They rode throughout the night and, at dawn, established a position near the oasis at Bir-el-Abd. Ross and his men remained there throughout a scorching day, their only refreshment coming from the brackish water they drew from the Sinai's ancient wells ('It's horrible stuff,' reported Ross).[11] One of the regiment's other squadrons had a brief skirmish with an Ottoman patrol and captured a pair of Turks. Having not fired their guns, Ross's section returned to Romani that night, riding back into camp at 1.30 a.m. on 12 June. 'As it was about full moon, I quite enjoyed it, although when one has to ride all night with a lot of gear round one's neck, and on the saddle, the pleasure of riding is somewhat diminished,' he explained to his mother.[12]

Overnight rides would become a characteristic of patrolling in the Sinai, and Ross would spend many long hours in the saddle hovering in that strange realm between wakefulness and sleep. 'The motion of the horse seems to make it worse,' he wrote. 'The white sand plays strange tricks with one's eyes and it appears as if the sand is really 20 feet below you.'[13]

It did not take long for Ross to acquire some non-issue kit to make life out on patrol a little easier. He was glad he had purchased a portable solid fuel camp stove—a 'Tommy Cooker'—from a department store in London. Brewing up a mug of Oxo after a long night in the saddle made life immeasurably better. From the camp canteen at Romani, Ross secured a supply of tinned fruit to add some variety to his rations and enjoyed some sultanas and chewing gum—'fine things to chew when riding along'—from parcels sent from home. Ross also asked his mother to send him a water skin to supplement the single army-issue canteen that did not 'go very far on a hot day', and a pot in which he could stew up the biscuits and bully beef provided in his field ration.[14] Riding out with these accoutrements slung from his saddlebags reminded him of his childhood at Mutooroo and made him feel like 'a real bushman again'.[15]

By the end of June, after a month of 'tired and monotonous work' in temperatures he described as 'hot as Hell with a capital H', Ross and his comrades were fed up.[16] He and the regiment's other Gallipoli veterans debated whether conditions in the Sinai might be worse than at Anzac (Ross thought they were) and they chafed to get into 'a real good fight'.[17] Besides his own discomfort, he also regretted the toll that the desert took on the machine gun section's horses. Ross clearly maintained the affection he had developed for these animals as a young boy at Mutooroo, where he had spent countless days riding and hunting far from the homestead. He named his mount 'Tango', reflecting his great fondness—and perhaps yearning—for dancing. 'They have to be nursed all I know and I had some anxious times on this trip but got them back without one blowing out,' wrote Ross after one particularly arduous patrol in late June. 'I'm finding my bush bringing-up is helping me in lots of ways.'[18] One trick he used to sustain Tango during long patrols was to share the biscuits that Jessie included in her parcels. The horse had grown quite fond of them, he reported.[19]

Ross had to acknowledge that, for all the desert's hardships, the camp at Romani provided comforts unknown at Gallipoli. The YMCA established a recreation tent and there, in between patrols, Ross and his friends enjoyed singalongs around a 'rather tinny' sounding piano and watched inter-regimental boxing matches. Leave passes were available to visit Port Said or the surrounding camps. When Ross heard that Colin, having recovered from typhoid, had again left Australia and was en route to France, he expected that he would stop over in Egypt and hoped they might see each other for the first time in two years.

While Ross was at Romani, a reorganisation of machine guns throughout the British Army saw him transferred out of the 3rd Light Horse Regiment. To augment the firepower available to them, regimental machine gun sections such as the one Ross led were combined to form machine gun squadrons that light horse brigades could deploy en masse. In mid-July Ross's machine gunners formed No. 4 Section of the 1st Machine Gun Squadron. Although still attached to the 1st Light Horse Brigade, his guns could now be deployed to support any of the brigade's three regiments. Ross felt sorry to leave the 3rd Light Horse after two years' service, but took comfort that he would be camped close to the old unit and still had his 'little guns' to operate.[20]

Although machine guns rarely came into action during patrols, Ross and his men had plenty of opportunities to use them against the German aircraft that appeared over Romani most mornings to drop bombs and take reconnaissance photographs. They typically came over at 6 a.m.—a 'most inconsiderate' time, thought Ross, whose shaving they sometimes interrupted: 'Twice now I've had to rush out to my horses with a well-lathered face.' The British had aircraft in the Sinai too—one squadron of the Royal Flying Corps (RFC) and a recently arrived unit of the Australian Flying Corps (AFC). During June and July, the sight of British aircraft became an increasingly common one for Ross and his friends; they regularly flew over Romani on their way to bomb and reconnoitre Turkish camps and sometimes they cooperated with light horse patrols. Neither side had many fighting aircraft so aerial combats were uncommon. It was a novelty, then, when one morning a British pilot engaged a German aircraft over Romani. Ross watched with fascination: 'They were doing 85 miles an hour and blazing away at each other with their machine guns, and doing all sorts of dives and turns,' he wrote. Having never seen anything like it before, Ross employed the most familiar analogy he had: the sight of hawks fighting at Mutooroo: 'One would get on top, and then swoop, and just as he was getting level with the other chap, the other chap would turn, and go almost straight up, guns rattling away all the time.'[21]

To Ross's great satisfaction, the German pilot left without dropping his bombs, although his British adversary had been badly damaged in the fight. Perhaps, in this spectacle, Ross was beginning to perceive something more arresting than horses and machine guns.

13

THE SAVAGE SATISFACTION OF SEEING THEM DROP

On 19 July 1916, the pilot of a British reconnaissance aircraft spotted a force of 8000 Turks advancing across the Sinai; they were just 35 kilometres east of Romani. The British generals expected that, after attacking the camp, they would continue their advance towards the Suez Canal.

For the following fortnight, Ross and his comrades rode out each night to watch and harass this Ottoman invasion force as it manoeuvred to attack Romani. 'At last,' reported Ross, 'we are getting a bit of what we came here for.'[1] The light horsemen fought 'sharp skirmishes' with Ottoman patrols among the sand dunes as they probed forward, closer to the British camp. Ross's machine gun section remained in reserve, usually occupying a defensive position a couple of kilometres behind the 1st Light Horse Brigade's patrol area. The tension built as the Turks pressed closer to Romani. 'For two weeks we did not have a single night in bed,' wrote Ross. 'We would leave camp at night, relieve the 2nd Brigade at dawn, and hang on to the Turks until relieved by the 2nd the following dawn.'[2] Out on patrol on 29 July, Ross wrote to his mother while 'sitting under a palm tree' with his machine guns: '1½ miles further out is the firing line, with the rifles breaking the otherwise still air.'[3]

The Turks finally attacked Romani in the early hours of 4 August 1916. The evening before, Ross had sited his machine guns on a 'slight ridge' to the south-east of the British camp. He was near a prominent sand hill known as Mount Meredith and situated so as to support his 'old pals' in the 3rd Light

Horse.[4] Although Ross did not yet know it, his section's position in the line lay at the centre of the area through which Ottoman commanders planned to attack Romani. The British commander, General Sir Archibald Murray, had anticipated this. He expected the Turks to bypass Romani's main, east-facing defences and attack the British camp from the south. Accordingly, he ordered the Anzac Mounted Division to establish a line of outposts along Romani's southern flank. He intended the light horse commanders to make a fighting withdrawal back towards the camp to wear the Ottoman forces down and, drawing them in, expose their left flank to a counter-attack by British cavalry units held in reserve, further to the west.

At about midnight, the advanced elements of the Turkish force began probing the light horse outpost line. From his machine gun position a few hundred metres to the rear, Ross listened as rifles began firing sporadically and intermittently. The attack 'started properly' at 1 a.m.; rifle fire suddenly leapt to a crackling crescendo accompanied by the Ottoman battle cry that Ross recalled from Gallipoli: 'Allah! Allah!' with 'Australia Finish' and 'an occasional "bastard" thrown in for good luck'.[5] Although accustomed to the gunfire, the horses were spooked by the Ottoman cries and, to Ross's horror, they bolted. Fortunately, he had ordered them to be tied together before the battle started and their handlers managed to get them under control before they had gone far.[6]

The Turks made ground to the right of Ross's position and soon occupied a ridge about 200 metres away from where they could see his machine guns. Bullets began swishing past Ross and his men, some striking the tripods on which their guns were mounted. Unable to return fire for fear of hitting comrades who had fallen back between them and the Turks, Ross ordered his men to stay low and dig in.

For some time—perhaps two hours—Ross and his 25 men held on in their forward position, under heavy Turkish rifle and machine gun fire. They returned fire but found that this only made things worse; the muzzles of their two machine guns emitted a flash that 'showed up like a comet'.[7] They held on, becoming increasingly desperate as it appeared that the Turks would cut off their line of retreat. Just as dawn began to pale the night sky, an officer from the 3rd Light Horse arrived and ordered Ross to withdraw his guns to a new defensive line further back.

Ross pulled his men back to Wellington Ridge, a prominent terrain feature situated across the axis of the Turkish advance. He had just established his guns on this high ground when the Turks launched a bayonet charge on the new light horse outpost line. Both machine guns opened fire, tearing into the waves of advancing Ottoman infantry: 'We knocked them back easily, and then had great sport at running targets at about 400 yards [366 metres],' reported Ross. Although he had often fired his rifle and thrown bombs from the confines of the trenches at Gallipoli, this was the first time he could be sure that he had killed. 'One gets worked up into it, and I wish I could describe my feelings as I sat [at] that gun with my thumbs on the firing button, and pouring 600 rounds a minute into living targets. The savage satisfaction of seeing them drop!'

Having fired hundreds of rounds, the water-cooling mechanism on Ross's guns boiled. They emitted huge clouds of steam that attracted the attention of Ottoman artillery and machine guns. 'They simply plastered us with lead,' wrote Ross. 'Shells seemed to burst right in our faces.' With no trenches dug, he could only order his men to lay down for protection. 'There was nothing to do but get as close to Mother sand as possible while their guns were firing, and then have a go with our own while they were not firing.' The men joked and laughed to conceal their fear; Ross smoked constantly.[8]

In the following hour, the Turks charged Wellington Ridge with fixed bayonets twice, each time coming closer to overwhelming the thin screen of light horse outposts there. When a party of Ottoman troops worked their way into a fold of dead ground just in front of Ross's guns, he assembled five volunteers and led a counter-attack. The Australians quickly overwhelmed their six adversaries; using his Webley pistol, Ross shot one Turk dead while his men shot and bayonetted the others. In the brief, bloody skirmish, a Turk killed one of Ross's men before being gunned down himself. It was all over in about a minute. Reflecting on it later, Ross realised the mortal danger he had put himself and his men in at that moment but claimed that he had reacted instinctively when he saw enemy troops so close. He felt absolutely no fear: 'it seemed to be the most natural thing in the world to do to walk out there and shoot them'.[9]

With their right flank collapsing, at 7 a.m. Ross and his machine gun section again received orders to withdraw. Under heavy fire, they struggled to load their two guns and ammunition boxes onto the section's surviving horses and then gallop 450 metres across 'fire-swept ground' to the next sand ridge—itself on the southern outskirts of the British camp. As they again set their guns up and prepared to meet a new onslaught, Ross was struck by the 'wonderful and awful sight' of his old regiment retiring to join this new, last-ditch defensive line:

> Horses half mad with excitement, riderless horses, dead horses, wounded horses just hobbling along, yelling men, dead men, men without horses, two men on some horses, other men carrying a wounded man across the saddle—all mixed up in a mad gallop.

He admired how, as this retreating crowd reached the ridge line, 'every man formed up again, and was ready for more'. The commander of the Anzac Mounted Division, Major General Harry Chauvel, meanwhile rode nonchalantly about in the Turkish artillery bombardment, 'as if he were out for exercise'.

A little after 7 a.m., the Turkish artillery opened fire on the British camp and German aircraft dropped bombs. The infantry attacks, however, ceased on the part of the line that Ross occupied and shortly afterwards he received orders to move his machine gun section to reinforce another part of the line where the Turks now focused their attacks. Ross and his men found another ridge on which to deploy their guns and, for the rest of the morning, fired long-range bursts whenever Turkish infantry columns came into view. Ross watched as British artillery shells 'pounded the enemy'. Further to the west, beyond what he could see through his binoculars, British cavalry counter-attacked the exposed left flank of the Ottoman invasion force. Hundreds of Turks surrendered. At sunset, Romani remained in British hands.

Ross and his men remained in a reserve overnight on 4–5 August. Exhausted, they 'had a beautiful sleep' and woke the following morning to news that the Turks had retreated. On the previous day's battlefield, Ross and his men found a 'ghastly' panorama: thousands of dead men and horses lay scattered throughout the sand dunes. Among the abundance of abandoned equipment, Ross's section came across three German machine guns just as General Chauvel and his staff happened to ride past. The general ordered Ross to salvage them and take them back to Romani. Souvenir collecting ('looting', in military terms) was forbidden but Ross managed to sneak a few items, including a 'wee coffee cup' from the kit of a captured German officer that he sent home to Jessie.[10]

Ross spent the following two days (6–7 August) in camp before riding out with the 1st Light Horse Brigade to pursue the Turks in their withdrawal back across the Sinai. He and his men covered 30 kilometres during an overnight ride and, early on 9 August, discovered the Ottoman rearguard dug in along a line at Bir-el-Abd. As the entire Anzac Mounted Division prepared to go into action against them, Ross and the rest of the 1st Machine Gun Squadron established firing positions on 'a steep sand ridge' overlooking the battlefield. They had their guns ready just in time to catch an Ottoman camel convoy passing across a ridge, 1600 metres away. 'We loosed off all 6 machine guns on to them, and carved them up,' said Ross.

Austrian artillery batteries, attached to the Ottoman Army, returned fire: 'They started pelting us with shrapnel and 5-inch stuff rather fast,' wrote Ross. One of them, a 'huge sharp solid pointed missile', landed beside one of Ross's machine guns but, mercifully, failed to explode. Most landed wide, showering the machine gunners with sand, but some found their mark among groups of men and horses, of which they 'made a mess', in the words of one of Ross's machine gunners.[11] One shell landed close enough to

No. 4 Section to kill one of the men under Ross's command, Private Joseph Radnell. A 26-year-old miner from rural Victoria, Radnell had been one of those who had charged alongside Ross against the Turks at Wellington Ridge on 4 August. 'We hurriedly buried Joe in a shallow grave and put a large wooden cross at his head,' recalled one of Ross's men.[12]

By the middle of the day, Anzac Mounted Division's efforts to break through the Ottoman line at Bir-el-Abd had failed. In response, the Turks launched a powerful counter-attack, well supported by artillery. The Australian machine gun sections provided covering fire while the division's artillery withdrew and then received orders to pull back themselves.[13] As Ross's men packed their guns, Ottoman infantry appeared on a sandy ridge just a few hundred metres away and opened fire. Shot through the wrist, Humphrey Kempe received a sharp rebuke from Ross when he stayed to carry on working. 'There was enough trouble about without having to care for the wounded,' Kempe recalled his lieutenant saying as he ordered him to retreat and find an aid post.[14]

Ross led his section in a wild gallop of 8 kilometres to Oghratina, where the Anzac Mounted Division had established a reserve line. Ottoman artillery shells followed them all the way, the high explosives erupting in great geysers of sand and the shrapnel whistling and cracking overhead. Ross saw a shell hit a comrade's horse, blowing it 'to bits'. To his amazement, 'the man was unhurt, and soon caught a riderless horse, and got away again'.

After the battle at Bir-el-Abd, Ross and his men remained in the desert for another three days (10–12 August) while the Turks retreated to the Palestinian frontier. The Ottoman invasion of the Sinai had been defeated.

On 13 August, the 1st Machine Gun Squadron returned to Romani for, as the unit's war diary describes it, 'taking stock of shortages—losses, etc.'[15] Ross heard that in facing the Ottoman invasion of the Sinai between 4 and 12 August, the Anzac Mounted Division had suffered about 230 casualties ('If you multiply my age by ten,' he cryptically told his mother in a successful effort to circumvent the censor). In fact, the division's casualties were closer to 800—although still substantially lower than those suffered by the Ottoman

Fourth Army—which Ross heard had lost nearly half the 13,000 troops it committed to the action (Turkish sources number their losses at 4000).[16]

Ross recognised that the two dozen men in his section had been remarkably fortunate. Despite their many hours under fire in the open, he had only three men wounded and one, Private Joseph Radnell, killed. On Ross's recommendation, Radnell was posthumously awarded the Military Medal for his work at Romani and Bir-el-Abd. 'He had been with me all through the fighting, and I feel his loss very much,' confided Ross to his mother. 'He was one of those chaps who don't know what fear is, and was very popular.'

Ross received a letter from the CO of his old unit, the 3rd Light Horse, commending him and his machine gunners for 'the very excellent work' they had done at Romani on 4 August. 'You were under a very hot fire and greatly helped the withdrawal of the C Squadron,' wrote Lieutenant Colonel David Fulton. 'I'm bringing it under the notice of the Brigadier.'[17] Ross told Jessie about this, and his experiences in battle, but with his characteristic modesty asked her not to share them with anyone else—especially the newspapers, as many soldiers' mothers did.[18]

For Ross, the battle's significance lay in the fact that it was the first occasion that the Australian light horse, which had acted as infantry at Gallipoli, had finally fought a battle in its proper mounted role. 'I am very pleased that I was in it,' he told Jessie at the end of a lengthy account of the battle that he sent home. 'Our only sorrow is for our gallant comrades who have fallen.'

The battles in the Sinai of August 1916, however, had a strategic significance that Ross slowly came to appreciate as newspapers arrived in camp carrying reports of the campaign.[19] What he read led him to predict correctly that the Ottoman defeat had secured the British position in Egypt. With the war beginning to turn against the Turks in other theatres too, they would not make another attempt against the canal. British success at Romani, in fact, would represent a turning point in the campaign. Whereas during 1915–16 the British command in Egypt had been content to defend Egypt from Ottoman invasion, following the battle of Romani the focus shifted towards mounting an offensive into the Palestinian lands that the Ottomans had occupied for the past four centuries.

From a personal perspective, the battle of Romani represented the most intense experience of combat that Ross would ever have. It was one that he unreservedly described to his mother as exhilarating. 'I felt absolutely bursting with life and energy, and I've never felt so vitally alive before,' he explained to her. 'Above all, there was a burning desire to kill.' Unlike in the trenches at Gallipoli, where enemies were rarely seen, at Romani and Bir-el-Abd, Ross had an intimate experience of killing. He had mowed down dozens of Turks in the open with his machine gun and, during the 'little charge' he led at Wellington Ridge, had shot a man dead at almost point-blank range.[20] Yet none of it weighed on his conscience. 'On the contrary,' he told Jessie, 'I am always rather pleased of the fact when I think of it.' To Ross, killing on the battlefield was not only enjoyable but a justified act of revenge—part of the 'long account' he had to settle for all of the 'pals' he had lost. Anticipating that his mother might think him 'blood thirsty', Ross assured her that the instinct to kill was only natural.[21] As he reminded her, the bellicose Scottish Highlands blood that coursed through his veins came from her. [22] In any case, he reasoned, 'we are no better than animals after all'.[23]

Reading these comments, it is easy to assume that two years of war had changed Ross profoundly—perhaps it had even brutalised him. This is difficult to determine, however, because as candid as he was in his letters from the Sinai in 1916, he had been guarded and evasive in his depiction of the fighting at Gallipoli. It may be that Ross was undergoing a desensitisation to the privations and violence of war that much of Australian society was also experiencing in 1916—either through direct participation in the fighting for the soldiers or vicariously, through letters, news reports and casualty lists, in the case of their relatives. Perhaps by mid-1916, both Ross and his mother were better equipped to talk about the reality of war than they had been a year before.

Yet it is also possible that, rather than profoundly changing Ross, the war had brought certain aspects of his personality into sharper focus. His pragmatism is certainly evident in the way he rationalised combat, as is his sense of the rightness of the cause for which he fought. Indeed, shortly after the battle Ross wrote to his mother describing his role as 'a privilege' and only regretting that he could not be in France where he might make a more significant contribution.[24] It is also clear that Darwinian notions of struggle figured more prominently in his rationalisation of killing than did any religious belief.

Finally, in the battles of Romani and Bir-el-Abd, Ross had also demonstrated his growing capacity for leadership. He had handled his 26 men and their horses adroitly, despite needing to move and redeploy his guns under heavy fire on three separate occasions. Like many successful Australian officers, Ross discovered that the success of his command rested on his standing among the men. To him, it was fundamental that he would never 'send men on a risky job without going myself, if it's possible'. Accordingly, the men of No. 4 Section respected and obeyed Ross; he 'never had the slightest trouble with any of them'.[25] They knew him as 'Smithy' or 'Gun-Boat Smith'. 'Froggy', his nickname in Adelaide, had not followed him to war.[26] He formed a strong bond with them and grieved the deaths of two during the summer (Radnell and Driver Donald Munro, who died in a German air raid on the camp at Romani).[27]

Still, despite the good working relationship Ross had with his men, these days there was an aloofness about him. On the one hand, it reflected the maturity he was developing as a leader that allowed him to recognise the limits to the closeness he could share with the men he commanded. But also at play, it seems, was a fear of getting close to men he may soon need to bury: since the death of his best mate, Gordon 'Timmy' Timbrell, at Anzac a year before, Ross had never 'had any particular pal', as he put it.[28] He got along well with those with whom he lived and worked but, it seems, he took care not to personally invest too much in these relationships.

When, shortly after the battle of Bir-el-Abd, the Romani camp canteen sold beer for the first time in months, the men binged. Ross, content to go to bed early, lay listening to them enjoy their well-earned revelry.[29]

PART THREE

'A LEADER BORN'

1916–1918

MAP 3 Egypt, Sinai and Palestine, 1916–18

14

THE COMING THING

For a month after the battle at Bir-el-Abd Ross and his machine gunners stayed in camp at Romani. 'We've . . . done absolutely nothing,' reported Ross on 22 August. 'I'm growing fat once more on our good tucker.' He and his men had plenty of spare time; they took picnics to the beach and swam with their horses in the surf. 'Of course, there is no jetty to promenade, or tea shops to visit, or pretty girls to talk to, but it's very nice all the same,' he reported. '[It's] hard to realise I am not just down at Glenelg or somewhere.'[1]

Within a couple of weeks, though, Ross chafed for action. He made inquiries about a posting to the Western Front ('where the work is being done'), but then heard about another interesting possibility.[2] The Australian Flying Corps' No. 1 Squadron had recently arrived in the Sinai and required volunteer officers to work as aerial observers. Back in April, while he waited for a posting at Tel-el-Kibir, Ross had come across some AFC officers. He found them 'a jolly decent lot of chaps' and it impressed him that their number included Bill Hart, an aviator from Sydney whose flying exploits before the war had made the Adelaide news. Ross referred to Hart in his letter home that week as that 'Sydney aviator, who used to break his neck pretty often just before the war'.[3]

That Ross would find the prospect of flying an aeroplane compelling is not surprising. For one thing, infatuations with various contraptions of the industrial age had punctuated Ross's adult life. It was motorcycles before the war, then rangefinders, trench mortars, wireless sets and, most recently, machine guns. As Ross put it, 'the same thing in me that made me take on bombing, and then machine guns, is now asking for flying'. Another appealing aspect was the good prospects the Flying Corps offered for promotion to the captaincy to which Ross had aspired since first enlisting. In the longer term, aviation seemed to promise big things for the future. 'It is the coming thing,' he predicted.[4]

Ross had good reason to think so. Within his short lifetime, aviation had gone from science fiction to a practical reality. Ross started boarding school in Adelaide in 1902—a year before the American Wright Brothers made history with their short flight over the sand dunes of a windswept beach in North Carolina. As a schoolboy, Ross might have joined the crowds who flocked to Adelaide's public parks when travelling 'balloonatics' visited town. In 1910, when the first aeroplane arrived in Adelaide, perhaps he went along with thousands of others to see it on display in the John Martin and Co department store on Rundle Street. A few months later, while in Britain with the mounted cadets, Ross witnessed French aviators flying (and crashing) at Brooklands—a spectacle that must have thrilled him and his seventeen-year-old friends. Back in Adelaide, in 1913 a visiting British aviator named Arthur Jones drew thousands of spectators to Cheltenham racecourse; even if Ross didn't go himself, he probably saw Jones make the first ever flight over the city—an event the press anticipated would go down as 'one of the notable events' of Adelaide's history.[5]

As a young man, Ross had vicariously experienced aviation's pioneering days through the newspapers, which he read keenly. Indeed, between Ross's sixteenth and 21st birthdays, two of Adelaide's largest circulating dailies, *The Register* and *The Advertiser*, published over 2000 articles mentioning aviation-related subjects.[6] Most reports concerned developments in Europe and America—many on the use of aircraft in military exercises and in small wars in the Balkans, North Africa and Mexico. In January 1913, Ross might have read in *The Register* of an exciting development in aviation closer to home: the Commonwealth Government planned to open a military flying school and to establish the Australian Flying Corps.[7] The school was set up in sheep grazing paddocks at Point Cook, west of Melbourne, and opened in August 1914. 'In the next war the flying machine will be a great factor,' predicted South Australia's military commandant.[8]

On 15 September 1916, Ross led his machine gun section out into the desert to support a raid by the Anzac Mounted Division against a Turkish outpost at Bir-el-Mazar. They were out in the desert for 72 hours—their longest ride yet—but remained in reserve the entire time. '[We] didn't see any of the fun,' grumbled Ross.

This 'long ride for nothing' to Mazar proved to be the final straw. As soon as Ross could get out of camp for a few hours, he visited the aerodrome at Mahemdia, a few kilometres from Romani, from where the AFC's No. 1 Squadron's aircraft operated. Drawing on his prodigious confidence and congeniality, Ross introduced himself to the squadron's CO, Major Thomas Rutledge, and managed to turn the conversation into an impromptu job interview. By the time he left, Ross had the major's word that he would endorse his application to transfer to the AFC.[9]

Securing Major Rutledge's support, however, proved to be only the first hurdle. It took 'a lot of persuasion' for Ross to convince his own CO to authorise the transfer.[10] He then needed to shepherd his application through the AIF's rather muddled administrative branch in Egypt and pass a series of tests and interviews administered by the British Army's Royal Flying Corps, in which the Australian squadron operated. Characteristically, Ross used a personal approach with great success. 'The only way to do it,' he reckoned, 'is to take your application about yourself, and sit on doorsteps for hours waiting for people.'[11] On 11 October Ross went to Ismailia for an interview with the AFC, where he 'had to give the usual age, weight and pedigree business'—the last of these is a reference to the importance that Flying Corps staff placed on one's education and social standing.[12] Besides his private education and the success of his father, Ross checked a number of other boxes: being young, physically fit and experienced with both machine guns and the tactics of the light horse, with which the airmen of the AFC typically cooperated. In short, Ross represented just the type of man the AIF's flying arm sought.[13]

Nearly a month after submitting his application, on 22 October 1916, Ross received notice that the AFC had accepted him. Further, despite 60 candidates preceding him on a waiting list, the squadron's CO, Major Rutledge, had prioritised Ross's acceptance into a training unit. It was two years to the day since Ross had left Australia. 'They gave me a great send-off when I left,' he wrote of his departure from the light horse. 'I felt quite embarrassed being cheered.'[14]

With a mixture of sadness and excitement, on 24 October Ross reported for duty at No. 1 Squadron's Headquarters at Kantara East aerodrome on the Suez Canal. The AFC had accepted him for training as an aerial observer—the second crew member of an aircraft, whose jobs included making reconnaissance reports, taking photographs, signalling the artillery and defending his aeroplane from hostile aircraft with a Lewis machine gun mounted on his cockpit. Ross hoped to train as a pilot, but Major Rutledge explained that he would first need to put in some time as an observer.[15]

When Ross joined the AFC, No. 1 Squadron had an important role to play in the theatre; at the time, the Australian squadron was the only complete British aviation unit on the Sinai front. A mixture of British and Australian officers served on its flying roster. Their job was to provide reconnaissance for the army; they cooperated with light horse patrols into the eastern Sinai but also sometimes ranged over the Ottoman front and into southern Palestine. While the pilot flew the aircraft the observer made notes of what he saw and used a camera to take photographs that military cartographers could use to map the largely uncharted territory in which British forces now operated. Besides reconnaissance, the airmen of No. 1 Squadron also worked with the artillery. Communicating via wireless or visual signals, the observers reported the location of targets to the gunners and provided corrections for their aim. Some aerial bombing took place—although, like most other equipment in the Middle East theatre, bombs were in short supply. As Ross would soon discover, the airmen in No. 1 Squadron improvised by modifying howitzer shells to drop from their aeroplanes.

To fulfil these various roles, Ross's new squadron had a motley assortment of biplanes cobbled together from what could be spared from the Western Front. While the squadron had a few single-seat fighters, most of its aircraft were BE2 types, which carried a pair of airmen (a pilot and an observer). A pre-war British government design that had soldiered on well into the war, the BE was easy to fly and provided a stable platform from which to take photographs. Its lack of power and manoeuvrability, however, and its awkwardly positioned Lewis gun for the observer to operate, made it relatively easy pickings for German fighters.[16] Like all aircraft of their era, the BE2s on which Ross would begin his flying career had timber airframes covered in fabric. Compared to what came later, their performance was modest; equipped with a 90 horsepower air-cooled V-8 engine, the BE2c could fly at a maximum of 116 kilometres per hour and climb to 10,000 feet (although it took 45 minutes to get there). It could remain in the air for a little over three hours. Mechanical failures—especially in the desert where units had limited access to spare parts—occurred relatively frequently, sometimes with catastrophic results. Like all British airmen during the Great War, the men who flew No. 1 Squadron's BE2s were not equipped with parachutes.

Major Rutledge took Ross up in a BE2c for his first flight six days after he arrived at the squadron. The major went easy on his newest observer but the pilots who trained Ross in the following days proved less accommodating. It was their custom to 'put the wind up' new observers. One of Ross's new colleagues took them up to 2000 feet and, without warning, shut the engine off. Ross saw the blue sky above suddenly replaced by the desert sands as the pilot rolled and fell into a spiralling dive. They plummeted 200 feet and then zoomed up before arching over and careering back down again in a series of side-slips.[17]

Despite the pilot's best efforts to unnerve him, Ross found flying exhilarating. It was unlike anything he had ever experienced. In his letters he struggled to adequately describe the sensation, likening it to 'riding in a motor car' (only smoother) for his mother and riding the roller-coaster at London's Hyde Park for Keith. Ross tried to describe what later air travellers would experience as turbulence—'when the air is full of pockets . . . and we drop'. He found it 'quite a pleasant sensation' and assured Jessie that the aircraft were sturdy enough to handle them. 'I've not seen a crash since I came here,' he wrote, trying to sound reassuring.[18] Ross's early experiences of aviation, however, also revealed some of the less comfortable aspects of flying in an open cockpit biplane. Unlike in later reconnaissance aircraft, in the BE2c the observer sat in the front cockpit. 'It's not all beer and skittles, sitting behind a red hot engine for a few hours, and swallowing exhaust gas and oil,' he wrote.[19]

Ross's training began with lessons on the squadron's wireless sets. He had to develop the basic knowledge of Morse Code that he already possessed and learn to apply it to the RFC's arcane signalling codes. Things moved quickly; just a week after joining No. 1 Squadron, Ross was airborne, transmitting the location of simulated artillery shell bursts on a practice range.[20] A fortnight later, he participated in a live fire exercise with a British field artillery brigade at Romani. The experience gave Ross a sense of the strange and unique influence over, yet detachment from, the battlefield that aviators had in this war. As he told Jessie, 'it gave me such a feeling of power to be away up there and controlling the fire of their 12 guns'.[21]

Major Rutledge posted Ross to the squadron's C-Flight, where he came under the command of Captain Richard Williams. A couple of years older than Ross, 'Dicky' Williams had been the first Australian soldier to qualify as a pilot at the Commonwealth's Central Flying School in 1914. Unlike Ross and most of the other men he commanded, Williams served in Australia's professional army; he was a career officer who brought exacting standards and a prickly temperament to his command.[22] But he liked Ross, describing him as 'a very solid, reliable type of man', and appreciating the thoroughness which Ross came to demonstrate in both the care of his aircraft and the mechanics who maintained it for him.[23] The earnest and conscientious approach to things that Ross had developed as an NCO and junior officer in the light horse were just what Williams sought in flying officers for his flight.

Ross had only been in the squadron for a few weeks when, on 4 November 1916, Williams took him on his first operational flight—a reconnaissance ('reco') out over the north-eastern Sinai where, until recently, Ross had patrolled with the light horse. They took off from Kantara just before 7 a.m. and flew across the Sinai as far east as Zagadan. The patrol lasted two hours. In his post-flight report, Ross noted that they had searched the country for Turks but had seen nothing: it was 'apparently all clear'.[24] That evening, in the privacy of a diary he had recently commenced, Ross sounded less confident about what he had seen, noting that while he had recognised areas over which he used to ride with the light horse, he 'found the sandy country hard to read'.[25] He still had much to learn.

Nevertheless, as he always seemed to, Ross fit in among his new colleagues with ease. He thought them 'a very decent lot' and continued to get on particularly well with the CO, Major Rutledge.[26] Ross struck up a friendship with Lieutenant Lawrence Wackett, a Permanent Forces soldier from Queensland, who had a reputation for being one of the unit's best pilots. Wackett took Ross under his wing and trained him; they would dive at flocks of ducks to give Ross practice with the Lewis gun.[27] He and Wackett also enjoyed 'the great stunt' of flying low along the canal and waving to girls aboard the boats. 'We saw one boat with 2 nurses on this morning,' he reported to his mother.[28]

As he came to know the other airmen in No. 1 Squadron, it occurred to Ross that the AFC represented something of an elite unit in the AIF. The technical nature of its work required highly skilled personnel. 'Everything is done so well and thoroughly,' Ross observed. 'There are no half measures.' And because competition to get into the Flying Corps was so strong, recruiters could be selective. As Ross put it, 'A chap knows exactly how he stands. If he's no good, out he goes.'[29]

Indeed, the NCOs and aircraft mechanics who worked in the hangars tended to be skilled tradesmen, hand-picked to apply their expertise to the wood and wire airframes, engines and instruments of the squadron's aircraft. Ross's fellow officers, meanwhile, represented an impressive group of young Australians—most had been privately educated and hailed from professional occupations.[30] They were men who, in later years, would shape the development of aviation in Australia and the empire. Besides his flight commander, 'Dicky' Williams, later founding Chief of the Royal Australian Air Force, Ross's flight in late 1916 included the future Air Marshal Sir Peter Drummond and Air Vice Marshals Adrian Cole and Frank McNamara. Another of C Flight's pilots, Allan Murray Jones, would go on to serve as a senior figure in the Department of Civil Aviation while Ross's pilot, later Sir Lawrence Wackett, is best known as Australia's premier aircraft designer and General Manager of the Commonwealth Aircraft Corporation.

If Ross felt any inadequacies among his new comrades, he may have been reassured by the fact that he was one of only a few officers in the squadron who had gone overseas with the AIF's first contingent and who had experience in combat. His familiarity with the tactics of the light horse, in particular, made him a valuable asset to the unit that the other pilots—most of whom had been teachers, engineers and university students a year earlier—probably appreciated. In any case, Ross's place in the squadron was confirmed on 22 November when he passed the observer's qualifying examination. The course had taken him a month, 'a good bit shorter' than usual, it pleased him to report.[31]

When Jessie heard news of Ross's new job, she gave her approval, any concerns apparently allayed by Ross's insistence that flying was safe.[32] Back in Adelaide, news that Ross had swapped his horse for an aeroplane spread around the town. To know someone who flew an aeroplane—the machine that was changing warfare and would soon change the world according to the papers—in 1916 was noteworthy to say the least. When Peter Waite, Andrew Smith's boss, heard that young Ross had joined the Flying Corps, he imagined having someone around to fly him between Adelaide and the Mutooroo station. The idea reached Ross in one of his mother's letters, firing his imagination and galvanising his determination to train as a pilot.

'If he'll provide the machine,' Ross responded, 'I'll do it like a shot, and we could just about do the trip in under five hours. Father will be able to get a landing ground ready for us.'[33]

First, though, Ross would need to get home to South Australia with an aeroplane—something to which he had also already turned his imagination. 'I always think of flying to Australia when I get away up, and I have a good look your way to see if I can see you,' wrote Ross to his mother in late November 1916. 'If we could carry enough petrol and oil, we would be able to fly to Australia in five days,' he predicted. 'Wouldn't it be nice? And I suppose it will be done in a few years' time.'[34]

15

HADJI

Ross's comfortable existence at Kantara aerodrome, on the Suez Canal, came to an end on 7 December 1916. With orders to move up to the front to support a British advance towards the Palestinian frontier, the men of No. 1 Squadron packed their gear and crowded onto open rail cars for the six-hour journey across the Sinai. At the village of Mustabig, a few kilometres from the Mediterranean coast, they pitched tents among sand hills overlooking a dry salt lake that would henceforth serve as an airfield. Rationed water and bully beef again became staples and Ross did his best to make an army bell tent feel like home.[1]

Flying from Mustabig, Ross and the other observers in No. 1 Squadron gathered intelligence on the Ottoman garrisons that remained scattered around the Sinai Peninsula—some, it turned out, in positions that could threaten the British line of communications.

On 9 December, Ross flew to Maghara, a Turkish enclave in central Sinai that had previously beat back a raid by the light horse. Ross's pilot, a Victorian school teacher named Lieutenant Frank McNamara, took them low over the settlement and dropped four small bombs. The Turks replied by firing artillery shells, timed to burst in mid-air, at the Australians. They exploded wide but then a horrible mechanical crash alarmed Ross and McNamara. Believing they had been hit, 'Mac' instinctively began looking for a place to land among the rugged hills below, but then realised that one of the aircraft's exhaust manifolds had come loose and blown off. Ross and 'Mac' had an unbearably noisy, but otherwise uneventful, flight back to Mustabig.[2]

Over the next couple of weeks, Ross settled into the routine of war flying. An operational flight every second day was typical, with half the time devoted to flying and the other half to writing reports and checking equipment. Besides this, as an officer Ross had responsibilities within his flight of 50 or so men, such as inspecting the tent lines and overseeing work in the hangars. Compared with the light horse, it wasn't too onerous; No. 1 Squadron held a minimum of parades, and relations between the officers and the mechanics was relatively relaxed. Ross had none of the discipline issues he had to deal with in his light horse troop. He had plenty of free time too. 'If I don't have to fly during the day,' he wrote, 'I can do exactly as I want.' For Ross, this meant 'mornings around the hangars', where he no doubt hovered inquisitively, as keen as ever to learn, and plenty of sport with his fellow officers.[3] Days typically finished with drinks and supper in the officers' mess tent where the squadron cook, previously the chef at the Menzies Hotel in Melbourne, reputedly had 365 different recipes for bully beef.[4]

A week before Christmas, Ross and the other observers began detecting signs that the Turks were preparing to abandon El Arish, the main Ottoman stronghold in north-eastern Sinai. A reconnaissance flight on 20 December reported the post empty and early the following morning Ross and Wackett scouted ahead of the light horse as they moved up to investigate. Arriving over El Arish, Ross could immediately tell that the Turks had indeed gone—'vanished in a night', he thought, just as the Australians had done to them at Gallipoli a year earlier. Ross and Wackett flew up the coast as far as the Palestinian border. Over verdant countryside that Ross thought looked 'like a picture from the bible', he saw little sign of the Turks, but plenty of civilians were about. Flying over one village, it amused Ross to see 'all the inhabitants standing in the street with their hands up, and an old man, evidently the Omdah or head man, waving a large white flag on a pole'. Wackett circled as the man climbed a nearby hill and planted his flag. Ross waved his handkerchief in response and wondered whether a town had ever surrendered to an aeroplane before.[5]

Other reconnaissance flights found the Turks digging in at Magdhaba, a settlement 30 kilometres to the south-east of El Arish. The light horse attacked at dawn on 23 December 1917, supported overhead by No. 1 Squadron. With Lieutenant Eric Roberts as his pilot, Ross took off mid-morning with orders to machine gun any Ottoman forces trying to withdraw from the battlefield. They arrived over Magdhaba to find the Turks' heavily fortified positions practically surrounded by the light horse, who were inching their way forward under heavy fire.

'The fun commenced', as Ross put it, when he and Roberts spotted a train of camels making off to the east. 'It was really most thrilling,' wrote Ross. 'I have never experienced anything quite like it before.' Roberts swooped down to 100 feet and Ross knelt up on his chair to angle his Lewis gun down and fire. The camels bolted, tumbled and contorted, reminding Ross of Catherine wheels: 'I nearly fell out from laughing once or twice.' Flying further behind Ottoman lines, they found a light railway and Roberts again dived, allowing Ross to shoot up several cars, leaving things in 'a pretty mess'.

Returning to the battlefield, Ross and Roberts tried strafing one of the Turkish fortifications, but they were hit by a volley of machine gun fire that punched eight holes through the fabric of their machine. Roberts then landed close behind the battlefield so Ross could collect messages from a light horse officer; they flew them back to Anzac Mounted Division headquarters, where Ross reported on the battle's progress to General Chauvel. Before returning to Mustabig, Ross and Roberts watched from 'a fairly safe hill' as the light horse made a final, victorious assault on Magdhaba.[6]

Writing home that night, Ross remarked on how different the experience of battle had been from the perspective of the air. On the one hand, he had endured few of the physical discomforts that his old comrades in the light horse had to face. 'I did my job, saw all the fun, and was back here having afternoon tea an hour later,' as he put it to his mother. At the same time, though, Ross felt that he had made an individual contribution to the attack's success—something of which soldiers on the ground rarely had a sense. 'It helped our troops a lot,' thought Ross, 'and put the fear of Allah into the Turks.'[7]

Ross had mixed feelings about his first Christmas with the Flying Corps. To his mother, he wrote about the lavish dinner he and the other officers shouted the men: 'plenty to eat' and 'a large quantity of champagne' that was 'thoroughly enjoyed' by all.[8] Writing to Keith, who remained in Australia, he admitted, however, to feeling homesick. 'Am sitting at my table wrapped in a coat and wishing I was home,' he wrote on a 'cold miserable' Boxing Day. 'I'm a bit fed up of this damned war seeing this is my 3rd Xmas away from home.' Brightening Ross's mood, however, was news that he had completed the required number of hours to officially qualify as an observer. Typically, he was not going to rest on this achievement: he wanted to train as a pilot as soon as he could arrange it.[9] Although he recognised the important contribution made by observers, he anticipated that piloting would be 'more fun' and would offer better prospects for the future: 'I want to be able to fly a machine after the war if I get the chance.'[10]

After the Turks lost Magdhaba, Ross and the other observers in No. 1 Squadron tracked them as they withdrew across the Palestinian frontier, leaving behind a garrison to hold the border town of Rafa. Ross spent the first days of 1917 flying sorties over Rafa to sketch maps of the Turkish defences. The empathy he had for his comrades in the light horse inspired a sense of diligence and a commitment to accuracy that some of his comrades who had only ever served in the Flying Corps did not share. 'It's a jolly responsible job,' acknowledged Ross, 'and some fellows don't realise quite that men's lives often depend on their report.' When one of his reports revealed errors made by another observer, the British staff amended their plans to capture the Rafa position.[11]

To support the British assault on Rafa on 9 January 1917, No. 1 Squadron established a forward aerodrome immediately behind the front line. Ross camped there the night before the battle and was airborne with Frank McNamara shortly after sunrise. He witnessed the start of the battle, an artillery bombardment against the Ottoman trenches, and then saw the British cavalry and light horse charge forward under bursts of Turkish shrapnel. 'Never in all my life have I seen such a beautiful and inspiring sight,' wrote Ross who, for the first time since joining the AFC, missed the light horse.

The fighting, however, quickly degenerated into something far less stirring, with the British and Australian troops edging their way forward through the crops that surrounded the Turkish positions. Ross dropped handwritten messages reporting their progress to British headquarters and used a wireless transmitter to identify targets for the artillery. With the shells of both sides exploding all over the battlefield, Ross found it difficult to control the gunfire, but at one stage in the afternoon he did manage to direct two batteries (eight guns) onto an Ottoman machine gun position that had pinned down some advancing cavalry. It gave him great satisfaction to see 'shrapnel bursting along the trenches and tearing up the ground' while 'our men were pouring in a hot rifle and machine gun fire, and there were little spurts of earth flying up all around the enemy's parapets'.

Ross spent nine hours in the air over Rafa that day, flying three sorties with two pilots—more than anyone else in the squadron, he believed. He and his pilot had to leave the battlefield at 4 p.m. to make it back to Mustabig before dark. When they landed, they heard that the final Turkish position had fallen. Over 2000 Ottoman troops had surrendered. 'A battle seen from the air is a truly wonderful and beautiful sight, and I'm never likely to forget it,' he wrote, unconsciously highlighting another contrast that fighting in the air had with fighting on the ground: from the sky, the killing was far more impersonal.[12]

Ross's work at Rafa confirmed his reputation as one of the squadron's most capable observers—something he readily attributed to his 'early bush life'.[13] Yet Ross had brought to the AFC a rather unique and valuable set of skills that had come to the fore in his role as observer. His familiarity with and interest in technical equipment allowed him to quickly master the wireless sets fitted to the squadron's aircraft while his keen eyesight and first-hand experience of the terrain and cavalry tactics helped him to produce detailed and accurate reconnaissance reports. Ross's personality played a role too, albeit in a less explicit way, with one of his pilots remarking in hindsight on the 'resource, initiative and [a] high degree of common sense' that he brought to the job of observing, while another noted in his work the 'intuition of a man who lived close to the earth'.[14] His affable, charismatic demeanour also allowed him to get the most out of his working relationships with others—a less obvious but important skill for an observer, who had to cooperate with everyone from generals to air mechanics. In one instance, when Ross had difficulty with some 'artillery people' who were sceptical about handing over control of their fire to an airman, Ross went to see them personally to 'discuss things'.[15]

Major Rutledge had also noticed Ross's skill as an observer. When the RFC accepted Ross's application for pilot school in January 1917, he asked Ross to remain with the squadron as an observer for the time being—at least until the next big battle was over. As Rutledge recognised, Ross's knowledge of the country now in front of British forces was second to none in the squadron. Ross didn't seem to mind, as he hoped not to miss out on the next battle: 'it's going to be some scrap too'.[16]

In the meantime, Rutledge selected Ross for some special jobs that broke the routine of reconnaissance sorties over the new Turkish front line in southern Palestine. On 19 January, Ross and Eric Roberts made the squadron's first long-range reconnaissance flight over Palestine. Escorted by two Martinsyde fighters, they flew one of the unit's new BE2e aircraft as far north as Jericho, crossing over Bethlehem, Jerusalem and Hebron. 'It was a perfect day and we could see nearly all Palestine from 10 000 ft', recorded Ross, who was glad for the big leather flying jacket and several layers of clothing he wore. Over Jerusalem, Roberts passed Ross his personal camera and Ross snapped what might have been the first ever aerial photographs of the city. He described it as 'a fine town' divided into the new and old cities. 'The old part is still enclosed by a high wall just like the old bible pictures,' he wrote. At Jericho, Ross tried unsuccessfully to see the remains of the walls 'that Joshua got his DSO for knocking over'; however, scanning the surrounding countryside he could see the Dead Sea and the Sea of Galilee, as well as all the way to the Mediterranean coast.

The patrol lasted four hours, during which time Ross and Roberts covered 350 kilometres. They landed back at Mustabig with, in Roberts' words, 'about a cup full of petrol'. Ross declared the flight 'the finest trip I have yet done' and felt proud that, out of the squadron's dozen or so observers, he had been selected to make this historic first aerial reconnaissance of the Holy Land. For many of Ross's comrades in the Flying Corps and other arms, the biblical landmarks of Palestine had enormous sentimental value. For Ross, however, biblically literate but not devout, seeing cities such as Jerusalem and Jericho for the first time was 'interesting' and 'strange', but ultimately a bit underwhelming: 'Personally, I don't think much of it,' he wrote.[17]

Being the first observer over Jerusalem earned Ross yet another moniker. He had been Froggy in Adelaide and Smithy or Gunboat Smith in the light horse, but from January 1917 Ross became known in the squadron as Hadji. The title was a Middle Eastern one given to pilgrims—both Christian and Muslim—who travelled to their respective holy cities of Jerusalem or Mecca.[18]

In mid-February, Ross was included on another special duty undertaken by the squadron. The British staff believed that a Turkish garrison at Nekhl, a remote settlement 100 kilometres into the desert east of Suez, represented the only substantial enemy force left in the Sinai. On 12 February, Ross and four other officers from No. 1 Squadron travelled to Ismailia, on the Suez Canal, to support two light horse columns sent to eliminate the Nekhl garrison. As the light horsemen worked their way out into the desert, Ross and the others flew out of Ismailia to support them. 'Our job was to watch the front and flanks . . . and to tell each column where the other one had got to,' wrote Ross.[19]

Bad weather and the central Sinai's desolate, rock-strewn landscape made for miserable flying—although it heartened Ross to think that the flights brought him closer to home than he had been in over two years. By 17 February, the light horse had made it to within striking distance of Nekhl and Ross, with his flight commander Captain Richard Williams as pilot, flew out to an improvised desert aerodrome to support the attack the following morning. Delayed by mechanical problems, Ross and Williams had not found the camp when the sun set. Anxious minutes passed as Williams flew about over the pitch-dark landscape. Then they saw a line of lights: tins of petrol lit by the other pilots to mark the rough, desert aerodrome.

Ross spent a 'bitterly cold night' huddled with the other airmen between boxes of spare parts. The next morning, as the light horse approached the town, Ross and Lieutenant Adrian Cole flew ahead of them. The village of Nekhl looked deserted and flying along the road leading to Akaba revealed no Ottoman forces. It had all been for nothing. When they landed so Ross could report to the commander of the light horse, his spirits were lifted by a cup of chicken broth from the colonel's campfire. As Ross put it laconically, the chicken was the only member of the Nekhl garrison who hadn't managed to get away.[20]

'Rather a costly business' is how Ross summed up the week-long expedition to Nekhl, an undertaking involving over a thousand Australian soldiers.[21] But if nothing else it confirmed that the Sinai belonged to the British Empire's forces. The generals could now focus, without concern for their southern flank, on an advance into southern Palestine.

Before returning to Mustabig, Ross and a few of the other AFC officers enjoyed several days' leave in Cairo. He relished the comforts of the Continental Hotel after his week flying over the desert and met some nurses, convincing them to join him and his friends for an excursion out to the pyramids followed by dinner at Mena House. Ross had a wonderful time, though dining at the Mena reminded him of his last meal there, before Gallipoli, with Timmy. The leave ended with a Saturday at the races, where Ross couldn't help but notice the number of pretty European girls. He had a bet, finishing 'up about square' (or so he told his mother).[22]

When Hadji returned to No. 1 Squadron at the end of February, Major Rutledge assigned him to one of the squadron's new pilots. With his three months' experience of war flying, Ross was now one of the squadron's more experienced and capable observers. Indeed, over the Sinai in early 1917, he had established the foundation on which, in the hard fighting ahead, he would build a reputation as one of the Great War's truly outstanding airmen.

16

GAZA

After losing Rafa, Ottoman forces withdrew across the Palestinian frontier and established a line stretching from the coast 7 kilometres inland to prevent the British from advancing into southern Palestine. The Turks set about fortifying this position and, during January, reports by Ross and the other observers in No.1 Squadron estimated that 13,000 enemy troops held the line.[1]

Known to the airmen as the Shellal position, it heralded a new phase of the war in Palestine. Previously characterised by movement and small-scale cavalry operations, the fighting began to transition to trench warfare. With the armies on both sides massed along more or less continuous lines, the firepower of the infantry and artillery began to supersede the mobility that the combination of cavalry and aircraft had previously given British forces in the Sinai. As it had on the Western Front, however, in the stalemate of trench warfare aviation offered a means of reconnoitring and striking the enemy beyond his front line, and enabling other arms such as the artillery to do this too. The concentration of aircraft above a fixed front line, however, also augmented the intensity of the war in the air. For the British and Australian airmen in Palestine, encounters with German aircraft would become more frequent in the early months of 1917 while Austrian anti-aircraft guns, concentrated around valuable Ottoman transportation and supply dumps, would introduce them to 'Archie'—the term the aviators of the RFC used for anti-aircraft artillery.

Ross first encountered Archie in mid-January while sketching the Turkish trenches at Weli Sheikh Nuran with his flight commander, Captain Richard

Williams. The shells exploded around their BE2, looking to Ross like 'big powder puffs' but rocking the aircraft violently with their concussion and punching holes through the fabric fuselage.[2] Amazed by how few vital parts an aeroplane actually had, Ross thought Archie a little less menacing than shelling on the ground, but admitted the unsettling experience of waiting for the next one to explode and the 'horrible racket' they made.[3] 'I'm beginning to understand the feeling a bird must have when it's being shot at,' he explained to Jessie, 'but like everything else, one gets used to it.'[4]

Still, Ross had no illusions about the danger posed by his regular flights over the Shellal position. One evening he approached his tent mate, Lieutenant George Mills, a dentist from Sydney who had also left the light horse to join the AFC as an observer. Ross asked Mills to countersign an updated version of his will and then explained which of his possessions he wanted sent home and which were to be distributed to other members of the squadron. According to Mills, Ross told him, 'I'm not breezy, but I'm not a fool either. You just can't do Shellal so often and get away with it all the time.' Perhaps noticing signs of strain in Ross, a couple of days later Captain Williams gave Ross a rest, assigning Mills to take his place as Lieutenant Eric Roberts' observer.[5] Shortly afterwards, Roberts and Mills were hit by Archie over Weli Sheikh Nuran. Shrapnel badly wounded Mills in the arm and he nearly bled to death before Roberts made it home. The experience traumatised Roberts and shortly afterwards he went home with a debilitating nervous condition.[6]

Ross had been lucky. Perhaps sensing the danger in her son's letters, which typically arrived weeks after he wrote them, Jessie became anxious about his new job. On 14 March she wrote to AIF Base Records after reading a vague newspaper report that a British aircraft had been shot down in the Sinai and its observer, an Australian, captured. 'I feel a little anxious,' she wrote, 'because in his letters he tells me he does a great deal of that work and frequently is the only observer who goes out with the patrols on special duty.'[7]

Throughout February 1917, Ross flew sorties over the Ottoman trenches to take photographs, make sketch maps and drop bombs. Sometimes when the moon was out he flew at night, taking bombs and parachute flares to drop on targets behind the Turkish front line. On other occasions, he and his pilots—usually Lieutenants Frank McNamara, Adrian Cole or Captain Williams—came down low to attack trains carrying Turkish troops and munitions. 'We found one steaming merrily along their line, and when it saw us it tried to get away, but didn't have a hope,' he wrote of one strafing attack. 'We came down quite low, and I had a fine target as we flew along it.' The train screeched to a halt and its passengers all jumped clear and fled for their lives. 'I nearly fell out laughing,' wrote Ross. 'Three silly old Turks hopped out while the train was going, and rolled down an embankment.'[8]

'The whole of the position has been EVACUATED.' So began Ross's reconnaissance report of the Shellal position on 5 March 1917.[9] Once again, the Turks had withdrawn. Two days later, flying with Captain Williams, Ross reported the Turks digging a new line of trenches stretching from the town of Gaza, on the coast, inland towards Beersheba. 'It looked as if this was to be their new line after the evacuation of Nuran and Shellal,' he observed in his diary.[10]

To disrupt the Ottoman withdrawal, the headquarters of the RFC's 5th Wing (in which No. 1 Squadron operated) ordered its squadrons to attack retreating enemy forces. Between 5 and 20 March the British and Australian airmen dropped nearly 5 tonnes of bombs on Turkish railway transport and troops as they withdrew into Palestine.[11] An agent working behind enemy lines reported that the raids did 'much to disorganise' the Turks.[12] German aircraft made little interference, but anti-aircraft guns continued to pose a danger to Ross and his comrades as they flew above crowded railway junctions and camps that the Turks were hastily packing up as they pulled back.

During his second sortie on 19 March, Ross spotted a British aircraft land, apparently suffering engine failure. Despite the rough terrain and the presence of an Ottoman camp nearby, Ross's pilot, Lieutenant Reginald

Baillieu, decided to attempt a rescue. He landed beside the British aeroplane and, as Ross later described it in a letter to his mother:

> The other pilot started to run toward us. Unhappily it was just near a big Turkish camp. They were nearly on him by the time we landed; but, I managed to keep them off with my revolver till we got into our machine. As soon as he was in we started off again, and it is a source of great wonder to everyone how the machine managed to lift us. However, we got clear of the ground very slowly, and never was I more thankful. The Turks showed their annoyance by peppering us with rifle fire. We had an awful ride home, as the rescued pilot was in my wee seat with me, and his face and hands were badly burned, poor beggar. We could not get higher than 500 feet all the way home and it was a 60-mile [96-kilometre] trip.[13]

A week later Ross learned that, 'for that landing stunt the other day', he and Baillieu had been awarded the Military Cross (MC).[14] He thought it 'a lot of rot, of course' and downplayed it among his comrades. To his mother, though, he admitted that he was pleased for her sake. 'It just shows how easy those things are to get, if only one has the luck to be noticed.'[15] The daring rescue that Baillieu and Ross made did have some precedent in the RFC in the Middle East. There had been at least a couple of attempts to land and rescue comrades in the squadron and, just ten days earlier, Headquarters of 5th Wing RFC had issued instructions regarding visual signals that its airmen should use if forced to land to communicate with other pilots.[16]

Ross and Baillieu's success perhaps inspired a similar action the very next day when Lieutenant Frank McNamara, with whom Ross regularly flew, landed and rescued another pilot, despite being wounded himself and under fire from Ottoman soldiers nearby. For his gallantry, McNamara received the Victoria Cross—the only one that would be awarded to an Australian airman during the Great War. 'It was a jolly fine stunt on Mac's part,' observed Ross.[17]

Headquarters of all British and Empire forces in the Sinai (known as 'Eastern Force') planned to attack Gaza on 26 March 1917. The operation had as its objective the capture of the town and destruction of the Ottoman garrison before it could, once again, withdraw to a line further back. Two cavalry divisions would encircle Gaza while a British infantry division attacked it directly. The British commander of the operation, Lieutenant-General Sir Philip Chetwode, had just one day to complete the city's capture. British logistics could not sustain his troops, who would be operating 30 kilometres beyond the British railhead, for any longer.

The RFC's 5th Wing came under Chetwode's command for the attack on Gaza. His staff would rely on Ross and the other observers to watch the exposed and extended flanks of the British cavalry as they encircled the city. Besides protecting the attacking force from German aircraft and informing Chetwode's staff of the battle's progress, the airmen would also cooperate with the artillery to spot enemy guns and direct fire against them.[18] Not yet as sophisticated as artillery cooperation techniques in France, Ross and the other observers in Palestine would have to mark targets with flares. The artillery batteries could respond by laying out cloth strips in prearranged patterns. For weeks before the attack, Ross and the other observers practised and conferred with Chetwode's gunners on an almost daily basis to prepare themselves for this important task. A couple of days before the battle, No. 1 Squadron moved closer to the front, establishing an aerodrome at the recently captured Rafa—'not a bad spot and nice and green,' described Ross, 'with the aerodrome on the side of a hill'.[19]

The first stage of the Gaza operation went to plan. The cavalry, including Ross's old comrades in the 3rd Light Horse, encircled the town to trap its garrison. Things went awry with the infantry attack, however, when fog delayed the deployment of artillery to provide fire support. When the infantry eventually advanced, they struggled to overcome the Turks holding the high ground south of the town. During the afternoon, Chetwode ordered the cavalry to join the attack on Gaza from the north. By nightfall, they had fought their way into the town but the approach of Turkish reinforcements and a lack of water prompted Chetwode to withdraw the cavalry. The infantry held the outskirts of the city overnight but had to retreat the following day. Chetwode's Desert Column ended the battle practically on their starting line; they had suffered 4000 casualties.[20]

Ross spent eight hours in the air on the battle's first day. Most of his work was artillery cooperation, a job of which he was 'very fond'. He found it thrilling to mark targets and then see shells 'go crashing right into the very places where they are most needed'. At one point during the day, he directed fire onto a Turkish gun, silencing it, and on another occasion he spotted a line of Ottoman soldiers leave their trenches and advance to counter-attack: 'We let them come on for about a mile, and then 3 batteries opened a terrific fire on them with shrapnel at close range, and plastered what was left of them right back to their trenches again.' As the Turks retreated, Ross also directed two of the heavy guns he was controlling onto them and watched 'the big shrapnel tearing up about an acre at a time'. The carnage he inflicted did not occur to him while over the battlefield but, reflecting on it that evening, admitted that it was 'horrible to sit here now and think of the poor devils who have been blown to bits'.[21]

Ross flew another eight hours' worth of sorties on the battle's second day, covering Chetwode's Desert Column as it withdrew from Gaza in the face of Turkish counter-attacks. The Ottoman infantry gave Ross 'some fine targets'; at one point he ranged a battery of 60-pounders onto a 'big lot' of Turks who had assembled in a wadi to draw water from a well: 'the big shrapnel carved them up in fine style'. He admitted it seemed 'very inhuman' to shell men 'who must have been half mad with thirst', but felt that his dead comrades lying on the Gaza battlefield justified his ruthless direction of the British artillery.[22]

Mercifully, the Turks had no anti-aircraft guns in Gaza but they did turn machine guns on Ross's aircraft on a number of occasions, which 'made it pretty hot for us at times'.[23] The German airmen also made an appearance over the battlefield. On 27 March, one attacked Ross and his pilot while they were focused on cooperating with the artillery. Ross initially thought they were being machine gunned from the ground and, by the time he realised what was happening, the German pilot had gone.[24]

Ross had a few more long and 'terribly hot' days of flying before the fighting on the Gaza front settled down.[25] Major Rutledge granted him a brief leave to Port Said to meet Keith, who was due to stop over in Egypt on his way to Britain. After several rejections from the AIF in 1915 and 1916, Keith had decided to pay for his own passage to Britain to join the RFC.[26] Ross felt proud that his older brother had decided to follow him into the Flying Corps and looked forward to seeing him for the first time in over two years. We can imagine the acute disappointment the brothers felt when they missed each other in Port Said by just a few days.[27] It would have been far more regrettable, however, had Keith not survived when a German U-boat torpedoed and sunk his ship in the English Channel a couple of weeks later.[28]

Meanwhile, the news on Colin was that he had reached Britain and deployed to the Western Front as a lieutenant in the 10th Australian Infantry Battalion. He had spent some time in hospital with influenza but had also been in combat—'over the top', as Ross put it, using the colloquial term for an infantry attack in trench warfare. Colin had apparently shared his experiences with Ross in letters with some candour. Ross passed none of the details onto his mother, but observed that his younger brother, who had been so eager to get to the war, had now experienced 'a taste of the real thing, and found it wasn't all it was cracked up to be'.[29]

Equipped with new aircraft, the German squadron in Palestine became more active over the battlefront following the failed British attack on Gaza. In late-March 1917, the Germans began bombing No. 1 Squadron's aerodrome, often arriving at dawn. On more than one occasion, Ross was forced to run from his tent in pyjamas to take cover or turn one of the aerodrome's machine guns onto the raiders.[30]

The German airmen also began to aggressively contest the skies over the Gaza battlefront. On 15 April, Ross and his flight commander, Richard Williams, were ranging artillery onto anti-aircraft guns in Gaza when a German aircraft attacked them. Ross spotted it as it dived from 2000 feet above, its machine guns hammering away. Ross angled his Lewis gun up and returned fire, prompting the German pilot to shear away. Williams pursued him and for the next fifteen minutes the two aircraft wheeled about the sky, exchanging fire. The German pilot broke off and dived for home just as Ross emptied his last drum of ammunition. Ross and Williams returned to their aerodrome at Rafa with a single bullet hole through their tail and a thrilling story to tell in the mess that night.[31]

Ross's first dogfight fired his enthusiasm. 'It was my first real fight in the air, and I must confess that I am eagerly looking for more,' he wrote to his mother. 'It's the proper way to fight, and just comes down to a man to man affair, which is more like the "Knights of Old" than anything else I've tried.'[32]

Ironically, in the most technologically advanced and industrialised expression of war fighting, Ross had found an experience of combat that emphasised the skill and prowess of the individual warrior in a way that had been obscured by industrialised warfare on the ground. For a keen sportsman like Ross, the personal skill involved in aerial fighting had obvious appeal. He found aerial combat to resemble a game in which the Germans became opponents, not enemies. Indeed, since joining the Flying Corps, Ross's attitude towards the German airmen had undergone a striking transformation. Initially, he had brought his hatred of Germans, fuelled by wartime press reports and atrocity-themed propaganda, into the Flying Corps, deriding them as 'a lot of cowardly swines' in January 1917. By March, however, he had come to see them as 'jolly sporting', their status as fellow aviators making them an exception: 'a much more decent crowd than their other soldiers'.[33]

Encouraging this shift in Ross's attitude towards the enemy was an informal system of communication that had evolved between the German squadron, *Fliegerabteilung* 300 (FA 300), and the RFC earlier in 1917. On 8 March, a German airman dropped a message on the Australian aerodrome containing letters from two captured British airmen; they reported that the Germans were treating them well and asked for some clothes and personal effects to be dropped to them at the German aerodrome. From this point on, the two opposing flying services communicated unofficially on a semi-regular basis regarding the fate of comrades who had been shot down. In some instances, the Australian and German pilots even exchanged gifts.[34]

As Ross understood it, the practice had started in France, where the aviators on both sides dropped news of shot-down pilots to each other and, in the case of a particularly well-known flyer being killed, a tribute and perhaps a wreath or flowers. Ross had heard how when the notable German fighter pilot Max Immelmann was killed in June 1916, 'Our fellows took up a big wreath, and tied it to a parachute, and dropped it for his grave.' Reflecting on this, Ross concluded that war was indeed 'a strange game', but he also saw the behaviour as an indicator of what set the Flying Corps apart from the other services. As Ross and his comrades understood it, they were fighting a new kind of war that gave them a distinctive identity and ethos in which they could take pride.[35]

After their failure at Gaza on 26 March, the British commanders planned a second assault on the city. Whereas for the first battle they had employed a cavalry encirclement, this time the extended Ottoman defences demanded more conventional siege warfare tactics—much like those employed on the Western Front. Following a preliminary bombardment by a reinforced heavy artillery group, the British infantry, supported by tanks and gas, would advance on 19 April against the Turkish trenches. They would be attacking across large expanses of open ground.

Ross flew two sorties over Gaza during the second battle on 19 April, artillery cooperation again being the focus of his work. It proved to be a difficult day for flying; the German aircraft ranged over the battlefield, aggressively fighting for control of it, while clouds down to 800 feet forced Ross and his comrades to fly at altitudes where they were easy targets for anti-aircraft fire. A new system of artillery cooperation, based on ideas imported from France, also proved problematic. When the British advance commenced at 6 a.m., Ross spotted one of the attacking tanks under fire from a Turkish battery. To his consternation, it took 22 minutes to get a British gun to open fire on it and, although silenced in five rounds, the British tank had been destroyed.[36]

Like many who took part in the Second Battle of Gaza, Ross summed it up with bitter resignation: 'The whole attack was a failure & after losing a lot of men we found ourselves back where we had started.' Eastern Force had suffered another 7000 casualties for no gain whatsoever.[37]

A few days after the battle, Ross received orders to report to the RFC's pilot training school in Cairo. Although excited at the prospect of finally learning to fly, he also felt some regret at leaving behind a role in which he felt that he had excelled in the 200 hours he had spent in the air as an observer.[38] Ross's sense of achievement was well founded: he would afterwards learn that Major Rutledge regarded him as not only the best observer in the squadron, but the most proficient that he had ever commanded.[39]

Ross left the squadron to commence training as a pilot on 23 April 1917. It was a day short of six months since he had reported for duty with the AFC.

17

QUITE AN AIRMAN NOW

Ross had demonstrated potential as a pilot from his earliest days with the squadron. Recalling how his 'one desire was to become a pilot', Ross's flight commander, Captain Richard Williams, often allowed him take control once he had finished making his reconnaissance notes and fly them back to the aerodrome.[1] Writing home in January 1917, Ross reported that he was 'doing famously' on these informal lessons.[2]

Nevertheless, Ross also happened to be in the right place at the right time to secure a place on the RFC's highly competitive pilot training course. In early 1917, the British War Office had expanded the aviation training establishment in Egypt, planning to send hundreds of pilots from Britain to learn to fly there. But in April 1917, the authorities in London suddenly reversed this decision, owing to an urgent need for pilots to replace the heavy casualties suffered by the RFC on the Western Front.[3] As a consequence, the new training squadrons in Egypt faced a shortage of pupils just as they were ready to begin instruction.[4] At the same time, the Australian Defence Department issued orders that units of the AIF (including the squadrons of the AFC) had to have all-Australian officers: they could no longer rely on British officers to fill vacancies as No. 1 Squadron had previously done. This created a shortage of Australian pilots in Egypt—a breach into which Ross gladly stepped in the spring of 1917.[5]

Following a few days' leave in Cairo, Ross reported to No. 3 School of Military Aeronautics at Abbassia on 30 April 1917. For three weeks he undertook an intensive course in the theoretical aspects of flying: seven lectures each day on subjects covering the principles of aeronautics, the role of aeroplanes in war and the inner workings of engines and airframes. Students had classes until 7 p.m. each day and, after a formal dinner in the mess, retired to comfortable stone barracks to write up their study notes. Ross found the course content 'fairly easy' owing to his practical experience as an observer, but did find its university lecture-style delivery challenging. He had always been more of a practical, hands-on learner than an academic. Sport was part of the program too, and here Ross excelled. He had the opportunity to play his first cricket match in years. He evidently still 'had it', making useful runs and taking a wicket.[6]

Despite the difficulties posed by formal, theoretical study, Ross passed the final examination at the School of Aeronautics 'easily enough', meaning that he could then begin practical flying lessons at Ismailia with the RFC's No. 57 (Reserve) Squadron.[7] To qualify for his 'wings' (the embroidered emblem of the AFC that pilots wore on the left breast of their uniform), Ross needed to complete twenty hours' solo on four different aircraft and then pass a series of practical tests in the air.[8]

Flying lessons commenced on 31 May 1917. Ross started on a Maurice Farman 'Shorthorn', an ungainly looking machine that one of his contemporaries described as 'a queer sort of bus like an assemblage of birdcages'.[9] Known colloquially as a 'Rumpty' after the sound its engine made, the Maurice Farman types were pre-war designs that the RFC had retired from combat service to use as training machines. Instructor and pupil sat in tandem in the aircraft's distinctive nacelle with the wings, braced by a maze of wires, the engine and the propeller behind them. Unable to speak over the tremendous racket made by the engine and rushing wind, Ross would have more or less learned by feel: holding the auxiliary control column in his cockpit while his instructor demonstrated on the main set of controls. He thus became basically familiar with the most elementary manoeuvres: taking off, climbing, turning and landing. Ross made his first solo flight on his third day at the training squadron. He had completed an hour and fourteen minutes in the air with his instructor.[10]

After a week at Ismailia flying Maurice Farmans, Ross graduated to No. 22 (Reserve) Squadron at Aboukir to learn on faster, more modern aircraft. He had a couple of hours with an instructor in an Avro 504 before taking one up by himself. Ross found the much faster aircraft tricky to handle at first, and made some rough landings; however, he soon got the hang of it.[11] He had a week of practice on Avros, then his instructor allowed him to take up a single-seat Bristol Scout, an aircraft that had been designed specifically for aerial combat. By the end of June, Ross had qualified to fly the BE2c, in which he had carried out reconnaissance and artillery cooperation with No. 1 Squadron.[12] In the month he spent at the flying schools, Ross realised that he had found his calling: piloting an aeroplane was a wholly captivating and absorbing experience, something that both thrilled and fascinated him. Ross was easily able to fit right in with the still rather exclusive fraternity of men who could call themselves aviators. 'We do nothing, and talk nothing, but flying all day long,' he wrote to his mother. 'I often dream I'm doing wonderful stunts at night.'[13]

Ross's characteristically indefatigable work ethic and self-confidence helped him to progress through the training course quickly. On 3 July, just over four weeks after starting, he flew his final practical examination. In a BE2c, he had to climb to 10,000 feet, take six photographs, drop some dummy bombs, direct artillery fire and complete a cross-country flight. Ross finished by looping the loop. The quintessential aerobatic manoeuvre confirmed his identity as an aviator. 'I consider myself quite an airman now,' wrote Ross.[14] He had 23 hours of solo flying in his log book.[15]

The limited experience Ross had from his informal lessons with Captain Williams during early 1917 probably helped him to move through the course so smoothly and efficiently. Nevertheless, the rapid transition that Ross made into the cockpit was fairly typical in the RFC in 1917. Competing demands for pilots to both raise new squadrons and fill chairs left empty by casualties forced British authorities to cut training programs to a barely adequate length. During the spring of 1917, British pilots usually joined service squadrons with a couple of dozen hours' flying and little or no specific instruction in aerial combat.[16] Besides producing pilots dangerously under-prepared for service flying, the RFC's rudimentary training equipment and shortage of experienced instructors made learning to fly a risky venture. Indeed, slightly more than half of the AFC's fatal casualties during the war would die in training accidents.[17] Ross had been fortunate to avoid an accident during his training course, though he witnessed some.[18] At least three RFC officers died in Egypt's training squadrons during the month when he learned to fly.

Ross might have realised that he had been fortunate in other ways too. On weekends spent in Cairo, he met friends on leave from the squadron and visited others recovering in hospital from wounds. Their stories from the front spoke of a hopelessly entrenched stalemate at Gaza and increasingly intense aerial combat overhead. Equipped with a new generation of aircraft that completely outclassed anything the RFC had, the Germans were inflicting heavy casualties on the Australian and British airmen who contested the skies over Gaza. In a letter home during May, Ross tallied the latest casualties he'd heard about: 'one a prisoner, one missing (Steele, an awfully nice fellow), two "nerves", and four wounded, and the rest of us, like Johnnie Walker, ready for more'.[19] Ross's steadfast outlook embodied the spirit of the RFC that the Australian service had inherited; however, the summer ahead would put his and his comrades' resolve to the test. By the end of July, No. 1 Squadron had suffered fourteen fatal casualties since the beginning of the year.[20] Ross would return to a squadron that desperately needed reinforcements and into what was bound to be a tough apprenticeship for a new and inexperienced pilot.

With a brand new set of AFC wings sewn on his dress tunic, Ross rejoined No. 1 Squadron on 16 July 1917. Much had changed in his three-month absence. The unit had moved aerodromes to Deir-el-Belah, a picturesque spot where the men pitched their tents among groves of fig trees and grapevines. As well as several new faces in the officers' mess who had replaced friends killed or wounded while Ross was away training, command of the squadron had passed to Richard Williams, who had previously been Ross's flight commander. Major Rutledge, who had played such an important role in securing Ross's transfer from the light horse and his development as an air observer, had been posted to a British squadron following the Australian government's stipulation that Australian units had to be commanded by officers of the AIF where possible.

Ross learned that the squadron's role had also changed. Whereas No. 1 Squadron had previously undertaken a variety of tasks—essentially whatever the army required—from mid-1917 it began to specialise in long-range reconnaissance and bombing, leaving the 'tactical' work, directly over the battlefield, to No. 14 Squadron, a British unit. Ross may have been disappointed to learn that this included handing over the artillery cooperation that he had enjoyed so much to his British colleagues.

The change to No. 1 Squadron's role reflected a broader reorganisation of British forces in the Middle East in mid-1917. The failure of the second attack on Gaza in April saw General Archibald Murray replaced; General Edmund Allenby took command of the Egyptian Expeditionary Force in June. Coming from an army command on the Western Front, Allenby arranged to secure reinforcements for the infantry, artillery and Flying Corps. The British Prime Minister, David Lloyd George, wanted him to use these to break the deadlock at Gaza and capture Jerusalem before Christmas.[21] Murray had generally been unpopular among the soldiers under his command, and many expressed relief when Allenby arrived to replace him at the end of June 1917.[22] Ross was circumspect: 'It will be interesting to see what the change of command will bring forth.'[23]

Another new face in the squadron was that of Lieutenant Les Sutherland. As Ross had done six months earlier, Sutherland had transferred to the Flying Corps from the light horse and trained as an observer. When Ross introduced himself, the two men realised that they had actually met before: Sutherland and Ross had been evacuated from Gallipoli together in

September 1915. Sutherland had been the other soldier quarantined along with Ross in the minesweeper's lifeboat, a makeshift isolation ward where the crew also kept their pig. Ross and Sutherland laughed at the memory and hoped that the pig was not about to join the reunion. 'I never heard a pig squeal like that one before,' recalled Ross, 'but no doubt he was made into Army bacon long ago.'[24]

The two men got along well, and Ross was pleased when Major Williams posted Sutherland to C Flight, where they could fly together. Sutherland shared a tent with Ross and they became 'best pals', according to Ross.[25] The two had a lot in common: they were the same age (24 years old in mid-1917) and, like Ross, Sutherland had a sharp intellect fostered by practical experience rather than formal education: he was witty, affable had a keen sense of humour, and he also enjoyed a drink. To Sutherland, Ross presented as 'a solid lump of a chap' who, for an Australian, had a fine command of English and excellent diction. 'He had a lovable smile, was intensely athletic, and was man all through.' Ross's bearing and intelligence made him 'a leader born', thought Sutherland, while in the air he seemed to be 'absolutely fearless'.

Curiously, Sutherland also observed that Ross 'was not a seeker of the other sex', despite often attracting female attention.[26] The comment echoes the impression provided throughout wartime correspondence that although Ross enjoyed female company—especially dancing—and noted the attractiveness of women from time to time, he apparently never pursued romantic relationships.[27] Indeed, he told both his mother and Keith on separate occasions that he had no desire to marry yet.[28] If this raises questions about Ross's sexuality, they will have to go unanswered given that the evidence is, at its best, implicit and circumstantial—unsurprising given the cultural taboo, and indeed illegality, of homosexuality throughout the British Empire during Ross's lifetime.

Ross flew his 'first job as a pilot' the day after rejoining the squadron.[29] With Sutherland as his observer, he reconnoitred the Gaza front, noting how extensive the Ottoman fortifications had grown since April. Near the coast, trench lines practically encircled Gaza, while a line of fortified redoubts extended some 40 kilometres inland to Beersheba.

To counter the superiority of German aircraft over Gaza at this time, Major Williams ordered that all reconnaissance flights had to go out in groups with at least one fighter to protect them. The situation frustrated Williams, who thought it 'an extraordinarily bad arrangement', but until he secured better aircraft from the RFC, he had little alternative.[30]

Ross began flying C Flight's escort fighter, a 120-horsepower Martinsyde 'Elephant'. Like most of No. 1 Squadron's aircraft, the 'Tinsyde' had been withdrawn from combat service on the Western Front after being outclassed by the latest generation of German fighters and relegated to secondary theatres such as Palestine. As Ross explained, the usual formation for reconnaissance flights became 'Three [BE]2e's in the shape of a triangle and a [single seat] Martinsyde or a BE12a above them as escort'. Taking an hour to climb to 6000 feet, C Flight's old BE2es would start half an hour before Ross, who would then take off and 'pick them up' above the aerodrome before 'the whole lot would move off'.[31]

In the middle of 1917, Ross usually flew operational sorties a few times each week. 'If we get a job to do the actual flying only takes about 2 hours,' he wrote, describing a typical day. 'But there are lots of arrangements to be made beforehand, and then we always talk over it afterwards.' When not in the air, Ross spent a lot of time in the hangars supervising the maintenance of his Martinsyde. He had a 'jolly good' pair of mechanics: Corporal Albert Luxton, a fitter from Brisbane, and Aircraft Mechanic Joe Bull, a Victorian shipwright.[32] The fact that Ross was an officer and dined in a different mess did not prevent them forming a warm and productive working relationship. The mechanics were the same age and shared a similar background to Ross. Indeed, as he put it, 'my life depends to a large extent upon their work'. Ross expressed his gratitude to Bull and Luxton by asking his mother to send them food parcels.[33]

During Ross's first weeks as a pilot in July and August 1917, it became clear that Allenby's Headquarters had an insatiable appetite for aerial intelligence.

With agents and prisoners providing little of value, General Headquarters (GHQ) staff relied on their airmen to both monitor Ottoman movements and to provide aerial photographs from which the British Army's cartographers could map the largely uncharted country behind Ottoman lines. During the summer, the number of aerial photographs British airmen exposed would triple, with the monthly total exceeding 1300; Ross and his colleagues in No. 1 Squadron were responsible for at least 80 per cent of these.[34]

Bombing represented another aspect of Ross's work at the time. Striking targets, especially railway yards and Ottoman camps, kept pressure on the Turks while Allenby prepared his army for its next major offensive, which allowed the RFC to retaliate for the raids that German airmen made on British camps.

It was on a bombing raid on 4 August that Ross had his first dogfight as a pilot. Les Sutherland had spotted a German aircraft on the ground near Sharia during the previous evening's patrol and early the following morning six No. 1 Squadron pilots, including Ross in a BE12a, went out to bomb it. The aircraft proved to be a decoy; as Ross and his comrades approached, focused on their target, two German Albatros scouts dived from above, their machine guns hammering. Ross hauled back on his control stick to meet them head on, firing a burst as the German fighters flashed past. Kicking the rudder pedals, Ross cartwheeled his aircraft back over and went 'nose to nose' with one of the Germans, both pilots firing. Ross turned to make another pass but the German pilot, perhaps hit or losing his nerve, broke away. Ross followed him in a dive, firing 40 rounds. 'He then made off,' reported Ross, 'with his nose well down, into his own Archies at Sharia.'

Turning back towards British lines, Ross found that the other Albatros, a distinctively painted machine of yellows, greens and browns, had cut him off. They met nose-on, Ross going 'like a bull at a gate' and opening fire at close range. The Albatros broke off under Ross's right wing and followed the other one home.[35] Ross returned to Deir-el-Belah, expressing to his mechanics his disappointment that the German pilots had not put up more of a fight.[36]

For a few weeks, Ross encountered no German aircraft, despite being over the lines every second day or so to drop bombs or escort the reconnaissance flights. Then, on 1 September, Ross and Captain Alfred Ellis were patrolling over Beersheba at 12,000 feet when, below, they spotted an Albatros escorting a reconnaissance aircraft. Ross and Ellis carefully manoeuvred to put the sun behind them and then dived together onto the German fighter's tail.

Ross opened fire at 40 metres out, but missed, hurtling past before zooming up to make a second diving attack. The startled German pilot turned sharply back to his own lines but Ross 'swung round head on to him'. This aggressive manoeuvre gave the German no alternative but to fight. The two aircraft sped towards each other and Ross pressed the firing button on his control column. Ross saw his tracer rounds find their mark on the enemy aircraft. In the next moment he was knocked senseless.

Blinded and dazed, Ross instinctively rolled his BE12a over and put it into a spinning dive. Working the control stick with one hand, he used the other to peel away his shattered and bloody goggles just in time to see the Albatros again. Another long burst from the machine gun and the German pilot broke away and dived towards his own lines. With his flying cap and tunic saturated with blood, Ross knew he needed to do the same: 'I turned for home and did 110 MPH all the way.'[37]

Ross and Ellis landed safely on the squadron's aerodrome at Deir-el-Belah. A doctor administered first aid, finding that bullets or bullet fragments had inflicted three wounds to Ross's head. One, a tracer, had passed through his face, its phosphorescent base burning Ross's cheek and smashing a tooth. Another projectile had grazed his right temple. The doctor applied field dressings and sent Ross to a local casualty clearing station. That evening he was on a hospital train bound for Cairo.

Ross spent a fortnight at No. 14 Australian General Hospital followed by ten days at the No. 10 Convalescent Home in Alexandria. He enjoyed the company of British and Australian nurses and sometimes arranged to spend time with them after hours. 'We would make up parties in the afternoons and go down to the harbour and get a boat and take our tea out with us.'[38]

Although undoubtedly painful, the wounds healed well, leaving Ross with 'fine little drawing room scars', on his left cheek, right temple and his scalp and a dark patch on his left cheek where the tracer had burned him. An artificial tooth replaced the broken one, making him, he wrote to Keith, 'as good as new again'.[39] Indeed, Ross remained characteristically upbeat; a photograph from the time shows him with his head in bandages, but smiling broadly.[40] He sent his blood-stained flying cap and tunic home to his mother as keepsakes (her thoughts on this have not survived in the records).[41] News from the front probably buoyed Ross's spirits too: an intercepted German wireless transmission confirmed that the German pilot Ross and Ellis had fought crashed following the dogfight. The transmission also indicated that the tables were turning in the skies above Gaza. The German squadron was running low on supplies and requested more fighters: 'One machine is not enough to get through the English blockade.'[42]

Ross returned to the squadron on 30 September 1917. He flew a new BE12a back across the Sinai to Weli Sheikh Nuran, where No. 1 Squadron had moved, ready to support General Allenby's planned offensive to advance into southern Palestine. It pleased Ross to be back among his fellow officers and to learn that Major Richard Williams had appointed him acting commander of C Flight following his flight commander's departure to join one of the new Australian squadrons then being raised. Williams also submitted the paperwork to secure the promotion to captain to which Ross had long aspired. He later recalled that this was 'by selection, not seniority'—Ross had impressed his CO with his coolness, courage and thorough attention to detail.[43] The news must have been satisfying for Ross: he had aspired to a captaincy since first joining the light horse.[44]

The promotion put Ross in command of one of the squadron's three flights. Each had six aircraft, a dozen flying officers and a ground staff of 40 mechanics, airframe riggers, armourers and other tradesmen. Besides being a larger command than the light horse machine gun section he had led in 1916, being a flight commander made Ross responsible for keeping C Flight's aircraft operational, as well as for the discipline and efficiency of its personnel and planning sorties—and continuing to fly himself.

Ross would report directly to Major Richard Williams—a man he respected but knew set exacting standards for his subordinates. With Allenby's offensive against Gaza about to recommence following a six-month stalemate, it was a trying time to take on the new role; nevertheless, Ross looked forward to the challenge with confidence and enthusiasm.[45]

18

VENGEANCE IS ONLY POOR CONSOLATION

Ross had only been C Flight's commander for a couple of weeks when he received the devastating news. Colin was dead. His younger brother had been killed in action on the Western Front.

It would take months for the details to filter through the bureaucracy of the Defence Department. Eventually, though, Ross and his family would learn that Colin had been killed on 6 October 1917 near Passchendaele in Belgium. Desperate for additional details, Andrew and Jessie paid the Red Cross to interview Colin's comrades, and from this they learned that he had been leading his platoon up to the front-line trenches when a German artillery bombardment began. It 'practically annihilated' the whole unit. Colin's right leg was shattered; he survived long enough to reach the 3rd Canadian Casualty Clearing Station at Lijssenthoek, 20 kilometres behind the front line, but he died the following day. He was just 22 years old.[1]

Back in Adelaide, Andrew and Jessie Smith listed Colin's death in the *Chronicle*. A brief, austere notice, it simply recorded that he had died from wounds in France on 6 October and was Andrew Smith of Mutrooroo's third son. Colin's notice was one of 58 published that Saturday—including one for Ross's friend Geoff Wells, also killed at Passchendaele the same day as Colin. Most families included a short epitaph ('his duty nobly done') but some featured lengthier tributes, such as poems expressing grief alongside religious and imperial sentiment. It was so very like Andrew and Jessie Smith to keep their grief private; they only published the barest details—enough to let the family's many friends know the dreadful news.[2] When it came time to select an epitaph for Colin's headstone, Jessie would choose the ubiquitous 'For God and Country'.

For Ross, who had been so protective of his younger brother, Colin's death was profoundly sad but not entirely unexpected. Through letters, he had followed Colin's journey to the front. Having been in battle himself and cognisant to the scale of the carnage in France, Ross had no doubts about the mortal danger an infantry officer faced.[3]

As it had done earlier in the war when he had lost Timmy and numerous other friends, Ross's grief manifested itself in an ardent desire for revenge. After Colin's death, killing for Ross would became increasingly personal: a form of retribution quite separate from more abstract ideals of 'God and Country'. Yet revenge would fail to assuage Ross's acute sense of grief. 'Vengeance is only poor consolation,' he would later reflect; 'however many Huns and Turks I can kill it won't make up for his loss'.[4] Ross would rationalise Colin's death through his increasingly fatalistic worldview, writing in June 1918 how he would 'often think of the Boy, and it's hard to think he's gone, but it's all chalked up somewhere, and we can't dodge our fates'.[5]

At the time, though, Ross had little opportunity to be too reflective or to become entirely consumed by his grief. News of Colin's death arrived in mid-October 1917, just as No. 1 Squadron was ramping up its flying operations to prepare for a new offensive to break the stalemate and advance into Palestine. Allenby intended to use an infantry corps to assault Gaza directly while another infantry corps and the Desert Mounted Corps attacked the inland flank of the Turkish line, at Beersheba. He planned to use the cavalry to outflank the main Ottoman centre of resistance in Gaza and then to cut the Ottoman Eighth Army's line of retreat.

Anticipating an advance deep into Palestine, Allenby's staff looked to the Flying Corps, and especially No. 1 Squadron, to photograph the vast area over which their army would need to operate. Keen to demonstrate the potential of aerial bombing, the RFC's leadership planned to use their squadrons to bomb Ottoman forces as they attempted to extricate themselves from Allenby's great pincer.

The Third Battle of Gaza began on 31 October 1917. Ross was over the right flank of the battlefield that morning; he observed the light horse manoeuvring into the position from which they would, later that afternoon, make their famous charge to capture Beersheba.[6] He flew on the following days too as the subsequent British attacks struggled to make headway against Ottoman forces in difficult terrain to Beersheba's north-west. Facing shortages of water, Allenby's cavalry took a week to capture objectives that he had intended them to secure within the offensive's first few days.

These were long days for Ross. He flew multiple sorties, sometimes staying out until dark to secure the most up-to-date intelligence. The photographs he took would be studied carefully by army surveyors attached to the squadron and any small change in the Turkish dispositions noted on updated maps. 'By this means the Staff knew exactly any alterations the enemy made in his defensive system,' wrote Ross. 'We were able to supply the Staff with these up-to date maps a few hours after the machine had landed with the exposed plates.'[7]

On 6 November, British forces finally overran Tel-el-Sharia, one of the main centres of Ottoman resistance on the inland flank. Ross and fellow pilot Lieutenant Ron Austin were over the battlefield that day in BE12as when they spotted three German Albatros fighters. Ross and Austin split up and attacked from two different directions. Austin turned to face the lone scout while Ross climbed towards the other two. 'The single fellow got over my wing, and I lost him for a few seconds, and before I knew what was happening he was right on my tail with both his front guns pouring tracers all round me.' Ross banked and turned as tightly as he could but the Albatros, both faster and more manoeuvrable, stayed behind him. With bullets shattering timber and tearing fabric all about him, Ross rolled his aircraft and put it into a spin; he dived 6000 feet before levelling out. Austin followed him and they regrouped; the Germans did not follow, allowing the two Australian pilots to make it back across the lines.

Ross felt disappointed; it was the first time his flight had abandoned a sortie without getting its photographs. He and Austin had not stood a chance though; the German Albatros fighters outclassed their antiquated BE12a aircraft in every way that mattered in air-to-air combat: speed, climbing power, manoeuvrability and firepower. Ross's plane had been extensively damaged in the few terrifying moments that the German had been on his tail. Bullets had torn through the cockpit, missing him by mere centimetres. Fragments from one projectile lacerated his leg. 'It's the first time I've ever had a Hun on my tail and it's not nice in a single-seater machine,' wrote Ross to Keith, who was part-way through his training course with the RFC in Britain. 'Take a tip and never let one get there if you can help it.'[8] Concerned for the welfare of his pilots, Major Williams urged his British superiors to provide new aircraft.[9]

With Sharia in British hands, the Ottoman commanders ordered Gaza's evacuation. British infantry occupied the besieged town early on 7 November. With the Turks in retreat, the staff at RFC Headquarters could finally issue orders for every available aircraft to be loaded with bombs. The first raid went out at two o'clock that afternoon, a formation of 32 aircraft from various squadrons, all led by Ross. 'It was a great sight,' he wrote. The formation assembled over No. 1 Squadron's aerodrome at Belah before setting out along the coast. They passed over the British 52nd Division, advancing north of Gaza before finding masses of Ottoman troops and horse-drawn transport retreating north towards Mejdel. With Ross in the vanguard, the formation of British and Australian aircraft dropped bombs and fired their machine guns into roads crowded with troops and transport. 'It was good bombing,' reported Ross, who heard afterwards that they had killed 700 Turks.[10] A German officer later described the scene as 'a sad spectacle with material strewn along the whole road, stationary lorries, broken up carts, dead horses, camels, bullocks and sheep, lying around with fugitives and wounded here and there'.[11]

Ross led another two raids the following day, this time against the railway station and aerodrome at Arak-el-Menshiye, where a German flying squadron was preparing to evacuate. 'We bombed from 3[000] to 4000 ft. and did great damage,' wrote Ross. 'After bombing the aerodrome most of us went down low and machine gunned it.'[12] German documents captured afterwards revealed how the squadron had only just arrived in the theatre and had to abandon most of its stores and equipment; it had to commandeer an Ottoman train at gunpoint to escape the advancing British cavalry.[13]

Each day for a week, Ross and his comrades pursued the Turkish Eighth Army north, bombing rail junctions and bridges to inflict the most damage possible. On 9 November Ross bombed the Ottoman rail yards and aerodrome at Et Tine, where thousands of Turkish troops were converging. Instead of the RFC's regular 20-pound bombs, he dropped 112-pound bombs. They made 'a great mess'; one hit a battery of Ottoman field artillery as it loaded its guns onto a train. Several Turkish soldiers were 'splashed' over the surrounding landscape, in Ross's words.[14] One German commander reported how the bombing caused huge explosions in the munitions dump, cut communications and resulted in 'wild excitement'.[15]

For the next three days the British airmen shifted their attacks north along the railway line to Junction Station, where a line branched off the main north–south route towards Jerusalem. While reconnoitring the station on 10 November, Ross dropped four 20-pound bombs from 11,000 feet and managed to land three in the station yard.[16] It was a fluke considering the rudimentary nature of the RFC's bomb-aiming equipment and Ross's minimal training and experience in bombing. Indeed, when Ross made another two 'trips' to Junction Station on 12 November with orders to cut the railway lines heading north, he found such precision targeting beyond his capabilities. 'On the first raid one of my bombs burst just outside a large shed in the station and the other failed to explode,' he recorded in his diary. 'On the second raid I miss[ed] the line with both bombs.'[17]

Ross flew eight raids during the week following the Ottoman withdrawal from Gaza. The RFC's Palestine Brigade dropped 10 tonnes of bombs and fired thousands of rounds of ammunition along the Ottoman Eighth Army's 90-kilometre line of retreat. 'We have never had such bombing before and some of our targets were impossible to miss,' wrote Ross. He found that the 112-pound bombs were particularly effective against masses of troops and transport: 'anything you hit with them just fades away in smoke'.[18] Given the day off on 13 November, Ross and Les Sutherland borrowed one of the squadron's cars and went out to explore the battlefield and hunt for souvenirs. 'All along the road were evidences of the Turks' retreat,' recorded Ross: 'broken transport, ammunition & dead animals were very plentiful.'[19] Indeed, while the air attacks had not prevented the Ottoman Eighth Army from withdrawing to a new defensive line north of Jerusalem, they had, in the words of one German commander, caused a 'disastrous panic' and made the retreat far more difficult than it might have been otherwise.[20]

As Allenby's forces closed in on Jerusalem during the second half of November, aerial photography again became No. 1 Squadron's priority. With the logistics of the whole Egyptian Expeditionary Force under strain, Ross struggled to keep C Flight's aircraft flying. A lack of transport postponed the squadron's move closer towards the new front line and a bad batch of fuel caused mechanical problems.[21] Flying an RE8 with Sutherland as his observer, Ross nevertheless spent most days during the latter part of November reconnoitring the Ottoman defences north of Jaffa. To assist Allenby's staff plan their assault on Jerusalem, on 27 November Ross and another pilot photographed the Turkish trenches east of the Holy City. Ross exposed 72 glass plates and, between them, the two Australian airmen covered 45 square miles (116 square kilometres).[22]

Two days later, Ross led eleven aircraft on a raid against the railway station at Tul Keram in northern Palestine. He had just crossed into enemy skies when his engine began misfiring. Being the flight's leader, Ross decided to press on. He made it to the target and had just released his bombs when the engine stopped altogether. Ross turned his aircraft for home and glided towards the line; he lost 2000 feet while working the controls to make the engine fire again. Finally it started. For the next hour, Ross watched his gauges anxiously as he nursed his aircraft on the long flight back to the squadron's aerodrome. 'I've never had such a "windy" trip and was very glad to be back on our side of the lines again.'

Ross was disappointed that the BE12a had let him down; it was his 'old machine'—the one he had flown regularly for two months, throughout the Third Battle of Gaza. He had his mechanics look over it and, confident that they had fixed whatever caused the problem, he took off on a test flight later that afternoon. Ross had just lifted off the grass aerodrome when the engine spluttered and stopped. He had to think quickly: 'I was faced with a row of tents & just beyond them a railway with a telegraph line beside it.' Resisting the impulse to turn back towards the aerodrome—usually a fatal mistake at such a low altitude—Ross put the nose down. He gathered enough speed to zoom up clear of the tents but not enough to miss the telegraph pole. The collision sent Ross's machine cartwheeling into the ground, leaving it a crumpled wreck. Remarkably, Ross emerged from the mess of shattered timber, torn fabric and tangled wires with only 'a few bits of skin off'. A laceration in his leg required a few stitches but he stayed with the squadron.[23]

Major Williams took Ross off the flying roster for a couple of weeks, although he had difficulty keeping him out of the cockpit. With his leg in a splint, Ross flew whenever he could to ferry aircraft around or take them on test flights; he ferried an aircraft up to the squadron's new aerodrome at Mejdel on 5 December and later that month acted as an aerial mail service to collect ballot papers for the Australian government's second conscription plebiscite.[24]

Jerusalem fell to Allenby's forces on 9 December 1917—an occasion trumpeted by the British government following a year of bloody stalemate in the war's other theatres. Ross appears to have been unaffected. 'We occupied Jerusalem' was all he noted in his diary that day.[25] Maybe it was the exhaustion of a year of flying combat operations; perhaps he realised that Allenby's great victory had not actually succeeded in bringing the war in the Middle East to a decisive conclusion. It now seemed certain that the war would continue into 1918—a fourth year away from home for Ross.

Had he paused to reflect on the past year, Ross might have recognised that 1917 had been one of the most important periods of his life. Not only had he realised his ambitions of learning to fly and securing a captaincy; he had thoroughly distinguished himself in combat. By the year's end, Ross had emerged as one of the most experienced airmen on the Middle East front; as an observer and pilot, he had 360 hours in his log book.[26] In November alone, during the advance of Allenby's forces, he had flown 68 hours—'more than any other pilot here', as he noted in a letter to Keith, in an uncharacteristically forthright summation of his achievements. 'I led nearly all the big bomb raids and took miles and miles of photographs with a few H[ostile] A[ircraft] patrols thrown in, as well as reconnaissances.'[27]

A few days before Christmas, Ross learned that he had been awarded a Bar to the MC he had received for his part in rescuing a downed British pilot in March. Unlike his first MC, which had been recommended for a single, gallant act, the second award referred to his conduct throughout the Third Gaza operations, which had been 'characterised by consistent gallantry'.[28] When Ross wrote to Keith to tell him the news, he sounded proud and it pleased him that the award would reflect well on their parents. Still, aware of how medal citations and press reports could exaggerate, Ross expressed some anxiety about how it would be 'worded' in the official statements.[29]

But while 1917 had been a triumphant year for Ross, it had also been one marked by loss. He had indeed become accustomed to attending the funerals of friends and colleagues—young men like him, whose bodies were shot or burned thousands of feet above Palestine, or crumpled and broken in accidents that had been caused by human or mechanical error.

In the previous nine months, fifteen of No. 1 Squadron's officers had been killed and numerous others had been wounded, captured or sent home with debilitating nervous conditions. The most recent, an observer named Lieutenant Harry Matheson, had become lost on Christmas night while walking home from a neighbouring aerodrome and died of exposure. Elsewhere, Ross's friends had died fighting with the light horse or in France and Belgium where, most poignantly, his younger brother Colin had been killed. The Smith family's experience of 1917 reflected that of the broader Australian community. Twenty-two thousand Australian soldiers were killed that year—more than any other year in World War I, or indeed the nation's entire military history.

But if the deaths of friends and family overwhelmed Ross with bereavement and hopelessness, then he did a good job at covering it up. In letters to friends and family he remained resilient, pragmatic and, at least ostensibly, optimistic and upbeat. Ross clearly missed his family and eagerly looked forward to the war's end—but he expected the fighting to continue for some time yet and he remained convinced of the righteousness of the British Empire's cause. It seems that Ross kept the death and maiming of comrades at a safe emotional distance, describing dead comrades as 'poor devils' who had 'gone west' and reconciling himself to the likelihood that his luck could not possibly last forever. 'Yours 'til my wings fold up' is his how Ross fatalistically signed off letters to friends in the Flying Corps (Jessie Smith continued to receive the more reassuring 'Your loving son, Ross').[30]

Ross's muted response to death reflected the stoic, masculine identity and the commitment to duty on which his generation had been raised.[31] It was an identity shared throughout the squadron, where funerals were brief and outwardly unemotional affairs and reinforcements arrived promptly to replace casualties.[32] The squadron's medical officer, Captain John Harris, found it 'astonishing how . . . accidents and losses are covered up by the men'. Everyone 'feel[s] it keenly', he suspected, but nobody articulated their grief: 'The only thing one notices is that the boys might take a few drinks more for a day or two.'[33]

Indeed, alcohol played an important part in the coping, with Ross revealing how he was 'inked most of the time' whenever he could get away from the aerodrome on leave or official errands.[34] The squadron's mess also offered opportunities to imbibe, with its bar serving wine, spirits and beer. Captain Harris remarked how he 'could get drunk every day' if he wished, while another of Ross's comrades fondly remembered the 'bouts of drinking and "playing hell"' that helped the airmen deal with the strain of war flying.[35]

Ross noted how, in early 1918, Major Williams ordered the mess to be closed at 10 p.m. in an attempt to curb some of the excesses.[36]

It was therefore, with a stoicism braced by alcohol, fatalism and a mutually silent code of grieving that Ross and his fellow aviators faced what would be the Great War's climactic year.

19

BRISFITS AND BAGGAGE

No. 1 Squadron's casualties had been so high during 1917 because of the tactical disadvantage that the Australian pilots usually faced in aerial combat. Throughout the year, the German squadrons in Palestine used aircraft, including the latest Albatros fighters, that out-performed the ageing Martinsydes and BEs flown by the Australians: the Albatroses were faster, more manoeuvrable and more heavily armed. In a dogfight, the German pilots always had the initiative; Ross himself had been wounded in two separate encounters with German fighters in 1917. As he realised when flying a frail, old BE12a, there was little even the most experienced pilot could do to shake an enemy aircraft off his tail.[1]

With the squadrons in France prioritised to receive the latest aircraft designs, the RFC in the Middle East had to make do until late 1917. In October, Ross's flight received a few RE8s—they represented an improvement over the BE2 but still required a fighter escort when ranging deep into enemy territory to take photographs. In December, however, No. 1 Squadron began refitting with Bristol F2bs. Known colloquially as the 'Bristol Fighter' or 'Brisfit', the F2b had a crew of two but the performance of a single-seat fighter aircraft. Squadrons using them in France had discovered that, by flying them like a fighter, pilots could well and truly hold their own in a dogfight.[2]

Ross put one of C Flight's new Bristol Fighters through its paces on New Year's Eve 1917. He escorted a pair of RE8s across the Jordan River to photograph Ottoman strongholds along the Hedjaz railway. The Bristol Fighter's 190-horsepower Rolls-Royce engine and its superb handling left a big impression on Ross, filling him with an unfamiliar sense of confidence that he could now match any 'Hun' aircraft that they came across.[3] To a friend, he described them as 'top hole, *believe me*', while to his mother, Ross introduced his new aeroplane as 'so nice looking . . . he's painted dark brown and his engine sticks away out in front just like a big dog's nose that is sniffing around for trouble'.[4]

For the time being, though, there was little trouble for Ross to find in the skies over northern Palestine. Allenby's campaign at the end of 1917 had incapacitated the five German flying squadrons in the region; they had abandoned much of their equipment during the Ottoman retreat and now struggled to obtain replacement aircraft and reinforcements from Germany. During the first few months of 1918, Ross would only occasionally see German aircraft and he found them frustratingly reluctant to fight. 'The Huns have got a colossal draught up now and very seldom cross the lines,' he wrote to a friend in late January. 'I was escorting photos this morning and met 3 scouts at 15,000 (they were about 16,500) but they weren't having any biff and cleared off.'[5]

With Allenby forced to relinquish parts of his army to reinforce the Western Front in early 1918, the war on the ground in Palestine also once again atrophied into a stalemate. A more or less continuous line of trenches ran across northern Palestine, extending from the Mediterranean coast at Jaffa to Jericho on the River Jordan. Off Allenby's right flank in Transjordan, the Turks held outposts that stretched south along the Hedjaz railway, towards Medina. Here an army of Arab nationalists, supported by the British, waged an insurgency against their Ottoman rulers.

In this operational context, aerial photography again became one of Ross's main responsibilities. During January 1918, he oversaw a major assignment to photograph an area extending 50 kilometres behind the new Ottoman front line. Allenby's headquarters lacked accurate maps of this territory and hoped to use mosaics of aerial photographs as the basis for a new series of sheets. On most days for a fortnight, Ross and Sutherland, flying one of the new Bristol Fighters, escorted other crews flying older machines equipped with cameras. Typically, five aircraft with cameras flew in a line abreast, about 1000 metres apart, to take strips of overlapping images. 'In this way we got a lot of country at once,' explained Ross. 'Two or 3 Bristols would escort the photo machines & it was rather a hard job because they were all spread out so much.'[6]

In a fortnight, Ross and the airmen in C Flight photographed over 1600 square kilometres of previously unmapped territory. The commander of the RFC's Palestine Brigade, Brigadier General Amyas Borton, hailed their efforts as 'probably the highest point which has yet been reached in map making photography'.[7] The photographic survey of northern Palestine by air would continue for the following few months, with Ross's C Flight emerging as the RFC's specialists in this kind of work. Major Williams assigned Ross the few available Bristol Fighters equipped with more powerful 275-horsepower engines and allowed him to handpick the best crews from the squadron roster to fly them.[8] Under Ross's leadership, C Flight would photograph three-quarters of the 5200 square kilometres surveyed by the RFC in Palestine during the first half of 1918.[9]

During this period, Ross flew an operational sortie about every second day. They typically lasted two or three hours and involved photographing enemy territory or recording the movements of Ottoman forces. Although Ross continued to get enormous pleasure from flying, this work tended to be tedious and physically strenuous. Flying at altitudes of up to 20,000 feet in an open cockpit without an oxygen supply, Ross experienced conditions similar to those a mountaineer might face when scaling some of the world's highest peaks. 'I've never been so painfully cold in my life before, and breathing at that height was quite difficult,' wrote Ross after spending nearly two hours taking photographs at 19,000 feet in January.[10] On another occasion, he described how his fingers went numb. 'I started slapping them on my knees to get them warm, and after I stopped I was quite puffed from the exertion of just doing that!'[11] The debilitating effects of altitude sickness frequently continued after the pilots had landed, and included headaches, shortness of breath, physical exhaustion and, in the long term, nervous strain.[12]

In February 1918, a visit to the squadron by the AIF's official photographer, Captain Frank Hurley, disrupted the monotony of Ross's reconnaissance sorties. Hurley, who had achieved some renown as the photographer on both the Mawson and Shackleton expeditions to the Antarctic, had come to Palestine in early 1918 to photograph Australian troops in action. Major Williams assigned Ross to fly Hurley around Palestine so he could take cinema reel footage and photographs from the air.

Hurley was impressed with the unique perspective provided by his flights with Ross. During one four-hour trip, Ross took Hurley up to photograph Jerusalem from 18,000 feet before descending and skimming along just above the surface of the Dead Sea. 'I am powerless and utterly incapable of describing the wild and tremendous grandeur of the view now stretched before us,' wrote Hurley of the scene that Ross had also found breathtaking when he first took to the skies a little over a year earlier. 'I was lost enraptured by the ineffable beauty of the scenery below . . . It was a glimpse of another world. A peep into the realms of the infinite.'[13]

During his few days with No. 1 Squadron, Hurley also took photographs around the aerodrome at Mejdel, immortalising Ross and his comrades and their aeroplanes in his carefully composed style. An early adherent of Paget process photography, Hurley created what is perhaps the only colour exposure of Ross in existence. He and an unidentified observer (possibly Les Sutherland) are posed in their long leather flying coats beside a Bristol Fighter, scrutinising a map. The flat, dusty expanse from which they would take off and land is immediately behind them and, on a slight rise in the background, there are lines of bell tents: the basic canvas accommodation that Ross and his comrades did their best to make feel homely.[14]

Hurley's flights with Ross finished with him riding along on a bombing raid against the Transjordan citadel of Kerak. Along with six other Australian aircraft, Ross took off in cold, gusty conditions and climbed to 8000 feet over the Judean Hills before crossing over the Dead Sea into Transjordan. 'Clouds rolled up, and the chaos of mountains and valleys were chequered with sunshine and shadow,' described Hurley. The formation released its bombs over Kerak, causing large explosions in the citadel's main square; pulverised masonry and smoke engulfed the town, obscuring it from view. Ross then led the formation home via Kutrani, where it descended to strafe a railway siding crowded with over 100 carriages and a neighbouring aerodrome. Despite an uncomfortably bumpy flight home through inclement weather, all seven aircraft made it safely back to Mejdel. 'After a wash,' recorded Hurley, 'we went across to lunch where the topic naturally was the raid, and we all wondered how many we had killed and wounded.'[15] Later that afternoon, Ross bid Captain Hurley farewell, unaware that their paths would cross again in the future.

As Hurley's visit indicates, Ross's role as a flight commander came with additional responsibilities. He had nearly 60 officers and men under his command, and he had to ensure that they cooperated in an efficient and disciplined manner to keep C Flight's six Bristol Fighters flying. Besides overseeing the work of the mechanics and arranging for the resupply of spare parts and equipment, Ross had to assign crews to fly the sorties that squadron headquarters ordered each evening. He needed to know the pilots and observers in his flight well—to appreciate their strengths and weaknesses, understand how they worked with each other and recognise who needed a rest. Being so personable and approachable, Ross seems to have handled this aspect of his command well. Indeed, he noted with some surprise how frequently his comrades confided in him with 'their troubles'.[16]

Ross brought other personal qualities to his role as flight commander that served C Flight well. Brigadier General Borton, who came to know Ross well during his visits to the squadron in 1918, recalled, 'It was an outstanding feature of his character that, even in the heat of the moment, he could bring a calm and sound judgement to bear on the situation.' In addition to this capacity to think clearly under pressure, Ross remained 'cheerful' even in the most difficult situations and demonstrated an 'indomitable courage' in his own flying that earned him respect throughout the Royal Air Force (RAF; as the RFC was renamed in April 1918) in Palestine.[17] Henry Gullett, the official Australian war correspondent in Palestine, recalled similar characteristics in Ross:

> Very fair, tall, spare, angular and powerful, Ross Smith's whole bearing suggests resolution and capacity. But the dominant will of the man is concealed beneath a charming modesty and a pretty self-consciousness. Success has not spoiled him. He always struck us on service as one of the happiest men in the war; his smile was one of the sunniest things in Palestine.[18]

After hours, Ross divided his time between the officers' mess and sport. At Ramleh, where No. 1 Squadron moved in April 1918, the men rolled out a cricket pitch on which Ross played a few wickets after tea each evening.[19] As the weather warmed up, Ross and the other officers also swam at a nearby beach; some nights they borrowed a squadron tender and drove to Jaffa for dinner.[20] He continued to write prodigiously, sending letters to his many friends, to Keith and to his mother. The diary he started the previous year, however, inexplicably stopped in February 1918. Every ten weeks or so, Ross earned a week's leave in Cairo—far more than his comrades in the light horse and infantry received but a reflection of the physical and psychological strain of war flying. More frequently, when he could secure a day off, Ross and the other officers went sightseeing. He visited Jerusalem for the first time in March 1918, landing on Judas Iscariot's field in his Bristol Fighter. Ross's indifference regarding religion again becomes apparent in his correspondence—this time in his response to a first-hand experience of Christendom's most significant sights. 'It's a filthy place and full of smells and holy places. I did the sights as quickly as possible,' he wrote.[21] Ross's second trip to the Holy City proved to be more to his taste: he went to a dance attended by many 'fine looking Jewish girls'.[22]

As summer approached, the German squadrons in Palestine became more active. Ross and his comrades began sighting enemy aircraft every so often during their patrols, but the German pilots kept their distance, apparently reluctant to fight. On 7 May 1918, however, Ross and another pilot, Lieutenant Alfred Tonkin, surprised a new type of two-seater 11,000 feet over Jenin. As usual, its pilot made to escape but, in their Bristol Fighters, Ross and Tonkin easily caught up and manoeuvred above him and into the perfect position for a diving attack.

Tonkin went first, with Ross following. When Ross pressed the firing button, he was close enough to pick out the distinctive red bands on the enemy machine's cigar-shaped fuselage. Its pilot dived towards his aerodrome with Ross and Tonkin in pursuit, firing as they went. From 2000 feet, they watched as their adversary crashed into a hillside and burned.[23]

During their flight home, Tonkin fired a flare, alerting Ross to a pair of Albatros scouts approaching them from below and behind. 'I turned quickly and got right on his tail and dived,' reported Ross, 'but my gun only fired one round, and then jammed.' Ross's observer, Lieutenant Ernest Mustard, opened fire on the German aircraft but Ross spoiled his shooting by pulling away to fix his own gun. By the time he had it firing again, Tonkin had shot both German fighters down. The three German aircraft they had claimed between them made it 'quite a good day's sport', thought Ross, although it irritated him that his gun had failed at such a critical moment: 'It was rotten luck my gun jamming because I had that scout absolutely "cold".'[24]

Mustard photographed the wreckage of their first victim and Ross sent a print home to his mother. In the accompanying letter, he noted that the usual satisfaction he felt at killing Germans had been tempered by the incendiary death of his opponent. 'I felt rather sorry for the pilot and passenger, because they were almost sure to be burnt too,' he wrote. 'I couldn't wish my worst enemy such an awful fate as that.'[25] Ross did not share more on this topic with his mother, but his response to seeing an adversary in flames suggests that, like many airmen in the First World War, the prospect of being caught in a burning aircraft was a horrifyingly real one that offered a stark choice:

either jump without a parachute or burn alive. It would be surprising if such a terrifying scenario did not, at least from time to time, play out in Ross's imagination—or, indeed, in his nightmares.

Ross's failure to shoot down his second opponent on 7 May reflects not only the 'rotten luck' of a gun jam but also his lack of experience in air-to-air combat. Although he had over 300 hours' flying time in his log book, up until this point Ross had fought in fewer than half a dozen dogfights—and these tended to be chaotically fast and confusing affairs from which general principles seemed difficult to draw and apply. But as it had in France, where the Bristol Fighter first deployed in early 1917, it was becoming clear to Ross and his comrades in Palestine that this unconventional aircraft's greatest asset in a fight was its observer—the '160 pounds of baggage' that Ross and the other pilots jokingly called their comrades in the back seat.[26] Armed with two Lewis guns, the observer could fire in an almost 360-degree arc, including forwards over the pilot's head and top wing. When in a dogfight, the most successful Bristol Fighter pilots flew to secure their observer the best shot; they used their own single Vickers machine gun as the aircraft's secondary weapon.

Ross had flown regularly with Les Sutherland as his observer in 1917, but during 1918 he mainly flew with two of C Flight's newer observers, Lieutenants Ernest 'Pard' Mustard and Walter Alister Kirk. (Sutherland stayed in C Flight and remained good friends with Ross. Perhaps Ross assigned him, as one of the flight's experienced observers, to fly with one of the newer pilots.) Mustard had been a clerk in Melbourne before the war and was the same age as Ross (25 years old in 1918), whereas Kirk was a few years older, came from Belfast and had worked in Sydney as a mechanic before the war. Both had joined the AIF at the beginning of the war and had fought in the light horse at Gallipoli and in Sinai before volunteering for the AFC. Like Ross before them, Mustard and Kirk proved to be outstanding observers and took an obsessive interest in their Lewis guns. Perhaps this was why Ross picked them to join C Flight and, later, chose to fly with them. 'In the East that was something of an accolade,' observed Sutherland.[27]

Two weeks after the gun jam incident, Ross and Kirk were on a reconnaissance sortie, several kilometres behind Ottoman lines at 11,000 feet over Nablus, when their escort pilot spotted two Albatroses above them. Despite having the tactical advantage of 1000 feet of additional altitude, the German pilots both turned and tried to make their escape.

Ross caught his opponent easily. 'The chap I went for was an awful ass, and got rattled and didn't fire a shot at me,' he wrote. This time Ross manoeuvred to give his observer a clear shot; he approached from behind and underneath the Albatros's tail, allowing Kirk to fire a 'full double drum' (nearly 100 rounds) into it. The Albatros emitted a 'puff of smoke' and its engine stopped. 'As the Hun fell, I gave him a good burst with my front gun, and he went down in a wide spin through the clouds, which were only about 1000 feet above the ground.'[28]

Encounters with German aircraft became more frequent during the summer. In June the RAF ordered its squadrons to mount 'Hostile Aircraft Patrols' just behind the Ottoman front line to engage any would-be intruders. For No. 1 Squadron this meant a daily routine of patrols at dawn and dusk, with pairs of Bristol Fighters covering each of the unit's allocated patrol areas.

During the summer, Ross regularly led C Flight's early patrol, flying with either Mustard or Kirk. On flying days they would emerge from their tents at 3 a.m. and take off before dawn. Climbing above the cloud bank before the sun's rays had touched the Earth produced some of the most arresting sights Ross had seen during the 400 hours he had, by this stage, spent in the air over Palestine.[29] Arriving at his patrol area, Ross and the crew of the other Bristol Fighter would fly circuits back and forth between two points for three hours. 'It's alright for the first hour,' he admitted, 'but after that the clock won't go nearly fast enough.' To pass the time, Ross sang—mostly the ragtime tunes to which he danced when on leave. 'The engine is a fine accompaniment,' he wrote, 'and quite drowns the noise I make.'[30]

Taking off at 4 a.m. on 11 June with a Bristol Fighter crewed by Lieutenants Ernest Stooke and Louis Krieg, Ross and Kirk noticed British anti-aircraft shells exploding a few thousand feet overhead. Climbing to investigate, they spotted a German Rumpler making off to the north. Ross pursued it across the front line and then a further 50 kilometres north before getting into gun range. 'I gradually crept up to him, and then got under his tail, and Kirk opened fire with his double guns.' As the German pilot dived away, Ross hit him with a burst from his Vickers machine gun. Stooke then fired another burst into the hapless enemy machine. 'The Hun finally landed in a field near a village and the pilot and observer got out and ran for cover,' reported Ross. 'We both went down and shot up the machine on the ground, and then came back and continued our patrol.'[31]

Ross and Kirk took off early on 19 June to surprise a German two-seater that British anti-aircraft gunners had reported over Jericho each morning at 6 a.m. They were waiting at 16,000 feet when the reddish-brown Rumpler with a camouflaged top wing approached. Spotting Ross, the German pilot turned and 'bolted'. Ross pursued him, catching up just across the Ottoman lines. 'And the fun started,' wrote Ross. 'I had expected him to put his nose down and try to land somewhere but this fellow was a real sportsman and put up a fine fight.'

Aware that he would be met with a 'hail of lead' if he approached from directly behind, Ross again used the tactic that had been proving so successful throughout the squadron. He carefully positioned himself underneath the Rumpler's tail, where the German observer could not traverse his gun. Far from being the 'mug pilot' Ross expected, though, this adversary proved to be 'a real artist at handling his machine'; he made steep banking turns each time Kirk brought his Lewis guns to bear. 'The Hun then tried again and again,' wrote Ross. 'But each time I beat him. Kirk was firing whenever he could, but we were manoeuvring so fast that accurate shooting was difficult.' For five minutes, they flew around in tight circles, the centrifugal forces compressing Ross into his seat. Then he got close enough to see the German observer, 'a little chap' trying to clear his jammed gun. When Kirk fired his next burst, Ross saw the observer drop into his cockpit.

At this, the pilot lost his nerve and made a break for home. Ross had a clear shot: 'I fired about 50 rounds right into him from close range with my front gun.' They kept diving, Ross's air-speed gauge registering over 200 miles (322 kilometres) per hour. Hit by two more bursts from Ross's Vickers gun, the German pilot turned underneath the Bristol Fighter's wing; Ross had to ease out of the dive to prevent breaking his airframe. Circling around, he spotted the Rumpler on the ground, having apparently made a rough landing. 'We came down to 1000 [feet] and my observer fired 300 rounds into [the] machine,' reported Ross. 'Judging by the tracers, his shooting appeared to be very accurate. Only one man was seen to run away from [the] machine.'[32]

That Rumpler marked the fifth enemy aircraft that Ross claimed to have forced down. Some, such as this one and the Rumpler on 11 June, appeared to have been wrecked (or at least severely damaged). Others, such as the Albatros of 22 May, emitted smoke and spun down, apparently out of control, but was lost to sight in the clouds. Taken together, these claims ostensibly distinguish Ross as an 'ace' pilot and earn him a place on the numerous lists of aviators with five or more aerial victories that aviation historians have produced in the decades since the First World War. Yet, despite the obsessive attention accorded the 'ace' pilots of the Great War, this qualification actually had no official basis or sanction and is, in fact, an historical anachronism. The notion of a 'fighter ace' is largely the product of post-war histories (and novels and films) rather than a metric by which pilots such as Ross used to measure their success.

French newspapers coined the term 'ace' in 1915, but it never really gained traction among British and dominion airmen.[33] The RAF and its antecedents did not officially tally the 'scores' of individual aviators or squadrons, and indeed remained reticent about publicising the exploits of individual pilots.[34] Ross himself recognised this; the modesty he characteristically demonstrated in his letters regarding his achievements not only reflected his personality, but also the culture of the organisation in which he served. In the British and dominion flying squadrons, pilots thought to be big noters or 'hot-air merchants' faced ostracism and ridicule. As one veteran Australian pilot put it years after the war, to have discussed one's 'score' or talked of 'aces' would have been considered 'vulgar'.[35]

Indeed, in none of the hundreds of pages of surviving letters and diary entries that Ross wrote does he use the term 'ace'—nor, indeed, does he refer to his own personal 'score' or 'tally'. Where Ross reflected on his successes in aerial combat, he tended to characterise them as a joint effort, a reflection perhaps of a youth filled with team sports and games. Ross clearly appreciated the contribution made by the ground staff who kept his Bristol Fighter flying and in his combat reports he acknowledged the part played in bringing down enemy aircraft by other pilots and especially his observers. Indeed, as Ross noted in most of his combat reports, his observer typically fired more ammunition than he did, and quite often fired the killing shots.

Ultimately the only score that Ross seems to have kept was that earned by Bristol Fighter number B1229—the machine he flew most frequently throughout 1918. The aircraft came to the squadron in March 1918 with 'New South Wales No. 11, The Macintyre Kayuga Estate' painted on its fuselage—an indication that it was one of 41 aircraft funded by a private subscription campaign in Australia during 1917.[36] Just as he had with his horses, Ross took great pride and interest in his aircraft, and he asked his mother to look up the Macintyre family, who apparently resided in Muswellbrook, New South Wales. He wanted to write to them and 'tell them about their machine': how the airmen of No. 1 Squadron's C Flight had earned six Distinguished Flying Crosses on it and that '1229 has so far accounted for 4 Hun machines destroyed, and at least 5 more driven down, and 1 driven down out of control'. The team for which Ross played and with whom he shared his success therefore evidently extended all the way back to a small town in New South Wales.[37]

In June 1918, Major Richard Williams was appointed to take command of No. 1 Squadron's senior formation, the RAF's 40th Wing. Williams had played an important part in Ross's development as an airman. In 1916, as his flight commander and regular pilot, Williams had encouraged Ross's ambitions to become a pilot and provided some unofficial flying instruction. Then, when he became a flight commander himself, Ross had been responsible for reporting directly to Williams—or 'the boss', as he referred to his CO.

The private papers of No. 1 Squadron members make it clear that Williams was a difficult man to serve: he was strict and idiosyncratic with a leadership style that some described as rigid and impersonal.[38] Yet Ross had a good working relationship with his CO. He acknowledged Williams' stringency, but he got along well with him—the gears of the relationship were greased by Ross's qualities as a leader and an airman, and probably also by his conviviality and well-practised ability to fit in and cooperate with others.[39] The feeling was evidently mutual, as Ross's advancement in the squadron and the MC and Bar that Williams recommended indicate. Williams also gave Ross considerable responsibility and latitude in running C Flight; he allotted it most of the special long-range work, assigned the Bristol Fighters with the largest engines to Ross's command and allowed him to hand-pick his own pilots and observers. After the war, Williams would speak glowingly of Ross's courage and skill as a pilot.[40] In his memoirs, he would write of the 'close friendship' they shared throughout Ross's flying career.[41]

Despite this, Ross did not succeed Williams in taking command of No. 1 Squadron. Instead, one of Ross's fellow flight commanders (and his tent mate), Captain Sydney Addison, was appointed as the squadron's new CO. Ostensibly, Addison's advancement ahead of Ross seems odd. A journalist from Hobart, he had embarked on active service in late 1916—two years later than Ross—and had only been with No. 1 Squadron since November 1917 (Ross had joined as an observer a year earlier). But within the AIF, Addison—who had been an officer in the militia before the war—had seniority to Ross. His captaincy and grading as a flight commander dated from August 1917, whereas Ross's had been gazetted in November.[42]

Despite Addison's seniority, Ross may, in fact, have been offered command of the squadron first and declined it—although there is no surviving evidence of this. As Ross would have realised, appointment as squadron commander would have effectively ended his flying career: COs in the RAF (and AFC) did not regularly fly, their deskbound responsibilities allowing little time for combat sorties. It is difficult to envisage Ross, so completely absorbed by flying, finding much satisfaction in paperwork.

Hindsight reveals that Addison's appointment as No. 1 Squadron's CO ahead of Ross had implications of immense historical importance. Had he moved from the cockpit to a desk in squadron headquarters in June 1918, Ross would almost certainly have missed the truly life-changing opportunities that lay ahead for him in the coming months—personal opportunities that would have ramifications of global significance.

Rank seniority and, perhaps, Ross's desire to avoid a desk job, kept him flying in 1918. But chance, providence or, as Ross would have probably described it, fate had also played a hand. Back in April, one of the squadron's pilots had lost control of his Bristol Fighter while taking off and crashed into C Flight's tent lines. The aircraft's propeller shredded the tent that Ross, Les Sutherland and Sydney Addison shared; Addison was asleep in his bed when the accident occurred.[43] To everyone's amazement, he emerged from the mess of torn fabric, flying papers and splintered furniture with nothing more than a 'slight abrasion' on his left knee.[44]

20

BIFFY AND THE BLOODY PARALYSER

Since March 1918, Ross and one of his regular observers, Ernest 'Pard' Mustard, had often 'amused' themselves by sneaking 'a bomb or two' aboard for reconnaissance sorties and hostile aircraft patrols. As Ross explained, 'Mustard carries them in his cockpit and when he sees a decent target he leans out with the bomb and I tell him when to drop it.' Ross enjoyed seeing Ottoman troops run for cover whenever he approached.[1]

Other crews in C Flight followed their flight commander's lead and began attacking any targets they came across during their long and usually otherwise uneventful patrols. For a few months, these 'unofficial' activities went unreported in the squadron's records, but on 21 June 1918 Ross and his observer Walter Kirk, with Lieutenants Carrick Paul and William Weir, demonstrated to the rest of the RAF in Palestine the potential that such tactics had in inflicting considerable damage.

That morning, Ross had dropped a message on the German aerodrome at Jenin for a captured Australian officer. He was on his way home when he spotted a train in a railway station and a large number of Turkish soldiers preparing to board. 'It was too good to miss,' wrote Ross afterwards, 'so down we went to 1000 feet over them and pasted them with lead.' After the Bristol Fighters made their first low-level pass, the train steamed out of the station. Ross and Paul followed, flying alongside it so their observers could rake it with Lewis gunfire. Climbing over a hill and dropping down into the next valley, Ross found another two busy railway stations: 'We shot up the first one and then flew along the road to the next one, shooting everything we saw.' The third railway station had a large camp and motor transport yard beside it. 'We gave them a fine old picnic and Kirk and I nearly fell overboard with laughter,' wrote Ross. 'You never saw such a mess, there were men, horses and carts and other things going in all directions. It was great fun twisting about among the hills and along the valleys.'[2]

Although he claimed to have done it 'for the sport of the thing', Ross's report impressed his former CO, Lieutenant Colonel Williams, and his staff at 40th Wing Headquarters. They forwarded it to Brigadier General Amyas Borton, commanding the RAF's Palestine Brigade, and the following day a letter arrived at No. 1 Squadron's aerodrome commending the 'fine piece of work on the part of Capt. Smith', Kirk, Paul and Weir. It predicted that such opportunistic aerial attacks would result in the 'demoralisation of the enemy'.[3] Shortly afterwards, the RAF issued orders that pilots on all sorties should carry bombs and use them to strike 'any favourable target' that they came across during the course of their regular duties.[4]

Ross continued to lead by example, frequently interrupting patrols and reconnaissance flights to bomb and 'shoot up' trains, Ottoman camps and enemy aerodromes. Frequently joining him on these sorties were Lieutenants Paul and Weir. The two crews developed a reputation—so much so that Paul and Weir's distinctive yellow Bristol Fighter apparently became known to and feared by the Turks.[5] Ross described Paul as 'a jolly fine pilot' and aggressively keen on strafing ground targets. Of Weir, he wrote, 'also an excellent chap, and doesn't care a damn for anything'.[6]

On 9 July, having not seen many German aircraft for some time, Ross, Kirk, Paul and Weir devised a plan 'to liven them up a bit'. They flew to Jenin and, after photographing the aerodrome, Ross circled at 2000 feet so Kirk could strafe the hangars. When the Germans wheeled out six fighters, Ross and Paul both dived to machine gun them:

> The Huns then evidently changed their minds, because they stopped their engines, and would not come up. We flew round for a bit more and did

> some more shooting, and everyone on the aerodrome was running all over the place, and then we started home again.[7]

They had been above the German aerodrome, unopposed, for twenty minutes. 'The whole show was great fun,' wrote Ross. Again, the brigade commander wrote to the squadron congratulating Ross. Two days later, during a quiet patrol up near Nablus, the Ross–Paul team repeated the exercise, strafing another aerodrome before following a main road back south, with Kirk shooting up 'everything he could see'.[8]

Ross had fought no aerial combats for a month when, shortly after sunrise on 17 July 1918, he and Kirk spotted a pair of German Albatroses at 11,000 feet over the Wadi Ajua, near Jericho. When Ross approached, they fled; he followed, chasing them down to tree-top height. 'We were going along the valleys and zooming over hills,' Ross recounted. 'I then got right on to one fellow's tail, and fired a burst with my front gun, and down he went, and crashed, and turned over on to his back.' Ross switched his attention to the other Albatros; by this time, they were down to 100 feet in altitude. As he closed to within 30 metres of the German fighter, Turkish soldiers fired at him. With the Albatros filling his gunsight, Ross clutched the firing lever: 'he fell like a stone' and ploughed into the Nablus road, cartwheeling onto its back. 'I'm fairly sure I killed the last chap, but the first one may have only been wounded,' Ross reported in that week's letter to his mother.

After Kirk photographed both wrecked aircraft, Ross resumed the patrol. It wasn't long before he spotted a German reconnaissance machine being shelled by anti-aircraft guns at Jericho. Ross pursued it back across enemy lines and had just come into firing range when his engine began missing. He smelled burning paint as he turned and put the Bristol Fighter's nose down. 'You can't imagine my next 10 minutes,' he later wrote, recalling the prospect of soon seeing the inside of an Ottoman prison camp. He had just crossed back over British lines when the propeller seized. The engine billowed smoke and made horrible grinding sounds. Being over the rugged

Judean hills, there were few places to make an emergency landing. With seconds to choose, he picked a patch of flat ground about twice the size of a tennis court, crowded by hills and rocky outcrops, and side-slipped down onto it. 'It was a very anxious few minutes and I was thankful when I got out of the machine and on to the earth once more,' he reported.[9]

Fortunately they had come down close to a main road, so Ross and Kirk hitched a ride into the nearest town and called Major Addison to send a tender from the squadron with some mechanics and a new engine. Eight mechanics worked into the night replacing B1229's engine and parts of its tail that had been damaged, while Ross and Kirk enjoyed the hospitality of a nearby Indian regiment's officers' mess. The following day, the mechanics pushed the Bristol Fighter out onto the road, from where Ross and Kirk 'took off in fine style' and flew home.[10]

Reports of Ross's outstanding work during June and July 1918 reached the top echelons of the RAF. Major General Geoffrey Salmond, General Officer Commanding the RAF in the Middle East, sent Ross and Kirk a wire congratulating them on their double victory on 17 July and he endorsed Lieutenant Colonel Williams' recommendation that both airmen be awarded the Distinguished Flying Cross (DFC). This decoration had been introduced by the recently established RAF to acknowledge 'acts of valour, courage or devotion to duty while flying'. Ross's citation referred to the two German aircraft he and Kirk had shot down in July as well as the 'gallantry and initiative' they demonstrated in frequently attacking targets on the ground from low altitudes: 'The keenness and fine example set by these officers cannot be over-estimated.'[11]

The news thrilled Ross. He immediately sent cables to his parents and to Keith, and a couple of days later wrote letters providing details. 'I am a very happy little boy at present,' he enthused in the account he sent his mother—although he also downplayed his actions, telling her that things like that happened all the time. Knowing that Captain John Harris, the squadron's medical officer, had already sent a somewhat hyperbolic description of the 17 July dogfight to Jessie, Ross urged his mother not to share it with the newspapers as she had done following the award of his first MC a year earlier. 'I would lose every bit of respect of the fellows here that I have got, in fact, I don't think I could stay in the Squadron,' he warned.[12]

When the DFC's conspicuous purple and white ribbon arrived the following month, Ross pinned it onto his tunic next to the colours he wore for the MC, but almost immediately wished that he had not. 'It's rather embarrassing . . . because as it's new and uncommon everyone stares at it, and several people have wanted to know what it is.'[13]

In early August 1918, Ross went to Cairo for a few days' leave. He and Major Addison had been invited to represent No. 1 Squadron at a formal dinner in honour of Brigadier General Amyas Borton, Officer Commanding the RAF's Palestine Brigade. Borton, Ross learned, was making the first-ever flight from Britain to Egypt.[14]

Ross had known Borton for over a year, first as the commander of No. 1 Squadron's senior formation, 40th Wing, and more recently as Officer Commanding Palestine Brigade, the senior RAF formation on the Palestine front. In these commands, Borton had much to do with No. 1 Squadron: he regularly visited the Australians and often dined in their officers' mess.

That Ross and Borton would become the closest of friends over the following few years is perhaps surprising, and an example of the way that war has a tendency of drawing the otherwise disparate threads of society together in strange and unexpected ways. In contrast to Ross's upbringing by self-made parents on the dusty fringes of the empire, Borton, six years older, hailed from an estate family in Kent. Like his grandfather and father before him, Borton attended Eton College before taking a commission in the British Army. His family had a distinguished army record: a grandfather who had fought in the First Anglo-Sikh War (1845) and the Crimean War (1853–56) and later served as Governor of Malta; an uncle who had fought in the Second Anglo-Afghan War (1878–80) and Boer War (1899–1902);

and a brother who, so far during the Great War, had received a Distinguished Service Order and a Victoria Cross.

Universally known as 'Biffy', Borton had qualified for a flying certificate in 1912 and before the war had served in one of the RFC's foundation squadrons. He flew in France during 1914 and 1915, had been badly wounded in aerial combat and recommended for a Victoria Cross (he received a Distinguished Service Order instead). Having gone to war as a lieutenant responsible for a single aeroplane in August 1914, by mid-1918 Biffy Borton had attained the rank of Brigadier General and command of the brigade in which all seven of the RAF's squadrons (126 aircraft) in Palestine served.

Yet, despite the differences in their life experiences, Biffy Borton and Ross Smith shared personality traits that makes it easier to understand how, in the relaxed confines of No. 1 Squadron's officers' mess, they could strike up a friendship. Both men had an easy-going and gregarious disposition, an irreverent sense of humour and a hands-on approach to leadership. It was probably a shared passion for flying, however, that really cemented their friendship.

In mid-1918, Borton had been in Britain on leave when he came across the Handley Page O/400, a twin-engine biplane bomber with which the RAF planned to attack German cities. The aircraft originated in late 1914 when the British Admiralty called for a twin-engine aircraft capable of carrying bombs on long-range maritime flights—'a bloody paralyser' of an aircraft in the words of the Director of the Admiralty's Air Department.[15] The bomber that the Handley Page company produced certainly pushed the boundaries regarding British aviation capabilities. With two Rolls-Royce 360-horsepower engines mounted on an imposing 100-feet wingspan, the O/400 carried a crew of four airmen. It could remain in the air for eight hours and deliver over 750 kilograms of bombs onto a target.

The 'Bloody Paralyser' impressed Borton; he had nothing like it in Palestine and perceived its potential to strike targets across the expansive Middle Eastern theatre. He acquired an O/400 for Palestine Brigade and secured permission from the Air Ministry to fly it back to Egypt. A crew had flown one to Lemnos a year earlier, but what Borton proposed involved a considerably longer over-sea flight, including a stop to refuel on Crete, where an airfield had to be built from scratch. Borton and his crew left Britain on 25 July 1918; their route took them across France, Italy and the Mediterranean, and finally to Heliopolis. The 4000-kilometre journey took fourteen days.[16]

Ross watched Borton land the Handley Page O/400 at Heliopolis at the end of his record-breaking journey. The colossal aircraft with its two large Rolls-Royce engines and ship-like hull fascinated him. That evening, Ross enjoyed the reception, relieved that he had been seated at the far end of the dining table with a somewhat rowdy bunch of pilots: 'mostly all the General's oldest flying officers'. After the official toasts, Borton came down to have a drink with 'the rough end', as he put it. Almost certainly filled with liquid courage, Ross took it upon himself to rise and gave an impromptu speech that turned out to be the evening's penultimate formality. At its conclusion, Ross and the other pilots hoisted Borton up, still seated in his chair, and paraded him around the reception hall to a raucous rendition of 'For He's a Jolly Good Fellow'.[17]

Ross returned to No. 1 Squadron at Ramleh but had only been back a few days when orders arrived recalling him to Cairo. Reporting at RAF Middle East Headquarters, Ross learned that Borton had assigned the Handley Page bomber to No. 1 Squadron. He and his staff felt that it suited the long-range reconnaissance and bombing roles in which the Australians specialised and recognised the experience that they had with Rolls-Royce engines (which the Bristol Fighters used too). Furthermore, Borton wanted Ross to fly the O/400 on operations.

The assignment pleased Ross. 'I think it is the greatest honour I've ever had,' he wrote to his mother, adding that General Salmond told him privately that he had been hand-picked him from all the pilots then stationed in the Middle East. (It seems likely that Lieutenant Colonel Richard Williams, commanding the wing in which No. 1 Squadron served, also advocated on Ross's behalf.[18]) That an Australian had received such a distinguished responsibility surprised and gratified Ross. 'It seems that the more decorations one gets, the more one has to live up to,' he mused.[19]

Ross knew, though, that the news would also bring some disappointment for his mother. Earlier in 1918, the Commonwealth Government had announced a special leave to Australia for men like Ross, who had been on active service since 1914. Ross was due to go to Australia later in the year, and in previous letters had expressed his eagerness to be home for Christmas. The new assignment would, he admitted to his mother, almost certainly postpone his departure.[20] While unquestionably genuine in his disappointment, Ross was secretly relieved. He had heard rumours that men returning to Australia for a rest were being demobilised and he still harboured ambitions to get to France to do some war flying there before the fighting finished.[21] Ross was torn: although he missed home terribly, returning to civilian life, and in particular work, had little appeal after his experiences as a pilot in the AFC.

For the next fortnight, Ross remained in Cairo, learning how to fly the Handley Page, instructed by one of the pilots who had flown to Egypt with Borton. Although the considerably larger size and weight of its airframe and engines gave the flying giant vastly different handling characteristics to the Bristol Fighter, Ross found making the transition 'quite simple'. The bomber, which Ross christened 'Tiny', actually reminded him of a small ship:

> The pilot's seat is in a sort of cabin built away out in front, and a gunner sits near me, and 2 more gunners some distance back and behind the engines. My seat is in front of the engines, and that's what makes it so nice to fly, because there is no hot air or oily smell blowing back on me all the time.

The aircraft was fitted with state-of-the-art equipment—a wireless set, electric instrument lights, navigation lights for night flying ('like a ship has') and electrical elements for warming the crew's flight suits. Ross's training involved night flying and, although he had done some over the desert, he had not yet flown over a city. 'You can't imagine anything more beautiful and wonderful than Cairo and the Nile by moonlight from 5000 feet,' he wrote. 'It is a most wonderful machine . . . I'm awfully happy it's going to be mine,' he wrote to his mother, adding 'I'm going to have a lovely time with it, poor old Turks!'[22]

Ross flew the Handley Page back to Ramleh at the beginning of September, taking Salmond, Borton and another general as passengers. To his great relief, the flight (and landing) went smoothly; he made the entire trip without needing to stop and refuel, as was normal when flying the Bristol Fighter across from Egypt.

On his return to No. 1 Squadron, Ross learned that, as Major Addison was ill, he was acting squadron commander. Between leading the squadron and preparing the Handley Page for combat, he had a 'strenuous' week.[23] His responsibilities kept him on the ground—a strange experience after flying so frequently during the last two years and one to which he did not readily take. 'I'd much rather be doing jobs,' he complained in a letter home.[24] Also irritating to Ross was the large crowds of spectators attracted to Ramleh by the giant Handley Page. 'Just about everyone in Palestine from the C-in-C [General Allenby] downwards has been round,' wrote Ross, who reckoned that he'd had more personal contact with generals since taking charge of the bomber than ever before. Answering the same 'silly' questions over and over tested Ross's patience.[25]

On 8 September a large crowd assembled to witness the Handley Page bomber's first flight from Ramleh. But this was, in Ross's words, only a 'joy ride'—a test to put his new aircraft and its crew, which included 'Pard' Mustard, through their paces. General Borton had forbidden him to fly the Handley Page anywhere near the front line for now. Although Ross did not yet know the details, the generals were saving it for something big.

21

ARMAGEDDON

Ross had the Handley Page and his crew ready just in time. For more than two months, British and Empire forces in Palestine had been preparing to launch a major offensive—one that General Sir Edmund Allenby intended to inflict a 'decisive defeat' on the three Ottoman armies in Palestine and Transjordan.[1]

Ross and the other airmen in No. 1 Squadron learned the details at a briefing provided by Lieutenant Colonel Williams on 18 September 1918. Early the following morning, General Allenby's three army corps would launch an attack across the Palestine front, extending from the Mediterranean coast to the Jordan River. The focus of the initial assault would be on the coast; the British infantry and artillery would break through the Ottoman trenches to open the way for Allenby's mounted troops. After charging through the breach in the Turkish line and advancing up the coast, the cavalry would swing inland onto the Plain of Esdraelon, the biblical battlefield Armageddon, from where they could interdict the Ottoman line of retreat. Meanwhile, east of the Jordan River, an army of Arab insurgents would cooperate with Allenby's forces by advancing north along the axis of the Hedjaz railway towards Damascus.

In briefing the RAF's staff, Allenby had asked his airmen for 'general assistance' in the battle.[2] For No. 1 Squadron, this predominantly meant long-range reconnaissance and photography. Elaborating on Allenby's broad directive, however, the staff at RAF Headquarters devised plans to exploit success on the ground through an aggressive bombing campaign.

During the opening stages of the battle, they would target communications and transportation centres to disrupt Ottoman command and control arrangements. Ross and his crew would play an important role in this, with the Handley Page's large bomb load providing the means to destroy enemy telephone exchanges and headquarters. When the Ottoman forces withdrew from the front line, the airmen of the RAF's squadrons would bomb and strafe them as they attempted to escape north.

At 1.15 a.m. on 19 September 1918, three hours before the ground forces launched their attack, Ross took off in the Handley Page from Ramleh. Besides Mustard, who occupied the aircraft's forward nacelle to aim the bombs, two other observers, Lieutenants Maxwell Lees and Ashley McCann, manned the guns in the rear cockpit. For this important job, Ross had selected a veteran crew—men like him who had all enlisted in 1914 and gone to war with the light horse before joining the AFC.

In clear moonlit skies, Ross flew north across the still-silent front line. It took an hour and a quarter to arrive at 4000 feet over Afuleh, where the Turks had a telephone exchange and a large railway station. From the forward cockpit, Mustard looked through the bombsight and directed Ross over the target before he released the sixteen 112-pound (50-kilogram) bombs they carried. Among the flashes and dull, percussive detonations below, Ross counted six large explosions in the railway yard. Only one bomb appeared to land near the telephone exchange. While Ross circled to survey the damage, Lees used a Lewis gun mounted in a trapdoor below the fuselage to spray the area with 850 rounds.[3]

'Good bombing' is how Ross summed up the raid that opened the battle of Megiddo: 'We did a lot of damage.'[4] Although he apparently failed to score a direct hit on the telephone exchange, the bombs had caused some damage in the railway yard. Later that morning, a squadron of British de Havilland DH9s launched two further raids against Afuleh's telephone exchange and rail yards, and when RAF staff inspected the site a few days later they found that telephone lines had been cut between Ottoman General Headquarters and the headquarters of the two Turkish armies on the Palestine front.[5]

Although the impact of Ross's raid is impossible to single out, the destruction of Turkish telephone exchanges by aerial bombing contributed to a critical breakdown in Ottoman communications during the first 24 hours of Allenby's offensive.[6]

While Ross and his crew prepared the Handley Page for another sortie that night, No. 1 Squadron's other crews spent the first day of the battle ranging behind Ottoman lines to secure intelligence and attack enemy troops. They brought back news that things were going to plan: the British cavalry had broken through on the coast at dawn and, by late afternoon, had arrived at Tulkeram, far behind the Ottoman front line. As Turkish forces attempted to fall back, Ross's comrades attacked them from the air; No. 1 Squadron alone dropped 3 tonnes of bombs and fired 16,900 rounds of machine gun ammunition on the battle's opening day.[7]

At sunset, Ross and his crew climbed back into the Handley Page and took off on what would be the first of two raids that night against the German aerodrome at Jenin. It was a place Ross and the others knew well from their regular patrols there over the summer. As Ross passed over the battlefield, he perceived its devastation, illuminated in the moonlight and stretching back kilometres from what had been the front line just that morning; he felt upbeat: 'everything below looked so helpless and absolutely at our mercy,' he thought.[8]

Indeed, of the 32 individual 112-pound bombs that Ross dropped during his two trips to Jenin that night, he counted '27 direct hits' on buildings at the aerodrome and in the adjacent railway yard—though he only classified his bombing as 'fair' on the official report.[9] Reconnaissance flights the following morning confirmed that Ross's bombs had, indeed, been on target. Photographs showed burned and smashed hangars and bits of aeroplanes scattered everywhere. Two days later, when the Germans abandoned the aerodrome, Ross flew up there to see for himself: 'It was an awful mess,' he noted.[10]

The Handley Page remained on the ground on 20 and 21 September. With the Turks in full retreat, there were no large, static targets for Ross and his crew to bomb. On 22 September, Allenby cabled London to report that the two Turkish armies west of the Jordan were practically annihilated and that his forces had captured an estimated 25,000 enemy prisoners. Two days later, he amended the figure to 'no less than 40,000 prisoners and 265 guns'; his own forces had suffered fewer than 5000 casualties in return.[11]

While Ross kicked about the aerodrome, frustrated that Major Addison would not let him join in operations in his Bristol Fighter, the other crews flew an almost continuous relay of sorties to bomb and strafe columns of retreating Turks. For two days, Ross listened to the gruesome stories his comrades told in the mess—accounts of firing thousands of rounds of machine gun fire into narrow mountain passes, crammed with helpless enemy troops and horse-drawn carriages. 'One could see the expressions on the faces of the poor devils below, could read the agony and the anguish in front of the gun-sights,' claimed Les Sutherland. 'One second it would be a team of horses; the next a bloody mass of shattered legs and carcasses.'[12] In two days the airmen in No. 1 Squadron clocked up 130 flying hours; they dropped nearly 450 bombs and fired 50,000 rounds at targets on the ground.[13] 'I'm missing a lot of fun,' grumbled Ross in a letter.[14] As the only pilot in the squadron trained to fly the Handley Page, however, he was too valuable to expose to the dangers of low-altitude bombing and strafing. A random bullet fired from the ground was just as lethal to an experienced flight commander like Ross as it was to a novice.

After an exasperating two days on the ground, Ross finally managed to get back into the air in his Bristol Fighter. The squadron had orders to send a few aircraft out to the camp of King Faisal's Arab army, which cooperated with Allenby's forces against the Turks in the Transjordan desert. The British Army's liaison officer with the Arabs, Lieutenant Colonel Thomas (T.E.) Lawrence—the famous 'Lawrence of Arabia'—had asked RAF Headquarters for some fighter aircraft to stop German airmen bombing the Arab camp.[15] Ross joined the expedition to see whether the Handley Page O/400 could operate safely from the landing ground at the Arab camp. It would be Ross's second meeting with Lawrence; back in May 1918, he had flown the eccentric British colonel from a meeting at Allenby's headquarters to the Arab army's desert camp near Kutrani.[16]

At first light on 22 September, Ross and Mustard led two other Bristol Fighters out to the Arab army's camp in the Transjordan desert. Arriving at Urn el Surab, where the Arabs had retreated after being bombed again, Ross inspected a stretch of the desert that they had cleared of stones. Lawrence watched as he 'anxiously paced the length and breadth of the prepared space and studied its imperfections', and was relieved when Ross wandered back over 'with a clear face': he would be able to land the Handley Page there, and thus bring the supplies necessary to sustain the Bristol Fighters while they cooperated with the Arab army.

Lawrence invited Ross and the other Australian airmen to breakfast. As sausages cooked and tea brewed, Ross listened to Lawrence's colleagues report on an exciting raid they had mounted the previous night to blow up a stretch of the Hedjaz railway.[17]

Suddenly one of the Arab lookouts gave a shout: three aeroplanes approached. In an instant, Ross and the other Australian airmen were sprinting to their Bristol Fighters. With the engines still warm, they took off immediately and climbed to intercept these raiders. The pilots of the two escorts, Pfalz DIII fighters, turned and fled while Ross and the other Australian airmen set upon the DFW two-seater. They briefly circled it, firing before the enemy pilot landed his aircraft in the desert. As the crew ran, Ross 'went down to within a few feet of the ground' so that Mustard could machine gun their aircraft. The two German airmen watched helplessly as their machine caught fire and exploded.[18] Mustard took pity on them, however, and did not turn his guns on them: 'We just gave a wave and returned to camp to finish our breakfast.'[19]

When Ross landed back at the Arab camp, he received a wild reception: 'One old Sheikh pulled out his revolver and fired its six rounds off as fast as he could.'[20] Ross and his comrades resumed the breakfast that Lawrence had kept warm and had just started on the fruit when 'again the watchman tossed up his cloak and screamed "A plane!"'.[21]

This time, only Ross and Mustard took off: they spotted three Pfalz circling the burning wreck of the two-seater that had been destroyed half an hour earlier. Ross dived on the closest one and its pilot immediately landed, taxiing to a nearby Turkish outpost. He then pursued the other two. Ross started firing at one, but its pilot also landed and ran for cover. By the time Ross and Mustard had caught up with the third German fighter, it was landing at its aerodrome at Deraa. Ross fired and the pilot panicked; he landed roughly in a cloud of dust. 'Without waiting to see the result,' reported Ross, 'we returned to the other scouts and found them still at the same places.' Mustard fired 50 rounds into each of them.[22] The behaviour of the German pilots on this day disgusted Ross. 'The miserable swine wouldn't stay and fight,' he wrote to his friend in Adelaide, Bobbie Warren. 'They are a rotten lot really and I wouldn't hate 'em nearly so much if they would stand up and scrap.'[23]

Having finally finished his breakfast, Ross returned to Ramleh to collect the Handley Page, which had been loaded with fuel and stores to supply the makeshift aerodrome at Lawrence's camp. He and Mustard flew it back out to Urn el Surab that afternoon, with Brigadier General Borton as their passenger.

Their arrival caused consternation among the hundreds of Arab fighters in the camp. 'You never saw such excitement,' wrote Ross. They swarmed around the Handley Page on horse and foot, firing rifles and revolvers in the sky and shouting.[24] The pilot of the Bristol Fighter that had escorted Ross from Ramleh had nowhere to land: it was pandemonium.[25] When Ross climbed down to clear them from the runway, they crowded in to touch him. Afterwards, Lawrence heard the Arabs refer to the Bristol Fighters parked nearby as the 'foals' of the large Handley Page bomber.[26]

Ross stayed at the Arab camp that night and the following day. That evening, with his regular crew of Mustard, Lees and McCann, he flew the Handley Page to Deraa to bomb the only remaining railway station through which Ottoman forces to the south could escape north. Dropped from 4000 feet in misty conditions, the sixteen high-explosives and ten incendiary bombs cut the railway line and exploded among tents and buildings.[27]

With Ottoman forces routed right across the axis of the British advance and retreating into Syria and Lebanon, No. 1 Squadron prepared to move to an aerodrome closer to the fighting. Some pilots and observers in the squadron expressed relief that, for now, the merciless bombing of retreating Turkish troops had let up.[28] Even Ross, who had been frustrated at missing the 'fun' of it a few days earlier, had a change of heart. 'We are all tired of the killing,' he reported. It was clear to everyone that they had won a great victory.[29]

Ross's flight moved first, flying to Haifa on the north coast of Palestine on 26 September 1918. They set up camp at the foot of Mount Carmel, a picturesque spot overlooking the town and its wide bay. 'It is an awfully pretty place,' Ross wrote. 'The tents are among olive trees and from my door I look out across the Bay to Acre and can see the Mountains of Lebanon and Mount Hermon away in the distance.'[30] Exploring the area, Ross and his comrades found an abundance of souvenirs left by the retreating Ottoman and German forces. The best, undoubtedly, came from a wine cellar that Ross and Sutherland discovered on the abandoned German aerodrome at Jenin: it had more than 30 cases of a 1904 vintage. Ross led a group of pilots on an unofficial mission to retrieve it for the squadron mess. They had the mechanics mount an aero-engine onto an abandoned railway cart and then used this to transport the champagne from Jenin to Haifa. According to Sutherland, Ross's decoration ribbons and captain's pips, as well as some Ottoman currency that he had obtained from a friend in the light horse, helped them get past the numerous guard pickets and railway stations that they encountered along the way.[31]

Still, work had to be done. Ross's flight had orders to support Allenby's cavalry as they closed in on Damascus, the enclave of the last surviving Ottoman army in the Palestine–Transjordan region. During the final days of September, the airmen of C Flight watched Damascus from the air and attacked Turkish columns as they fled deeper into Syria. On 30 September,

Ross's airmen provided close air support to light horse units battling their way into the city against Ottoman rear guards. Allied forces occupied Damascus the following morning.

Ross had only been at Haifa for a few days when he learned that he had been awarded a Bar to his DFC. The recommendation, probably made by Lieutenant Colonel Williams at 40th Wing Headquarters, has not survived; however, the citation that was subsequently published referred to Ross's work throughout the battle of Megiddo, including his 'numerous engagements involving flights of 150 to 200 miles', the damage he had inflicted on Ottoman targets with the Handley Page and the German aircraft he forced down in the desert while working with Lawrence and the Sheriffian Arab army: 'Captain Smith displayed most consistent gallantry in all his work, whether bombing night or day or in personal encounters in the air.'[32]

'That makes sixteen DFCs the Squadron has been awarded, and all since the end of July,' he wrote to Jessie in an effort to cast his personal success in the broader context of teamwork and comradeship that he genuinely believed had enabled it.[33]

With scattered remnants of Ottoman forces still retreating, Ross made some long-range reconnaissance flights during October in his Bristol Fighter, ranging deep into Lebanon and Syria; he went as far north as Aleppo. These flights typically took the entire day, with eight hours spent in the air and a stop to refuel at a landing ground near Allenby's advanced cavalry and armoured car units. With these flights, Ross's log book filled quickly. By the end of October, he had clocked up 800 hours in the air altogether, 600 as a pilot and 200 as an observer.[34]

The German squadrons in Palestine had been all but wiped out during the Megiddo campaign, either by bombing or by being forced to abandon their equipment in the retreat. Ross encountered one of the few surviving German aircraft, a DFW, on 19 October near Homs. They had just landed to refuel when it flew high overhead. Ross and his observer, Ashley McCann, took off in pursuit. When they finally caught up with it an hour later, at 18,000 feet, the German two-seater's pilot began a spiralling corkscrew dive. Ross followed, struggling to get the enemy aircraft in his sights, all the way down to the ground where it made a good landing in an open plain, about 50 kilometres behind Ottoman lines. As the German pilot and observer fled from their aircraft, Ross circled overhead, allowing McCann to machine gun it. 'Fed up' that it would not ignite, Ross suddenly had an idea: what if he could land, set the German aircraft on fire and then take its crew prisoner?

After touching down, Ross taxied up beside the DFW. He hopped out and looked around while McCann kept his guns trained on the two enemy airmen who stood by helplessly with their hands up. To his great disappointment, Ross found the ground soft—too soft to risk taking off with the additional weight of two Germans crammed into the Bristol Fighter's cockpit. While Ross prepared for take-off, McCann walked over to the German aircraft and fired a flare into its fuel-drenched cockpit, setting it ablaze. 'You should have seen the Huns' expressions, as their machine went up in smoke,' described Ross. 'I've never laughed so much in all my life.' At that moment, a force of Bedouin fighters came galloping over a nearby rise. McCann sprinted back to the Bristol and Ross took off, just in time, leaving the German airmen to their fate.[35] 'We then continued reconnaissance,' concluded Ross in his report of the incident.[36]

Ross's combat report, written in the prosaic language that such official documentation required, stood out among the dozens of reports that made their way up the Air Force's chain of command that month. When it reached RAF Middle East Headquarters, Major General Salmond cabled Ross and McCann personally, congratulating them on a 'unique performance'.[37]

To Ross's enormous surprise, on 23 October 1918, Lieutenant Colonel Williams recommended him for a *third* DFC; Brigadier General Borton endorsed it immediately.[38] 'The getting of it was all so simple too,' he explained to Jessie. 'And for once I know what this Bar is for, without having to wait a few months until they publish something in the *London Gazette*.' Indeed, whereas his first two DFCs had been for a period of sustained and outstanding performance, this one—like the first of his two earlier

MCs—had been for a specific act of gallantry. 'It was a very simple little stunt, but they seem to think it was something rather more, hence the new Bar,' he wrote.[39]

Ross's third DFC made him one of the most decorated British Empire pilots of the Great War. Indeed, just three airmen received the DFC three times during the First World War: one of them was fellow Australian Captain Arthur 'Harry' Cobby, who flew with the AFC in France; while the other was Captain Walter Longton, a British airman who also served on the Western Front. Ross had secured himself a place in a very exclusive fraternity.

Ross flew what would be his last mission of the war on 23 October 1918: an escort to a 'strategical reconnaissance' into Syria as far as the Muslimie railway junction. The Ottoman troops who he reported seeing were few and far between, scattered and withdrawing through Syria with British cavalry and armoured cars close behind them.[40] One week later, on 30 October 1918, the Ottoman government agreed to an armistice; the war in the Middle East had ended.

In the war's final days, Ross suddenly began to feel 'very homesick'. He wrote to his mother towards the end of October describing his pride at having contributed to the decisive campaign that defeated the Turks but also expressing regret that he had not taken up the opportunity to secure the leave offered to 1914 volunteers by the Australian government earlier in 1918. To Keith, he expressed his disbelief that after more than four years the war had finally ended. 'It seems wonderful to have come through alive.'[41]

Two years earlier, in November 1916, Ross had quipped to his mother about flying back to Australia to see her. It had been a fanciful notion then—at a time when no aeroplane in the world could have conceivably made such a journey and when, indeed, Ross had yet to learn to fly. In late October 1918, however, Ross returned to the idea when his British superiors, Brigadier General 'Biffy' Borton and Major General Geoffrey Salmond, began planning to fly the Handley Page O/400 across the Middle East from Egypt to India. During the war's final week, they approached Ross—the most experienced multi-engine aircraft pilot in the region—to be their pilot.

The prospect of flying all the way to Calcutta excited Ross and prompted him to revisit his idea of flying home to Australia. He could not resist writing to both his mother and Keith to tell them what he had in mind. 'It is very unlikely at present but I want to *fly* all the way if I can!' he told his mother, explaining that he could not yet share any particulars.[42] Apparently putting more trust in Keith's discretion, he revealed a little more to his older brother: that he would be flying the 'big fellow' to India and would sail back to Adelaide from there. 'I'm trying to work it to fly all the way, but it's very doubtful if it can be arranged. Some stunt if I could, eh!'[43]

Jessie Smith, mother of Ross, Keith and Colin.
(SLSA PRG 18/1/12)

Andrew Smith, their father. *(SLSA PRG 18/1/13)*

From left: Colin, Keith and Ross Smith, c. 1902. *(SLSA PRG 18/1/11)*

The homestead at Mutooroo where Ross spent his first ten years and school holidays while at the Queen's School. He regarded it as home. *(SLSA PRG 18/2/3)*

Staff and students of the Queen's School, Adelaide, in 1902—Ross's first year of boarding. Ten-year-old Ross is seated on the ground, second from the right. Keith is standing in the back row, tenth from the right. *(SLSA B29751)*

Rundle Street, in the centre of Adelaide, as Ross knew it in 1920. Kindermann's Café, where Ross, Keith and the Howards convened for lunch each week, is on the right. *(SLSA B2221)*

In 1910, at the age of 17, Ross toured Europe and North America with the mounted cadets. *(SLVIC H84/448/8/16)*

The aviation journal *Flight* reported on the flying display at Brooklands that Ross and his friends in the mounted cadets witnessed in August 1910. They saw French aviator Robert Cordonnier crash his Hanriot monoplane into the River Wey. *(*Flight*, 6 August 1910)*

Ross at Morphettville camp in August 1914. Within a fortnight of enlisting he had been promoted to sergeant. *(SLSA PRG 18/11/1A)*

Ross sent home this photograph of the 3rd Light Horse Regiment's camp at Maadi, in Egypt, in January 1915. 'My tent was the bell tent in the centre of the photo with the man standing just on the left of it.' *(SLSA PRG 18/4/2)*

Ross took this photograph of two comrades in the 3rd Light Horse at Quinn's Post, in August 1915. They are lighting a bomb to throw at the Turkish trenches which are situated fewer than 20 metres away. *(AWM P05584.001)*

A view of Pope's Hill and Quinn's Post from behind ANZAC lines at Gallipoli. Ross spent most of his time on the peninsula garrisoning these two positions. *(AWM C02705)*

Ross took this photograph of his men watering their horses at the Bir-el-Abd oasis during a patrol in the Sinai Desert, mid-1916. *(SLSA PRG 18/4/21/49)*

Mount Meredith, close to where Ross's machine gun section was positioned at the beginning of the battle of Romani, 4 August 1916. *(SLSA PRG 18/4/21/72)*

Captain Richard Williams, Ross's flight commander and mentor, in the cockpit of a BE2c aircraft. As an observer, Ross occupied the forward cockpit. *(SLSA PRG 18/4/14)*

Ross (left) and fellow No. 1 Squadron airmen Reginald Baillieu and Frank McNamara enjoy a tea break in between sorties during the battle of Rafa, 9 January 1917. *(SLSA PRG 18/4/13)*

Apparently no worse for his experience, Ross recovers in hospital after being wounded in an aerial dogfight, September 1917. '. . . as good as new again' he wrote to Keith. *(SLSA PRG 18/4/10)*

No. 1 Squadron's aerodrome at Mejdel, February 1918. The aircraft in the foreground is a Martinsyde G.100. The other machines are Bristol Fighters. Ross flew both during 1917–18. *(AWM B01617)*

Ross and one of his regular observers, Ernest Mustard, aboard Bristol Fighter B1229—the aircraft they usually flew in 1918. *(SLSA PRG 18/4/19)*

Ross and Amyas 'Biffy' Borton in the cockpit of the Handley Page O/400 during the flight to India in December 1918. *(SLSA PRG 18/16/10)*

The Handley Page O/400 lands at Calcutta race track, 18 December 1918. *(SLSA PRG 18/6/2)*

The mechanics: Walter 'Wally' Shiers and James 'Benny' Bennett. These men worked with Ross during the war and then during the Egypt–India and England–Australia flights. *(SLSA PRG 18/8/7)*

Vickers Vimy G-EAOU in the workshop at Vickers' factory in Weybridge before the great flight. The airframe was reinforced and modified to carry a substantial cargo of spare parts. *(SLSA PRG 18/9/1/5B)*

Hounslow, 12 November 1919, the crew of Vickers Vimy G-EAOU say farewell to friends and supporters before starting the flight to Australia. Snow covers the ground; bad weather lies ahead. *(SLSA PRG 18/9/1/9A)*

Jim Bennett captured this dramatic view of the French Alps during the flight from Lyon to Pisa, 13 November 1919. *(SLSA PRG 18/9/1/12B)*

G-EAOU's cockpit: Ross flew half way around the globe with only the most rudimentary instruments. *(South Australian Aviation Museum)*

Shiers and Bennett in the rear cockpit, as viewed from Ross's and Keith's perspective. *(SLSA PRG 18/8/6)*

The crew's view of the pyramids during the flight from Suda Bay (Crete) to Cairo, 18 November 1919. *(SLSA PRG 18/9/1/13A)*

Ross in flying cap and goggles during the flight to Australia. Numerous journalists remarked on his well-groomed appearance, even at the end of lengthy stages. *(SLSA PRG 18/9/1/1C)*

Arrival at Calcutta, 28 November 1919. As always, Ross and Keith wear the broad smiles that endeared them to the public. *(SLSA PRG 18/9/1/23A)*

The Vimy arrives at Rangoon racecourse, 30 November 1919. Tens of thousands of people came to greet the aviators. *(SLSA PRG 18/16/14)*

G-EAOU prepares to take off from the waterlogged and stump-strewn aerodrome at Singora, Siam, 4 December 1919. *(SLSA PRG 18/7/20)*

The runway of bamboo matting that Ross used to extricate G-EAOU from the mud at Sourabaya in the Dutch East Indies, 8 December 1919. *(SLSA PRG 18/9/1/31E)*

The Vimy lands at Darwin, 10 December 1919. Ross Smith and his companions have become the first airmen to fly from England to Australia—and they've done it within 30 days to claim the government's £10 000 prize. *(SLSA PRG 18/9/3/1A)*

Stranded at Cobb's Creek: after the port propeller split, Ross and the crew spent two days in the remote Northern Territory while Bennett (right) fashioned a replacement. *(SLSA PRG 18/9/1/32E)*

Frank Hurley, with his camera, joins the crew at Charleville, Queensland, in February 1920 to document the flight across Australia. *(SLSA PRG 18/9/1/36A)*

Shiers and Bennett look down on Sydney Harbour, 14 February 1920. *(SLSA PRG 18/9/1/58D)*

Crowds greet the Vimy crew at Mascot, Sydney, 14 February 1920. *(SLSA PRG 18/9/1/41D)*

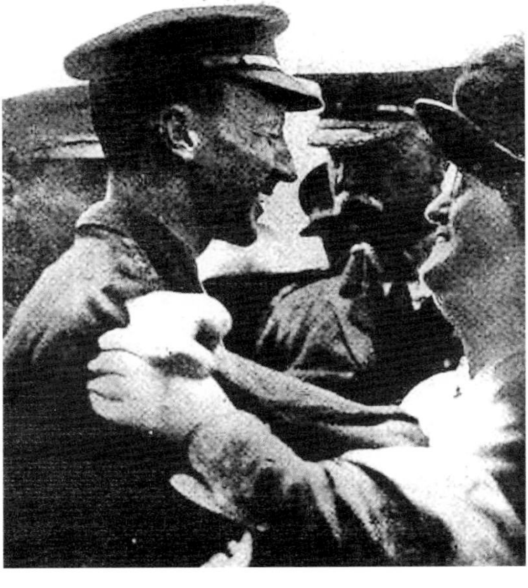

Mother and son embrace at their first meeting in five years, Mascot aerodrome, 14 February 1920. *(*Sunday Times*, 15 February 1920)*

Family reunion at Mascot, 14 February 1920. *(SLSA PRG 18/16/28)*

Prime Minister W.M. Hughes presents Ross, Keith, Bennett and Shiers with a cheque for £10,000 at a lunch at Federal Parliament House, Melbourne, 27 February 1920. *(SLSA PRG 18/16/25)*

Arrival over Adelaide, 23 March 1920. *(SLSA PRG 18/9/1/47B)*

Mounted police try, in vain, to keep the crowds back at Northfield aerodrome, Adelaide, 23 March 1920. The aircraft was damaged in the crush. *(SLSA B 46272/6)*

William McInnes' portrait of Ross, painted in 1920. The portrait suggests the strain and exhaustion that Ross experienced in the aftermath of the flight. *(AWM ART03179)*

Ross with the Vickers Viking, the aircraft he intends to fly around the world. Taken at Weybridge in April 1922, possibly the day before he was killed in this aeroplane, these are the last known photographs of Ross Smith. *(SLSA PRG 18/13/3; PRG 18/13/2)*

The wreck of the Vickers Viking in which Ross and Jim Bennett were killed, 13 April 1922. (*Illustrated London News*)

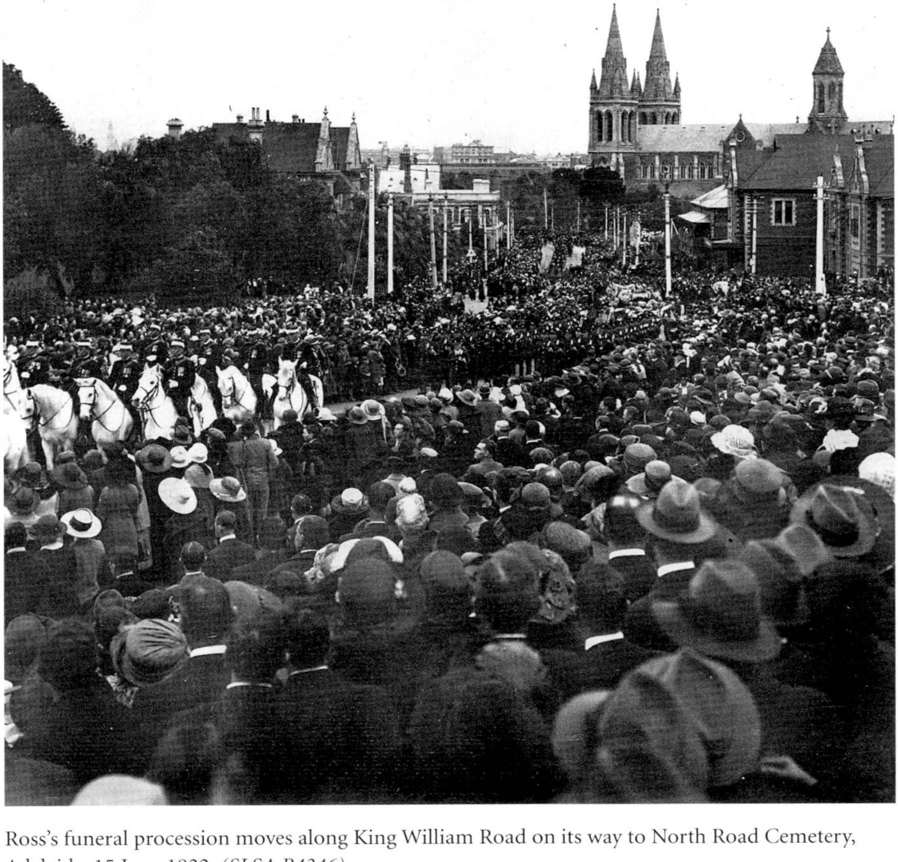

Ross's funeral procession moves along King William Road on its way to North Road Cemetery, Adelaide, 15 June 1922. *(SLSA B4346)*

Among thousands of mourners, Andrew, Jessie and Keith Smith farewell Ross at North Road Cemetery, 15 June 1922. *(SLSA B899)*

PART FOUR

'14,000 MILES THROUGH THE AIR'

1918–1919

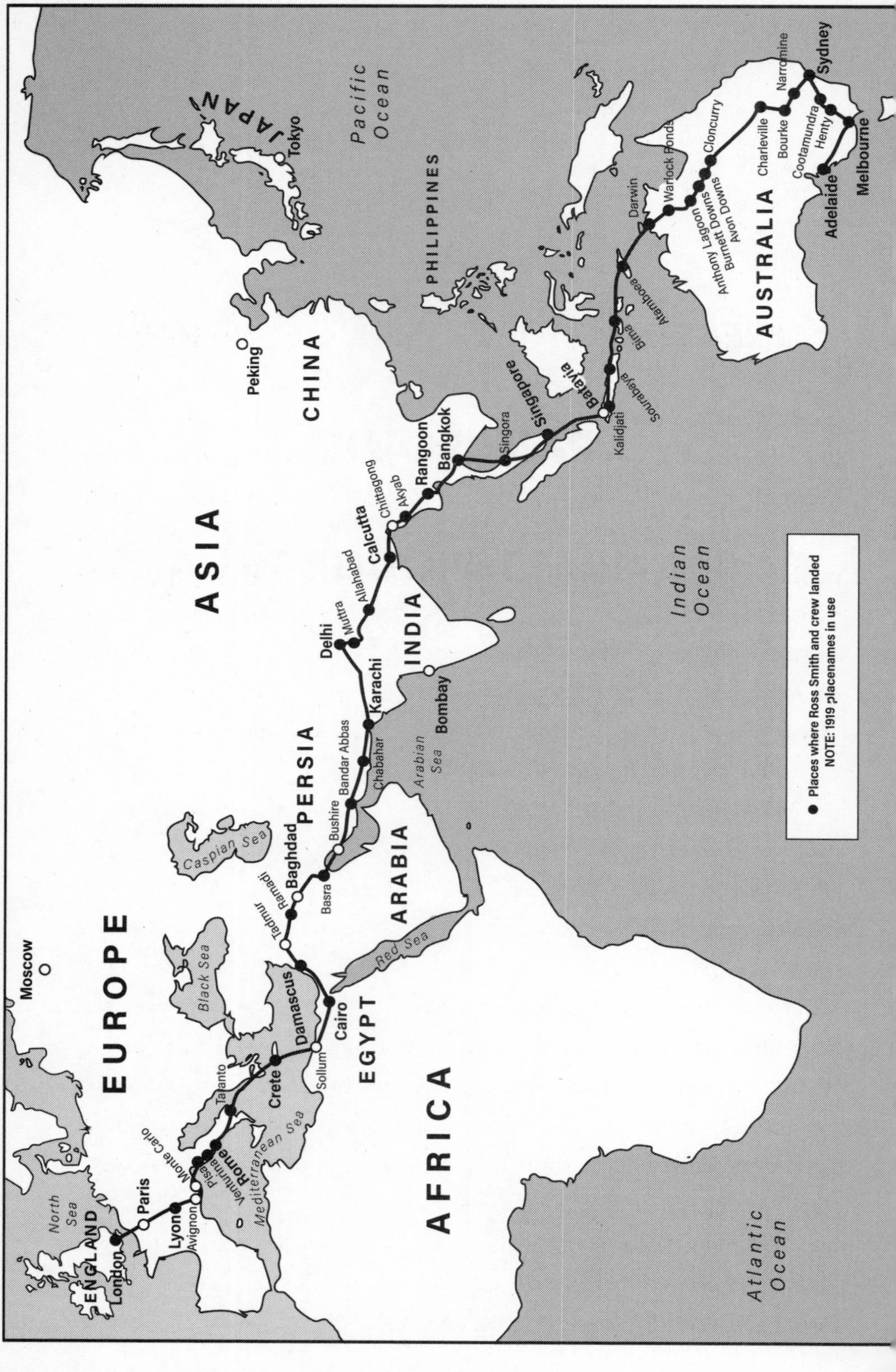

MAP 4 The route followed in the first flight from England to Australia, 1919

22

PREACHING THE GOSPEL OF THE RAF

Ross happened to be in Cairo on leave on 11 November 1918 when he heard the news that Germany had surrendered. 'It is quite hard to realise that peace has come at last and that there is no more war,' he wrote to his mother the following day. Whatever else Ross felt, he mostly kept it to himself. Perhaps, like many others in the AIF at that moment, he struggled to express the bewildering tangle of emotions evoked by the realisation that he had survived when so many others had not—and that, after four years of living in the moment, he suddenly had a future with which to contend.[1] All Ross could manage to articulate in this moment was his hatred of the Germans, which he still felt acutely: 'We have licked those damned Huns,' he declared. 'The only pity is that we can't go on killing them'.

The end-of-war celebrations in Cairo got out of hand. Soldiers rioted, ransacking Egyptian businesses in a reprisal of the scenes Ross had witnessed there in early 1915. Half a battalion of troops was deployed to protect Shepheard's Hotel, in which Ross was staying. He didn't join in, but he felt the soldiers were justified and admitted that he might have taken part had he still been a private. It was a revealing comment: after four years of war and extensive experience of leadership, Ross remained a citizen soldier at heart. He and the other officers staying at Shepheard's staged their own celebrations, turning the lounge into a 'stadium' to host a boozy night of games that included tug-of-war with the hotel's carpets, pillow fights and indoor rugby.[2]

Ross expected to return to No. 1 Squadron in Palestine at the end of his fortnight's leave in Cairo, but orders arrived detailing him for the 'special duty' to which Brigadier General Amyas 'Biffy' Borton had alluded shortly before the Turks surrendered. As it turned out, the RAF had brought another Handley Page O/400 to Egypt to ferry Major General Geoffrey Salmond around the various air units that he commanded across the Middle East. First, Ross would fly this aircraft across the Mediterranean to Salonika, in Greece, to collect Salmond before returning to make an inspection tour of aerodromes in Palestine, Syria and Mesopotamia.

It was the next part of the assignment that really thrilled Ross.[3] After taking Salmond to Baghdad, he and Borton would fly the O/400 to India. From there, they planned to survey an aerial route to Australia, first by sea to identify suitable landing grounds and arrange fuel and oil supplies, and then later by air. Ross realised that it would be a formidable task; while the RAF had some rudimentary aerodromes in Mesopotamia, Persia and India, practically no aviation infrastructure at all existed between India and Australia. Still, the element of adventure promised by this scheme proved irresistible. 'Doesn't it sound thrilling!!!' enthused Ross in a letter reporting the news to his mother. He had the sensitivity, though, to apologise to her that this new endeavour would undoubtedly delay his return to Australia. 'I think I could have got home on the next 1914 leave boat, but I did not want to miss the chance of such a wonderful and unique trip,' he reasoned. He hoped to be home by April 1919 at the latest.[4]

In an account published later, Ross claimed that the idea for a flight to India and a subsequent survey expedition to Australia originated in a whimsical exchange with 'Biffy' Borton shortly before the war's end. The general, he claimed, had instructions to fly Salmond to Baghdad to 'link up' the RAF in Egypt with air force units in Mesopotamia. Ross recounted: 'There was a further proposal that after reaching Baghdad we should shape a route to India "to see," as [Borton] jocularly remarked, "the Viceroy's Cup run in Calcutta".' Ross responded by suggesting that they 'fly on to Australia and see the Melbourne Cup'.[5]

Whether or not this conversation actually happened, the idea of flying to India and then on to Australia appears to have originated with Borton.

As the war in the Middle East drew to a close, Borton had privately worried that when the Turks surrendered his command would 'disintegrate' and leave him 'stranded' with limited career prospects. 'The one thing I want to avoid,' he wrote to his father, 'is being caught at home when peace breaks out, and getting mixed up in the tidying process.'[6] In early October 1918—still a few weeks before the Ottoman government agreed to an armistice—Borton conceived a flight to India as a means of promoting the air force's interests on the subcontinent ('to preach the gospel of RAF out there', as he put it). After the Air Ministry sanctioned this flight to India, Borton began thinking about how he might convince the authorities in London to authorise a survey of the air route between India and Australia, with the intention of then flying it himself. 'If this comes off,' Borton wrote to his father, 'it should give me a good claim to a job in the organisation of air routes in the future.'[7]

For their flight across the Middle East, Ross and the generals would be joined by two of the mechanics who had been responsible for the O/400's maintenance while it was attached to No. 1 Squadron. Ross knew both of them well, having worked with them in C Flight since he had joined the squadron in late 1916. Sergeant James 'Benny' Bennett came from Melbourne. A couple of years younger than Ross, he had worked as a motor mechanic before the war. Benny joined No. 1 Squadron as one of the unit's original members and went overseas with it in March 1916. He had considerable experience on the Rolls-Royce engines that both the squadron's Bristol Fighters and the O/400 used.

Air Mechanic 1st Class Walter 'Wally' Henry Shiers had been born and raised in Adelaide. He left school at thirteen years of age and learned electrical engineering in the mines at Broken Hill. In April 1915, at the age of 23, he enlisted in the light horse, later transferring to No. 1 Squadron at about the same time as Ross. According to one account, the two men got off to a bad start. Originally a batman (an officer's assistant), Shiers was assigned to work for Ross. They didn't get along and, after Ross complained that Shiers refused to cooperate, some of the other officers in the squadron intervened to diffuse the situation. Shiers was re-mustered as a fitter and turner.[8] If true, the account is unusual as, by all other accounts, Ross got along with most people. Whatever the nature of their apparent disagreement, Shiers and Ross had resolved their differences by September 1918 when they were assigned to work together again on the Handley Page. Indeed, Ross would privately express great admiration for both Shiers and Bennett in the coming months.[9]

In mid-November, the flight to Salonika was cancelled because of bad weather in the Mediterranean. Salmond returned to Egypt by sea and ordered Ross and his mechanics to prepare to fly to Baghdad. He planned to start in a few weeks but abruptly changed his mind on 26 November when news arrived that the Air Ministry was preparing to send a larger, four-engine Handley Page aircraft, the V/1500, to survey the route to Asia. Determined to be first, Salmond gave Ross two days to be ready.[10] They had a 'very strenuous time', but Ross, Shiers and Bennett managed to prepare the O/400 to start on 29 November.[11] 'This will be the first aerial trip to Baghdad, and there is great excitement about it,' wrote Ross, the night before their departure. It was probably his association with Generals Salmond and Borton that secured Ross an invitation that evening to a ball hosted by the exiled Russian Grand Duke Dmitri Pavlovich—the man, as Ross noted, credited with assassinating the tsar's infamous mystical adviser, Grigori Rasputin. 'It was a nice little show,' he wrote, 'but as I'm flying tomorrow I had to leave early.'[12]

With General Salmond, and Bennett and Shiers, aboard, Ross took off from Heliopolis at dawn the following morning and set a north-easterly course towards the Mediterranean coast. They flew over Romani, where Ross and his machine gun squadron had fought for their lives two and a half years earlier, and by 7 a.m. the shadow of the O/400's broad wings was being cast onto the overgrown trenches and rusted tank hulks scattered about Gaza. An hour later, Ross landed at No. 1 Squadron's aerodrome at Ramleh to collect Borton. For the remainder of the flight, Borton, Salmond and Ross would occupy the O/400's forward crew compartment, sharing a pair of seats abreast in the open cockpit and a crawl space below, just large enough to stretch out and sleep. Although Salmond was in command (and would receive most of the credit in the press), the three pilots shared the flying and navigating in hourly shifts while Ross and Borton took turns with the landings.[13] Bennett and Shiers shared the aircraft's rear cockpit. They could crawl through the aircraft's empty bomb bay to communicate with Ross and the generals. Although designed for long flights, without a toilet on board the crew probably used a tin can and tossed it over the side when they had to go.

From Ramleh, they followed the River Jordan north into Syria, passing the snow-capped Mount Hermon before turning north-east towards Damascus, where the crew planned to stop for the night. The 700-kilometre flight had taken just under six hours. Flying conditions had been perfect, but frigid: 'It was jolly cold,' noted Ross.[14]

After struggling to get the O/400's frozen engines going, the crew made an early start for Baghdad, setting an easterly course that would take them across the northern fringe of the Arabian Desert. Salmond described how, after leaving Damascus, the country below became a featureless expanse of black lava rock: 'no living habitations can be seen for miles and the majestic solitude of the desert surrounds and penetrates every fibre of your being.'[15] If they had to make a forced landing in this landscape, their lives would depend on the ten days' worth of water they carried and a letter in Arabic, from King Faisal, whose Arab army Ross had assisted in October 1918.

Without landmarks by which to navigate, for the next couple of hours Ross, Salmond and Borton plotted their course 'solely by compass'. They used an instrument known as a speed and drift indicator to calculate how wind affected their course. As planned, a couple of hours into the flight, the O/400 passed over the ancient ruins at Palmyra; Ross turned east and after another two hours the shimmer of the Euphrates River appeared on the horizon. Ross and Borton's navigation was accurate: they arrived over the river exactly where planned and then followed it south to Ramadi before turning east again for the journey's final stage. Six hours after leaving Damascus, the majestic domes of Baghdad took shape in the haze and shortly afterwards Ross landed on the RAF aerodrome just outside of town. Altogether, the 1500 kilometres from Cairo had taken just under thirteen hours—a journey by sea usually measured in weeks. As the *Chicago Daily Tribune*, one of many newspapers around the world to publish cables from London regarding the flight, remarked, 'In three days the airmen had visited three countries—Egypt, Syria and Mesopotamia—and linked up the two great Asiatic expeditionary forces of the British Empire.'[16] To Ross, it seemed novel that he had eaten his breakfast in Shepheard's in Cairo on Friday and then his lunch in Baghdad on Saturday.[17]

For three days, Generals Salmond and Borton inspected the RAF units stationed near Baghdad. Ross meanwhile enjoyed the hospitality of Colonel Bradley, an Air Force wing commander who lived in a charming old style 'Eastern house' that backed onto the Tigris River. The colonel had a motor boat and took Ross joyriding on the river; he also showed him around Baghdad, a city that had been under Ottoman control from 1534 until captured by British Indian forces in 1917. From Ross's Anglo-centric perspective, the end of nearly four centuries of 'Eastern' rule could only have been to the city's benefit. 'For a native town,' he thought Baghdad, 'quite clean'—something to which he attributed the occupying British Army. 'Our troops have certainly done wonders there in the way of improving the place.'[18]

While Ross took in the sights, Shiers and Bennett prepared the Handley Page for the flight to India. Ross admired the hard work they did each evening during the flight, despite spending several hours each day exposed to the elements in their open cockpit. 'As soon as we landed at a place,' he observed, 'they would start right away on the engines and go over them and clean them up, etc.' Refuelling after each stage of the journey proved a particularly strenuous task. The O/400's tanks took nearly 1000 litres of petrol at most stops, which Shiers and Bennett needed to decant from 20-litre tins, through a chamois, into the machine's tanks.

Salmond had originally planned for Ross to fly him back to Cairo and then to return to Baghdad, collect Borton and continue on to India. His belief that the four-engine Handley Page V/1500 was close behind them, however, compelled Salmond to press on to India as soon as possible. As Ross later acknowledged, 'We were really spurred on by the knowledge that the other big machine was somewhere behind us and we knew that once he caught up to us our chances of being the first to fly to India were practically nil.'[19] (In fact, Ross and his party had been misinformed: the V/1500 was yet to leave Britain.)

Salmond, Borton and Ross considered two possible routes to India: a northern one that would take them across Persia (what would later become Iran) to Quetta and a southern route along the Persian Gulf coast to Karachi. Both posed difficulties and uncertainties; neither had been completely traversed by air and the crew had limited information about what they might expect in terms of landing grounds and fuel. Considering the risks posed by winter weather along the mountainous northern route, Salmond decided to take the coastal route. The RAF had some rudimentary aerodromes along the Persian Gulf coastline, but none had been prepared to handle an aircraft as large as the O/400. The contingency plan was to land on beaches if the Air Force's bases appeared unsuitable.[20]

The O/400 left Baghdad on 4 December 1918, which was Ross's 26th birthday. He and Borton followed the Tigris south, stopping for the night at Basra before turning east to follow the Persian coastline towards India. Each day they flew for between five and six hours, covering up to 800 kilometres. After Basra, they made stops at Bushire, Bandar Abbas and Chabahar—isolated outposts on the fringes of the British Empire that Ross mostly found to be dreary, depressing and garrisoned by soldiers who would have preferred to be anywhere else. Of the locals, Ross observed, 'They were much impressed but thought we were evil spirits!'[21]

With the exception of a heavy landing by Borton at Bandar Abbas, which delayed them for three days to repair a broken undercarriage, the flight across Persia proved uneventful. The weather was excellent and from 8000 feet, Ross and his companions saw some spectacular scenery along the Gulf coast—snow-capped mountains that ran parallel to the sea and looked 'wonderful' when caught in dawn's auburn rays. Further east, the Persian coastline became rough and foreboding, making Ross and his companions grateful that the Royal Navy had agreed to dispatch ships to search for them if they failed to arrive at a scheduled stopover. 'I have never seen more desolate or rugged country,' he wrote. 'It was the same all the way to Karachi with just occasional flat strips near the coast'.[22]

At Karachi, the local garrison had spent four days clearing and levelling a field next to the town's zoological gardens for the O/400. Ten thousand people gathered there on 11 December to welcome the first aircraft to fly all the way from Britain to India.[23] 'I think the whole of Karachi must have turned out to meet us,' said Ross. The lumbering aircraft touched down gently at 2 p.m. close in front of the crowd, and after completing its landing roll, it turned and taxied back towards a group of tents pitched for the official guests. As one journalist described it, 'The crowd streamed across the ground to see General Salmond and General Barton [sic], as spick and span as if they had merely travelled a few miles in a motor car, alight to be welcomed by Brigadier General Fowler, Commanding Karachi Brigade.'[24]

The log books of the flight have not survived, but at the time the press reported that the O/400 had taken 36 hours of flying time to reach Karachi from Cairo: a distance of 2548 miles (4100 kilometres).[25] Ross accounted for their apparently slow average ground speed of 71 miles (114 kilometres) per hour by explaining that they had not always flown the most direct routes and had made diversions to survey interesting features on the ground.[26] Arriving in Karachi had particular significance for Borton, who had previously flown a Handley Page O/400 from Britain to Egypt, thus making him the first pilot to fly the all the way from Britain to India. On hearing the news of his son's achievement, Borton's father would reflect how Biffy's grandfather had taken nearly four and a half months to sail from Britain to India in 1840 to fight in the first Afghan war. Two generations later, his son had made the same journey in fewer than four days' flying time (and eleven days overall). 'I wonder how long it will take Biffy's grandson, say in 1998?' he mused in the pages of his diary. The

68-year-old Borton Snr's prediction, as radical as it might have seemed in 1919, would still prove too conservative at '300 miles an hour—say 16 hours'.[27]

The O/400 set off for Delhi the following morning, with the crew planning to break the trip overnight in Nasirabad, a cantonment town 725 kilometres away in Rajasthan. It proved to be an 'uninteresting trip', thought Ross, mostly over the Thar Desert of north-western India. Ross climbed to 8000 feet in an effort to freeze a pair of rats that Salmond had spotted aboard the aircraft the previous day and that the crew feared might chew through a control cable or bracing wire: 'It was too much for the rat in the top plane— he tried to climb down a strut but the wind caught him as soon as he came out of the plane and away he went into space!' They found the other one a couple of days later in the starboard engine, apparently electrocuted after touching a spark plug.[28]

Despite being 15 kilometres outside of town, the improvised landing ground prepared by British authorities at Delhi attracted a large crowd of spectators, including the Commander-in-Chief of the British Indian Army and a number of senior military and government personnel. While they waited, the commander of the RAF in India put on an aerobatics display before flying out to meet the O/400 and escort it in to land. A journalist reported:

> The huge Handley Page hovered over the ground and coming down made a perfect landing amidst the cheers of the crowd. What struck the spectators most was the wonderful steadiness of this aerial monster.

As the crowd surged in around the aircraft, Ross, Borton and Salmond took a moment to 'solemnly' shake hands. 'It was a great relief to know that we had done what we set out to do,' wrote Ross.[29]

The generals and Ross were received by the Commander-in-Chief, Sir Charles Monro, who congratulated them on their successful journey. To Ross's delight, as the crowd pressed in around them, someone passed him a telegram from his mother. That afternoon, the crew showed Sir Charles and Lady Monro through the Handley Page before joining them at the races. They attended an official reception that evening at the Commander-in-Chief's residence where, at one point, Ross found himself speaking with his host, who he knew had commanded the Mediterranean Expeditionary Force at Gallipoli. Over drinks, Ross and Sir Charles—the station manager's son and one of the British Army's most senior soldiers—conducted an impromptu post-mortem on the campaign informed by the perspectives of one who had fought in the trenches and another who had advised the government to abandon the campaign and who oversaw its evacuation. 'He is an awfully nice old chap and very well liked over here,' concluded Ross.[30]

Ross remained in Delhi for three nights. 'We were made a great fuss of and asked everywhere,' he wrote. Such were his options that Ross turned down an invitation to stay at the home of General Sir George Kirkpatrick, the Indian Army's Chief of the General Staff. He chose instead to stay at Delhi's most luxurious hotel, Maiden's, to be closer to where the generals were staying.[31]

Borton and Salmond had planned to remain in Delhi for Christmas, but an invitation from the Viceroy to spend the holidays (and the horse racing season) in Calcutta changed their minds. The crew flew to Allahabad on 16 December, passing over Agra on the way and photographing the Taj Mahal—the first time ever from the air, believed Ross. Yet another 'large and enthusiastic gathering of the people' met the O/400 at Allahabad.[32] 'We were met there by a terrific crowd of natives, rajahs and one thing and the other, and they couldn't do enough for us,' recalled Shiers. 'They took us over into their villages and gave us a most wonderful spread, wines and different things, plenty of beer. We had a wonderful time.'[33]

After spending the night as the Bishop of Allahabad's guests, the crew set out for Calcutta, a 750-kilometre flight that would take nearly seven hours. Arriving over the city in mid-afternoon. Ross could see 'thousands of people streaming out to the racecourse where we were to land'. He had never seen such a mass of humans; newspapers would later estimate that as many as 300,000 people came to see the O/400 land.[34] A reporter for *The Bengalee* described the scene on the ground:

> Motor cars, motor bikes, motor lorries, phaetons, drawn garries, cow carts, bullock carts and pedestrians jostled one another . . . to secure an advantageous position near the Race Course affording a better view of the much expected aeroplane from Allahabad. There was a sea of human heads from Esplanade to Kidderpore Bridge. Lakhs and Lakha [hundreds of thousands] of pairs of eyes from roofs of houses, trees, decks, staircases and spires were turned towards to horizon to catch the first glimpse of the biplane.[35]

For half an hour, Ross and Borton circled the racecourse while police and soldiers struggled to clear a space for the aeroplane to land. Borton brought the O/400 in to land, somehow managing to clip the only tree on the racecourse as he taxied; the collision smashed the tip of the aircraft's upper-starboard wing. The Handley Page came to a stop in front of the marquee that had been erected for the dignitaries, and the crowd surged forward onto the polo ground.[36] 'There was a stampede,' wrote one observer. 'European ladies and gentlemen were seen climbing over the several railings that separated them from the machine and within the space of a few seconds the aeroplane was surrounded by a seething mass of humanity.'[37]

At the marquee beside the aircraft, Salmond and Borton introduced their Australian crew to the Viceroy, His Excellency the Right Honourable Lord Chelmsford. Ross, thought one reporter, 'appeared to be well bronzed' and, like the generals, a soldier of 'daring and determination'. He also observed how 'the two Sergeants', Shiers and Bennett, 'stepped up to His Excellency in their uniform and slouched hats' and assumed that they 'no doubt' appreciated his Excellency's attention.[38] Perhaps—but, as Ross would write to his mother, after spending seven hours in the air he 'did not feel much like meeting Viceroys and such people'. He realised, however, that 'it had to be gone through' so, smiling politely, he braced himself for another round of introductions, interviews, speeches, official receptions and toasts that represented the gulf that now separated Captain Ross Smith the aviator from the warehouseman who had left Adelaide four years earlier.[39] Newsreel footage shows Ross, just a few minutes after landing, wearing an immaculate dress uniform and chatting comfortably to Lady Chelmsford beside the giant aeroplane.[40]

In the following days, details of General Salmond's journey appeared in newspapers all around the world.[41] The flight, which had by Ross's calculation covered 4088 miles (6578 kilometres) in 59 hours' flying time, represented a watershed moment for aviation, demonstrating the trans-continental capabilities that aeroplanes had so rapidly developed during the Great War.[42] The Anglo-Indian press enthusiastically agreed, anticipating how airmail would revolutionise communications in Britain's Asian colonies: 'From every point of view, commercial, administrative and strategic, it is important that India be equipped as soon as possible with an adequate supply of aeroplanes and pilots.'[43] Speaking to a journalist in Calcutta, Salmond reflected on the broader implications of the air age for the British Empire, predicting how, in future, aircraft would prove to be as important to imperial defence as the navy had been in the past. He imagined, as a first step, the establishment of 'an All-Red Route' (i.e. all British) extending out from Britain via Egypt to South Africa and throughout Asia to Australia.[44]

For his part in the journey to India, Ross received the Air Force Cross—an equivalent award to the DFC, but for non-operational flying. Shiers and Bennett each received the equivalent for other ranks: the Air Force Medal.

Although Major General Salmond attracted most of the attention in the press, a few reports mentioned Ross by name (Shiers and Bennett, however, were usually simply 'the mechanics'). On 12 December, as the crew approached Delhi, news service cables arrived in Adelaide carrying details of the flight, one noting that General Salmond 'was accompanied by Capt. Ross Smith, an Australian, and a brother air-force commander'.[45] Ross's involvement gave the story an interesting local angle and, in the following days, at least half a dozen Adelaide newspapers reported Ross's connection with the flight, some mistakenly inferring that he had flown the Handley Page O/400 all the way from Britain.[46] Adelaide newspapers profiled Ross's wartime career in columns that were then reprinted in newspapers all around the country. Although he had occasionally been the subject of news stories in the Adelaide press during the war, this was the first occasion in which Ross became the subject of national news. Readers of newspapers from Broken Hill to Brisbane were thus introduced to the 'intrepid South Australian aviator' in columns that detailed notable events from his wartime service.[47] Sydney's *Sun* would go as far as dubbing Ross 'the Australian Captain Ball'—a reference to one of the most famous British fighter pilots of the war, Captain Albert Ball. 'Although quite a young pilot [he] was easily the most outstanding figure in the flying world on the Palestine front,' it claimed.[48] A few days after Ross's arrival in Calcutta, Australian newspapers began speculating that he would shortly fly to Australia—although when questioned about this ambition of Borton's, Air Ministry officials refused to comment.[49]

On 16 December 1918, while Ross was in the air somewhere between Delhi and Allahabad, the Queen's School in Adelaide had its annual speech day. Headmaster Jacomb-Hood, the severe disciplinarian who had once dismissed young Ross as never likely to 'set the Thames on fire', had apparently changed his mind about the ex-pupil whose name now appeared in news columns all over the world. The old boys who represented 'the highest glory of Queen's School' were, he claimed, the 187 who had gone to war, 35 of whom had made 'the supreme sacrifice'. Of those who survived to now return home, Jacomb-Hood singled out the quiet, unassuming little boy who had gone by the nickname 'Froggy' while at Queen's. Having flown all the way to India, forecast the headmaster, Ross Macpherson Smith 'would soon be seen arriving in Adelaide from the clouds'.[50]

23

AN AWFULLY GOOD TIME

The two months Ross spent in India immediately after the Great War were the most enjoyable that he had ever known. He arrived on the subcontinent looking forward to some time off. He found himself subject to the lavish hospitality of India's colonial masters, with whom Borton was well-connected.

Following their triumphant arrival there on 18 December 1918, Ross and the members of the Handley Page crew spent the holidays in Calcutta. Described by contemporaries as 'the queen of the east', the city represented the commercial epicentre of Britain's sprawling imperial venture in Asia. Generations of British rice, jute and coal money had funded the development of a comfortable and well-appointed European quarter where 'many beautiful old houses tinted with yellow ochre exist in spacious and full-leaved compounds'.[1]

At the Viceroy's invitation, Ross stayed in one of Government House's 90 rooms. He celebrated Christmas and New Year 1918–19 with 'a very strenuous' schedule of parties, dinners and balls and, alongside Borton, found himself 'promptly elected members of all the best clubs & so forth'. Ross discovered that the three ribbons and three bars he wore on his chest, which had caused him embarrassment when among his peers, now proved 'certainly very useful'.[2]

In a Rolls-Royce motorcar, borrowed from one of Calcutta's benevolent officials, Ross zoomed between social engagements at speeds of up to 110 kilometres per hour. He enjoyed the attractions of the Maidan, the verdant parkland on the east bank of the Hooghly River where Europeans motored, had picnics, played cricket, football and polo and went to the races. As Ross and Borton anticipated when planning the flight to India, the Championship of India racing season coincided with their visit. 'It's very good racing and I have managed to make a little money,' Ross reported to his mother.[3]

Despite this additional income, Ross found it impossible to get by on his captain's salary. At the end of December, he faced the minor indignity of cabling his mother to ask for more money. 'I am having an awfully good time but a very expensive one,' he explained. 'Everyone has made a great fuss of us all over India and as I am living with the best in the land it costs a lot to do it.' Jessie wired her son £100.[4]

A few days after Christmas, Ross said farewell to General Salmond, who sailed home to Britain for a short leave before returning to Egypt. Along with Borton, Shiers and Bennett, Ross remained in India, intending to undertake a voyage through Southeast Asia to locate sites for aerodromes along the route to Australia. Since their arrival in India, they had received sanction from London to undertake the voyage but now waited on the Government of India to prepare a ship and crew for them.[5]

On 13 January 1919, Ross and Borton flew the O/400 to the RAF station at Lahore to have its engines overhauled. They made planned stopovers at Allahabad and Delhi, but also had to make an emergency landing when a fuel line became blocked.[6] The aircraft remained at Lahore while Ross and Borton went to Delhi, where they spent three weeks that blurred, for Ross, into 'one long succession of lunches, tea parties, dinners and dances'. Four nights in succession, Ross stayed out until sunrise. With the Anglo-Indian newspapers covering Ross's and Borton's movements, they assumed the status of celebrities. 'Everyone knows who we are and all about us,' wrote Ross. Apparently, not all of the attention proved unwelcome, with Ross admitting to his brother to falling in love 'temporarily' with 'numerous' girls.

While in Delhi, Ross joined a hunting expedition to Jaipur at the invitation of the British Resident, Colonel R.A.E. Benn. He stayed for four days in the 'huge and magnificent' residency house, where he enjoyed the company of 'two charming girls' who he had met while in Delhi. 'We went out shooting black buck one afternoon,' wrote Ross in a letter to Keith. 'I kept up Australia's reputation and bagged two of them, fine big ones too.' While a guest of Jaipur's colonial administrator, Ross also had the opportunity to try his hand at pig sticking, 'the finest sport I've ever tried', as he reported. Despite having done little horse riding in over two years, Ross managed to spear two wild pigs with a lance. 'They can travel at some pace and dodge,' he wrote. 'I got the second one after a fine run, and once he was stuck he turned and fought.' Ross arranged to have one of the bucks' heads and a pig's tusk mounted, possibly looking forward to telling the story to guests in his mother's drawing room at Aviemore, back in Adelaide.

Ross and Borton returned to Calcutta on 7 February. In a letter to Keith, he described his three weeks in Delhi as the best of his life: 'It's been great, old son, especially after 4 years of war.'[7] The dancing, dining, socialising—the carefree days of leisure that blurred together—reflected something, albeit in grander style, of what Ross's life had been before the war. Perhaps for fleeting moments during his Indian sojourn it seemed like the years 1914–18 had not happened at all.

While Ross and Borton enjoyed themselves in Delhi, arrangements for their Southeast Asian survey expedition progressed. General Salmond had set the wheels in motion with a cable from Delhi on 14 December 1918. In it he asked the Air Ministry in London to sanction a sea expedition to reconnoitre the air route to Australia from India 'to prove' its passage by aeroplane 'possible' and to distribute supplies of fuel and oil throughout the region. He also advised authorities in London to make arrangements with their counterparts in Australia and the Netherlands to develop a string of aerodromes extending south from the Dutch East Indies to Melbourne. As Salmond pointed out, the development of an aerial route across Asia would 'materially assist' these governments too.[8]

Salmond's superiors in London agreed. Major General Sir Frederick Sykes, Chief of the Air Staff, thought it 'a most desirable and worthy request', while the RAF's Director of Flying Operations, Colonel Percy Groves, concurred given the 'strategic' and 'commercial' possibilities offered by an air route to Australia.[9] Finances presented a problem, though. Post-war cuts to defence budgets were forcing the services to reduce spending to a bare minimum. At the time of Salmond's proposal for the establishment of an air route across Asia, Treasury had allocated the Air Ministry just £5000 for the development of civil aviation.[10]

Consequently, Borton and Ross received permission to proceed with their proposed voyage, but only to reconnoitre and report on possible aerodrome locations. They had no authorisation to purchase land or commit money to the development of aerodromes along the route.[11] Despite Salmond's appeal to his superiors in London that Borton should have a 'free hand' to spend money, they remained unmoved: it was to be a reconnaissance expedition only.[12]

On the eve of their departure, Ross wrote to Keith, explaining that they were sailing aboard the Royal Indian Marine Ship (RIMS) *Sphinx*, a 900-tonne paddle-steamer commissioned in 1883: 'It's the best we could get and we will be quite comfortable.' With a crew of Indian sailors, and the assistance of Shiers and Bennett, they planned to explore the Burmese and Malay coasts before sailing through the Dutch East Indies as far south as Timor. The *Sphinx* carried a cargo of 320,000 litres of fuel to leave behind along the route for use during their planned flight to Australia in the Handley Page O/400. 'We will have to find aerodromes about every 350 to 400 miles [560 to 640 kilometres],' wrote Ross, 'so we should see something of the country if nothing else.' Returning to India, they would then prepare the Handley Page O/400 for a flight to Australia: 'when we hear that the aerodromes are ready we start off, and away we go for home'.[13]

24

SOUTH ASIAN SURVEY

The *Sphinx* left Calcutta on 10 February 1919 and two days later arrived at Chittagong, a port in the apex of the Bay of Bengal. After inspecting several possible sites, Borton selected one and wrote a report on it for the Government of India, which planned to establish an airmail service extending into this region.

The *Sphinx* had just set sail at 9 a.m. the following day when Ross heard 'a hell of an explosion' in the ship's rear cargo hold. Within moments, flames had engulfed the stern, including Ross's cabin, which by remarkable fortune he had only just vacated.

Ross later admitted that he had never been so terrified in his life. But he pulled himself together and joined the crew in a vain attempt to save the ship.[1] With the onboard fire-fighting equipment incapable of battling such a blaze, the *Sphinx*'s captain decided to beach the vessel, flood the holds and order the crew to abandon ship. A fire-fighting boat from the harbour soon arrived, and Ross and Borton went back aboard to help. The two airmen proved less than effective in their first attempt at fire-fighting. As Ross wrote:

> Most of the time we were fighting the fire the General and I were howling with laughter . . . A fire hose with a good pressure of water in it is a strong thing to handle and it jumps about in the most alarming way. I caught the General square in the middle of his back once with the stream of water from my hose and he went over in a heap of spluttering profanity! Another

> time one of the crew was caught under the chin at close range & you never saw a more comical expression. We all got sopping wet and almost black with smoke.[2]

It took until late afternoon to bring the blaze under control. The ship had been gutted. Ross lost almost everything except the clothes on his back. His flying gear, £100 worth of uniforms and kit, and the photos he had been taking on his personal vest-pocket camera throughout the war had been incinerated. But it was the loss of his flying log book that stung the most. After half an hour of exertion, Ross managed to pry open his charred suitcase; all that survived were fourteen gold sovereigns 'none the worse for their experience'.[3] Over a year later, he would receive £70 compensation from the Air Ministry for his loss.[4] Although a welcome surprise, this could not come near to replacing his wartime records. Their destruction represented a profound loss of both personal and historical proportions.

In a letter written to Keith, Ross cryptically claimed that while they did not know for certain what had caused the explosion, 'we have our suspicions' and that he would tell him about it when they saw each other again: 'I can't now.'[5] Borton reported to his superiors that the fire had started in the cargo hold, which was filled with drums of fuel, and the newspapers said likewise.[6] Perhaps one of the *Sphinx*'s crew had carelessly tossed a cigarette butt.

Ross returned to Calcutta dejected about the prospect of waiting for months to find a replacement ship. Within a matter of days, however, the Indian naval authorities offered Borton the use of the RIMS *Minto,* a 1000-tonne vessel armed with four guns—'a much better ship this time', in Ross's assessment.[7]

While the *Minto*'s crew prepared for the voyage, Ross and Borton visited Cooch Behar on a ten-day hunting expedition. 'I went up with the General as the guests of the Maharajah, and had a wonderful time,' wrote Ross. The party claimed two tigers, eight leopards 'as well as a lot of smaller stuff and birds'—although none of the larger game fell to Ross's rifle. To scare up the game, the Indian gamekeepers used a line of 30 elephants to crash through the jungle towards Ross and the other hunters. 'It really was the experience of a lifetime, and I was very lucky to get the shoot.'[8]

Ross and Borton left Calcutta aboard their replacement ship on 13 March. Bennett and Shiers went along too and took charge of the *Minto*'s motor boat; they would use it to ferry Borton and Ross ashore to look for aerodromes.

During the following fortnight, they searched the coast of Burma for possible aerodrome sites, stopping at Akyab, Rangoon, the Mergui islands and Victoria Point. At each location, Borton and Ross met and interviewed colonial administrators and British business owners to identify possible locations and then reconnoitred them by car (and, in some instances, bicycle). Without authority to commit funds to the development of aerodromes, Borton sought expense estimates from local contractors that he could then include in an official report for the Air Ministry. Ross acted as Borton's adjutant, taking notes and sketching rough maps in his pocket notebook, and recording data about local weather conditions. Most sites required extensive work: raising ground prone to waterlogging, clearing jungle or rubber plantations and removing obstacles such as telegraph lines. Ross recorded the names of influential individuals they met at each stopover—people who might come in handy during the flight that he and Borton still hoped they could shortly make to Australia.[9]

Indeed, during the expedition Ross and Borton had their eyes open for two types of sites: those that could be turned into permanent aerodromes along a future trans-Asian air route (which might take many months to develop) and temporary landing grounds that they might soon use themselves on their way to Australia in the O/400.[10] The permanent sites for which Borton and Ross searched reflected the performance of contemporary aircraft. To be suitable, an aerodrome needed to be relatively flat and dry throughout the year; it could be either grass or dirt, but it had to be clear of obstructions and at least 1200 x 800 yards (1097 x 731 metres), with the longer axis facing into the prevailing wind. To service an airmail or passenger route, an aerodrome also needed to be situated close to a road or rail line. Importantly, pilots required a place to land every 800 kilometres between Calcutta and Darwin. Ideally, the route would take pilots over regions in which they could make a forced landing with a reasonable prospect of rescue. For their own flight to Australia, though, Borton and Ross were less particular: any relatively flat piece of ground that could be cleared at short notice might do.

At Akyab on Burma's west coast, the pair identified a potential site among rice paddies, just outside of town. It needed clearing and levelling—and even then, in Borton's opinion, should only be used by a pilot who had inspected the ground first.[11] They had greater success at Rangoon; exploring the countryside in a car for 25 kilometres around town, they identified a potential site near the rifle ranges at Cambe which the colonial government already planned to clear and develop. In the meantime, Borton and Ross could land on the local racecourse, just as they had in Calcutta—although again Borton felt that only a pilot who had 'made a personal examination of the ground' should attempt to land there, given that it was relatively small—750 x 300 yards (686 x 274 metres) and surrounded by houses and trees.[12]

Late one evening, while sailing along the Burmese coast, Ross spotted the Southern Cross. It was the first time he had seen the constellation since November 1914, when he had been on his way to Egypt with the AIF's first contingent. 'It was nice to see the dear old thing again,' wrote Ross to his mother.[13]

When the *Minto* reached the Mergui Archipelago on 24 March, Borton and Ross explored one of its larger islands but failed to find anything suitable among its mangroves, rubber plantations and thick jungle. The beaches were too muddy to land an aeroplane.[14] 'All this coast is a mass of dense jungle or cultivation and it is a hard job to find the sort of ground we want,' recorded Ross. 'General Borton and I spent the day before yesterday walking through swamps and thick jungle and I've never felt such heat in all my life.'[15]

The *Minto* next stopped at Victoria Point, close to the Malay border. Ross and Borton cycled 10 kilometres through densely wooded slopes and valleys to the only site that local authorities thought might be suitable. It was 'the only open space for miles around', as Ross noted, and 'a good site, requiring clearing and a certain amount of levelling'.[16]

Seventeen days after leaving Calcutta, the *Minto* reached Penang. Ross thought it a paradise, describing how 'the streets are lined with trees . . . in flower. Hills rise almost abruptly to 2500 ft behind the town.' At night, the sea around the *Minto* glowed bright with phosphorus so that Ross and his companions 'could follow the tracks of fish swimming about in the water'. While Borton tried in vain to find a suitable aerodrome on the rugged, narrow island, he sent Ross by rail to Alor Setar in the north-west Malayan state of Kedah. Ross stayed with the British commissioner there and 'motored about' for two days, identifying a landing ground near Ketri Station, 110 kilometres from Penang.[17] Returning to the *Minto* that evening, Ross found that the ship's officers had invited members of the local British community aboard. 'I danced away until the early hours,' wrote Ross. 'It was great fun and there were quite a lot of people on board.'[18]

After spending a week in Malaya, the *Minto* continued its voyage south through the Strait of Malacca. While at sea, Ross passed the time comfortably. 'There is quite a lot of deck space and I have got a nice cabin,' he wrote. The ship reminded him of one of the yachts on which his family had explored the coast of Scotland when he was a boy.[19] Ross enjoyed the company of the ship's officers (who all came from the Royal Navy); for an hour before lunch and dinner, they played poker in the officers' mess, betting drinks. Having taught himself how to use the ship's typewriter, Ross tapped out a letter to Keith: 'I'm getting quite hot stuff at it as you will observe,' he quipped (though soon 'fed up' with the contraption, he switched back to a pen).[20]

It is easy to imagine that Ross and Borton, perhaps with Bennett and Shiers too, devoted hours to discussing their plans to fly the O/400 from India across the seas on which they now sailed. Although Ross wrote optimistically to Keith ('we have had no trouble about aerodromes'), in reality the expedition was highlighting the enormous difficulties that such an undertaking would entail. Indeed, after inspecting sites in Burma and

Malaya, Borton was beginning to realise that, without considerable investment in the development of aerodromes in the area, a flight beyond Calcutta in a land-based aeroplane would be impossible.[21]

After Penang, they made a five-day stopover in Singapore, where Ross and Borton identified land for a permanent aerodrome a few kilometres out of town ('will require considerable drainage') and a temporary one on the local racecourse. Although presently serving as a golf course, Ross thought that its eight bunkers could be removed. He imagined landing there in the O/400: at only 600 yards [550 metres] long and surrounded by a ditch, he would need to make a hard right during the landing roll and double back, allowing him to 'finish up in front of the stand'.[22]

From Singapore, a two-day voyage conveyed Ross and Borton into the Dutch East Indies; they docked in Batavia on 14 April. From London, the Colonial Office had arranged their visit with the Dutch government. Count Johan Paul van Limburg Stirum, the Governor-General, welcomed Ross and Borton to his 'very fine house' and expressed his enthusiasm for developing aviation in the region. He 'was very interested in our proposed flight to Australia and did all he could to help us in our search for landing grounds', reported Ross.

Provided with two cars and an officer to assist them, Ross spent a fortnight exploring Java with Borton. 'It is one of the prettiest places I have ever seen,' remarked Ross. 'Nearly everything seems to grow there and every bit of land is under cultivation of some sort.' On one occasion, after stopping for lunch at a large estate owned by a British firm, they attempted to drive along a steep mountain road. Ross had never seen a road with such sharp hairpin bends. 'It was also raining hard,' he wrote, 'and the real fun started when the car I was in stopped on a steep hill and started slithering back. We finally managed to get to the top after getting very muddy and wet, and by dint of much pushing'.

In another instance, at Sourabaya, Ross and Borton came to a 3-kilometre section of road that had a foot of water over it. They walked along an adjacent railway line while the soldiers accompanying them pushed the car through the snake-infested floodwaters. 'The General and I had great sport bombing [the snakes] with stones.' While in the tropics, Ross would have a few close encounters with snakes and, on one occasion, a 'mad dog' chased him. He also came across some of the island's German settlers. Ross thought the venomous looks they gave him and Borton as they went about in their uniforms 'rather fun really'.

At Bima, on the island of Sumbawa, Borton became seriously ill with malaria and returned to Batavia to see a doctor. Ross continued without him to Timor, where he spent a week looking for places to build the penultimate aerodrome along the route to Australia. He found sites that could work at Koepang and a remote but otherwise well-situated one at Atamboea, but nothing near the Portuguese settlement at Dili. At Koepang, Ross went sightseeing to some nearby volcanoes and watched 'mud bubbling out'. He bought several 'curios' to send home to his mother.[23]

Ross returned to Batavia after nearly a month exploring the Dutch East Indies to find Borton still too sick to carry out his official duties. He reported to the Governor-General and a committee of local Dutch officials who were planning the establishment of a local aviation service. In a 'prolonged interview', the Dutch Governor-General questioned Ross about his thoughts on the future of aviation in the Dutch East Indies. Ross described the several sites he had identified among the islands that might be developed into aerodromes and incorporated into a route to Australia. A three-hour meeting with local officials followed, during which Ross conveyed what he knew about recent aviation developments in Europe and the capabilities of aircraft for carrying passengers and mail. Although topics beyond his own direct experience, Ross probably drew upon what he had picked up from the newspapers, from discussions with Generals Salmond and Borton and from his work on the O/400. At this time, and in this part of the world, this knowledge and experience would have well and truly distinguished Ross as an expert on the subject. Borton, indeed, reported that Ross did well in these meetings.[24] Ross thought so too: 'I'm becoming hot stuff at making speeches,' he joked in a letter to Keith.[25]

In mid-May, Ross and Borton returned to Singapore, stopping briefly at Muntok on Banka Island, where they identified a strip that Ross thought could be cleared and ready to use in two or three months.[26] From Singapore, Ross and Borton went their separate ways: Borton took the *Minto* to British North Borneo while Ross travelled by rail to Bangkok.

Visiting Siam (Thailand) had not been part of Borton's plans, but during the voyage he had received a cable from the British Chargé d'Affaires in Bangkok indicating the Siamese government's desire to participate in a trans-Asian air route.[27] Given the paucity of suitable landing sites that he and Ross had located on the west coast of Malaya, Borton had indeed already considered that routing aircraft through Siam might be necessary. In the shorter term, he saw value in the Handley Page O/400 visiting Bangkok for 'political reasons'—that is, as a demonstration of British air power to the Siamese government, the only regime in the region not under the direct influence of a European colonial administration.[28]

Arriving in Bangkok on 28 May, Ross met the British Chargé d'Affaires and the other consular officials who would assist him during his stay in the Siamese capital. In the days that followed, he had audiences with His Royal Highness Prince Chakrabongse Bhuvanath of Pitsanuloke, Chief of General Staff for the Siamese army, and His Royal Highness Prince Purachatra Jayakara of Kamphaengphet, an army engineer and head of the government's railway department. Both seemed enthusiastic about the development of aviation in Siam; they had been instrumental in the recent establishment of a Royal Siamese Aeronautical Service and now hoped to connect the country to an international air route. Ross inspected the air force's aerodrome at Don Muang, 15 kilometres north of the city, where he found two large hangars and six old Nieuport monoplanes. One hundred Siamese pilots had gone to France to train and procure 50 new aircraft.

Ross thought that they could stop at Don Muang on their flight to Australia. In the longer term, however, it would require considerable work to raise it above seasonal flood levels—'a serious' and expensive undertaking, he concluded after speaking to British officials attached to the

Siamese government's Survey, Irrigation and Agricultural Departments. A better option, thought Ross, would be the establishment of an aerodrome at Nakon Patom, a high, level plateau 40 kilometres west of Bangkok on the railway line to Penang. In either case, though, the ruggedness of the Siamese countryside, which Ross had spent many hours watching from the window of his train, would give an aviator little chance of surviving a forced landing. He recommended that any air route over the interior of the country include some emergency landing grounds 'at frequent intervals'.[29]

After six days in Siam, Ross travelled by rail to Penang where, on 6 June, he rejoined Borton and the crew of the *Minto*. Their three-month survey of aerodromes across Southeast Asia now complete, they set sail back across the Bay of Bengal towards Calcutta.

In Ross's official report of his expedition to Siam, we are reminded of just how comprehensively wartime service had transformed his life. He had enlisted in the AIF in 1914 as a private and here he was, not quite five years later, representing the British government to a sovereign power, regarding an issue of commercial and strategic importance to the empire. As he had done previously in the Dutch East Indies when Borton fell ill, in Siam Ross handled audiences with diplomats, royalty and senior service personnel adroitly—all the while surreptitiously gathering intelligence.

Indeed, besides his 'official' report, which Borton sent to the Air Ministry, the Governor of the Straits Settlements and the British Embassy in Bangkok, Ross also wrote a separate report for the Colonial Office. In this second document, he provided an assessment of the Royal Siamese Aeronautical Service's capabilities and, from what he could gather, its plans for expansion. He also explained that the Siamese Government seemed 'most anxious to have full control and possession of any aerodromes that may be made in their country'. From the British Chargé d'Affaires, however, he learned that 'the Siamese Government would promise to do anything but did not always carry it out . . . it would be preferable for a [British] commercial firm to have its own aerodrome and so not be dependent upon the Siamese for anything'.[30] To resolve this dilemma, in a cover letter to Ross's reports,

Borton reaffirmed his original idea that the air route 'should follow the West Coast of Burmah [sic] and the Malay Peninsular [sic]' and that, if it wished, the Siamese government could connect a 'branch line' to this at Mergui.[31]

Ross's motivation for gathering this intelligence while in Siam is unclear. Had he done it on his own initiative, or had he been briefed by British authorities while in Singapore? If so, no record of such instructions appears to survive. Perhaps Ross's secret mission originated in the Long Bar at Raffles Hotel with Colonial Office officials and a round or two of Singapore Slings.

Either way, to his lengthy and diverse resume of wartime experiences, Ross could now, albeit quietly, add another: spy.

25

THE GREAT RACE

Their survey voyage complete, Ross and his companions aboard the *Minto* returned to Calcutta on 13 June 1919.

Their three-month expedition had produced the first ever survey of a trans-Asian air route. Documented in dozens of pages of typewritten reports, the 30 aerodrome sites that Borton and Ross identified proved that India could, in theory, be linked to Australia by an air route passing through Burma, Siam, Malaya, Singapore and the Dutch East Indies. To be capable of supporting a commercial service, however, most of the sites would require extensive work and the investment of large sums of money. Indeed, the estimates for the purchase and construction of the aerodromes recommended by Borton came to £167,000—such a staggering amount, in fact, that when the cable with this figure arrived in London a shocked clerk at the Air Ministry assumed that there must have been an error in the transmission and asked for the cable to be repeated.[1] It would be many months—perhaps even years—before a permanent airmail and passenger route could be established across South Asia.

To Ross and Borton, though, the expedition had also demonstrated the feasibility of a flight to Australia in the near future using racecourses and parks as temporary aerodromes. Upon their return to Calcutta, however, Ross and Borton were 'chagrined' to learn the RAF had sent their machine, the Handley Page O/400 that they had flown from Egypt, to India's North-West Frontier.[2] A squadron had been preparing to use it against an invading Afghan army when a great storm hit its aerodrome, wrecking the aeroplane.

According to an account later written by Ross, things initially seemed hopeless but his 'heart pangs were mitigated' when he shortly afterwards learned that the Australian Commonwealth Government had offered a £10,000 prize to the first airman to fly from Britain to Australia within 30 days. Soon after this, claimed Ross, Borton was recalled to London, which 'opened the avenue of transport for myself and my two mechanics'. Accordingly, with Borton (who could not enter the competition because he was not Australian), Ross, Shiers and Bennett sailed for Britain shortly afterwards, intent on entering the Commonwealth Government's England-to-Australia air race.[3]

Yet this version fails to corroborate with other surviving primary sources. According to both Borton and Shiers, the party had learned of the England-to-Australia air race in Singapore before returning to India in mid-June. Neither recorded the date on which this occurred, but it was probably between 6 and 11 April when the *Minto* was docked at Singapore, although it might also have been in late May when Ross and Borton passed through again on their respective journeys to Siam and Borneo.[4]

Borton simply claims that, 'On return to Singapore we heard news of the prize' and that, as it was only open to Australian competitors, 'this ruled me out'.[5] According to Shiers, they were relaxing in the Dominions Club in Singapore when a ship's captain handed them a newspaper from Australia. It reported an announcement, made by the government in March that, 'with a view of stimulating aerial activity', it would award a £10,000 prize to the first Australian airman to fly from England to Australia. The idea originated with Prime Minister William Morris Hughes who, while visiting Europe for the Paris Peace Conference, had been impressed by the potential that aviation offered Australia. Although the rules had yet to be determined, the competing aircraft would need to be 'manned by Australians' and supplied by the crews themselves. Competitors would also be responsible for making 'all other necessary arrangements' for fuel and supplies along the route.[6]

It seems likely, therefore, that Ross returned to Calcutta in June already aware of the competition. If this is true, it did not alter his plans to attempt the flight to Australia from India, with Borton, as soon as possible. In a letter written to Keith on 29 April from the Dutch East Indies, Ross expected Borton to return to London to report on their expedition while he waited in India for his return. 'We expect to start our flight from India to Australia about 1st Jan. next year [1920],' he explained.[7] As late as August 1919, several weeks after their return to India and after they had learned about the unfortunate fate of their Handley Page O/400, Borton and Ross were still planning to fly to Australia, independently of the Australian government's prize. Writing to Ross's mother, Borton explained that he hoped, on his return to London, 'to persuade the Air Ministry to give us a machine to fly out to Australia so that we can complete the work which we have already done'. He looked forward to meeting Jessie Smith upon their arrival in Adelaide.[8]

It isn't surprising that Ross would, at this stage, pass up the opportunity to compete for the Australian government's £10,000 prize: he had at least three good reasons for doing so. First, he had experienced at first hand the challenges a crew would face in attempting to fly from India to Australia, where the few possible landing grounds posed both danger and difficulties ranging from the logistical and meteorological to the political. As the earliest reports on the Australian competition indicated, competitors would need to make all such arrangements themselves. It would be understandable if Ross believed that he had a better chance of successfully flying the route with official British government support than doing so independently. Second, to compete in the Australian competition, Ross would need to acquire his own aircraft. He had no contacts in the British aircraft industry and no capacity to acquire some from India. Finally, Ross must have felt a sense of loyalty to Borton, whose British nationality precluded him from the competition. Indeed, the two men had become the best of friends. As Borton wrote to Jessie Smith, 'there is no man I would sooner have with me on such a trip than your son. As you know, he and I have been together for 2½ years and I have the greatest admiration and affection for him.'[9] Indeed, six decades later, shortly before the end of his life, Borton would describe Ross as 'one of my greatest friends'.[10]

Borton arranged for Ross, Bennett and Shiers to accompany him back to Britain, where they could report to the Air Ministry on their survey expedition and try their best to acquire an aircraft with which to attempt the flight to Australia. Before leaving India, however, the party travelled to the North-West Frontier where the RAF and Anglo-Indian Army were fighting what would become known as the Third Anglo-Afghan War. Ross had heard about the conflict while in the Dutch East Indies and hoped to 'get back in time to get mixed up in it'.[11] As things turned out, he was—although there is practically nothing documented about his involvement in the three-month war that occurred in mid-1919 along the Indian–Afghan border. Bennett and Shiers were attached to No. 31 Squadron RAF at Risalpur between 7 July and 16 August to supervise the rigging of Bristol Fighters.[12] Ross was likewise 'temporarily attached' to this squadron, although it appears for only a few days in late July 1919, before he was posted to RAF HQ in Simla (Borton apparently was too).[13] The squadron's record books have not survived, so the only evidence of Ross's activities comes from an account that an elderly Shiers provided some 50 years later. He remembered that Ross 'got into a couple of the light machines they had up there' and reconnoitred the mountainous passes connecting British India and Afghanistan. 'Eventually Ross went up and he did some good work bombing in these Bristol fighters, and after about a week the Afghan threw it in.'[14] Given to exaggeration and muddling details, Shiers' account is questionable. Without further corroborating evidence, however, we can only assume that Ross did some flying on the North-West Frontier while Shiers and Bennett put their experience in maintaining aircraft under service conditions to good use. Of the three men, only Shiers would live long enough to claim the British Army's India General Service campaign medal with its 'Afghanistan N.W.F. 1919' clasp—a somewhat unusual award for a member of the AIF.

Along with the others, on 25 August Ross embarked from Bombay aboard a British troopship bound for Southampton. As officers, he and Borton had a pleasant enough voyage but, as the only Australians below decks, Shiers and Bennett experienced some difficulties, apparently being locked in the brig at one point as suspected stowaways.[15]

Arriving in Britain in mid-September, Borton took the three Australians to stay with his family at Cheveney House, the Borton family's estate in Kent. 'My word, it was a most marvellous place, we couldn't believe our eyes,' recalled Shiers.[16] On various occasions during the following two months, Ross and his mechanics would enjoy the hospitality of the Borton family, and the bucolic charms of their estate's extensive gardens and lakes.

Shortly after arriving in Britain, Ross telephoned the AIF Administrative Headquarters on Horseferry Road in London to report in and ask for orders. He was, perhaps, surprised to be put through to his old CO and mentor, Lieutenant Colonel Richard Williams, now serving as the AIF Staff Officer for Aviation. Although Williams' principal work concerned the repatriation of the AFC's personnel and equipment, he had also become responsible for organising the England-to-Australia air race on behalf of the Commonwealth Government.[17] Hearing that Ross and Borton had recently surveyed the route themselves, Williams immediately arranged with the Air Ministry to have them come to London to brief him and the competitors.[18]

The conference took place at the Air Ministry's headquarters at Adastral House on 19 September and attracted several Australian airmen who were interested in entering the competition. Senior RAF staff, representatives of the Royal Aero Club and a number of British aviation firms also attended.

Proceedings began with a commitment by the RAF to provide competitors with all the support they required at its aerodromes between Britain and India. Indeed, the Air Ministry's Controller General of Civil Aviation regarded the competition 'as more than a mere prize competition', recognising its potential to 'contribute to aerial development'.[19]

Borton then provided a briefing on what pilots could expect to find beyond Calcutta. He emphasised the difficulty they were likely to face given the few landing grounds likely to be available to them in the near future and he emphasised the danger some would pose to a pilot who had not inspected them personally. Ross spoke about what he had found in Siam and indicated a couple of places that might be suitable for landing an aircraft on the eastern coast of the Malay Peninsula. Ultimately, concluded Borton, the lack of aerodromes probably restricted pilots to using seaplanes if they hoped to make it to Australia. Even then, he predicted that it would be 'extremely difficult' to complete the journey inside the 30 days stipulated in the competition's conditions.

The briefing thus poured cold water on the government's air race plans. Suddenly and unequivocally, the reality of what competitors would face had been laid out by the only two men in the world qualified to speak authoritatively on the subject. On his copy of the agenda, next to the point 'Whether the route can be considered available for aeroplanes beyond Calcutta', one of the RAF personnel in attendance annotated 'NO'. Recognising this too, Williams pointed out to those in attendance that to cross the Dutch East Indies (where there were currently no prepared landing sites), a competitor would require an aircraft with a range of 2000 miles (3200 kilometres)—an endurance beyond any aeroplane's capabilities at the time. The meeting concluded with Lieutenant Commander Harold Perrin, Secretary of the Royal Aero Club, offering to refund the entry fee of any competitor who wanted to withdraw.[20]

26

GOD 'ELP ALL OF US!

Surprisingly, after Ross and Borton's briefing at Adastral House on 19 September 1919, four of the Australian entrants and the aircraft companies that backed them remained in the competition.[1] A few days later, these plucky competitors attended another meeting, this time at AIF Administrative Headquarters, where Ross provided another detailed briefing on what he thought needed to be done to prepare aerodromes in Burma, Siam, Malaya, Singapore and the Dutch East Indies.[2] Williams secured the Australian Defence Department's permission to fund the conversion of racecourses at Rangoon and Singapore into temporary landing grounds and to dispatch a party of AFC officers, including some of Ross's former squadron mates, to survey an aerial route between Darwin and Melbourne.[3]

At some point during the following few weeks, Ross decided that he too should enter the England-to-Australia air race.[4] This apparently followed the Air Ministry's refusal to provide him and Borton with an aeroplane to attempt the route themselves. The reason is not recorded, but we do know that in August, the Chief of Air Staff, Air Marshal Sir Hugh Trenchard, expressed reservations about allowing Borton to continue with his work on the air route to Australia, given the RAF's shortage of senior personnel.[5]

Before Ross could enter the competition, however, he needed an aeroplane. On his behalf, Major General Sir Geoffrey Salmond and Borton approached Vickers Limited, one of the nation's premier arms manufacturers. The managers of the firm's aviation division were interested in backing an Australian crew for the race but, while they had considered several pilots (including some with external financial backing), they had not found any that they felt qualified to trust with one of their machines.[6]

With Salmond and Borton's endorsement, however, Vickers' management agreed to sponsor Ross: the company would supply him with an aeroplane and the spare parts and fuel to enter the race to Australia.[7] Ross would later gratefully acknowledge the crucial support of Salmond and, in particular, Borton, in securing Vickers' support.[8] But it is also likely that the executives of Vickers aviation department recognised that, of the 1500 or so Australians who had learned to fly during the war, Ross possessed skills and experience that uniquely qualified him for this venture. He was perhaps the only Australian who had experience in flying large, twin-engine aircraft long distances and, besides Borton, the only pilot in the world who possessed a first-hand knowledge of landing sites between Cairo and Timor.

Vickers offered Ross one of its F.B.27 Vimy bombers. Designed to raid Berlin but deployed too late to contribute to wartime operations, the Vimy had nevertheless achieved international recognition in June 1919 as the aircraft flown by Captain John Alcock and Lieutenant Arthur Brown on the first non-stop trans-Atlantic flight. Although slightly smaller and lighter than the Handley Page O/400, the Vimy employed the same basic design, being a twin-engine biplane with two open cockpits—one forward and the other aft of the wings—and an open nacelle in the aircraft's nose.

Peter McMillan, who in 1994 built and flew a replica Vimy from Britain to Australia, recalled that 'you can't help but be awed by the size of the machine'. Its bottom wing was about shoulder height, while the top wing sat about 5 metres off the ground. The ailerons alone, he observed, were each nearly the size of a Cessna 172's wing. Each of the propellers' four blades was the height of an average-sized man. Like the Handley Page O/400, the tail of the Vimy resembled a large box-kite. 'There's two of everything,' explained McMillan: 'Two rudders, two vertical fins, two elevators, two stabilizers. And all the control cables are external, so the rear fuselage looks like a giant guitar.'[9]

Although powered by the same 360-horsepower Rolls-Royce Eagle VIII engines as the O/400, in its standard flying configuration the Vimy had a longer range. Cruising at 80 miles (128 kilometres) per hour, it could fly nearly 1500 kilometres between refuelling stops.[10] With its bomb load replaced by additional fuel and oil tanks, the Vimy's range could, in theory, nearly be doubled.[11]

Vickers entered into a partnership with Ross, expecting to invest between £5000 and £6000 on the aircraft, spare parts and fuel.[12] It was a considerable sum, considering that Ross's AIF salary at the time was £410—and indeed, a relatively large investment when measured against the £10,000 prize on offer. The company was not interested in a financial return, however, informing Ross that if he won, he could keep the cash and that the aircraft should be presented to the Commonwealth Government as a gift. Rather, Vickers was in the race for the publicity. With the war over, it needed a new civilian market for its aircraft. It wanted to demonstrate that Vickers aircraft were not only capable of trans-continental flight, but safe and reliable too. Accordingly, the assistant manager of Vickers' aviation department, Walter Caddell, emphasised the importance of the flight's success. 'A great deal of business is tied up with a successful trip,' he explained to Ross. 'On your side the question of the prize is important but from various talks we have had I believe that you will not sacrifice a safe arrival on account of being hurried by some other competitor for the sake of the prizemoney.'[13]

To maximise publicity, Vickers also negotiated a deal with Keith Murdoch's United Cable Service for exclusive coverage of the flight. In doing so, the company ensured that 250 newspapers around the world would report on the progress made by its aeroplane.[14] In exchange for £500 if he won (and £100 if he did not), Ross agreed to send an account of each stage of the journey by cable to Murdoch's agency in London. The contract he signed forbade him from speaking to other news agencies or, indeed, anyone who might allow a rival news agency to scoop the story. Murdoch instructed Ross to provide him with 'graphic accounts' and 'good, long racy despatches', and to ensure that 'at all hazards news gets through'.[15]

The Royal Aero Club received Ross's race entry on 18 October 1919.[16] By this time, five other crews were busy preparing their own aircraft for the long flight to Australia. Captain George Matthews and Sergeant Thomas Kay planned to fly a 'Wallaby', a single-engine prototype built by the Sopwith Aviation Company, to compete in the race. The small Alliance Aviation Company entered its P.2 Seabird crewed by Lieutenants Roger Douglas and James Ross. Blackburn sponsored a four-man crew led by Captain Hubert Wilkins to compete in one of its twin-engine RT1 'Kangaroos'. Captain Cedric Howell and Lieutenant George Fraser had convinced Martinsyde to provide them with a Type A Mk 1—a version of its 'Buzzard' fighter that had been adapted for long-range flying. Lieutenants Ray Parer and John McIntosh were in the process of finding a benefactor to purchase them a single-engine Airco DH.9 from surplus war stocks to enter into the race. Unofficially, French aviators Etienne Poulet and Jean Benoist had also announced that they would attempt the flight in a twin-engine Caudron biplane. While not eligible for the Australian government's prize, they had expressed determination to be first to fly from England to Australia.[17]

Reviewing the entries at AIF Headquarters, Richard Williams told his wife that, of all of them, Ross alone possessed the experience and resources to reach Australia within 30 days.[18] The lateness of his entry did, however, put him at a disadvantage: by the time Ross signed an agreement with Vickers, the first of his competitors were ready to begin. With his entry, Ross notified the Royal Aero Club and the press that he intended to leave Britain within a fortnight.[19]

Selecting a crew seems to have been relatively straightforward.[20] Bennett and Shiers were obvious choices, having proven themselves during the Cairo-to-Calcutta flight: they readily agreed to join as the Vimy's mechanics. Competition rules stipulated that each crew also required a 'competent navigator'.[21] To Ross, the natural choice seemed to be his older brother, Keith, who was at the time still in Britain waiting to be repatriated.

Ross did not record anything about the first meeting he had with Keith after returning to Britain in 1919. Shiers, however, recalled standing outside a club on Horseferry Road in London when 'all of a sudden a chap sang out "Hullo, Ross!" And he said "My God, there's my brother!" . . . So he walked over and they shook hands.'[22] Ross and Keith's reunion must have been a jubilant one. The two brothers, who had been inseparable as children and shared the same circle of friends as young adults, had not seen each other in five years. Perhaps, however, the conversation soon turned to their younger brother, Colin, who had died at Passchendaele two years earlier, and from there to other friends from home who had not survived the Great War.

After several unsuccessful attempts to join the AIF, Keith had paid his own passage to Britain in 1917, where he joined the RFC. He learned to fly and then served as an instructor, training other pilots in Britain. During two years of death-defying work training novices how not to kill themselves (and him), Keith earned a reputation as a 'keen and efficient' officer and a pilot of 'unusual ability'.[23] Despite not seeing combat, he gained extensive experience in the air—some 459 hours on twenty different aircraft types. Keith's navigational experience appears to have been comparatively limited though: his log book records a three-week stint at the Admiralty Compass Observatory at Slough in January 1919 and only a few cross-country flights in Britain. Indeed, the vast majority of Keith's many hours of flying had been on short, instructional flights within sight of his aerodrome.[24] Clearly, there were more qualified navigators in Britain but Ross nevertheless chose his brother.

Vickers left planning the route up to Ross.[25] He worked out a schedule of landings that would see them fly on eighteen days, on each covering distances of up to 1500 kilometres. They would rest on seven days and, if everything went well, arrive in Darwin with five days to spare.[26]

As far as Calcutta, Ross would use the aerodromes of the RAF and its counterparts in France and Italy. Beyond India, however, he had to make his own arrangements. Stopping in Singapore was mandatory under the competition's rules; a 'control station' there would inspect seals on competing aircraft to ensure they had not been substantially modified en route.[27] Reviewing the notes he had made during his survey expedition with Borton, Ross decided that Rangoon's and Singapore's racecourses, and the Siamese air force base at Don Muang, represented his best options for landing grounds in the Far East—he hoped to avoid landing anywhere else between Calcutta and Singapore.[28] All Vickers needed to do was arrange local distributors of Shell fuel and Wakefield oil, both of which had agreed to sponsor the competition, to have stocks ready at these locations by Ross's planned arrival dates.

The flight's final 3400 kilometres, between Singapore and Darwin, posed greater difficulties. 'Coming as it does after some 10,000 miles of flying,' considered the editor of the weekly aviation magazine *Flight*, this stage would be comparable in difficulty to Alcock and Brown's trans-Atlantic flight.[29] Besides a Dutch aviation school at Bandoeng on Java, a third of the way between Singapore and Darwin, there were as yet no other prepared grounds in the Indies archipelago. Ross had identified a handful of locations where airstrips might be cleared and levelled, but all required work before a pilot could safely use them. Concerned that official approaches to the Dutch Government via the British Foreign Office were taking too long, Ross took matters into his own hands. On 14 October, he personally cabled the Governor-General of the Dutch East Indies, Count Johan Paul van Limburg Stirum, to whom he had reported in Batavia in May, asking him to prepare a landing ground at Bima on the island of Sumbawa; he anticipated reaching Java on 15 November.[30] On Ross's behalf, General Borton also cabled one of his counterparts in the Dutch aviation corps at Bandoeng asking for his assistance.[31] Ten days later, a reply from Dutch authorities reported that several aerodromes were being prepared, including one at Bima, but that it would not be ready until 1 December.[32]

The news that the Dutch were building additional aerodromes between Batavia and Port Darwin 'greatly eased' Ross's mind. It meant that he would now be able to make shorter flights in the final stage of the journey and that the Vimy could carry a smaller fuel capacity. The saving in weight made the aircraft easier and safer to fly and put less strain on the engines.[33] The additional time required by Dutch authorities to prepare the aerodrome at Bima, however, forced Ross to delay his start from England by two weeks, until mid-November. On 31 October, Vickers cabled the Dutch Governor-General on Ross's behalf, indicating that he now planned to arrive in the Dutch East Indies on 1 December.[34]

With the 'office work' in London complete, Ross, Keith, Shiers and Bennett moved to Weybridge, where Vickers had its aircraft factory at the Brooklands aerodrome.[35] Arriving there, Ross perhaps recalled with fondness the summery bank holiday Monday he had spent at Brooklands with the mounted cadets back in August 1910. Maybe he reflected on how far aviation had come in less than a decade: from the frail contraptions he and his young friends had watched trundling across the grass and pitching into the adjacent stream to the Vimy that he now planned to fly halfway around the globe to Australia.

Vickers provided Ross with the aircraft that had been the back-up machine for Alcock and Brown's trans-Atlantic flight. It had an RAF serial number (F8630) but to comply with new international regulations for civilian aircraft, the Air Ministry issued it a new number, which Vickers' staff painted on the wings and fuselage in large white letters: G-EAOU. Ross and the others wryly decided that, given the challenges that lay ahead, this represented a fitting acronym: 'God 'elp all of us!'

The staff at Weybridge threw everything they had behind getting the aircraft ready for Ross and his crew as soon as possible. 'It was gratifying to observe that these same men and women, who had produced the great machine flown by Sir John Alcock, felt that their efforts were something more than labour,' he wrote.[36]

Assisted by Shiers and Bennett, the Vickers mechanics stripped the aircraft's fabric and reinforced its airframe by replacing the standard-issue tacks with screws.[37] They also removed G-EAOU's gun mountings and bomb racks to make space for additional fuel and spare parts. The challenge here emerged as a compromise between carrying enough to support the crew in far-flung and poorly supplied aerodromes and maintaining a safe operating weight. Ross knew that Alcock and Brown had flown across the Atlantic with a Vimy weighing 6350 kilograms. Faced with a significantly longer journey, he was determined to shed at least 500 kilograms to help preserve the engines. Accordingly, they increased the Vimy's fuel and oil capacities to provide only a couple of extra hours' endurance beyond the aircraft's standard configuration.[38] Capable of staying airborne for thirteen hours, G-EAOU had a range of 1600 kilometres. Ross described this as 'ample' in his post-flight account and, for most of the stages he planned, it would be.[39] But G-EAOU's range was, in fact, only 80 kilometres greater than the longest stretch that Ross and Keith planned—the flight from Singapore to Kalidjati in West Java.[40]

The brothers debated whether or not to carry a wireless set but decided to leave it behind. 'It would weigh a hundred and fifty pounds and would not be worth it,' reasoned Ross. 'Unless we had the means of giving an absolutely accurate position, what would be the use of sending out a SOS call and wasting people's time looking for us?'[41]

Ross and Keith would occupy the aircraft's forward cockpit, squeezed in together side by side with the tips of the huge, four-bladed propellers passing a couple of feet from their heads. The Vimy's cockpit had only one set of controls—a large wheel on the right side, mounted on top of a control wheel, and a set of rudder pedals, both connected to the aircraft's control surfaces by a system of chains, wires and pulleys. Keeping the aircraft in level flight required constant physical effort so, to assist Ross in maintaining this for several hours at a time, the mechanics at Vickers installed adjustable shock-absorbers to both the rudder pedals and control column. With these, Ross could fly practically 'hands off' during spells of good weather.[42]

Without time to ship supplies ahead, the crew assiduously compiled an inventory of what they determined to be the essentials in terms of spare parts and tools to carry. Besides thousands of screws, nuts, washers and springs, G-EAOU's cargo would include a replacement axle, tail skid and a wheel.[43] This vast inventory of spares was 'stored in every corner of the machine and tied on outside'.[44] The crew would carry a couple of cameras and a supply of film that Kodak had provided to each of the competing crews to document their journey. The company announced that it would award £800 to the crew that produced the best set of 50 negatives.[45]

A compulsive smoker, Ross commissioned an inventor to design a device that would allow him to smoke safely in the cockpit; he had something in mind along the lines of the Davy safety lamp that miners used. The inventor failed to come up with anything suitable in time so, alongside the other discomforts of flying for several hours at a time in an open cockpit, Ross would have to endure nicotine withdrawal.[46]

In case of an emergency landing, the Vimy's cargo also included a small survival kit with some fishing tackle and seven days' worth of biscuits, chocolate, tinned meat and Bovril. The crew also carried a rifle and a revolver 'in case', as Ross explained to journalists, 'of a forced landing among hostile natives'.[47] In any case, as Borton told the aviation press, much of the terrain between Calcutta and Darwin would offer a pilot only a 'slight chance' of surviving an unscheduled landing.[48]

After long days in the hangars at Brooklands, Ross and Keith spent evenings in a Weybridge hotel plotting their route across the globe.[49] Using indelible pencils, they marked out a course, measured in 20-mile (32-kilometre) increments across dozens of navigational charts representing Europe, the Middle East and Asia.[50] 'Long before we left England,' wrote Ross, 'we had practically visualised most of the country that we were to fly over.'[51]

In clear weather, Keith would track their progress by visually identifying landmarks. When clouds obscured the ground, however, and when flying over deserts and oceans, he would need to estimate their position by 'dead reckoning': a calculation based on a compass reading and data from an instrument known as a speed and drift indicator that measured the effect of wind on the aircraft's speed and bearing. It is not recorded whether Keith—or Ross, for that matter—had doubts that his limited navigational experience in England had equipped him to navigate them across continents and oceans.

At the final weigh-in G-EAOU's cargo of fuel, spare parts and navigational instruments came in at just under 3000 kilograms—as much as the aircraft weighed empty. This was heavier than the maximum weight with which Ross wanted to fly but, unwilling to sacrifice any of the spare parts, he insisted the crew leave behind most of their personal luggage. Ross and his companions would leave Britain carrying only a small bag of kit each.[52]

As October drew to a close, it must have become evident to Ross that they would not have been ready to start before the end of the month, even if the Dutch airfields had been ready to receive them.[53] A pair of new Rolls-Royce engines only arrived at Weybridge in the final week of October and it was 4 November before G-EAOU received its airworthiness certificate from the Air Ministry.[54] Ross and his team found it 'galling' to wait while watching the winter weather close in and the first of their competitors begin their journey to Australia.[55] The French crew, Etienne Poulet and Jean Benoist, started first, leaving on 14 October in a twin-engine Caudron G4 biplane. The first of the official entrants, Captain George Matthews and his mechanic Sergeant Thomas Kay, left England in their Sopwith Wallaby on 21 October. They made it to Cologne a couple of days later; there, snow storms grounded them for the next ten days.

On 31 October, in wet, misty conditions, G-EAOU made its first test-flight. Vickers gave the responsibility to the trans-Atlantic flyer, Captain Sir John Alcock. Ross and Keith joined him as passengers. It was apparently their first time flying together and their first trip in a Vimy.[56] Presumably, Ross sat in the forward cockpit beside Alcock where he could scrutinise his handling of the controls.[57] After Alcock's test flight, G-EAOU remained on the ground for the next eight days. The weather was 'abominable' this week, according to Ross: 'driving sleet and pelting rains fell almost without intermission'.[58] The mechanics took the opportunity to make some final adjustments to the aircraft. Discovering a fault in the starboard engine's radiator, they replaced it with the equivalent part from the Vimy that Alcock and Brown had flown across the Atlantic.[59]

On the afternoon of 9 November, Ross and Keith took advantage of a short break in the weather to take the Vimy up for another test. They put the aircraft through its paces in the overcast skies above Surrey for 55 minutes before landing back at Brooklands. Ross enjoyed flying the Vimy and found it a superior aircraft to the Handley Page O/400 'in every way'. While we might have expected him to say this publicly, given his obligations to his sponsors, he also voiced his admiration of the Vimy privately.[60]

During his 27 years, Ross had had more experience of international travel than many of his peers. As he realised, though, this journey represented something else altogether—something that, besides the prospect of an enormous cash prize and international renown, might have historical significance. If successful, Ross's journey home this time would be the longest ever continuous flight: over 20,000 kilometres, the equivalent of halfway around the globe at its equatorial circumference. It would demonstrate the possibility of trans-continental aviation and connect Australia to Europe—if not yet practically, then at least theoretically—by air.

Though they did not mention it in any record that survives, we might well expect that Ross and his companions felt some measure of anxiety about the thousands of kilometres of wilderness, weather and rough, makeshift aerodromes and that stretched out ahead, separating them from home and family—not to mention the possibility of fame and fortune.

27

CLASS 5—UNFIT FOR ALL FLYING

Tuesday, 11 November 1919 found Ross and his companions 'pottering around' the hangars at Weybridge.[1] G-EAOU stood ready, loaded with spares and fuel, safe from the bitter squalls, sleet and rain outside.

At 3 p.m., the storm abruptly stopped: the clouds cleared and the sun came out, soon burning away the fog that had concealed Brooklands aerodrome for days. Seizing the opportunity, Ross called the Vickers' mechanics to wheel the Vimy out onto the tarmac and start its engines.

At 4.15 p.m., with indications of 'a bright, fine evening' ahead, Ross, Keith, Jim Bennett and Wally Shiers climbed aboard and took off.[2] Turning north-east, Ross flew over London's outer suburbs towards Hounslow aerodrome, the official starting point for the race. It irked Ross that he could not simply start from Brooklands; it was, after all, only 10 kilometres from Hounslow. When he requested an exemption, Richard Williams had refused, concerned that it might attract criticism given their relationship.[3] In this, Williams demonstrated great foresight as Ross would later need to defend himself against accusations that he had received preferential treatment that unfairly advantaged him over the other competitors.

With G-EAOU ready to start from Hounslow the following morning, Ross and his companions spent the night with Walter Caddell, assistant to the aviation branch manager at Vickers. They woke before daylight and, peering outside, were encouraged by the sight of stars in the sky; a thick white frost covered the ground. At 6.40 a.m., as they ate breakfast, Keith scribbled a short note to his parents, explaining that they hoped to start for home in a couple of hours' time: 'this morning very cold and the ground all white'.[4]

Caddell drove them to the aerodrome, where they found a small group of spectators—mostly officials and journalists—waiting to see them off. By the time they arrived, a heavy ground mist had settled and shortly afterwards a meteorological report from the Air Ministry predicted weather across the first stage to Lyon as being 'Class 5'—unfit for all flying.[5] Ross had made his mind up, though: they were going. Aerodrome staff wheeled the Vimy out of its hangar and filled the radiators with water. An official from the Royal Aero Club inspected the machine and attached five seals to its airframe which Ross would need to produce, intact, in both Singapore and Darwin to claim the prizemoney.

Just before climbing up into the cockpit, Ross spoke with one of Murdoch's journalists. He seemed confident, telling the reporter that they would not only reach Australia but that they would do so within the competition's 30-day time limit. The crew had prepared thoroughly—although, as Ross admitted, the weather represented a variable that they could not control: 'We are going to pass through every variety of climate. We are all fit, the machine is fit and everything is as right as possible. Whatever happens, Australia can feel that we have left nothing undone for the success of this great enterprise.' The reporter stood back and watched as Ross joined his companions aboard G-EAOU:

> The natural-tinted Vimy looked the picture of sturdy strength as it stood there against its chocks on the sward of long grass, turned to feathery white by the thick frost which the whirring propeller whisked into the faces of bystanders in cold dust . . . A few minutes before 9 o'clock the machine taxied slowly to the centre of the field, and with no further adieus than the waving of arms the brave airmen were away.[6]

Just as they lifted clear of Hounslow's grass runway, the crew heard a 'bang'. They presumed that the Vimy's undercarriage had hit a camera, set up on a tripod on the airfield by a press photographer keen to secure a photograph.[7]

As Ross circled, climbing to 2000 feet, the ground rapidly disappeared in the mist. Satisfied that the engines were running well, he used the large, prismatic compass on his instrument panel to set a course towards Folkestone on the English coast.

The weather conditions deteriorated as G-EAOU made its way south-east across Surrey and Kent. Unable to see the ground, Ross missed a final generous gesture from the Bortons: 'GOD SPEED' painted in 15 feet-high letters on the lawn at Cheveney.[8] As they neared the coast, Keith spotted the railway line to Ashford through a break in the clouds: they were on course. Above Lympne, Ross saw clearer skies ahead: for a few moments, he could see all the way across the white-capped sea of the Channel to Boulogne, their next waypoint. Ross would recall feeling confident as they left Britain behind, reassured by the 'one long-sustained rhythmic' drone of the aircraft's engine exhausts. 'This melody of power boomed pleasantly in my ears,' he recollected. 'My mind sought to probe the inscrutable future as we swept over the coast of England at 90 miles per hour.'[9]

The Vimy had a clear run across the Channel, but over the French coast Ross was confronted by a wall of clouds. Hoping this represented only a local storm cell, he tried steering G-EAOU into the towering barrier of nimbus, only to be blinded by a deluge of snow. Ross banked, turning the aircraft around, and the Vimy emerged into the sun above the French coast. Shutting off the throttles, he glided down to try to fly beneath the storm. Finding a whiteout and unsure of where he might encounter mountains, he again withdrew from the snow-storm's maelstrom and circled.

Perhaps Ross contemplated turning back for home to try again another day, but instead he opened the throttles and climbed in wide, ascending spirals off the western edge of the weather system. Finally, at 9000 feet, the crew could look down onto a sea of cloud extending out across Europe to the horizon. Keith provided Ross with a south-easterly compass bearing that would take them across France to Lyon, 550 kilometres away.

For three hours, Ross held the Vimy in a level cruise over an epic cloudscape that obscured the ground from view. Unable to fix the plane's position visually, Keith used the Vimy's airspeed and bearing to estimate the position, marking it off every fifteen minutes on his map.

Although the sun shone brightly above the clouds, at 9000 feet the temperature dropped to –14°C. The crew 'just about froze to death', wrote Ross. 'It was intensely cold. Our breath froze on our face masks.'[10] From time to time, they encountered immense columns of cloud that offered Ross no alternative but to fly right through them. Snow filled the Vimy's cockpits and ice formed on its wings; the aircraft's pitot, which measured airspeed, froze and stopped working. In the midst of these snow clouds, Shiers sometimes lost sight of Ross and Keith sitting just a few metres away in the forward cockpit.[11] When his goggles iced over, Ross had to remove them so he could read the compass: 'We suffered much agony . . . straining into the 90-mile-an-hour snow blast.'[12] Later, Ross admitted to Biffy Borton that he was 'thoroughly frightened' during this stage of the journey.[13]

At lunchtime, Keith reached for their packed sandwiches only to find them frozen solid. He was glad they had worn lambskin-lined boots and gloves, as well as balaclavas.[14] Still, the cold penetrated their bodies and, as the afternoon wore on, Ross 'was almost too frozen to operate the controls'.[15]

Around 2.30 p.m., five frigid hours since leaving Hounslow, Ross spotted a break in the clouds. Circling down to 1000 feet, he and Keith found themselves over a town that, to their enormous relief, appeared to be Roanne. Despite not seeing the ground for three hours, they had remained on course. Ostensibly a vindication of his navigational skills, Keith privately admitted: 'we were lucky.'[16] Forty-five minutes later Ross landed on the snow-covered aerodrome at Lyon. The crew were so stiff and sore that they could barely walk.

But the day's work had not yet finished. As would become a ritual at the end of each leg, after landing Shiers and Bennett checked over the aircraft for anything that needed repairing or adjusting. They emptied the radiators so that the water would not freeze overnight and crack them. Normally

Ross and Keith would refuel the aircraft, decanting petrol from dozens of individual cans into the Vimy's tanks through a chamois. Lyon aerodrome, however, appeared deserted and there was no sign of the fuel Vickers had ordered before leaving Britain. It was only as night was falling that some French aviation service personnel arrived, shaking their heads in disbelief that anyone had flown in such impossible conditions. Unable to speak French, Ross and Keith did their best to communicate that they required fuel and oil delivered in the morning.

The French had no hangars to offer nor anyone to guard the aircraft overnight so Shiers and Bennett volunteered to camp out beside the Vimy while Ross and Keith, hitching a ride into town, booked into a hotel. Sleeping out in the snow must have been a bitter proposition for the mechanics after the day they had just endured, and it illustrates their commitment to what they saw as 'their' aircraft. Ross would come to admire the way Shiers and Bennett 'refused to leave the machine after dark' unless on a RAF airfield under guard. 'Even during daylight I had difficulty in getting them away from the machine to have their food,' he said.[17]

Arriving in their room four hours after landing, Ross and Keith opened their toiletry bags to find their few personal possessions still frozen into a solid block. They felt jubilant though, having completed their great journey's first 800 kilometres in the face of unimaginably bad flying conditions. 'Sleep that night was very welcome,' wrote Keith in his diary. 'And we required no rocking.'[18]

28

CROSSING THE MEDITERRANEAN

Ross and Keith returned to Lyon aerodrome at dawn to find it deserted. Their fuel was nowhere to be seen.

It took two hours for Keith to find their 1300 litres and then another couple of hours to fill the Vimy's tanks and radiators. The language barrier presented further frustrating delays when Ross approached one of the airfield's French mechanics and asked for 100 litres of hot water to fill the radiators. The Frenchman returned shortly afterwards with a freshly boiled kettle. A second attempt, this time by Keith, employing 'that Australian tongue, famed alike for its potency and rhetoric', saw the man return with a second kettle.[1] Shires and Bennett improvised, using a blowtorch to heat water in discarded petrol tins. 'The French were very nice but messed us about,' wrote Ross, diplomatically.[2]

Finally, just after 10 a.m., Ross took off and circled to gain altitude before setting a southerly course towards the French Riviera. He and Keith planned to reach the Mediterranean and then follow the coastline most of the way to Rome—a journey as long as the one they had made the previous day but, they hoped, in better weather. It looked promising: 'hazy but otherwise alright for flying', according to Keith's diary.[3]

Ross followed the Rhône River south as far as Avignon, with the weather improving along the way. 'Today was great flying with only a few clouds about and a bright sun shining,' wrote Ross. 'The Alps all snow covered looked very fine in the bright light.' Ross added that it was 'not so cold today' at their cruising altitude of 8000 feet, only a few degrees below zero.[4]

At Avignon, Ross turned south-east and shortly after G-EAOU arrived over the coast, just west of Cannes. 'We were then experiencing splendid weather and the Mediterranean was a beautiful colour,' recalled Ross. 'We wanted to stop for a week it looked so lovely.'[5] From Cannes, Ross followed this striking coastal geography east. He circled over Nice, while the crew waved to a large crowd on the Promenade des Anglais. Next came Monte Carlo, where Ross picked out the town's famous casino and terraced gardens. Bennett, Shiers and Keith did their best to capture the stunning scenery with the cameras and film that Kodak had provided to each competing crew, along with the promise of a cash prize for the best set of negatives.

Ross continued above the coastline as far as Sanremo before setting out across the Gulf of Genoa towards Pisa. The crossing, which took them 80 kilometres over open water, was uneventful until, close to the Italian coast, one of the port engine exhaust manifolds 'blew out badly'. It made the engine noise considerably louder but, of greater concern, Ross noticed how the uncontained exhaust flame burnt a hole in an aluminium tray beneath it and then began licking at the engine's petrol strainer.[6] Perhaps it was this moment that produced an alarming note scrawled in the pocketbook that Ross and Keith used to communicate with each other in the air: 'ANY CHANCE FIRE[?]'[7]

Ross thought so: he had planned to finish the day's flying in Rome but, considering it too dangerous to continue, decided to land at the nearest available aerodrome: Pisa.[8] In his published account of the flight, Ross would make no mention of the blown-out manifold, instead attributing the diversion to the fact that it was getting dark.[9] Yet G-EAOU's log book and Keith's diary both indicate that they reached Pisa had 2.45 p.m.—leaving enough time to reach Rome before sunset had it not been for the problem with the exhaust manifold.[10] This would not be the only time during the flight to Australia that Ross would contrive to avoid publicly mentioning mechanical issues that might reflect badly on Vickers and Rolls-Royce.[11]

From the air, Ross thought the aerodrome at Pisa looked safe.[12] As he eased the Vimy onto its grassy surface in a whirlwind of mud and water, however, it became clear that the recent storms had waterlogged the airfield. The Vimy safely completed its landing roll but then, while taxiing towards the hangars, the undercarriage sank into the sodden airfield and became bogged. A team of Italian mechanics armed with shovels and planks came out to assist but, despite their best efforts, could not get the aircraft free. Each time Ross gunned the engines, the wheels stuck fast, lifting the tail up but producing no forward movement. With night closing in, Ross instructed Shiers and Bennett to drain the radiators and replace the broken exhaust manifold. They would again spend the night with the aircraft while Ross and Keith stayed at a hotel in town.

Ross and Keith woke early on Friday, 14 November, eager to start for Rome. Back at the aerodrome they were dismayed to discover the Vimy standing in the middle of what now resembled a lake. With the assistance of 30 Italian mechanics, Ross and the other Australians worked for an hour and a half before they finally extricated the undercarriage. With rain falling heavily and the crew drenched and muddy, Ross decided to postpone the day's flying. He and Keith, 'feeling somewhat fed up', returned to town, where they spent the afternoon sightseeing in Pisa.[13] Fulfilling his obligations to Keith Murdoch, Ross also wrote an account of the flight so far and gave it to the local British air attaché to cable to the United Cable Service for distribution to newspapers around the world. His words from Pisa would appear in Adelaide's press five days later for friends and family to read. At this stage, they made no mention of either the blown exhaust or the aircraft becoming bogged: 'Our machine is OK and the crew are well.'[14]

The weather improved overnight and at first light the two brothers once again trudged back to the aerodrome; it was drizzling rain and a cold, southerly wind chilled their bones. The airfield remained waterlogged but, pacing around it, Ross found sections that might support the weight of the Vimy during its take-off roll. With the crew aboard, he taxied to the end of the aerodrome and had just turned into the wind when the wheels again sank into the morass. For the third time, the crew worked with shovels and planks to manhandle the giant biplane onto more solid ground. Wet and muddy, Ross, Keith and Shiers climbed into their cockpits while Bennett sat on the tail to stop it rising against the resistance of the boggy ground. Ross gunned the engines, sending showers of water and mud cascading in all directions. As soon as the aircraft started rolling forward Bennett 'jumped off [the] tailplane as if he was running for a drink', and dashed around to the fuselage, where Shiers pulled him 'headfirst into the cockpit'.[15] Bennett only just made it aboard as they gathered speed, reported Ross. 'We resembled a seaplane taking off and all got wet through as most of our run was through water and we just cleared a ditch and fence at the side of the aerodrome.'[16]

Although relatively brief, the flight to Rome was unpleasant. 'We encountered strong head winds . . . and had a hazy, bumpy trip,' wrote Ross. 'Our ground speed was only 50 miles [80 kilometres] an hour.'[17] A short way down the Italian coastline, Ross ran into a furious deluge of rain. He flew out over the ocean and climbed to 5000 feet before finally getting above the storm. Soon afterwards, he had to make an unscheduled landing at Venturina to repair an oil gauge that 'went dud'.[18]

The crew continued on, arriving over Rome at 3 p.m.; Ross landed on Centocelle aerodrome, on the city's south-eastern outskirts, shortly afterwards. It was tricky to land on, being situated on a slope. Ross perhaps knew that Colonel T.E. Lawrence ('of Arabia'), with whom he had worked in 1918, had nearly been killed in an accident here a few months earlier. Both the pilots had died; it was one of a disturbing number of crashes along the RAF's so-called 'No. 1 Aerial Route' between Britain and Egypt.[19] Ross and his crew landed safely, though, and must have felt a palpable sense of relief to be done with the day's flying. 'Feeling somewhat tired,' noted Keith mildly in his diary.[20]

Ross and Keith now had a decision to make. They had originally planned to fly non-stop to Athens and then on to either Cairo or Damascus. The British air attaché in Rome, however, provided unconfirmed reports that British forces occupying Damascus were planning to withdraw from the town, making it potentially unsafe for Ross and his crew to stop there. Ross also learned that the aerodrome at Suda Bay on Crete, which he had assumed would be flooded at this time of year, might in fact still be dry enough to use. To confirm this, Ross decided to fly first to Taranto, in Apulia, on the 'heel' of the Italian peninsula, to consult the staff at RAF headquarters there. 'It appeared best to use Suda Bay if possible and so cut the long stage across the Mediterranean into two,' he reasoned.[21]

The crew started from Rome at nine o'clock the following morning, 16 November. 'We passed over Capua and Naples,' described Ross, 'and then turned east over the mountains and flew low over Vesuvius.'[22] Keith had his camera ready, but clouds completely obscured the famous volcano. G-EAOU picked up a strong tailwind that propelled it across the Apennine range. 'Had a very bumpy trip over the mountains and dodged several storms,' logged Keith.[23] Ross would later describe the turbulence over the Apennines as some of the roughest of the whole journey: 'On one occasion our altimeter did a drop of 1000 feet, and bumps of 400 and 500 feet, both upward and downward, were frequent.'[24]

G-EAOU arrived above Taranto shortly before noon. Ross admired the town's picturesque bay and was struck by how busy its port appeared to be. He also noted how the area, a major logistics base for the Royal Navy and British Army during the war, still held numerous military camps.

The Australians were welcomed at Taranto by a number of RAF officers—some of whom Ross knew from Palestine. After lunch in the officers' mess, Ross and Keith went to inquire about the route ahead while Shiers and Bennett, assisted by mechanics from the RAF station, changed the oil and repaired a frayed rudder control wire. Anticipating a long sea crossing ahead, they also carefully checked the engines.

From his RAF colleagues, Ross learned that, contrary to what he had been told to expect before leaving Britain; the aerodrome at Suda Bay on Crete was still dry enough to land upon. With the situation in Damascus still unclear, Ross decided to make for Cairo, breaking up their crossing of the Mediterranean on Crete and shortening the overall journey by 320 kilometres.

Taking off from Taranto at 8.15 a.m. the following day, Ross set an easterly course across the Ionian Sea. With the Italian coastline behind them, he soon spotted the Greek island of Corfu. Reflecting the attention he paid the newspapers, Ross recalled that Germany's now deposed monarch—'Kaiser Bill'—had once owned a 'nice palace' there.[25] Just south of Corfu, Ross flew into some 'big patches of heavy clouds and rain' that compelled him to descend to 1500 feet so that Keith could confirm their location.[26] It was crucial that he had a known point and an accurate bearing from which to set their course to Crete: an error of a few degrees at the beginning of the sea crossing might cause them to miss the island altogether—a potentially fatal outcome.

As Ross picked his way south-east along the rugged Peloponnesian coastline, the weather conditions deteriorated. Soon, he was flying at 800 feet in an effort to follow the coast. The fog and rain reduced visibility to almost zero and, in one instance, Ross narrowly missed the heights of an island that suddenly loomed up ahead. 'We nearly crashed on it as I pulled the machine around sharply.'[27]

> It was heavy, stinging rain . . . our goggles were useless on account of the rain. We could not see through them and the wind glass [i.e. windscreen] was just as opaque. We had to sit with [our] heads down getting soaking wet and now and again cover our faces with our hands or take [a] quick [look] over [the] sides.[28]

After what must have seemed like an age, Keith identified Cape Matapan, the southernmost point of the Peloponnesian peninsula and the waypoint from which he could set a south-easterly course for Crete.

Over open water, the weather improved. After 40 minutes, Ross and Keith spotted Crete's high mountains ahead, emerging from a layer of mist 'that encircled the island like a great wreath'.[29] Ross had been warned that Suda Bay's aerodrome was tricky to land on, having a rough surface and being surrounded by steep hills on three sides. He nevertheless brought

G-EAOU down safely, concluding an uncomfortable six hours and 40 minutes in the air.

The small RAF contingent at Suda Bay welcomed Ross and his companions, showing great interest in the airmen and their machine. Ross probably thought of his good friend 'Biffy' Borton, whose pioneering flight from England to Egypt in a Handley Page O/400 in July 1918 had made the construction of the airfield necessary. One hundred Greek labourers using shovels and a small steamroller had done the work.[30]

After giving the aircraft 'a particularly thorough overhaul', including the replacement of a worn-out magneto on one of the engines, Ross and Keith joined one of the RAF officers for a tour of Canea—'an extremely picturesque and interesting old place,' thought Ross. 'Our pilot excited our admiration by the expert way in which he steered us through a maze of rough-surfaced alleyways, our Ford causing a great scattering of children and dogs—both of which appear to thrive here in large numbers.'[31] They dined at their host's house before turning in for the night at the local British Army hospital. Bed bugs forced the brothers to abandon their beds and spend the night on the floor.

Ross woke at dawn to the sound of rain—the first that had fallen on Crete in three months. Anxious that the Vimy might become bogged again, he and Keith hurried back to Suda Bay aerodrome and got the engines started. They were in the air, bound for Cairo, at 8.12 a.m. Climbing through low cloud, Ross found the sky above likewise overcast. To the south, filling the sky in between the two layers of cloud, towered Crete's imposing Lefka Ori mountain range.

With some of its cloud-obscured peaks exceeding the heavily loaded Vimy's service ceiling, Ross did not want to risk flying over the range. Rather, he headed into a pass that Air Force colleagues indicated would safely lead him across the island. 'We appeared to be only a few feet above the rocks when we cleared the crest, but it was preferable to having to barge blindly through the clouds, running the consequent risk of hitting a mountain crag.'[32] For half an hour, Ross steered through the narrow pass, hemmed in by the pale rocky slopes on both sides and a dense cloud ceiling just above.

Over Crete's south-eastern coast, the low cloud cleared, although the overcast remained. Keith took his bearings from the island's southernmost point and set a course for Sollum—the shortest possible route to the north African coastline, 370 kilometres away. It is telling that Ross and Keith took this bearing rather than setting a direct course for Cairo. Although a few hundred kilometres shorter overall, the latter course would have nearly doubled the distance that they had to fly over water, increasing the risk of both navigational errors and an emergency landing in the sea with little prospect of rescue. As a contingency, before setting out Shiers had inflated the spare rubber tyre tubes that they carried to use as improvised flotation devices. At first Ross laughed at the suggestion, but then he came around to the idea.[33]

Aided by a tailwind and generally smooth flying conditions, crossing the Mediterranean took nearly three hours, with Ross flying at 1000 feet to stay below the clouds. Although more comfortable than the earlier stages, the flying proved monotonous and Keith passed the time by writing letters. Without any visual landmarks to steer by, Ross had to keep an eye on the compass that was mounted on the Vimy's instrument panel. At times like this, he must have appreciated the shock-absorbers that Vickers had installed on the aircraft's control column and rudder pedals, which took much of the physical effort out of keeping the aircraft on a level and consistent bearing. About halfway across, G-EAOU passed over two steamers, allowing Keith to use the speed and drift indicator to check their ground speed and bearing.

At 11.35 a.m., Ross spotted North Africa's barren coastline—the welcome sight brought to an end the anxieties that stalked even the most confident pilots during sea crossings in aviation's early days. Over Sollum, he turned east and set a course for Alexandria from where he would head inland across the Nile Delta to Cairo. A four-hour flight over Egypt's desert coastline followed before Ross finally spotted the comfortingly familiar sight of the pyramids on the horizon. He landed on the RAF aerodrome at Heliopolis at 3.45 p.m., bringing to a successful end the longest stage of the journey so far. G-EAOU had covered just over 1000 kilometres.

Ross had conceived the flight to Australia in four stages, the first of them being from London to Cairo. While each would present its own particular challenges, on this part of the journey, Ross and his crew needed to contend with difficult weather. They had undertaken the majority of the stage's 30 hours' flying time in wet and freezing conditions that made it not only more uncomfortable but more dangerous than it would have been at other times during the year. Writing to Borton, Ross claimed that he had 'never before experienced such a bad run of cloud & rain'. They made it, he claimed, because of Keith's 'excellent navigation'.[34] The flight to Cairo had also involved one of the journey's few lengthy water crossings. Both publicly and privately, Ross and Keith expressed their relief at having made it safely across the Mediterranean.[35]

Indeed they should: in the preceding seven months, the RAF had lost seventeen Handley Page and Vickers bombers and eight airmen had been killed while attempting to fly the same route that Ross and his crew had just completed. A third of the aircraft that the RAF despatched from Britain during 1919 failed to reach Egypt. Within a fortnight of Ross's safe arrival in Cairo on 18 November, the Air Ministry shut down the route and ordered a court of inquiry into these accidents.[36]

29

DO YOUR BEST BUT DO NOTHING FOOLHARDY

In his original schedule of landings, Ross planned to rest for a day in Cairo. But he arrived three days later than planned because of unscheduled stops in Pisa, Taranto and Suda Bay.[1] 'My inclinations wavered,' recalled Ross. 'We were at a hospitable aerodrome, surrounded by old friends; rain had begun to fall and we were all very tired.'[2]

Despite these enticements, Ross decided to press on the following morning, stopping overnight in Damascus before flying to Baghdad. He and Keith spent their night in Cairo at Shepheard's Hotel but declined an invitation to attend a dance in the ballroom—an indication of their exhaustion. Shiers and Bennett undoubtedly enjoyed sleeping indoors that night—one of the few occasions they would do so during the journey to Australia.

From Cairo, Ross wired an account of the recent days' flying to Keith Murdoch's cable service. His words were then disseminated to English-language newspapers around the world. In Adelaide, the crew's friends and family followed their progress in the 'special messages' from Ross that the *Daily Herald* published. Reports on the flight appeared most days and, while congestion in the cable system delayed their arrival in London, Ross's words got through to readers in Australia at surprisingly short intervals. His despatch from Cairo, sent at 10.50 p.m. on the evening they arrived, appeared on news-stands in Adelaide just 24 hours later.[3]

In his cables, Ross mentioned some of the difficulties and discomforts the crew faced, but he avoided embellishing them in the 'graphic' or 'racy' manner Keith Murdoch (and perhaps his readers) expected. According to Ross, despite the challenges they faced, the crew were perennially 'well' and optimistic, the aircraft ran reliably and the RAF and colonial authorities provided essential assistance. The tone and style of Ross's despatch covering the flight from Suda Bay to Cairo were typical:

> Weather again bad. Low clouds met crossing Crete. Mountains difficult. Wind slightly favourable. Steered south course after leaving, but had to fly through rain most of the way across the Mediterranean. Passed two steamers half way. Checked ground speed and drift on them. Cruising took two and a half hours. Struck African coast close to Sollum, then flew east to Cairo . . . All very pleased to have got here. Hope for better weather now . . . Vimy going perfectly.[4]

Notably, his account does not emphasise the difficulties he had navigating through Crete's mountains or the danger posed by the sea and desert crossings involved in this stage; nor does he mention needing to once again replace blown exhaust manifolds on the Vimy's engines in Cairo.

While in Cairo, Ross also received cables from friends and family, wishing him well and congratulating him on his progress so far. One, from Prime Minister William Hughes, who had originally conceived the England-to-Australia air race, commended Ross and his crew on their safe start but urged him to avoid 'unnecessary risks. Do your best but do nothing foolhardy. If you cannot make Australia in 30 days, never mind. Good luck.'[5]

We don't know what Ross made of the prime minister's expression of concern, but some Australian newspaper editors thought it disingenuous that Hughes should conceive an air race that required pilots to fly halfway around the globe and then expect them not to take 'unnecessary risks'. Sydney's *Sun,* for example, mocked up a satirical cable from Ross titled 'Safety First', in which he narrated how one of the crew climbed out of the Vimy and hung upside down from the undercarriage because of his concern that the cockpit floor might give away.[6]

The prime minister had sent a near identical message to George Matthews and Thomas Kay, the first Australian team to start. Despite leaving Hounslow in a Sopwith machine nearly three weeks before Ross, they remained in Germany, held up by snow storms.[7] The only other Australian crew that had started by the time Ross arrived in Cairo had met a tragic end: their Alliance biplane crashed shortly after taking-off at Hounslow. The crew, Lieutenants Roger Douglas and James Ross, died in the accident.

By the time they reached Cairo, therefore, Ross and his crew had a comfortable lead in the running for the £10,000 prize—they just had to make it to Australia in the remaining 24 days. Whether or not they would be the first airmen to do so would now depend on whether they could catch up to the French crew, Etienne Poulet and Jean Benoist, who were unofficially attempting the flight to Australia in a twin-engine Caudron biplane. The Frenchmen had nearly a month's head start, but bad weather and mechanical problems had delayed them. The day the Vimy reached Egypt, Poulet and Benoist landed at Karachi.

The Vimy took off at Heliopolis in overcast conditions on the morning of 19 November 1919. The weather forecast predicted heavy rain along the route to Damascus but, confident in his knowledge of the country, Ross decided to begin his journey across the Middle East anyway.[8]

From Cairo, Ross followed the Ismailia Canal north-east towards Kantara where, as a light horseman, he had first stepped into the Sinai in mid-1916. 'I knew the country pretty well,' he wrote.[9]

For 40 minutes, the Vimy tracked on an easterly bearing across the Sinai, Ross navigating by the railway and water pipe that British forces had constructed during 1916 to support the desert campaign. Places below represented a chronology of Ross's wartime service: Romani, where he had once camped with the 1st Machine Gun Squadron and fought in his first major battle; El Arish, Rafa and Gaza, where he had earned a reputation as one of the best observers in No. 1 Squadron; and then, crossing into Palestine, the aerodromes from which he had flown, as a pilot, during 1918—Mejdel, Ramleh and Haifa.

From Haifa, on Palestine's northern coast, Ross turned G-EAOU inland, making for the Jordan River. In heavy rain, he descended to a few hundred feet and followed the valley north to the Sea of Galilee. 'All this time we were having a pretty rough time dodging storms in the hills and it was very bumpy at times,' recorded Keith.[10] 'The torrential rain cut our faces and well-nigh blinded us,' wrote Ross. 'We were soaked through and miserably cold.'[11]

G-EAOU landed on the RAF aerodrome at Damascus just as the town was receiving its first drenching of the wet season. Ross knew its reputation as a 'bad wet weather ground' and desperately hoped that they could avoid being bogged—especially given the plans of the British garrison to evacuate the city in a few days' time.[12] After refuelling, Ross and Keith borrowed one of the Air Force's Fords to drive into town and find a hotel for the night. It broke down on the way, leaving them stranded for three hours before another passing vehicle stopped to give them a ride.

'It was raining hard at Damascus next morning,' wrote Ross, 'but as the ground was getting sticky I decided to move at all costs.'[13] The crew spent a couple of hours sheltering under the Vimy's wing before a break in the storm allowed them to take off. Ross gunned the engines and G-EAOU trundled across the saturated aerodrome in a whirl of mud that covered the crew. 'The aerodrome stands at 2000 feet above sea level and we only just got off after a long run,' reported Ross.[14]

Unable to climb the heavily loaded Vimy above the storm clouds, Ross levelled off at 1500 feet and set a north-easterly course across the Syrian desert. The featureless landscape presented Keith with few landmarks with which to fix their position; for most of the day, he would navigate by dead reckoning. The first confirmation that they were on course was Tadmur, a settlement among the ancient ruins of Palmyra. From there, Ross set a compass bearing for Abu Kemal on the Euphrates River, which he intended to follow to Baghdad. Although the weather cleared as the day wore on, Ross kept the Vimy at a low altitude. They passed over Bedouin camps from time to time, alarming both the inhabitants and their livestock.[15]

Ross had hoped to reach Baghdad that day, but over the Euphrates G-EAOU ran into a strong headwind. With only an hour or so of light remaining and still 100 kilometres west of their destination, Ross picked out a small landing ground at Ramadi, where he knew the RAF had a supply of fuel and a wireless station.

The officers of the 10th Indian Lancers, whose troops camped nearby, welcomed the Australian airmen, providing them with both an 'excellent dinner' and beds for the night in town. In exchange, Ross and Keith passed on the latest news from London—a home many of the regiment's officers had not seen for months or years.

Ross and Keith woke at 11 p.m. to the roar of a gale force wind. Hurrying back to the aerodrome, they discovered that Bennett had already roused some Indian cavalrymen from a nearby camp to help him hold the Vimy down.[16] Ross started the engines and turned G-EAOU to face into the wind. For the next few hours, he and the crew, assisted by 50 Indian troops, strained against the wind to hold the aircraft down. 'It was a pitch-dark night, and the gale whirled sand into blinding eddies, cutting our faces and eyes,' recalled Ross. A powerful gust wrenched one of the ailerons and stretched a control wire, allowing 'all four ailerons to flap about in a very dangerous manner'. Ross thought the aircraft's control surfaces might be torn off.[17]

The wind died down at dawn, revealing that all the Vimy's aileron wires had either broken or stretched. Sand covered the aircraft; it had worked its way into every corner and crevice of the machine. But Ross felt relieved: it could have been much worse—'very nearly a disaster', as he later admitted to his benefactors at Vickers.[18]

It was 1.15 p.m. by the time Shiers and Bennett had replaced the damaged control cables and cleaned out the engines. This time, a tailwind worked to Ross's advantage, propelling G-EAOU south along the Tigris at over 160 kilometres per hour. Ross decided to bypass Baghdad and head for Basra, 500 kilometres downstream in southern Mesopotamia.

For the first time since leaving London, the weather remained fine throughout the day's flying. 'We flew over Baghdad, Kut and the Garden of Eden,' noted Keith, apparently sharing his younger brother's irreverent sense of humour: '[We] didn't meet Eve and the garden wanted water but otherwise looked OK.'[19] After three and a half hours, Ross landed at Basra.

Exhausted and concerned about the battering the Vimy had taken the previous night, Ross decided to stay at Basra the following day to give the aircraft a proper overhaul before setting out on the next stage. 'We commenced work at daylight and worked until dark,' wrote Ross. Shiers and Bennett replaced two stretched rudder-control wires and adjusted the valve clearances on both engines, managing to secure an additional 25 revolutions per minute out of each.[20]

While Shiers and Bennett worked on the aircraft, Ross ventured into Basra to send cables and post some letters, including one to his mother that he hoped he and Keith would beat to Adelaide. 'We are getting along famously but it is hard work,' it began.

> We still have great hope of being the first people to do the job and in 30 days too. It is very nice Keith and I being together, he is, as you know, a great chap to work with and has done some very fine navigating work when we have had to fly over clouds. We are all very happy and quite fit and today's rest here has done us a world of good. Very much love to you and Paw.[21]

30

CHASING POULET

Feeling rested and confident in the work that they had done on the aircraft, Ross and his crew started from Basra at 6.35 a.m. on 23 November 1919. Determined to catch up with Poulet and Benoist, who had been delayed in India for a fortnight with mechanical problems and illness, Ross planned to push the aircraft and his team hard. During three long days of flying, they would follow the Persian coastline to India, stopping overnight at Bandar Abbas and then Karachi before reaching Delhi on 25 November.

Excellent flying weather aided the Vimy's journey along the Persian Gulf towards India. 'Following wind and weather conditions best of trip,' logged Keith. 'All feeling very cheerful.'[1] Just as Ross had done on his first flight over Persia a year before, Keith found the Gulf's mountainous coastal terrain striking, especially as the sun's first rays illuminated them in the morning. He snapped photographs on his Kodak and described them in a letter written to his father from '4000 ft over Gwadar':

> It is most appalling country, one great mass of jagged rocks and hills. I have never seen such a curious formation of rock before, the tops are all sharp edged and I doubt if a person could walk along one. The hills are all in terraces, the lowest nearest the sea shore and extending to highest some distance back.[2]

The ruggedness of this terrain concerned Ross. If the Vimy suffered a mechanical failure, there were few places he could make an emergency landing. He also worried about how the locals might treat them. He carried a letter, written in Farsi, from the British Consul at Bandar Abbas, appealing for help from anyone they might encounter. If this did not persuade them, Ross had his pistol.

The three-day flight to Delhi involved stretches of between seven and a half and nine hours in the air each day. Finding the scenery monotonous, Ross soon became bored; the ideal flying weather allowed him to practically fly the Vimy 'hands off'. To keep himself awake, Ross devised a mental routine of checks around the aircraft. He began with the starboard engine gauges, checking the oil pressure and revolutions, then he listened to see if he could detect any irregularities in the engine's running noise. Next Ross glanced at the engine itself, checking for leaks on the oil-pipe connections and reading the gauge displaying the radiator water temperature. Looking back to the instrument panel, Ross would check the altimeter, airspeed and petrol-flow indicators. He then turned to the left to repeat the process with the port engine. The routine finished with a scan of the landscape: where might he land if an engine failed now? It was then time to begin the whole process again.[3]

During their overnight stops at Bandar Abbas and Karachi, the crew performed the maintenance schedule on the Vimy that had by now also become routine. 'As soon as the machine landed, Bennett and Shiers would don their overalls and set to work on the engines,' wrote Ross. 'The sparking plugs would be taken out and cleaned, magnetos examined and all parts of the engine inspected and cleaned.' Keith meanwhile organised delivery of the fuel and oil that Vickers had ordered for them, while Ross found the nearest post office to send cables to Murdoch's news service and a letter to his parents. By the time he returned to the aircraft, Keith usually had the fuel ready to load onto the aircraft. 'This was very tiring and monotonous,' described Ross. 'I would open the four gallon [18 litre] cans and lift them up to my brother, a distance of about six feet, and he would empty the cans into the tanks through a large funnel with a chamois leather strainer.' By these means, Ross and Keith often transferred half a tonne of fuel into the

Vimy's tanks; for longer flights, such as the nine-hour trip from Karachi to Delhi, they manhandled a tonne of fuel. They finished by topping up the oil tanks with Castrol—a job that left them black and greasy. Looking back, Ross regarded this work as the 'hardest part of the whole flight'. He admitted sometimes being tempted to delegate it to local RAF mechanics but remained adamant that his crew should take responsibility for the aircraft themselves.[4]

This daily post-flight routine usually finished late in the evening—sometimes after 9 p.m. Bennett and Shiers usually camped with the aircraft while Ross and Keith ran 'the gauntlet of functions and ceremonies' that local authorities held in their honour. 'It was difficult to make folk understand that work had to be done,' recalled Ross of the well-meaning (but in some cases disruptive) hospitality extended to him during his journey to Australia. 'We deeply appreciated every one's generous kindness, but I fear that on some occasions people must have thought us very discourteous.'[5] Ross and Keith averaged five hours' sleep each night during the flight to Australia, a factor that contributed to their exhaustion as the journey wore on. Unfortunately, at Karachi the officers of the local RAF squadron tempted Ross and Keith to stay for a dinner that lasted into the small hours. They embarked on the nine-hour flight to Delhi—the second longest stage of the entire journey—the following day with only three and a half hours' sleep, and most likely still reeling from the effects of the previous night's celebrations.

Feeling 'very tired', the crew took off from Karachi at 7.40 a.m. on 25 November.[6] The heavy fog 'changed into a golden mist as the sun mounted higher [and] hid the earth from view' described Ross: 'Passing over Hyderabad, the vapours rolled away and we had a grand view of the River Indus.'[7] Beyond that stretched out the Sind, 200,000 square kilometres of arid desert terrain; for three hours, Ross followed the railway line that ran north-east across its barren expanse. 'It's pretty rotten country,' explained Keith in a letter written to his father from the cockpit, 'sand and more sand.'[8]

Finally, Ross spotted Ajmer, 'a delightful little city, beautifully situated in a basin of green hills', on the desert's north-eastern fringe. Further on the terrain morphed from drab browns and yellows to a tapestry of deep, lush, green tones: 'a vast verdant carpet irrigated from the great rivers'.[9] The change in scenery delighted Ross: it was the first they had experienced in several days of flying over the Middle East. He also welcomed the 'boisterous' turbulence that bounced the Vimy about during the afternoon and disrupted the monotony of good-weather flying.[10]

Ross and his comrades spotted Delhi from 80 kilometres away: 'a white streak in a haziness of green plain'.[11] Over the city's outskirts, Wing Commander Norman MacEwan, the RAF's commander in India, met the Vimy in a Bristol Fighter and escorted the Australians towards their landing place: a dirt airstrip at Safdarjung constructed by the RAF. The crowd that gathered to meet them was smaller this time, with only 'brief notice' having been given of the Vimy's arrival in Delhi. 'Captain Ross-Smith [sic] made an excellent landing,' reported one journalist, 'and on alighting received many congratulations from numerous officers of the RAF and a number of old friends.' Despite having flown 2500 kilometres in two days, thought the reporter, 'neither Captain Ross-Smith, his brother, nor the two mechanics seemed weary, on the contrary the whole party were in excellent spirits'.[12]

In fact, Ross felt somewhat the worse for wear: exhausted, cramped, probably desperate for a cigarette and deaf from nine hours of engine noise. He struggled to hear the people who crowded in, shaking his hand and congratulating him. He did, however, pick up an encouraging piece of information: Poulet and Benoist had only left Delhi that morning, bound for Allahabad. By pushing his crew and aircraft to their limits during the past week, Ross had closed the gap between themselves and the Frenchmen to less than a day's flying. They certainly had pushed themselves. Ross reported to Vickers:

> We left Basra at 6.35 a.m. on November 23rd and 58 hours later were in Delhi, a distance of 2100 miles [3380 kilometres]. Out of that 58 hours we spent 25 hrs 10 mins in the air and during the remaining 33 hrs we had overhauled the engines twice and loaded by ourselves, by hand, approximately 2¾ tons of petrol and oil into the machine.[13]

Two of the stages had involved non-stop flights of nine hours: 'We felt pretty dead at the end of them,' explained Ross.[14] By making it to Delhi from London in fourteen days, Ross and his crew had also set a new record for the route.

In his published account of the flight, Ross claimed that he decided that evening to spend the next day in Delhi resting.[15] In fact, he had intended to fly to Allahabad the following morning to catch the Frenchmen but, when warming up the Vimy's engines, he discovered that its starboard engine was 'missing slightly'.[16] On inspection, Shiers and Bennett discovered that the induction pipe had cracked. 'We could have bound it up with tape, but I thought it best to get another and I knew a day's rest would do us all good,' explained Ross in his confidential report to Vickers.[17] Wing Commander MacEwan cabled the RAF station at Lahore and arranged to have a spare induction pipe flown to Delhi.

The crew spent six hours on 26 November overhauling the Vimy, including replacing some stretched elevator control wires and a punctured tyre. In the evening, Ross took Keith sightseeing in Delhi. It felt good to play tourists for a few hours away from the aircraft.[18] Keith, who had not been to Delhi before, enjoyed himself and noted that Wing Commander MacEwan and his fellow Air Force officers 'looked after us very well'.[19]

With a new induction pipe fitted, the Vimy left Delhi at 10.20 a.m. on 29 November. Forty-five minutes into the trip, the starboard engine's oil gauge dropped to zero, compelling Ross to land at Muttra and repair what turned out to be a faulty gauge before continuing. Passing over Agra, he circled so that the crew could photograph the Taj Mahal.

The afternoon's route took G-EAOU across the central plains of India: 'a great flat tessellation of cultivated patches that gave an impression of the earth being covered with green and brown tiles'.[20] As Ross approached Allahabad, he scanned the aerodrome, looking for Poulet's aeroplane, hoping they might have finally caught up with the Frenchman. He couldn't see it and, after landing, learned that Poulet and Benoist had started that morning for Calcutta. A correspondent for the Australian Press Association reported that when Ross climbed down from the Vimy at Allahabad, he was 'cheerful, fresh-looking and spick-and-span . . . He is very optimistic concerning his future flight.' Ross said to the journalist, 'Tell them in Australia I hope to see them soon.'[21]

The crew started for Calcutta at 8.30 a.m. the following day—a five-hour flight covering 750 kilometres. Ross described the day's flying as 'uneventful' and even Keith, for whom all of this was a greater novelty, recorded in his diary that it was a 'Good but uninteresting flight . . . Hot day but clear sky.'[22]

Unsure of when the Vimy would arrive, by 1.50 p.m. a crowd of spectators had gathered at Calcutta's polo field, many waiting throughout the morning in the hot sun. When the aircraft finally emerged from the heat haze above Howrah, to the city's south-west, it 'was received with tremendous cheering' that grew into a 'deafening noise' as Ross approached and circled the landing strip that had been marked out on the polo ground.[23] The crowd applauded as Ross brought the Vimy in for a gentle landing on the grassy field.

As G-EAOU rolled to a stop in front of a tent occupied by the city's military and political dignitaries, 'several military officers immediately ran towards the machine, followed by a crowd of European ladies and gentlemen anxious to meet the airmen'. Ross pulled off his flying overalls and climbed down from the Vimy's high cockpit wearing his AFC uniform, one reporter noting the numerous decorations he wore on his breast.[24] Another described how 'the brothers who are spare built, but apparently wiry men, looked remarkably fresh and fit even after so tiresome a flight from Allahabad'.[25]

Noting the number of spectators to be smaller than it had been when Ross landed in Calcutta the previous year with Borton and Salmond, the press speculated that the novelty of aviation had already started to wane.[26] The crowd that came out to meet Ross and his crew was nevertheless larger than the 'some dozen' who had gathered to greet Poulet and Benoist two days earlier.[27] Ross had made many friends during his stay there at the beginning of 1919, and now they pressed in, eager to congratulate him. 'The Captain was soon surrounded by an army of photographers,' described one journalist. 'Several ladies carrying Kodaks rushed through the crowd to snapshot the airmen at every point of vantage.'[28]

> A lady friend forced herself through the dense crowd and after the customary greetings exclaimed 'How are you?' to which the Captain smilingly responded, 'Oh very well, thank you.' 'But,' said the lady, 'you are looking thin!' He replied, 'Yes, I am.' A gentleman friend who was standing alongside humorously remarked, 'Oh, yes, had nothing to eat.' This met with [an] equally witty response from the Captain—'Only air'.

A few minutes later, while Ross was being led away by friends, another young lady broke through the crowd and presented him with her visiting card and a request for an autograph. Ross 'courteously complied . . . and handed the card back to the girl'.[29] Signing autographs—and dealing with the attention of young ladies—would be something to which Ross would need to become increasingly accustomed.

Ross spent the night with some friends and claimed that he slept well. 'We had crossed India and were now more than halfway to Australia.'[30]

He originally planned to fly from Calcutta to Rangoon in Burma, but the Rangoon Turf Club had a meeting scheduled for 29 November at the track on which Ross planned to land. He claimed that they 'sportingly offered to postpone their races' but, considering they had 'time in hand' to reach Australia, he declined their offer. Instead, Ross decided to fly to Akyab, in Burma, where Poulet and Benoist might still be situated, then continue to Rangoon the following day. Ross's decision appears to have reflected his optimism that, despite some unscheduled stops, his crew still had enough time to reach Australia within the 30 days allowed to claim the Commonwealth Government's £10,000 prize. They had covered 10,800 kilometres in seventeen days; from Calcutta, Port Darwin lay 4400 kilometres away.

By the time Ross and Keith returned to the polo field the following morning, a large crowd had assembled around the aircraft. They climbed out of their motorcar to 'ringing cheers and shouts of applause'. The four Australian airmen got into their flying overalls beside the Vimy, quickly farewelled their hosts and then started the engines.[31] Ross didn't show it, but he felt nervous: the polo field seemed too short to take off safely.

From the perspective of those on the ground, Ross's take-off appeared to go smoothly: the Vimy 'taxied towards west at great speed and in doing so shot up gracefully over the trees and soon disappeared in the cloud'.[32] Yet that moment had been one of terror for Ross and his crew. Just as the Vimy's wheels left the ground, a pair of hawks dived into its path, one striking a wing and the other going through the port-engine's propeller. 'There was a crash as if a stone had hit the blade, and then a scatter of feathers,' recalled Ross, who was instantly gripped by the terror of losing a propeller blade ten feet above the ground with a line of trees directly ahead. 'My heart stood still,' he wrote—but he resisted the urge to panic, dodged another large flock of birds and narrowly cleared the trees on the polo field's perimeter.[33] 'I was deeply relieved when we had climbed to 1000 feet and were clear of the pestilent birds,' he wrote.[34] Ross appreciated his luck: he had previously seen something as small as a stone shatter a spinning propeller in an instant of terrifying mechanical violence.

But anxiety continued to nag at him: had the propeller been damaged? Would it hold together for the day's flying that lay ahead? Ross took a risk by pressing on as, throughout the morning, the Vimy would be passing over the Ganges Delta, a vast, tangled expanse of tropical forest, tributaries and swampland. Ross thought it 'a dreaded span of country'—certainly not a place where he would like to attempt an emergency landing.[35]

The engines ran well, though, and it was with relief that Ross spotted Chittagong, where he and Borton had narrowly escaped the fire aboard the RIMS *Sphinx* in February. With the Burmese coastline to follow, Keith easily tracked their course south to Akyab, where shortly before 1 p.m., Ross spotted the triangular clearing in paddy land, just west of the town, that he had identified as a potential spot for an aerodrome during the survey expedition. As he descended, Ross noticed Keith and the mechanics waving and pointing excitedly. There it was: Poulet and Benoist's Caudron parked on the aerodrome!

The Frenchmen were waiting to greet Ross and Keith as they climbed down from the Vimy's cockpit. Poulet 'came forward with a cheery smile and outstretched hand—a true sportsman,' thought Ross. Regarding the two aircraft parked alongside one another, they reminded Ross of an eagle and a sparrow.[36] Poulet's Caudron G4 looked small and flimsy next to the Vimy; the two machines had a similar wingspan but the French aeroplane was half as long and, most strikingly, its tail was attached to the wings by a pair of long timber booms—a reflection of its early-war design. The key difference, however—and the one that had allowed Ross to catch the French crew despite their month-long head start—lay in the engines. Compared with the Vimy's 360-horsepower Rolls-Royce Eagle VIIIs, the Caudron used two 80-horsepower Le Rhone radials. Besides being slower, Poulet had to run his engines much harder than Ross did, increasing the chance of mechanical failure. Ross was filled with admiration as he realised that these Frenchmen had attempted to fly halfway around the globe in *this*. It surprised him that Poulet and Benoist had made it this far.

31

THE FAR EAST

The Australian crew felt jubilant: they had made it as far as Burma; they had caught up with their only serious competitor; the Vimy remained in good working order; and they had twelve days make it to Australia to claim the £10,000 prize. This seemed achievable, given Ross's plan to make six more landings before reaching Port Darwin: Rangoon, Bangkok and Singapore, followed by three stops in the Dutch East Indies.

Ross also realised, though, that they now faced the most difficult and dangerous flying of the entire journey.[1] Behind them was the assistance of the RAF and the security of its airfields; ahead lay vast expanses of wilderness over which no aircraft had ever flown. Places to make unscheduled landings would be few and the aerodromes that did exist were improvised and untried. Although the wet season had finished for the year, the region also remained prone to violent tropical storms.

G-EAOU started for Rangoon in good weather on 30 November 1919. After following the coast east for an hour and a half, Ross turned inland, setting a course over the rugged and heavily timbered slopes of the Arakan range. He climbed to 6000 feet to clear its mountain peaks and shortly afterwards spotted the Irrawaddy, which he followed south towards Rangoon.[2] As Ross had anticipated, the terrain of heavily timbered slopes and irrigated rice paddies offered few options if he needed to make an emergency landing.[3]

Arriving over the Burmese capital, Ross easily picked out the racecourse: 'a green patch framed by a compact ring of cheering humanity'.[4] The crowd, in fact, was the largest that had yet turned out to welcome the Australians. Ross estimated there were 40,000 people and afterwards learned that many had camped out overnight, eager to see the first ever aeroplane to visit the city. The Vimy landed to 'a great ovation of cheering'; they were welcomed by Sir Reginald Craddock, Governor of Burma and his wife, Lady Craddock, who invited Ross and Keith to stay that night at Government House.

'The most striking and picturesque scene is provided at the racecourse at the present moment,' described Ross in a cable sent to the press that afternoon, 'the most modern aeroplane, 19 days from England, surrounded by interested Burmese, gaily dressed in all colours.'[5] Indeed, throughout the afternoon thousands of Burmese and Europeans watched as the crew prepared the Vimy for its next day's flying. The 'entire population turned up and made a day of it,' observed Keith.[6]

Despite starting before the Vimy that morning, Poulet and Benoist landed at Rangoon an hour after the Australians, illustrating the difference in the speeds of which the two aircraft were capable. Ross nevertheless agreed with the Frenchman that they should fly the next leg to Bangkok together in case one of them went down in the remote, rugged jungle that covered most of the route. Engine trouble, however, held Poulet up the following morning and the Australian crew proceeded without him. It was the beginning of the end for Poulet's attempt to be the first man to fly from Europe to Australia. He would only make it a couple of hundred kilometres further before his aircraft's mechanical problems would force him out of the race altogether.

The Vimy took off at 7 a.m. the next day, 1 December 1919, barely clearing the trees and houses that surrounded Rangoon's racecourse. Ross felt the undercarriage clip the treetops as they left the ground. 'It was over in a breathless moment,' he wrote, 'but had the machine been but a single foot lower, disaster must have overtaken us.'[7]

From Rangoon, Keith directed Ross along a course across the Gulf of Martaban. Their first navigational waypoint was Moulmein, which Ross—like any good child of the empire—knew from Kipling's 1890 poem, 'Mandalay'.[8] Keith's navigational charts for this region lacked detail; some of it had not previously been surveyed. The maps did, however, indicate that to reach Bangkok, Ross had to fly over the Dawna mountain range that extended along the border between Burma and Siam. According to the charts, some of its peaks reached 7000 feet—the same altitude as the Vimy's service ceiling. To make matters more difficult, that morning Ross found the range's peaks obscured by clouds.

From the charts, Keith thought that he had identified a valley through which they might pass at lower altitudes. After flying along it for a short distance, however, Ross noticed its sides begin to narrow. Alarmed that they were being funnelled into a dead end, Ross pulled the Vimy through a tight turn, narrowly missing the jungle-covered slopes, and returned the way they had come.

Conferring via scribbled notes, the two brothers agreed that they needed to try to get enough altitude to fly over the mountains. Circling, Ross climbed through the clouds, emerging above them at 8000 feet.[9] Flying by compass bearings, they set off across the mountain range, just above the cloud cover; it reminded Ross of their first day's flying by the map in France—although it was nowhere near as cold.[10] Using the speed and drift indicator, Keith calculated that they faced a 30 kilometre per hour headwind, decreasing their ground speed by around a third.

In the following hour, Ross encountered several big storms over the mountains. He attempted to climb over them, even running the Vimy's engines at full power for the first —and as it would turn out only—time on the journey to Australia. Unable to coax any more altitude out of his aircraft, he had no option but to fly through some of the higher cloud formations.

Ross found these stints of flying completely blind, without the sky or the ground to orientate himself, the ultimate test. He had to ignore all other sensations and rely solely on his airspeed indicator, compass and inclinometer to keep the aircraft level and on course. Ross had to fight the urge to panic as he lost all sense of direction.[11]

While turning in his seat to check the gauges on the engines, Ross inadvertently applied some rudder, turning the Vimy off course by 10 degrees.

He applied opposite rudder, but without any horizon or ground by which to judge, over compensated, sending the compass needle swinging 45 degrees in the opposite direction. As he worked to get the aircraft back on the correct bearing, he noticed that the airspeed had increased by 25 miles (40 kilometres) per hour. Although he could not physically feel it, the Vimy's instruments told Ross that his aircraft was slipping sideways and on the verge of getting into an out of control spin. 'It is useless attempting to describe how I acted,' wrote Ross. 'A pilot does things instinctively, and presently my instruments told me that we were once more on our course and on an even keel.'[12] The Vimy emerged into clear skies after what felt like hours to Ross; checking his watch, he realised just twelve minutes had passed. Reflecting on this later, he would admit that the strain and exhaustion of the past two weeks had left him ill-equipped to face such 'tense and nerve-racking conditions'.[13]

After an hour, Keith reckoned that they should be clear of the mountains. Throttling back the engines, Ross put the Vimy into a slow glide down through the thick overcast. As he watched the altimeter approach 7000 feet, Keith, Shiers and Bennett peered over the sides, anxiously looking out for the tops of mountains. They were safe, though: at 1500 feet the Vimy dropped through the cloud base into clear sky above a dense jungle. 'It was an unspeakable relief,' recalled Ross, the end of an hour that represented 'the veriest nightmare experiences I have ever passed through'.[14]

The Vimy landed at Bangkok's Don Muang aerodrome just before 1 p.m.—six hours after leaving Rangoon. Progress had been slowed by headwinds and the climb above the Dawna Range. The crew felt relieved to be finished with the day's flying. 'Not at all a nice trip,' recorded Keith in his diary.[15]

The Australians were welcomed by the British Consul General, who had hosted Ross during his visit earlier in 1919, and the officers and men of the Royal Siamese Aeronautical Service, at whose aerodrome they were now guests. Taking advantage of their offer to provide any assistance that the crew should require, Shiers and Bennett spent the night in the aerodrome's workshops, grinding two of the starboard engine's 'badly pitted' exhaust valves.[16] Otherwise, it pleased Ross to note that the engines remained in excellent condition.[17]

At 5.30 a.m. the following day, the Siamese Army's Chief of Staff, Prince Chakrabongse Bhuvanath, arrived at the aerodrome to have breakfast with the Australians and inspect the Vimy. Ross had originally planned to use the aircraft's maximum range to reach Singapore from Bangkok (a distance of nearly 1500 kilometres). While at Don Muang, however, officers from the Siamese air service informed him of a suitable aerodrome about halfway along the route at Singora, close to the Malay border. It was stocked, Ross learned, with 500 gallons (2273 litres) of aviation fuel.

This news presented Ross with a conundrum. A stopover would conserve the aircraft's engines and mitigate the risk of attempting a flight at its maximum range. But Ross had never been to Singora; if he decided to use it, he would be relying on the accuracy of the Royal Siamese Aeronautical Service's assessment of its suitability for the Vimy.[18] Considering that a non-stop flight to Singapore represented the greater risk, Ross decided that they would fly to Singora and continue to Singapore the following day. It was a decision he would soon regret.

Things began to go badly just an hour into the flight to Singora on 2 December. After starting from Bangkok in good weather, the Vimy ran into a storm over the Gulf of Siam. Unable to see anything, Ross descended to 500 feet so he could follow the coastline. He had never flown in such heavy rain before. Water sprayed in over the windscreen, drenching the two brothers; soon even their googles filled with water. Removing them, Ross and Keith took turns to look out into the torrent of air and water rushing past the cockpit. 'It was almost impossible,' wrote Ross. 'When my eyes became too sore he would look out and direct me and I would carry on again when he could not see anymore.'[19]

For three hours, Ross and Keith followed the gulf coastline south through violent tropical thunderstorms. They searched for somewhere to land but found the coastal flats covered in waterlogged rice paddies or thick jungle. When he finally spotted the aerodrome at Singora, six hours after leaving Bangkok, Ross was utterly dismayed.[20] The ground was saturated; large pools had collected on its surface and tree stumps remained, scattered across the airfield. Unable to see any alternative, Ross picked out a relatively dry strip running perpendicular to the wind.

Easing the Vimy onto the sodden ground, he braced himself. Remarkably, G-EAOU rolled to a stop with just one jolt as a stump tore off its tail skid. Walking back along the strip afterwards, Ross would discover that the tyre tracks missed several of the obstacles by mere inches.[21] Keith's disgust is palpable in that day's terse diary entry: 'Got down on so called landing ground at Singora at 1.50. Very bad ground tree stumps and holes everywhere'.[22]

Ross's mood darkened further when he learned that the 500 gallons of aviation fuel said to be at Singora was in fact 500 *litres*—nowhere near enough to sustain the Vimy's flight to Singapore—or, indeed, a return to Bangkok. If at any moment in the journey to Australia Ross came close to despair, it must have been this: stranded on a remote, waterlogged and stump-strewn aerodrome with a damaged aeroplane and no fuel. It was also raining heavily.

Acquiring more fuel represented the most urgent and potentially most difficult problem to solve. Fortunately, Singora was situated on a railway line. From the local cable office, Ross sent a telegram to the Asiatic Petroleum Company in Penang, requesting the urgent delivery of an additional 750 litres of aviation spirit.[23] Aware of 'all sorts of restrictions about carrying petrol on the Siamese Railways', he also prudently sent cables to the Railways Commissioner in Bangkok and the Governor of Penang asking for their assistance. Ross then visited the Governor of Singora and requested help in clearing the tree stumps from the aerodrome's surface. Yet again, Ross's confident and personal approach worked; the governor agreed to put 200 convicts from a nearby prison to work clearing the airfield the following morning.

The Viceroy of Southern Siam, Prince Yugala Dighambara, provided the Australians with a bungalow for the night. They did not get much rest, however. Storms lashed the aerodrome all night, the wind becoming so strong that at 2 a.m. Ross and the others returned to the aircraft, worried that it would blow over. They spent the miserable hours before dawn sheltering under the wings and holding onto them whenever a new squall swept across the airfield. The Vimy 'so strained at her lashings' that Ross feared it would be flipped over and wrecked. Eleven inches (279 millimetres) of rain fell at Singora. 'It was the heaviest rain I have ever seen in my whole life,' reported Ross. 'We were wet through.'[24] At dawn, the Vimy stood on an 'island', surrounded by water 30 centimetres deep in places.[25]

As promised by Singora's Governor, a working party of 200 convicts arrived at the aerodrome in the morning. They spent what must have been a miserable day, shackled together by the legs, pulling stumps out of the flooded landing ground to clear a strip, 400 x 50 yards (365 x 45 metres), on which Ross hoped to take-off the following day.

Shiers meanwhile worked on the Vimy's starboard engine, which despite having had some of its valves ground in Bangkok, ran badly during the flight to Singora. Sheltered from the weather by a few tarpaulins rigged around the engine, Shiers identified the culprit—a worn needle valve that upset the fuel mixture going into the carburettor—and repaired it.[26] Despite the torrential rain, he had a 'curious crowd' of locals looking on as he worked.[27]

Bennett spent the day repairing the Vimy's tail skid. Somehow, he needed to fashion a new metal bracket to re-secure it to the aircraft's fuselage. In the backyard of a local Chinese man, Bennett found a pile of scrap metal, from which he obtained a suitably sized piece of steel. At a nearby rice mill, he then located a lathe on which to turn it. The machinery was antiquated: hand-powered by four workers—'coolies', as Ross and Keith described them.[28] The Australians paid the mill's foreman to hire the lathe and four labourers. They cooperated at first, but when they went on strike late in the afternoon Ross had to produce more cash. Stopping work again just fifteen minutes later, Ross called the mill's foreman, who beat the workers to get them back on task. Bennett emerged from the mill that night with a new tail skid bracket—'a remarkable piece of workmanship and skill,' thought Ross.[29]

Late that evening, the fuel arrived by rail from Penang. The weather improved overnight and by the following morning, 4 December 1919, had cleared: it was Ross's 27th birthday, the sixth he had celebrated since leaving Australia. By 9.30 a.m., the crew had refuelled the Vimy and pulled it into position at the end of a makeshift runway. The prison inmates had 'made a bad job' of clearing the tree stumps and three large sections of the runway lay submerged underwater.[30]

G-EAOU began its take-off roll nearly 50 metres from the first submerged section. The aircraft hit the water with such a tremendous impact that it nearly pitched forward onto its nose; water sprayed in all directions. The Vimy picked up speed again in the next dry run of 65 metres before the next large pool. 'Each lot of water would practically stop us as we charged though it,' described Ross. On the final 90 metres of runway, Ross gathered just enough speed to lift the biplane's wheels off the ground, bouncing them back down in some gorse bushes at the aerodrome's perimeter, then back into the air. It surprised Ross that they did not lose the undercarriage.

Thinking about it later, Ross admitted that the take-off from Singora had been 'desperate' and incredibly risky: 'I still wonder how we managed it.'[31] Writing in his diary that evening, Keith described it as a 'thrilling take off amongst the stumps and water, a very near thing and only just got away with it'.[32] Indeed, after landing they would discover that the water and mud whipped up by the propellers had lifted the brass binding on the propeller blades and stripped the protective nitrocellulose dope covering from the fabric on the wings.[33]

With visibility limited, Keith directed Ross to follow the railway line across the Malay Peninsula. 'We had a nasty trip for the first 50 miles [80 kilometres],' reported Ross. 'Low clouds and rain kept us down and most of the way we flew at 100 feet just above the railway line.' The brothers reasoned that if they stayed directly above the tracks, they would be unlikely to encounter any hills unexpectedly.[34] After crossing from Siam into Malaya, Ross followed the peninsula's west coast south as far as Penang, over which observers on the ground reported them at noon.[35] From there the weather improved. Ross climbed to 1500 feet and, for three hours, flew south along the coastal side of the Titiwangsa Mountain range, passing Kuala Lumpur at 3.30 p.m. At Malacca, Ross adjusted his bearing east and tracked south along the coast towards Singapore.

Excitement about the Vimy's arrival had been building in the city for days. Only once, six years earlier, in the words of one local news editor, had an aeroplane 'demonstrated to gaping crowds the possibilities of aviation'.[36] Spectators began arriving at Singapore's racecourse in the morning, taking seats in the grandstand or staking out positions along the fences. By 4.30 p.m., reported the local press, 'throngs of people of all nationalities . . . including a large proportion of the fair sex' had gathered: 'the stand was quite filled, and the crowd round the course and on the lawn was close packed and excited'.[37] Announcements of the Vimy's progress throughout the day, relayed from towns along the route, fuelled the anticipation and excitement.

The Vimy came into view at 4.45 p.m. 'The excitement of the vast concourse was manifested into cheering and waving of hats and handkerchiefs,' described one reporter.[38] Ross circled the city, giving everyone in Singapore a good view of the aeroplane. At the Alhambra Theatre, where St Andrew's School was holding its annual speech day, the headmistress had just started reading out the names of prize-winners when the Vimy roared low overhead. Despite the best efforts of the school's chaplain to maintain order, the students leapt from their seats and made 'an excited rush for the doors'.[39]

Ross 'had been dreading' landing at Singapore. As he knew from his inspection of it earlier in the year, the racecourse was 'altogether too small for our large machine' and closely surrounded by buildings. He approached from the west, keeping the Vimy just above stalling speed. As the wheels touched the ground, Bennett—apparently on his own initiative—climbed out of his cockpit onto the rear fuselage and slid down towards the tail to weigh it down.[40] Still, without wheel brakes, Ross had to swing the Vimy around in a 180-degree turn to avoid colliding with the boundary fence. The machine came to a stop directly opposite the stewards' stand.

It served as a dramatic and effective piece of theatre. 'The spectators cheered continuously as the machine was coming to earth, and three final cheers were given as it drew up,' wrote the *Straits Times*:

> From all sides people ran excitedly towards the aeroplane, gathering round in a dense crowd and only with difficulty being kept back by the police. A chorus of congratulations was shouted up to the airmen still in their seats, and Captain Ross Smith, smiling happily, shouted back his thanks, though his words were lost in the general clamour.[41]

According to another account, Ross's first words to the crowd as he stood in the cockpit were, 'Glad to be back with you all again.'[42]

Like journalists at other landings along the way, it surprised these reporters that the Australian airmen appeared so fresh and cheerful. 'The sergeants chatted gaily with the people who surged around, answering the volley of questions which came at them from all sides,' reported one journalist, who noted Ross's handsome and dashing appearance, adding that 'ladies may be interested to know' that he was 26 years old and unmarried (Ross apparently kept it to himself that it was his 27th birthday).[43]

The official party, led by Singapore's Assistant Colonial Secretary, escorted Ross to the Golf Club for refreshments while Keith, Bennett and Shiers stayed behind to check over the Vimy. Throughout the evening, locals came in their hundreds to see the aircraft. Some made it through the police cordon around the machine and signed their names onto the large white letters, G-EAOU, painted on its fuselage—a practice started by spectators at previous stops and one that Ross deplored.[44]

The Singapore Club hosted an exclusive dinner for Ross and Keith. The 26 invited guests represented the social, commercial and political elite of Britain's empire in the Far East. After lengthy speeches by a number of dignitaries, congratulating the brothers and emphasising the historical significance of their journey, Ross rose and delivered a reply that was notably brief and characteristically self-deprecating.[45] He extolled the brilliance of the Vickers Vimy and attributed their success to the assistance provided at each stop. Above all, Ross explained, he and Keith had only made it this far due to the skill and tireless efforts of Shiers and Bennett—the crew members who did 'the real work' to keep the machine airworthy.[46]

Following the meal, Ross and Keith went to the Victoria Theatre with their hosts to see a performance by Singapore's Amateur Dramatic Society. To his great embarrassment, as Ross entered the box that had been reserved for them, the whole crowd rose and gave 'ringing cheers'. For an awkward moment, he simply stood there, looking uncomfortable and apparently unsure of how to respond.[47] Then, regaining his bearings, Ross stepped forward to the balcony with Keith and the two brothers bowed to the audience in acknowledgement. The 'episode was one which quite thrilled the audiences,' reported one journalist.[48] Ross's feelings about his rapturous reception in Singapore are not recorded, although given what we know about his modesty and distaste for adulation, it was perhaps with mounting apprehension that Ross now began to conceive the fame that awaited him at his journey's end.

32

THE BAMBOO RUNWAY

It had taken 22 days for the Vickers Vimy to reach Singapore from London. Eight days now remained to reach Australia in time to claim the £10,000 prize. To journalists, Ross seemed 'full of confidence' that his crew would make it to Darwin in time.[1]

Ross had good reason to feel optimistic. Waiting for him in Singapore was a letter from the Netherlands Consulate, which reported the construction of several new aerodromes in the Dutch East Indies.[2] With these, the Australian crew would be able to break up the 3700-kilometre flight to Darwin into four fairly modest stages. Ross planned to follow the main islands of the Indies archipelago as far as Timor, from where he could make the final flight, across the Timor Sea, to Darwin. He had always anticipated this to be the most challenging and dangerous part of the journey. Not only were the crew utterly exhausted, but by this stage the Vimy had flown over 14,000 kilometres without a thorough overhaul. The condition of the aerodromes in the Dutch East Indies also remained to be seen.

The Australian airmen stayed in Singapore on 5 December to service the aircraft. Despite the sweltering heat, a large crowd surrounded the aeroplane throughout the day and watched the four Australians as they worked. 'We adjusted the valve clearances on the engines and generally overhauled everything,' reported Ross. They did their best to tighten up the bracing wires that held G-EAOU's airframe square; in the tropical humidity the timber and canvas had begun to warp. 'The machine was not climbing so well now,' Ross noted, with some concern. It 'took longer to get off the ground'.[3] As a precaution, the crew discarded 900 kilograms worth of equipment, mostly spare parts they reckoned they no longer required but also their personal kit and the cinema camera, which was shipped back to Vickers in London. The Australians finished the day feeling drained; having come from a European winter, Singapore's diabolically hot climate affected them severely. Ross even declined an invitation to a dance that evening.[4]

By 6.30 a.m. the following day, a large crowd had assembled at the racecourse to see the Australians off. Ross must have felt anxious: he only had a short run to gather enough speed to get airborne and rain had fallen overnight, soaking the ground and causing the aircraft's fabric covering to sag again. The two brothers wandered around the racecourse debating whether or not they should attempt it.[5] 'I carefully studied the aerodrome,' wrote Ross, 'and concluded that we might just get out with luck.'[6]

The Vimy started from the southern end of the course. Ross gunned the engines and, in the words of one observer, 'with a bound forward the plane raced right across the course'.[7] 'It was a tense and anxious moment' for Ross. 'When fifty yards from the rails, I pulled my control-lever back,'[8] G-EAOU pitched up into the air at an 'alarming, steep angle', clearing the racecourse's boundary fence and buildings but then stalling. Fortunately, the ground behind the racecourse dropped away, allowing Ross to recover speed and regain control of the aircraft. He climbed away to the north-east before turning and flying back over the crowded grandstands. As Ross circled, the other crew members waved. He then set a south-westerly course over the harbour. 'The thousands on the Racecourse watched in silence till the machine disappeared from their view, at about 6.55,' wrote one news correspondent. 'It was obvious that everyone was deeply impressed and stirred by the unique and significant spectacle which they had seen.'[9]

From Singapore, Ross followed the Durian Strait south. G-EAOU made landfall over Sumatra just after 8 a.m. As they did so, Keith wrote a large, triumphant note across a double-page spread in his notebook and showed it to his crewmates: 'EQUATOR AT THE FRONT'.[10]

Ross maintained a southerly bearing, following the Sumatran coastline but altering his course several times to avoid dark thunderstorm clouds.[11] A headwind slowed the Vimy's groundspeed and caused some rough turbulence. 'Are you alright? I'm feeling b____ sick personally,' wrote Keith to his brother on another page of the notebook.[12] Ross kept up his instinctive vigil for places to land in an emergency but, apart from a partially constructed Dutch aerodrome on Banka Island, he saw nothing: 'The coast of Sumatra is quite impossible for forced landings . . . either dense forest or mangrove swamp.'[13]

After passing Banka Island, Ross set a compass course across the Java Sea towards Batavia. The airmen marvelled at the sight of the Thousand Islands, hundreds of irregular blobs capped with green jungle and fringed by narrow rings of white sand that made them stand out brilliantly against a sea that varied in hue from an iridescent turquoise to a deep, dark blue.

Arriving over Batavia, Ross circled, looking for the aerodrome at Tangerang, but he and Keith could not see it.[14] Conferring via notes, the brothers decided they had enough fuel to continue on to the Dutch aviation school at Kalidjati, 130 kilometres to the south-east.[15] Ross followed the railway and, an hour later, spotted the 'large and good' airfield 'nestling at the foot of the mountains'.[16] At nine hours' flying time, the 1000-kilometre stage from Singapore to Kalidjati had been one of the longest of the trip.

The Dutch airmen at Kalidjati received the Vimy and its crew 'with huge enthusiasm'. They carried Ross from the aircraft on their shoulders to the Governor-General, who had flown from Batavia that morning to greet them.[17] The colonial Dutch press were taken with Ross, describing how 'when he gets out of the plane it is as if he gets out of a taxi,' and adding, 'for the ladies', that he was both handsome and unmarried (though the newspapers also noted that he seemed surprised and embarrassed by all the attention). Local journalists were frustrated in their attempts to get an interview. Keith explained that they had an exclusive deal with a news service in London.[18]

After a hearty lunch in Kalidjati's mess, it took Ross and Keith six hours to refuel the Vimy. They only needed 1500 litres, as the next leg, to Sourabaya on the eastern side of Java, lay a relatively short 560-kilometre flight away. That evening, the Dutch Governor-General and the leaders of colonial Dutch society hosted Ross and Keith at dinner. His Excellency gave a speech, heralding the Vimy's flight as evidence that Java could be connected to Europe and Australia by air, to the commercial advantage of all countries concerned.[19]

The Vimy took off from Kalidjati at 7.30 a.m. the following day and, with good weather, had an 'uneventful' flight to Sourabaya, where Dutch authorities had built the aerodrome for the benefit of the England-to-Australia air race competitors.[20] It had only been finished a few days when Ross eased G-EAOU's wheels onto its surface, shortly before noon on 7 December. The landing was a good one, but as the Vimy taxied Ross felt the machine begin to drag—a sensation he would have recalled from Pisa and Singora. As the Vimy's wheels sank, the aircraft lurched to a stop and pitched forward onto its nose. Ross shut off the engines and it rocked back onto its tail, stuck fast in the mud.

Climbing down from the cockpit, it became apparent that the aerodrome had been built on recently drained paddy land. A superficial crust, baked firm in the sun, obscured a sticky, muddy morass underneath.

Sourabaya had a busy harbour, with both commercial and naval docks. Ross called the Harbour Board's chief engineer, who arranged to send 'a horde of coolies' and some mats made from woven bamboo to help extricate the Vimy.[21] Two hundred labourers arrived at the airfield soon afterwards and, with their combined strength, managed to extricate the aircraft's undercarriage and push the Vimy up onto some bamboo mats. Hoping they had been unlucky in striking an isolated wet patch, Ross made it fewer than 50 metres before G-EAOU's undercarriage again sank into the mud—this time it disappeared entirely and the lower wings almost touched the ground. Using timber planks and bamboo mats, the Australians again dug the aircraft out and, with the assistance of the work gang, hauled the aircraft along a rotating section of bamboo mats towards the end of the runway, 350 metres away. Nails in the mats punctured the Vimy's tyres, making the process all the more difficult. It took six hours in the scorching sun.

The four Australians worked late into the evening by the light of electric lamps, refuelling, checking the engines and repairing the punctured tyres. The last of these proved particularly difficult when the jack kept sinking in the mud. Dejected, and without having eaten since breakfast, Ross and Keith left the aircraft. 'I don't think I have ever felt so tired or so miserable in my life as I did then,' admitted Ross. As he recognised, they were only 2000 kilometres from Australia with four days remaining to claim the prize but apparently hopelessly stuck. 'It seemed as if victory were to be snatched from us at the last moment.'[22]

At some point during dinner late that evening, Keith suggested that if they could get enough bamboo mats to cover the length of the runway, they might be able to get off the ground. Ross put the idea to the Harbour Board's engineer; he was sceptical but agreed to help.[23]

The next morning Ross and Keith returned to the airfield to find 'Natives . . . streaming in from every direction, bearing sheets of bamboo matting'. Already, an enormous pile of them lay beside the Vimy. As with most accounts of the flight, Ross's 1922 book, *14,000 Miles Through the Air*, implies that the 'natives' willingly and even gladly contributed their bamboo mats to assist the Australians. In one version, though—written by Ross for Murdoch's United Cable Service immediately after the flight—it appears that Dutch authorities had to coerce the locals. As Ross wrote, 'During the night the engineer had collected as many bamboo mats as possible from the whole district: in fact, he had pulled down numerous native houses to get a sufficient quantity.'[24] Years later, Shiers put it more bluntly: '[They had] to rob the natives of their huts to give us more mats.'[25]

From the hundreds of woven mats they created a runway nearly 40 metres wide and 275 metres long. On its first attempt at taking off, the Vimy's prop wash lifted the mats, causing the aircraft to swerve off the bamboo runaway and into the mud; the wheels sank again to their axels. The Australians again dug the wheels out, with the help of local labourers, then manhandled G-EAOU back onto the makeshift runway. It was a frustrating and anxious experience for Ross: 'Of course the Coolies had no idea which parts were safe to pull and which were not and to try and watch 200 of them and get anything like team work out of them was somewhat of a problem.' He later remarked that this experience, above all others, illustrated the sturdiness of Vickers' aeroplane.[26]

Having lashed all of the mats together, at noon the Australians made a second attempt. 'Only just got off,' recorded Keith in his diary afterwards: 'matting flying in all directions but no damage done. Very pleased to have got away.'[27] The thousands of spectators felt relief too; according to one Dutch news correspondent, the prevailing expectation had been that the Australians would 'fall into the sea'.[28] Ross summed up their miserable experience in Sourabaya by noting that they had been there for 24 hours, thirteen of which he had spent 'digging the machine out of the mud'.[29]

Ross climbed G-EAOU to 3000 feet and set a compass course across the Madura Strait. The five-hour flight to Bima, on the island of Sumbawa, proceeded without mishap. With Java behind them, Ross navigated past the northern tip of Bali and then over the Lombok Strait, where the crew saw schools of flying fish.[30] The Vimy reached Lombok at 3 p.m., the 3765 foot-high volcano Rindjani providing a conspicuous navigational marker. 'Very pretty at times,' noted Keith.[31] Ross followed Lombok's north coast and crossed the Alas Strait to Sumbawa; from several kilometres away, he spotted the large white cross marking the aerodrome at Bima.

To everyone's relief, although this aerodrome had also been constructed only recently, its surface proved to be dry and firm, and Ross landed without mishap. Unlike Sourabaya, a city of 150,000 people and bustling commercial centre, Bima was a tiny outpost; it had no cable office and few Europeans lived there. The region's Sultan and Dutch Commissioner welcomed the Australians and entertained them that evening. Ross and Keith had the use of a bungalow a few kilometres from the airfield. Exhausted, the brothers had little patience with the locals who surrounded the hut and peered in through the slats as they tried to sleep. Fed up, Ross fired his flare pistol out the door, which sent them fleeing in terror.[32]

The Vimy left Bima at 9.45 a.m. on 9 December and followed an easterly course across the sprawling archipelago of tiny, jungle-covered islands that separate the larger islands of Sumbawa and Flores. When planning the flight two months earlier, Ross believed that he would need to make the final flight across the Timor Sea to Australia from Flores—then the eastern-most aerodrome in the Indies. In Singapore, however, he had learned of two new airfield constructions on Timor, at Atamboea in the north and Koepang in the south. The former was not due to be finished for another week, but Ross had to fly over it on his way to Koepang; if Atamboea appeared ready, he could land there; if not, he would continue to Koepang.[33]

Throughout the morning, Ross followed the northern coast of Flores, Keith noting on his chart the 'very pretty' coral reefs that fringed the island's turquoise waters.[34] They flew low enough to perceive the 'great interest ... being taken in our machine by the natives'.[35] Shortly before 1 p.m., Keith directed Ross across the island to Flores' southern coast, from where they flew an easterly course along the southern fringe of the Solor Archipelago. As G-EAOU passed the numerous volcano-crowned isles, some emitting smoke, the crew detected the sharp smell of sulphur. The weather remained mostly fine but on a few occasions Ross skirted close to thunderstorms, one giving the Vimy a 'hell of [a] bump', as Keith noted on his navigational chart.[36]

Over the Ombai Strait the Vimy picked up a tailwind. 'Get there by 3.15 easy,' Keith wrote in a note to his brother on their map. Ross responded, 'Good oh.'[37] Keith's navigation proved spot on: after the 100-kilometre sea crossing, the Vimy arrived over the Timorese coast just a few hundred metres from where his dead reckoning had estimated them. From a couple of thousand feet, Ross spotted the aerodrome at Atamboea, sitting on a high plateau and surrounded by bush. It looked ready, so he put the Vimy down, making a good landing. Ross learned afterwards that preparations for their arrival had been completed the previous day.[38]

The Australians found the region's Dutch Commandant waiting to greet them; he had a supply of aviation fuel and oil ready. While Bennett and Shiers overhauled the machine and made some repairs to the tail-skid, the commandant showed Ross and Keith around the area. The two brothers thought that Atamboea, with its abundance of gum trees, looked like Australia. It excited them to be so close to home—just a little over 700 kilometres to go, a shorter flight than they had made on numerous days, including that one.[39] Ross and Keith stayed in the nearby Dutch Army camp that night. 'It is hardly necessary to say that none of us over-slept,' recalled Ross. 'We were too excited at the prospect of tomorrow.'[40]

33

THE SUPREME HOUR OF OUR LIVES

The most significant day in Ross Smith's life began with a startling wakeup call. It was not yet dawn on Wednesday, 10 December 1919 when a large Malayan man, tasked with rousing the Australian airmen, beat on the door of their hut. In the muddled moments it took his mind to register what was happening, Ross assumed that they were experiencing one of Timor's frequent earthquakes.[1] Then he remembered: he and his brother were flying to Australia that day. Just one more flight separated them from a homeland they had not seen in years, not to mention international fame and a £10,000 prize.

Still exhausted, the brothers returned to the aerodrome at Atamboea to find a crowd of Timorese already assembled in the dark to see them take off. Ross hoped to start at first light so that they could complete the 650-kilometre crossing of the Timor Sea during the morning and arrive in Port Darwin around lunchtime. While warming up the engines, however, the ears of the airmen, by now well attuned to their rhythmic drone, detected a slight anomaly. Investigating it, Shiers and Bennett discovered a faulty spark plug and replaced it. Finally ready to go, Ross telephoned the cable office in Koepang and ordered a cable to Darwin explaining that they would take off at 8.30 a.m.[2] Although early, it was already stiflingly hot. The atmosphere was hazy and conditions seemed just right for a thunderstorm.

The aerodrome at Atamboea was yet another that put Ross's skills to the test. Besides being short and surrounded closely by tall gum trees, it sat on a high plateau, 2000 feet above sea level. Starting with the Vimy's tail against the airfield's rear boundary fence, Ross had only just managed to get the aircraft to take-off speed when the fence at the other end of the grass strip appeared out of the haze. The Vimy's undercarriage left the ground just in time and the lower starboard wing brushed the tops of the surrounding gum trees. 'We only just got out,' admitted Ross.[3] 'It was one of the closest shaves of the trip.'[4]

Ross climbed the Vimy gradually to avoid overheating the engines. He skirted around Mount Ramelau, the island's 3000 metre-high peak, and at 9.14 a.m. they arrived above the island's southern coast to find an overcast at 2500 feet and a 'slight haze' below.[5] Keith marked their position on his map, adding, 'Port Darwin next stop'.[6]

The momentous departure from Timor soon settled into the monotony of fair weather ocean flying. Ross held a steady course, not altering it as much as a degree, and flew most of the way at 500 feet. They encountered a few rain squalls, but nothing like Southeast Asia's tumultuous summer climate had presented them with during the previous week's flying. While Ross made his routine of checks on the instruments and engines, Keith and the mechanics watched the horizon for the light cruiser HMAS *Sydney,* which the Defence Department had stationed to patrol the waters between Timor and Darwin in case the Vimy came down in the sea. At 11.48 a.m., two and a half hours after leaving Timor, Keith spotted smoke on the horizon, directly on their bearing—a 'very cheery sight', he thought.[7] Twenty-minutes later, Ross flew over the warship low enough to see the faces of sailors looking up and waving. Keith dropped a bottle containing a message to the *Sydney*'s crew. Addressed from 'the air' and signed by G-EAOU's four crew members, it said, 'Very glad to see you. Many thanks for looking after us. Going strong.'[8]

When a wireless transmission from the *Sydney,* reporting the Vimy's position, reached Darwin a few minutes later, the news spread quickly. An exodus from homes and workplaces began, reminding one journalist of 'an old time gold rush in the west'. Riding horses, walking, a minority in motorcars, the people of Darwin headed for the cliffs above Fannie Bay, where the Defence Department had cleared a space for the Vimy to land.

Within a couple of hours, most of the town's population had assembled; they watched the horizon anxiously, as tens of thousands of others had done during the previous month at aerodromes scattered across the globe from Hounslow to Fannie Bay. A pelican flying over the bay caused a false alarm.[9]

For nearly two hours after passing the *Sydney*, Ross and the crew of G-EAOU saw little except ocean. It was 1.30 p.m. when Ross and Keith began to make out an indistinct hazy smudge on the port horizon. Within a few minutes, it took on the solid form of land: Bathurst Island—Ross's first glimpse of Australia in five years. His feelings in this moment went unrecorded: we can only imagine the exhilarating sense of relief and achievement he felt, mingled perhaps with sadness that his good friend Biffy Borton could not be there to share it.[10] Maybe, too, he felt apprehensive about the overwhelming attention and acclaim that his success would shortly attract.

Within half an hour, the crew could see the coastline of the Australian mainland, including, from 60 kilometres away, the town of Darwin. Approaching from the north-west, the Vimy made landfall close to Point Charles lighthouse and then flew across the mouth of Port Darwin towards Fannie Bay. Ross easily spotted the airfield, encircled by a large crowd. He would later estimate that 2000 people—more than the town's permanent population at the time—had come to see them.[11] At the first sound of the Vimy's engines, there was an excited rush to the edge of the cliffs. 'All at once a tiny speck playing hide and seek with the passing clouds was seen scudding towards the land,' wrote one observer. 'Within a few minutes the outline of the great machine could be plainly discerned far above Fannie Bay sailing along with a mighty roar, and showing a long trail of white vapour from its exhaust.'[12]

Ross switched off the Vimy's engines and glided down in wide circles above the airfield. He eased the biplane onto the ground with what one observer described as 'the grace and ease of some giant bird': it was a perfect landing.[13] The local time was 3.50 p.m.; G-EAOU rolled to a stop on Darwin's coarse grass 27 days and twenty hours since it had lifted off from

Hounslow's frosty surface. The aeroplane and its crew had been in the air for 135 hours. The £10,000 prize was theirs.

As the Vimy rolled to a stop, 'every man, woman and child yelled and cheered and rushed towards the machine'. Ross, Keith, Bennett and Shiers stood slowly in their cockpits and began to peel off their flying gear. To *The Sun*'s reporter, they appeared as 'four weary-looking fellows, who, all the same, did not seem much distressed as a result of their remarkable and nerve-trying experience'.[14] Indeed, Ross again surprised those present by emerging from the cockpit well groomed. He donned a pith helmet and climbed down, 'with his uniform spick-and-span'.[15]

The four airmen stepped down onto terra firma and shook hands. Ross would recall how their hearts swelled 'with those emotions invoked by achievement and the glamour of the moment'. He predicted that 'it was, and will be, perhaps, the supreme hour of our lives'.[16]

The first to greet them was Hudson Fysh, with whom Ross had served in both the light horse and the Flying Corps. Fysh was in Darwin on behalf of the Defence Department and had been involved in surveying an air route across northern Australia for the race competitors. He shook hands with Ross and passed him a bundle of 50 telegrams—the first of many the crew would soon receive. Fysh recalled that Ross's first words were, 'Well, we're here. I did not recognise you at first—where's your uniform?'[17]

Two officious public servants then intervened: they were Darwin's quarantine doctor and customs officer. Examining the airmen before the gathered crowd, the doctor confirmed that they carried no communicable diseases. Not so easily satisfied, the customs official insisted on inspecting the aircraft's cargo then and there. An argument started, with Ross and Keith insisting they carried nothing but some spare parts, their pyjamas and a few tins of bully beef (they apparently neglected to mention the bag of letters G-EAOU also had on board—the first airmail to ever arrive in Australia from overseas). Irritated, Ross pointed out that at no other airfield between London and Darwin had they been subject to such demands. Perhaps because this played out in front of an audience of hundreds, the customs official backed down. He handed Ross a list of dutiable items and declared that he would return the following day to inspect the aircraft.[18]

Next to struggle forward through the press of spectators who had gathered closely around the Vimy was Alderman Robert Toupen, the Mayor of Darwin. After greeting Ross and his comrades, he launched into a florid speech that drew on the imaginary but compelling relationship between aviation and medieval chivalry that wartime literature, art and propaganda had established. Although too polite to show it, Ross probably cringed inwardly at the sort of rhetoric he had previously derided as 'hot air'. Toupen exalted them as the 'valiant knights of the air who have crossed the wide continents and oceans of the world' and, in doing so, had conquered the last great element for mankind. As the Anzacs had done on the battlefields, the mayor declared, Ross and his companions had 'enshrined Australian chivalry and resource in the pantheon of nations where the whole world will do homage to your unique exploit'. Not to be outdone, Mr Staniforth Smith, the Northern Territory's Acting Administrator, spoke too, claiming that the crew of G-EAOU had surpassed the deeds of the mythical Greek hero, Icarus.[19]

The crowd, rowdy and impatient to hear from the airmen, called out and interrupted as the officials pontificated. As the administrator concluded his remarks, people surged forward, hoisting Ross and his three comrades shoulder high before carrying them off across the field towards the neighbouring gaol. Ross found himself planted on a large tree stump to the chant of 'speech, speech!'[20] He obliged, but only briefly, thanking the crowd for its kind welcome and paying tribute to the work of Shiers and Bennett, without whose dedication and expertise he and Keith could have never succeeded.[21]

Mercifully, the gaol's governor intervened, inviting the four weary fliers into his residence for some tea and homemade cakes. When he expressed regret that he had not been able to cater more elaborately, Ross assured him that the spread was more than adequate and thoroughly appreciated.

After they had secured the Vimy, a car took the airmen to Government House, where Acting Administrator Smith invited them to stay. That evening, they dined at the Victoria Hotel in town, at what the local press described as a 'little impromptu dinner arranged hurriedly'. If Ross and his tired crew thought they might escape further formalities, they were mistaken. Another round of speeches followed dinner, including another from the Mayor and the Acting Administrator. Justice Norman Ewing, who presided, also gave an acclamatory speech that finished with a toast to 'These young Australians, four of the foremost men in the empire, who have just performed one of the greatest achievements in the history of the World'.[22] It must have been an enormous relief to Ross, Keith, Bennett and Shiers when they could finally retire, exhausted, to their rooms at Government House.

As Justice Ewing's presence that evening indicated, Ross's arrival in Darwin coincided with a Royal Commission into the administration of the Northern Territory. A year earlier, extensive industrial action in Darwin had culminated in the resignation of the Territory's Administrator. Ross, indeed, had read some sensational news stories about this so-called 'Revolution in Australia' and 'Bolshevism in Darwin' while overseas. He admitted to feeling a little apprehensive as to what they might find upon their arrival in the Northern Territory, yet any concerns about how the top end's rough breed of working men might respond to the Vimy's arrival must have been allayed by the delivery at Government House, the following day, of a letter from the North Australian Meat Company. It had 200 signatures appended. 'Some of us do not know anything about flying, but we saw the final direct flight to the landing paddock,' it read. 'The undertaking is one that requires all the best qualities of mankind, and we take our hats off to the party who manipulated the airship.'[23] Though as yet lacking the experience—and indeed idiom—of aviation, and the ornate oratory skills of Mayor Toupen, Darwin's working men nevertheless appreciated that they had just witnessed something extraordinary—something that not only represented the best of their country to the world, but also heralded a new era in human civilisation.

This was a realisation that, in the hours following the Vimy's landing at Fannie Bay, was dawning not only on people all around Australia, but across the world. Ross and his crew had a great achievement behind them, now, they needed to fly the Vimy south, to Melbourne, where Vickers had instructed Ross to hand the aircraft over to the Commonwealth Government as a gift. 'The aviators have still to cross a continent,' reported the newspapers, 'but that is a minor matter after crossing parts of three continents and two oceans.'[24] This prediction, however, would soon prove to be wrong.

PART FIVE

'THE FOREMOST LIVING AVIATOR'

1919–1922

34

EVERYONE HAS GONE QUITE MAD

The significance of their achievement began to dawn on Ross and his companions during the two days following their arrival in Darwin. Each hour, great bundles of cables arrived at Government House, conveying congratulations from all over the world. Along with many from friends, family and ordinary people who Ross had never met, there were messages from the King, Prime Minister David Lloyd George and Secretary of State for Air Winston Churchill. There was even a telegram from the Warriston School in Moffatt, Scotland, where the Smith brothers had studied in 1906–07: 'Well done, Ross and Keith. Warriston is proud of you.'[1] Newspapers around the world proclaimed the Vimy crew's success. Ross, the *New York Times* declared, 'must be hailed as the foremost living aviator'.[2]

The crew spent two days at Fannie Bay preparing G-EAOU to fly across the Australian continent. Shiers and Bennett did their best with the engines, patching up the worn-out exhaust manifolds and checking the valve clearances. The starboard engine needed a top overhaul, but Ross did not intend to linger in Darwin. With the wet season just starting, he feared the damage a tropical storm might do to the Vimy. Although Ross told the press that Vickers' aircraft remained in excellent condition and could indeed be flown back to London after a proper overhaul, he knew his aircraft to be in a fragile state. The fabric hung slack in places and the airframe had warped, requiring regular adjustments to the bracing wires. The engines had blown six exhaust manifolds during the flight and there were no more spares; to fly across Australia, the port engine would be running with 'practically open exhausts'. The propellers were in bad shape too.[3]

Ross and Keith planned to fly south along the route that the Defence Department had surveyed and stocked with fuel—a monumental undertaking in itself, which involved the first flight across the continent, from Melbourne to Darwin, and to which the Commonwealth had committed more than £2000.[4] Following this trail, blazed by some of their ex-AFC comrades, Ross and his crew would fly across the Northern Territory's Barkly Tableland, through Central Queensland via Longreach and Cloncurry, then to Bourke and Narromine in New South Wales. Ross did not plan to stop in Sydney, but changed his mind when petitioned by the city's Lord Mayor and a number of other prominent residents who felt outraged that Melbourne should be honoured by a visit from the famous aircraft and its crew while Sydney, 'the mother city of the Commonwealth', missed out.[5] The directors at Vickers expected Ross to conclude the flight in Melbourne, where he would present G-EAOU to the Commonwealth Government. But Ross harboured aspirations to fly all the way home, to Adelaide—and, indeed, perhaps even out to Mutooroo. For now, though, he told the press that he expected to reach Melbourne in about four days.[6]

The Vimy began its journey south on 13 December 1919, with Ross hoping to reach Anthony Lagoon, a cattle station about 1000 kilometres south-east of Darwin. With no decent navigational charts available, Keith sketched some of his own, based on conversations with drovers and the pilots who had recently surveyed the route. For some sections, he was instructed to follow the tracks left by large mobs of cattle. 'It is bad country for flying,' observed Ross, 'mostly scrub and waterless.'[7]

About 480 kilometres from Darwin, the Vimy's starboard engine lost power. Ross picked out a dry swamp bed and landed. Known as Warlock Ponds, the place was, Ross reckoned, 'about 100 miles away from anywhere'.[8] Shiers and Bennett fixed the problem by adjusting the engine's valve guide, but not before sunset. The four airmen camped overnight beside the Vimy among swarms of mosquitoes. 'Soon our faces, arms, and legs were just a mass of lumps,' wrote Ross. They tried lighting a grass fire and wrapping themselves in blankets; in desperation, Ross splashed whiskey onto his skin—which only seemed to increase the insects' appetite. 'I was forced to watch Keith and Bennett and Shiers drink their portions while I vainly tried to lick up the drips that were running down my face.'[9]

Continuing its journey the following morning, the Vimy made it to within 30 kilometres of the Anthony Lagoon cattle station when a loud crack, this time from the port engine, startled the crew. The whole aircraft vibrated. Realising with horror that one of the propeller blades had split, Ross switched the engine off and looked for a place to land.[10]

The blade had come apart along its entire length, from tip to boss. Ross suspected the bird they had struck in Calcutta, though in truth the propellers had suffered much abuse on improvised and often muddy airfields.[11] G-EAOU had landed at Cobb's Creek, an uninhabited spot in the Barkly Tableland, 700 kilometres from the nearest railhead. Obtaining a new propeller or dismantling and shipping the aircraft would prove difficult, if not impossible: they would have to make repairs themselves.[12]

They had been lucky in one respect, landing near the campsite of an engineer who was working on a sub-artesian bore. He agreed to leave them some food and water and carry a message from Ross to the nearest cable station. For two days, the airmen camped in the wilderness while Bennett did his best to repair the propeller. He used pieces of a timber crate, scavenged from the engineer's campsite, to replace the missing splinters; after gluing them, he bound the blade with strips of galvanised sheet secured by screws extracted from the Vimy's floorboards. 'We worked under the most trying circumstances,' reported Ross.[13] It got so hot during the day that they had to stop work and shelter beneath the Vimy's wings. The heat warped the laminated glass of their flying goggles and the aircraft's windscreens. When they ran out of water, they made themselves ill on the brackish stuff from the bore.[14]

When the Vimy failed to reach its destination, 'the wildest rumours' circulated in Australia's towns and cities.[15] 'In hotels, in clubs, in the trains, even in the State Parliament,' reported one Melbourne newspaper, 'it was whispered that the Defence department had received news that Captain Ross Smith had "crashed", and that he and all his party had been killed.' It was not until 17 December, three days after G-EAOU's forced landing at Cobb's Creek, that the newspapers reported Ross and his crew safe.[16]

With the propeller repaired, Ross and his companions continued their journey south, nursing the Vimy through several short stages. 'I am taking no risks with [the] machine now,' cabled Ross to Vickers.[17] It took seven days to fly the 1500 kilometres between Cobb's Creek and Charleville in South-Central Queensland. 'We found it almost impossible to fly during the middle of the day owing to the intense heat,' reported Ross. 'Our machine was literally tossed about like a cork and we all became violently air sick . . . we had to spend a whole day at Cloncurry tightening up our wires, which had become quite slack.'[18] The crew stopped overnight on the pastoral stations at Burnette and Avon Downs and then at Cloncurry and Longreach, before reaching Charleville on 23 December. Four hundred locals gathered in a dusty paddock at Glengarry, 17 kilometres out of town, to meet the aviators. The airmen enjoyed refreshments under the shade of a tree before attending a dinner in their honour in the Shire Hall.[19]

News was waiting in Charleville that the King had conferred knighthoods on Ross and Keith. Receiving the telegram in his hotel room, Ross reportedly responded in disbelief, exclaiming, 'Oh rot! What a joke!' Flopping backwards onto his bed, Keith said, 'Great Scott! What on earth will Mother say to having two knights knocking about the place?'[20] The recommendation for the titles came from the British Controller-General of Civil Aviation, Sir Frederick Sykes; in his submission, he had cited the precedents of Alcock and Brown, who were similarly honoured for their trans-Atlantic flight. While acknowledging the value and achievement that both flights represented, Sykes nevertheless believed that 'the Australian flight is a greater thing and will have more far reaching results'.[21]

The press immediately took to referring to them as 'Sir Ross' and 'Sir Keith'. Privately, Ross felt uncomfortable with his new title, expecting that it would 'only be a nuisance to me'.[22] Publicly, he expressed gratitude and, as usual, accounted for their success by pointing to the work of others—Shiers and Bennett in particular, for whom the British Government announced the more modest honour of a Bar to the Air Force Medal each had received following the flight to India with Salmond. The British Controller General of Civil Aviation had, in fact, recommended Shiers and Bennett for the receipt of a higher award, the Air Force Cross, but as sergeant NCOs they did not qualify for it.[23]

The disparity in honours for G-EAOU's crew would raise some questions as to why the mechanics, who played such a vital role, were not equally honoured. When the matter came up in the House of Representatives, the disparity between classes, which Australians traditionally believe does not demarcate their society, became apparent. Responding to a question from a Labor member as to why Shiers and Bennett had not received knighthoods, Nationalist member for Ballarat Edwin Kerby reasoned, 'They would probably not know what to do with a title.'[24] The Defence Department would promote the mechanics by one rank, Bennett to Warrant Officer Class 1 and Shiers to permanent sergeant, and later award them honorary commissions.

The journey's next stage began on Christmas morning. From Charleville, Ross intended to make overnight stops at Bourke and Narromine, and to arrive in Sydney on 27 December. According to the newspapers, 'nearly all Charleville and its numerous visitors' turned out to farewell the four airmen: 'Handkerchiefs, hats and sticks were waved by the sightseers as the plane ascended.'[25] With the engines apparently running well, Ross climbed to 3000 feet and had just set a course south when there was a 'terrific bang'. Flames flashed out of the port engine past Bennett and Shiers in the rear cockpit, followed by smoke.[26] Shutting down the engine, Ross returned to Charleville and landed.

It was immediately apparent that the port engine had been critically damaged. Two of the connecting rods were broken; one had punched a hole clean through the crank case and fallen to the ground, while the other lay broken in the engine cowling. A couple of the piston heads had been damaged too. While they could not be certain what had caused such a catastrophic engine failure, Ross initially suggested to Vickers that the makeshift repairs to the port engine's propeller had caused a slight vibration that weakened and then broke the connecting rods.[27] In a private letter to Borton, he revealed that a mechanical failure had been the cause: 'The main oil pump drive went wrong and caused the rest.'[28] To the public, he downplayed the damage, reminding people that 'nothing mechanical would last forever' and joking that perhaps the engine had objected to working on Christmas Day.[29]

The crew were dismayed: 'Looked like end of flight,' noted Keith in his diary.[30] Ross thought so too, cabling Vickers' office in Sydney to express his doubts that they would be able to get the aircraft flying without a new engine from Britain. Considering the situation hopeless, he proposed coming to Sydney via rail to arrange for G-EAOU to be dismantled and shipped to Melbourne.[31]

Vickers' Australian agent agreed. It was a 'sounder policy', he thought, for Ross to 'take no risks' with the aircraft.[32] In the following days, however, Ross had a change of heart. Bennett reckoned that, with the right tools, he could fashion some replacement pistons and a new propeller. When the Government of Queensland offered Ross the use of its railway workshops at Ipswich, he gratefully accepted.[33] Writing to Vickers about his new plans, Ross explained that he was 'more disappointed than I can say that we should have been held up so near the end' and that he was determined to 'see the job through'.[34]

Ross, Keith and Bennett arrived in Ipswich with the damaged engine on 2 January 1920. They stepped off the train into a crush of hundreds of people who crowded the platform, eager to welcome them. Ross did his best to put on a gracious smile and an appreciative demeanour, but to some it was apparent that he was uncomfortable with all the attention. His reputation for modesty and distaste for 'hero worship' had, indeed, preceded him.[35]

The repairs that Ross predicted would require a fortnight ended up taking nearly six weeks.[36] While Shiers remained at Charleville to give the starboard engine a top overhaul and repaint the airframe, Bennett, assisted by mechanics from the railway works and Defence Department, machined a new pair of connecting rods and piston heads, and patched up the damage caused by the engine's failure. They also fashioned a new propeller from Queensland maple.

Ross and Keith spent most of January in Brisbane, where they were feted, day and night, at receptions and functions. 'Everyone has gone quite mad about the flight,' reported Ross. 'There is an awful lot of hot air business going on which bores me stiff and I would like to crawl away to the hollow logs but suppose we must go on with it.'[37] Ross found the constant demand to make speeches particularly bothersome, but by all reports he played the part well. He and Keith charmed audiences with their self-deprecating humour, their broad smiles and their charismatic modesty.

Indeed, this is the impression Ross and Keith, now free from their exclusive deal with Murdoch, gave to the journalists who interviewed them in Brisbane. The *Daily Mail*'s reporter noted that 'he does not seem at all surprised at the fact that he has flown here from London and would not bring up the matter in conversation for worlds'.[38] They left a similar impression with a journalist from the *Brisbane Courier*, who noted that 'one of the most pleasing attributes of both brothers is their perfect naturalness of manner and their complete freedom from self-consciousness'.[39] *The Mail*'s correspondent was taken by their 'perpetual' smiles and lack of pretence: 'They carry their honours well.'[40]

Perhaps it was all the attention in Brisbane that compelled Ross to get in touch with Captain Frank Hurley, the famous Antarctic adventurer and official war photographer with whom he had flown in Palestine in 1918. When Ross asked him to join the crew to film and photograph the remainder of their flight south, Hurley needed little convincing. He knew a lucrative opportunity when he saw one, and he lost no time in packing his cameras and heading for Charleville to fly in the aeroplane 'that had obliterated space and held the world enthralled'.[41]

35

FAME AND FORTUNE

With the Vimy's port engine repaired, Ross and his party left Charleville on 12 February. From the nacelle at the front of the Vimy's fuselage, Hurley was awed by the 'soul-stirring spectacle of the drought-stricken plains of Southern Queensland—desolate, dreary, and dead'.[1] After stopping for the night in Bourke and then Narromine, on Saturday, 14 February, Ross and his crew headed for Sydney. They followed the railway line, passing over Dubbo, Orange, Bathurst and Lithgow—regional towns whose residents filled the streets to see the aeroplane that had flown all the way from England. They waved, rang bells and blew whistles in a 'clamour', reported one journalist, 'reminiscent of the din on Armistice Day'.[2] After crossing the Blue Mountains, G-EAOU was met by three escorting biplanes. Ahead lay Sydney and its harbour, bright and clear in the summer sun: 'a spectacle of exquisite charm and beauty,' thought Ross.[3]

Ross flew over the city from the north-west. He headed over the eastern suburbs towards the Heads and then made two wide circuits of the harbour so that Hurley could take pictures and shoot film. The photographer described how Ross descended to 600 feet as they came in for their second pass over the city.

> We were not very far above the roofs of the buildings; and we could distinctly make out the crowds in the streets, and even the patches of colour of the ladies' dresses. We were all waving then; the sergeants were leaning out and waving to the people; while Sir Ross stood up with his hand on the joy-stick.[4]

Normal life in the city stopped as an estimated three-quarters of a million people came outside to watch the Vimy's arrival; they crowded onto roofs, balconies and hilltops and packed the foreshores. 'Never,' declared *The Sun*, 'have so many people crowded on to Sydney's skyline'.[5]

Tens of thousands of men, women and children travelled south of the city to Mascot, where, in a paddock beside Botany Bay, Ross had been promised 500 yards (460 metres) of level ground.[6] The site, later to become Sydney's international airport, had only been operating as an aerodrome for a few weeks, after being purchased by the Australian Aircraft & Engineering Co. Ltd, agents for Avro in Australia.

'An army' of police had established a cordon around the airfield, but as the Vimy touched down, the mass of spectators swept them 'ruthlessly aside' and surged forward to surround the aeroplane.[7] Looking down onto the sea of hats—bowlers, boaters, fedoras and gardeners—Ross and Keith would have eagerly sought the faces of their parents, who they had arranged to come to Sydney to meet them. Parting a little, the crowd allowed Andrew and Jessie Smith through. 'Leaning from their high seats,' reported the *Daily Telegraph,* 'the boys seized their parents' hands in steel grasps. There were looks of affection exchanged, a murmured word—that was all.'[8] Ross climbed down and embraced his mother, a photographer from the *Sunday Times* capturing the moment: both mother and son smiling broadly as they stared into each other's faces—the joy they felt as five years apart came to an end is palpable in the image.[9]

Before a representative from the Premier's Department could explain the official program to Ross, a group of men wearing the uniform of the Australian light horse seized the airman and carried him off through the crowd on their shoulders. 'He was helpless,' described the *Sydney Morning Herald*'s correspondent with some admonition. 'There was little or no respect for the airman's comfort.'[10] Ross and the other crew members found themselves jostled towards a tent, where the Premier's welcoming party attempted to serve refreshments. With the crowds pressing in, threatening to collapse the marquee, the reception was abandoned and, with difficulty, the four airmen, along with Andrew and Jessie Smith, were 'hustled into motor cars and hurried off' into the city.[11]

First there was a reception at the Town Hall before an audience 'packed like sardines'. To rapturous applause, the Acting Lord Mayor proclaimed the flight 'the world's greatest aviation exploit', while in response Ross humbly apologised for the delay and paid tribute to his crew.[12] Afterwards the airmen had afternoon tea with the Prime Minister and that evening attended a dinner, hosted by *The Sun* at the Australia Hotel, where the party stayed as guests. Excited crowds mobbed the airmen as they moved between engagements. 'Their motor car was rushed; people fought to shake hands with them, and Sir Ross Smith was patted on the back by 20 people at once,' described a reporter. 'All round amateur photographers took snapshots.'[13]

For a week, Ross and Keith found themselves the focus of an entire city's adulation. 'Sydney was the worst place,' Ross would later recall. 'The whole town appeared to go quite mad and we were led around like bears on a string.'[14] It was an extraordinary thing—perhaps the first example in the city's history of public mania over a visiting celebrity. *The Sun,* which had the greatest access to Ross through his association with Murdoch, reported how his room at the Australia Hotel 'is besieged from breakfast-time till midnight with importunate callers'. Letters, telegrams and autograph books arrived in great bundles.[15] 'We tried to do our best,' explained Keith, 'but when 60 came in in one lot for both our autographs I thought it was too hot.'[16] Besides congratulatory messages and pitches for commercial opportunities, the brothers were inundated with requests from new and expectant mothers to name babies after them and with marriage proposals from Sydney's young and eligible ladies. In three days, *The Sun* reported receiving 130 poems and songs written in their honour.[17]

Ross received the public's overwhelming and gratuitous demands with good grace and humour—although it proved exhausting and, given his aversion to adulation, almost unbearably embarrassing. He gave dozens of speeches, paying tribute to Vickers and his crew *ad nauseam*, and expressing gratitude to the people of Sydney for their hospitality. 'I had to make 7 speeches in one day there!', he reported to Borton. 'I said the same thing exactly each time but they didn't seem to mind a bit.'[18] In only one recorded instance did Ross refuse to indulge his public; it was during a performance at Her Majesty's Theatre on 18 February, when an unruly section of the audience vocally demanded that he take to the stage. When he declined, Keith addressed the audience 'quietly and firmly' from their box: 'My brother will not go on the stage. He is not a member of the company, and had nothing to do with the performance . . . We have to thank [the manager] Mr Ward for his most pleasant entertainment, and you for the most handsome reception you have given us.'[19] It was an awkward moment, handled adroitly.

The crew began their flight to Melbourne from Richmond aerodrome on 22 February. The New South Wales Premier, William Holman, accompanied them as a passenger to Cootamundra so that he could deliver a campaign speech for the state's upcoming elections. Three thousand people welcomed G-EAOU and its crew in a paddock beside Cootamundra West railway station. The presence of 150 motor vehicles in town suggested that spectators had travelled from far and wide. For many, it was the first time they had seen an aeroplane.[20]

Ross intended to fly to Melbourne on 24 February where, at Flemington Racecourse, Victorian authorities had organised a large and elaborate reception.[21] During the day, 60,000 people turned up, paying at the gate to see what promised to be quite a spectacle. Bands played throughout the afternoon and some biplanes from the Defence Department's aerodrome at Point Cook put on a flying display, but there was no sign of the Vimy. Then, late in the afternoon, it was announced: Sir Ross Smith and his crew were not coming; the aircraft had been forced to land with mechanical problems.

Ross had landed three times that morning after leaving Cootamundra. The port engine kept losing oil pressure; he stopped at Bon Accord, 20 kilometres south-west of Wagga Wagga and then at the Rock, only a short distance further on, before abandoning the day's journey at Henty, 70 kilometres from the Victorian border. Ross felt 'fed up at disappointing' so many people who had paid to see him arrive at Flemington.[22] Clearly in no mood for more speeches, when representatives from Henty's returned services branch tried to compel the crew to attend an impromptu function, he bluntly told them: 'We are going to bed, and don't you forget it.'[23]

Ross woke the following morning with renewed determination to reach Melbourne that day. The crew stripped everything they could from the aircraft to make it lighter and, after taking off under the power of both engines, he shut down the port one. The Vimy flew the remaining 400 kilometres to Melbourne on the starboard engine alone. Few saw the aircraft as it passed over the city, its arrival being unannounced and largely obscured by fog. Ross landed at Point Cook, 30 kilometres south-west of the city.

An inspection of the port engine revealed that the big end bearings had worn out—a prelude to the kind of catastrophic engine failure they had suffered at Charleville two months earlier. 'It must have been inferior metal badly put in at Ipswich,' speculated Ross in his official report to Vickers. Whatever the cause, it would take nearly a month to repair, during which time Ross and his party would remain in Melbourne, as guests of the Prime Minister's Department at the Menzies Hotel.[24]

The crew had arrived in Melbourne utterly exhausted. Ross explained to the city's 'Sir Ross Smith Reception Committee' that he and Keith were 'eager to buy some mufti, and that they want rest and quiet and to dodge official functions as much as possible'.[25] He would be disappointed: for their first fortnight in town, the schedule of official receptions would almost rival the intensity of what they had experienced in Sydney.

Ross delivered around 320 letters to the federal postal authorities in Melbourne—the first airmail ever delivered in Australia.[26] Some had been carried all the way from Britain; Ross collected others along the route. Before forwarding them on to their addressees, the Prime Minister's Department ordered a specially designed stamp to be affixed to each cover. These few hundred 'Ross Smith Covers', with their blue stamp featuring the title 'First Aerial Post' and an image of the Vimy, immediately became valuable to collectors.

The largest and most important event on the Melbourne itinerary occurred on Friday, 27 February at Parliament House, where Prime Minister William Morris Hughes presented Ross with a cheque for £10,000. Acknowledging that all the crew members had shared the risks and hard work, he divided the prize equally with Keith, Shiers and Bennett. Kodak also awarded the crew £800 for the photographs they took during the flight, while Murdoch's United Cable Service paid Ross the £500 agreed for his exclusive reports on the flight.

But these represented just the beginning of the commercial opportunities that now presented themselves to Ross and the members of his crew. While in Melbourne, dozens of proposals came from businessmen, hopeful of associating all manner of products and ventures with the now world-famous aviators. 'Callers were more numerous than ever at the Menzies Hotel today,' reported a journalist on 1 March. 'Before the airmen entered the breakfast room persons were waiting to see them and there were times when Sir Ross was approached by three or four callers almost simultaneously.'[27]

Frank Hurley, who appears to have become the party's spokesman and publicist, announced that he was making a film of the flight and booking a lecture tour for the airmen. They had, he claimed—perhaps with some exaggeration—already turned down a contract for an international speaking tour worth £10,000.[28] With Hurley's assistance, Ross also started work on a book and negotiated deals with publishers in the United States, Australia and Britain. Despite its many irritations, fame—as Ross was beginning to discover—also brought with it the prospects of fortune.

36

LEAVING AN OLD AND TRUSTY FRIEND

Since his earliest days in the cockpit, Ross had entertained aspirations of flying all the way home to Adelaide—and perhaps even out to Mutooroo.[1] During the long journey south from Darwin, journalists had reported him discussing this ambition and, indeed, on 1 January 1920, newspapers published a cable Ross sent to the South Australian Premier expressing his wish to fly the Vimy to Adelaide.[2]

While in Melbourne preparing for this, the final stage of a 22,500 kilometre flight from London, Ross received a cable from Vickers instructing him to hand the Vimy over to the Australian Government at once.[3] Considering the numerous mechanical problems Ross and his crew had experienced since arriving in Australia, the company's managers were now unwilling to push their luck any further. They did not want him to attempt the flight to Adelaide in G-EAOU.

This put Ross in an awkward position. He had publicly announced his intention to fly to his hometown and had repeatedly claimed in speeches that the Vimy remained in excellent shape. It could, he said, be flown back to London after an overhaul. As he reasoned to the managers at Vickers, withdrawing the aircraft from the flight to Adelaide 'would have been almost an admission that the Machine was done for after under 200 hours' flying'.[4]

On 19 March, Ross did as instructed by his sponsors and went to the Prime Minister's office, where he formally signed ownership of G-EAOU over to the Commonwealth. He then asked permission to borrow the aeroplane to make the first flight between Melbourne and Adelaide—a request the Prime Minister 'readily granted'. Ross announced his plans to the press: he would fly to Adelaide and then return the Vimy to Melbourne. He had changed his mind about flying to Mutooroo, citing a scarcity of places to land and the difficulty the crew would face if they broke down in such a remote place.[5] The reaction of Vickers' directors is unrecorded; it seems likely, however, that they would have felt apprehensive that an accident might now reverse the publicity Ross's success had secured the company. Perhaps, too, they felt that Ross had acted with perfidy. He had abided by the letter, but certainly not the spirit, of their agreement.

Ross and his crew set out for Adelaide early on 23 March 1920. Hurley flew with them but Andrew and Jessie Smith went by rail. As the crew prepared to depart Point Cook, journalists peppered Ross with the usual questions about how he felt about the flight ahead. 'What can I say to express my feelings?' he asked, his patience apparently wearing thin. 'I have had a splendid time, and I would like to thank everyone. But it is the business of you people to spin words—express my feelings for me, tell them how grateful I am. Say what you will—you can't say too much—but don't make it flamboyant.'[6] It is a revealing comment; behind Ross's easy-going and charismatic good humour, his frustration with his new-found fame was growing. He resented the loss of control, describing in private correspondence how he and Keith had become 'more or less public property' and that they 'had to do many things which I would have liked to avoid'.[7]

After taking off at Point Cook, Ross had to climb through a thick overcast. It was cold and turbulent, and the crew couldn't see the ground again until Ballarat. The 760-kilometre flight took a little over six hours. Ross approached the city from the south-east, coming in over Mount Lofty. 'Adelaide showed up beautifully and well-defined in the sunlight,' said Ross. 'The hills presented a glorious picture.'[8] The Vimy flew over the centre of town, where according to Shiers they could 'discern the people like ants crawling about the streets and perched upon the roofs of houses and buildings'. It gave him 'a queer thrill' to see his hometown again.[9] Ross then deviated from his course slightly to pick out Aviemore, the family home at Walkerville: 'It was a dear old spot after five years of absence.'[10]

Local authorities arranged for Ross to land on the privately owned Northfield aerodrome that had recently been established in a paddock 10 kilometres north of the city. The Vimy arrived at 2.12 p.m., the drone of its engines joining the discord of tooting motor horns and screeching sirens, and the shouts and cheers of the 'multitude' of people who had travelled out from town. 'Flying at great speed, and often rocking gently, it was an inspiring sight,' described one observer. 'Then facing the westerly breeze it came down with a swoop that suggested the grace and power of a huge bird.'[11] As the wheels touched down, though, they ran through a depression that bounced the great biplane back into the air. Ross pushed the throttle levers forward and took off again to go around and make a second attempt. 'If my engine had failed at that stage,' Ross later reflected, 'we would have crashed into 60 or 70 motor cars.'[12] It is the only recorded instance in more than 40 landings since leaving Hounslow that Ross needed to go around for a second attempt.

As in the other capitals, thousands of people turned out to see the Vimy land. Adelaide's *Daily Herald* estimated that 10,000 'fathers, mothers and children crowded along the roads and around the fences near the flying grounds'.[13] Bennett thought there might have been as many as 20,000.[14] Either way, the police detachment proved inadequate to manage this mass of people. As Ross taxied, the crowd broke through the cordon and surged onto the aerodrome. The Vimy edged forward, its propellers still spinning, with Ross and Keith standing in the cockpit, frantically waving their arms to compel the spectators to move back. Fearing someone would be killed, Ross switched off the engines, bringing G-EAOU to a stop in the middle of the airfield.

Thousands of people closed in around the aircraft; to escape the crush, some began climbing onto its wings. One of the aircraft's timber skids was broken. Officials and mounted police scrambled to get the situation under control but in the wild excitement the crowd refused to disperse. For several minutes, Ross and Keith stood in the cockpit trying in vain to reason with the masses. 'The two brothers conversed together quite calmly,' reported a journalist, 'but let it be understood that the programme was suspended until they could be sure that the machine which was entrusted to their care was in safe hands.'

The South Australian Premier made it to the front of the scrum and appealed to Ross and Keith to come down. At first they refused: 'Not while they are tearing our machine to bits,' explained Keith. 'We have to get back to Melbourne in this.' Several tense minutes passed before Ross accepted that the crowd was not going to leave the aircraft alone while he occupied it; he and Keith climbed down from the cockpit to be greeted by the official party. The crowd seized the brothers and hoisted them shoulder high with deafening cheers. 'The people were bubbling over with enthusiasm and admiration,' described a journalist. 'Girls called them by name and threw kisses, and old comrades in arms hailed them gladly. Both knights recognised many old friends.'[15]

If anything, the first week Ross spent in Adelaide proved even busier than his time in the eastern capitals. But unlike the public appearances in Sydney and Melbourne, in Adelaide, Ross (along with Keith and Shiers) was among his own people: friends and family he had not seen in years. Every group and organisation with which Ross had ever been associated clamoured to secure a spot on his itinerary. In one four-day period, Saturday, 27 March to Tuesday, 30 March, between them the Smith brothers attended at least ten different functions.[16] For Ross, this included an appearance at the Adelaide Race Club's meet at Victoria Park, laying a war memorial's foundation stone in Glenelg, lunch with the Lieutenant-Governor, afternoon tea with old colleagues at Harris, Scarfe & Co., a reception at the Adelaide Rowing Club, a fundraising event with the Boy Scouts and an address to the pupils at the Queen's School.

On Sunday, 28 March, Ross took the Vimy on a flight over the city so that Hurley could secure some footage for his film. Andrew and Jessie Smith, as well as Ross's old friend Roy Howard, went along as passengers. Forty minutes into the flight, an alarming grinding sound from one of the engines prompted Ross to return to the aerodrome. To Vickers, Ross dismissed the episode as 'slight engine trouble', while Keith assured the press that 'it was not a serious defect'.[17] In reality, the engine's epicyclic reduction gear, responsible for moderating the propeller's speed, had failed. Ross knew that he and his passengers had been lucky; a few minutes more in the air and they may have lost the propeller altogether.[18]

It took a week for the crew, assisted by some local mechanics, to cobble the gearbox back together; it was a 'big job', wrote Ross. When the crew flew the Vimy back to Melbourne on 5 April 1920, Ross 'had the wind up', anxious that it might fail again.[19] It held together, but part-way through the flight the port engine lost oil pressure and the aircraft once again limped to Point Cook on a single engine. As Ross expected, it would be the last time G-EAOU ever took to the air.[20]

As the Vimy was wheeled into one of Point Cook's hangars, Hurley stood in the forward nacelle, filming what would be the final scenes of the film he was producing to accompany Ross's upcoming lecture tour. It was a bittersweet moment for Ross, marking the successful conclusion of his great endeavour—his '14,000 miles through the air', an adventure into which he had poured every ounce of his energy, skill and resources. It also marked the end of Ross's association with the aeroplane that had carried him and his crew safely halfway around the globe. 'In a way I am very sorry to be leaving the Vimy, for during the past few months I have grown attached to it,' he explained to one of the journalists there. 'Today I feel that I am leaving an old and trusty friend that has borne me many thousands of miles.'[21]

37

THE ARISTOCRACY OF ACHIEVEMENT

With G-EAOU safely ensconced in a hangar at Point Cook, Ross, Keith and Frank Hurley caught the next train to Sydney. They had no time to lose—there were just three weeks before the national film and lecture tour that Union Theatres, the largest syndicate of performance spaces in Australia, had booked for them. For the remainder of April, the trio worked at the studios of Australasian Films Limited, in Rushcutters Bay, to assemble a silent film from the footage and images that Hurley and the crew had taken during the flight and to write a script from which they could narrate it for audiences.

Known as a 'lecture film' or 'travelogue', this type of entertainment had become popular in the United States and Europe around the turn of the century. Hurley gained experience in the medium by producing features on the Mawson and Shackleton expeditions to Antarctica, which he accompanied before the war. They blended the new technology of cinema with older forms of media such as the lecture, music played by an in-house orchestra and still images (drawn and photographed) to produce shows that, their creators claimed, were entertaining as well as educational.

Ross had to work closely with Hurley to synchronise his words with the film's images; the timing needed to be precise, with producers of the genre typically allowing two spoken words for every foot of film stock.[1] It proved to be a tedious and exacting job, but Ross was determined to do it well, deciding 'to defer the opening until I had carefully prepared and diligently rehearsed the lines of my story . . . as each section [of the film] reaches completion, I synchronise the vocal text.'[2]

The final cut of *The Ross Smith Flight from London to Australia*, as they titled the feature, ran for two and a half hours.[3] Hurley would narrate the first part, which consisted of the footage and photographs he had taken between Charleville and Adelaide. Besides aerial photography of the crew and of various towns and cities, Hurley included sequences depicting life in the Australian outback: stockmen, horse trainers and an Aboriginal ceremony. He also included footage of the port engine being repaired at Ipswich railways workshops and of the crowds that welcomed the Vimy in Sydney, Melbourne and Adelaide. After an interval, Ross would take to the stage, lecturing to film and stills that Keith had shot during the flight from London to Charleville. The footage included a striking diversity of visual fare—snow-covered Alps, Middle Eastern deserts, tropical jungles and Australia's outback—that emphasised to audiences the Vimy's extraordinarily rapid crossing of geography and the seasons.

The film exploited the technological and stylistic conventions of the day to produce a spectacle every bit as modern as its subject. Hurley filled gaps in the pictorial record with 'trick' shots: picture postcards dangled before a camera lens to create the illusion of footage shot from the air.[4] The show opened with Ross addressing the audience in front of a screen onto which Hurley projected a view of the Swiss Alps, across which flew a silhouetted model of the Vimy, operated by Hurley behind the scenes.[5] During the feature, an animated map tracked G-EAOU's journey across the globe.

Hurley ensured that he received as much credit and exposure as possible from his partnership with Ross. Despite including footage shot by the crew, the feature opened with an intertitle stating it had been 'Edited and photographed by Captain Frank Hurley—Late Official Photographer, Australian Imperial Force, & Shackleton and Mawson Antarctic Expeditions, etc.' and, in the promotional articles he wrote for the newspapers, Hurley implied that he had been part of the entire expedition.[6] The division of the film into two distinct and non-chronological sequences made little sense in terms of narrative, but ensured Hurley a distinct platform from which to address the huge audiences that he expected Ross to attract.

Little is known about the dynamics of Ross's relationship with Hurley. After Ross's death, the photographer would write an article recalling their friendship warmly and quoting a letter from Ross, written in 1922, that suggests the pair shared a friendship and esteem for one another.[7] Still, it is difficult to see how Ross, whose modesty and distaste for 'big noting' defined his personality, could have appreciated Hurley, the consummate self-promoter. Perhaps their association had a pragmatically reciprocal nature: in Ross, Hurley saw an opportunity to further his career as a photographer and filmmaker, while Ross perceived the lecture tour as an opportunity to make some money and fill in time while he planned his next endeavour. Indeed, he seems to have regarded the whole thing with some ambivalence. 'It is not a bad job,' he wrote to Biffy Borton, 'certainly not very hard, and I have to do something.'[8]

Ross, Keith and Hurley previewed the film to members of federal parliament in Melbourne on 29 April 1920. Union Theatres had booked a three-month run of dates; Ross and Hurley would perform in the capital cities and large regional centres while Keith, Bennett and Shiers toured, with additional prints of the film, to regional areas.

Union promoted the film extensively, one newspaper advertisement proclaiming:

> You'll feel a Better Australian when you HEAR THE STORY and SEE THE FILM Personally Related by Sir Ross Smith himself. It's more than just entertainment—it's history relived—brought to your very eyes so that you might thrill at, and understand the amazing experiences of our pioneers of the air who have indelibly imprinted the glory of Australia's name across the skies of four continents.[9]

Hurley energetically spruiked the film too, declaring that its images—his images—were 'unusually clear and stereoscopic . . . in some cases the pictures are uncannily realistic and give the spectator the sensation experienced during an actual flight'.[10]

Ross's first run of performances opened at Adelaide's Town Hall on 3 May 1920. He and Hurley did eight days there, both matinee and evening shows, before moving to West's Olympia for a five-day season so that 'Picture Theatre patrons'—that is, working people—could come.[11] Whereas seats at the Town Hall performances cost 5 shillings each, tickets for the theatre dates went for as little as a shilling. The South Australian Education Department also arranged for Adelaide's state schools to attend the matinees at West's. In five days, 14,000 school children experienced Ross and Hurley's spectacle.[12]

Similar performance schedules followed in the other capitals, with a run of town hall gala performances followed by a season in one of Union's theatre houses. Ross performed eleven dates in Brisbane during the latter half of May and then seventeen in Sydney and the nearby regional centres of Newcastle and Bathurst during June. The tour moved to Melbourne for the first half of July before wrapping up with a fortnight of performances in Perth, Fremantle and Kalgoorlie—Ross's first visit to Western Australia.

In 96 days, Ross and Hurley gave close to 140 performances before audiences ranging in size from a few hundred in the regional venues to over 3000 in the cities. Records of ticket sales are not available but, according to reviews, the shows sold well. *The Evening News* reported, for example, that on the final evening at Sydney's Town Hall nearly 1000 people were left outside, unable to get tickets.[13] Ross may have spoken to over 200,000 people during his Australian lecture tour, while many thousands of others saw the shows presented by Keith, Bennett and Shiers in the country towns. Union Theatres did not publicly disclose how much the tour grossed, but the newspapers speculated that it may have been an amount that rivalled the £10,000 prize the airmen had received from the Commonwealth.[14] Judging by the size of the venues and reports of crowd sizes, this seems plausible; however, how much of this Ross made personally is not known. Given the value of his estate at the time of his death (about £5500), it appears he earned at least a few thousand pounds from the tour.[15]

Critics praised *The Ross Smith Flight*, acclaiming the uniqueness of its aerial photography as well as Ross's confident and compelling narration.

'The pictures were a revelation,' declared a typical review in Adelaide: 'It is a film that will live long in the memories of those who are fortunate to see it.'[16] A critic in Brisbane was taken by the 'charmingly simple' manner in which Ross related the story of the flight.

> He is a man of deeds, not words, and all the time one feels that he would very much rather say nothing about it. Honours have been showered upon him, but he wears them ever so easily. He is of the aristocracy of achievement. And at times he sidles away from the formality of the lecture platform and breaks out into some delicious touches of dry humour, which are all the more effective because of their unexpectedness.[17]

In Sydney, Ross reportedly spoke 'in a well-modulated, clear voice which can be distinctly heard' throughout the large auditorium. 'During his lecture there was perfect silence, punctuated by bursts of applause when he mentioned some specially heroic deed as though it was an every-day occurrence.'[18]

Some reviewers did, however, criticise the film's oddly non-linear narrative structure, whereby Hurley's footage of the journey's final stage preceded Ross's story of the flight to Australia. In Sydney, the *Sun*'s critic felt that this resulted in repetition that tended to 'dissipate rather than concentrate one's interest in the flight'. He thought that what should have been a one-hour feature had been 'spun out' to two and a half hours 'with no advantage either to the aviator-lecturer or his audience'.[19] A female correspondent who saw one of the Melbourne performances made a similar point, describing some of the aerial footage as 'rather monotonous, for as town after town appeared upside up, so to speak, they all seemed much the same'.[20]

Ross also faced criticism from those who felt it unbecoming for a Knight Commander of the Order of the British Empire to earn a living performing in theatres. This mostly came to Ross via gossip, but it made it into the newspapers on at least one occasion. In Bathurst, the local branch of the Returned Sailors and Soldiers Imperial League of Australia debated whether it should send a delegation to a reception planned by council to welcome Ross to town. As one member claimed, 'He was prepared to extend a welcome to Sir Ross Smith the airman, but not to Sir Ross the showman.'[21] Ross angrily dismissed such elitism as 'rot'. He explained to Borton, 'I tell them that it isn't my fault I've got it. Anyway I don't see anything wrong with it.'[22]

During the tour, Ross had a few opportunities to get back into the cockpit during some brief—but thrilling—exhibition flights. Over Brisbane, he flew a BE2e with John Butler, an ex-comrade from No. 1 Squadron who owned the aerodrome in Adelaide. In Sydney, Ross made two flights over the city in a De Havilland DH9. The first, with Hurley on 10 June, involved an aerobatic display only a few hundred feet above the city's buildings and the second, on 16 June, marked the Prince of Wales' arrival in Sydney for his royal tour of Australia. During the first flight, reported the *Sydney Morning Herald,* Ross had flown 'at such a low altitude that he seemed every moment to be in danger of crashing into one or other of the high buildings he was encircling'.[23]

At least one member of the local aviation community was unimpressed with Ross's flying. Lebbeus Hordern, of the prominent Sydney business family and a budding aviation entrepreneur, publicly charged Ross with 'foolishness' and claimed that he endangered the public by stunting so low over the city. The pilots of his company, he explained, were banned from flying below 2000 feet over populated areas. When *The Sun* put this to Ross, he 'smilingly refused to comment . . . beyond saying that he flew low in order to enable Captain Hurley, who was with him, to take some photographs'.[24] The incident highlights one of the tensions that wartime aviators faced as they sought to sell the idea of flying to the public. The death-defying approach to flying that had given them success in combat and enthralled the public now represented the antithesis of the message ordinary people needed to hear: that flying was a safe and reliable means of transport. Ross would need to learn this if he was going to make a living from flying in the post-war world.

This, indeed, appears to be what Ross intended—though he kept his plans to himself when journalists questioned him about the future.[25] Ross was apparently disappointed by the slow progress aviation was making in Australia at the time. During 1920, a number of his wartime comrades were attempting to start aviation companies, but they were having nothing like the success of their counterparts in Europe and North America, where the existence of aviation industries and larger populations made airmail and passenger services more viable than they were in Australia. Some of the burgeoning flying businesses in Australia tried to attract Ross and Keith with promises of lucrative salaries, but the brothers turned them all down, Ross dismissing them as 'sharks and speelers'.[26] The beginning of any future in aviation, Ross appears to have concluded, lay overseas. He made plans to sail for Britain in October, telling the press that he was going on 'private business'.[27]

Ross returned to Sydney after the tour's final lectures in Western Australia, arriving there on 22 August. *The Sun* reported that he came to see his co-competitors in the England-to-Australia air race, Raymond Parer and John McIntosh, land at Mascot. Flying a single-engine De Havilland DH9, they had started from Hounslow on 8 January 1920. It took them 208 days to reach Darwin, their journey marked by 'a trail of broken propellers, smashed undercarriages, damaged tail-skids, ruined radiators, crumpled wings, and bent fuselages'.[28] Ross greeted the airmen and, in awe that they had made it on a single engine, declared Parer and McIntosh's feat one of the greatest in the history of aviation: 'No one could be more proud of them than I am because I know more than anyone else what a wonderful thing they have done.'[29]

Parer and McIntosh would turn out to be the only other crew of the seven who started the race to make it all the way to Australia by air. The French team, Etienne Poulet and Jean Benoist, abandoned their flight in Burma with mechanical problems a couple of days before Ross's arrival in Darwin. Captain George Matthews and Sergeant Tom Kay crashed their Sopwith Wallaby in Bali on 17 April 1920. Ross 'heartily' greeted them upon their return to Sydney by steamship—he was reportedly one of few people to turn out and meet them; he also paid them tribute at a dinner hosted by the Australian Aero Club. The Blackburn Kangaroo crew, led by Hubert Wilkins, wrecked their machine in an accident at Crete, but survived. The remaining airmen perished in fatal accidents. Lieutenants James Ross and Roger Douglas crashed shortly after taking off at Hounslow, and Captain Cedric Howell and Lieutenant George Fraser drowned after ditching in St George's Bay at Corfu. The Commonwealth Government decided to divide the proceeds (£1768) of the Vimy's cancelled arrival at Flemington in February among the runners-up and the families of the dead airmen.[30]

While in Sydney during September, Ross became the subject of potentially scandalous allegations from Cedric Howell's bereaved father, who called for a government inquiry into his son's death. Mr Howell published a pamphlet claiming that Commonwealth authorities had amended the race's rules and postponed its start date to favour the Vimy crew and that Ross had misled the other competitors by reporting that there were no landing places between Calcutta and Singapore, while he had 'several private ones of his own'.[31]

The charges stung Ross, calling into question both the validity of his crew's success and his own integrity. He wrote to the Defence Minister, Senator Sir George Peace, urging him to launch a public inquiry into Mr Howell's allegations. They 'so seriously reflect upon my character and are made so publicly that I feel that some step ought to be taken to prevent the repetition of the charges and to secure public refutation'. Ross considered legal action but graciously decided against it—all he wanted was his name cleared. 'I make every allowance for Mr Howell's grief and mental disturbance due to the tragic loss of his son and have no wish to punish him by the bringing of a libel action against him,' he explained to Pearce.[32]

The press reported Mr Howell's calls for an inquiry but largely overlooked his charges against Ross. Perhaps for this reason, the Defence Department did not hold a public inquiry—although it did look into the allegations. Richard Williams, who represented the government in organising the race, submitted a letter in which he explained that the decision made to postpone the start date until after 8 September 1919 was undertaken because the governments of some countries along the route had not yet granted permission for civilians to fly over their territory. Ross had nothing to do with this; indeed, at the time he had not returned to Britain from India or expressed any intention to compete. Fellow competitor George Matthews also wrote an unsolicited letter in Ross's defence. Matthews claimed that Ross had 'ungrudgingly' shared the information that he and Borton gathered during their survey voyage with the other competitors.[33] Further, it was on the public record that during the flight Ross had offered Poulet and Benoist use of the airfields that he had asked Dutch authorities to construct in the East Indies.[34] Obviously without basis, the allegations made by Mr Howell seem not to have done any damage to Ross's reputation.

Ross remained in Sydney for nearly two months between August and October 1920. The newspapers reported his attendance at a few dinners and balls, but otherwise he kept a low profile.

It was probably during this time that he and Hurley worked together to finish a 30,000-word account of the England-to-Australia flight, for which they had secured a series of publishing contracts. For Australian readers, Hurley secured an exclusive deal with *Life* magazine, to serialise the story in seven parts between May and November 1920.[35] In the United States, they sold the rights to *National Geographic*, which published the entire account in its March 1921 edition.[36] The New York–based publisher Macmillan would publish a very slightly expanded version of the account as a book titled *14,000 Miles Through the Air* in June 1922. As literary scholar Robert Dixon notes, Ross's published account proved so popular with readers because, like Hurley's lecture film, it 'associated the flight and aerial vision with individual heroism, colonial nationalism and imperial patriotism'—comfortingly familiar themes through which they could conceptualise trans-continental flight.[37]

Ross is attributed as the account's author, but he thanks Frank Hurley in the preface for 'his generous and energetic help in the writing of this book'.[38] It appears to be based on a 5000-word narrative that Ross wrote during the flight itself and provided to Murdoch's syndicate the day after his arrival in Darwin.[39] The prose of this shorter version reads like Ross's cables and his personal correspondence: it is understated, conversational and unpretentious. In contrast, the longer book-length treatment features passages that are lyrical and florid, reflective of Hurley's characteristic style. The existence in Hurley's private papers of a 35-page manuscript in his handwriting confirms his considerable contribution to the final, published version.[40] At the very least, Hurley co-authored *14,000 Miles Through the Air*; it is possible he was its ghost writer.

While in Sydney during August and September 1920, Ross also sat for a portrait commissioned by the Commonwealth Government. The artist, William McInnes, represents Ross as weary and worn thin by four years of war, a flight halfway around the globe and six months living in the glare of publicity. His hair is receding and his distinctive hooded eyes seem tired—perhaps even sad; he looks considerably older than his 28 years. Sitting low in the frame, against a large, drab background, Ross seems to have been diminished, not magnified, by fame. He desperately needed a break, but plans were already underway for his next great adventure.

38

VIKING

If Frank Hurley is to be believed, Ross's ambition to circumnavigate the world by air originated in a private office at the Menzies Hotel. It was March 1920 and the crew of the Vimy were in Melbourne, waiting for G-EAOU to be repaired so they could fly to Adelaide. Talking one night in an office the hotel's management had placed at Ross and Keith's disposal, Hurley claimed to have 'casually' suggested that a flight around the world in 60 days would provide an excellent subject for a film. For several evenings afterwards, recalled the photographer, he and the brothers met in the office and began sketching a route onto a world map. 'The present absorbed further interests,' wrote Hurley, 'and the flight around the world became a subject that was taboo while the lecture season was in progress.'[1]

Despite Ross's best efforts to keep the idea of a round-the-world flight secret, while lecturing in regional Victoria in August, Jim Bennett let some information slip that the press seized upon. Newspapers around the world reported that Ross would soon go to Britain to prepare for a global flight in an aeroplane designed by Vickers.[2] Ross was in Adelaide at the time and he called at the office of the *Daily Herald* to set the record straight. He was going to Britain, he said, but on 'private business'—not to plan another flight.[3]

With the secrecy of his aspirations somewhat restored, Ross left Sydney on 22 October aboard the RMS *Ormonde*. When journalists in Fremantle pressed Ross about his plans a few days later, his responses remained vague. To one he claimed to be going 'home' for a holiday and had no plans for the future; a second reported that he was unsure whether he would bring an aeroplane back to Australia to start a business; to another journalist, Ross suggested that his future work in aviation would be guided by what he discovered in Britain.[4] At Colombo on 5 November, Ross spoke optimistically to the press about the potential of civil aviation in Australia: 'The distances covered are very large, excellent weather is experienced practically throughout the year, fogs are very infrequent, the landing grounds would be in most places easy to prepare.'[5]

Ross described the *Ormonde* as 'a dull ship'. It carried around 100 passengers and was 'nothing a bit romantic looking'. He travelled alone, Keith having taken the Pacific route to Europe so that he could present the lecture film in New Zealand and, it seems, reconnoitre landing sites in North America for their round-the-world-flight. 'I don't know anyone at all and it's not much fun being all by myself,' Ross reported in a letter written from the *Ormonde*. 'I've quite made up for all the sleep I lost in Sydney and feel very fit and well.'[6]

Ross appears to have disembarked in France and spent some time exploring the Riviera, where he met up with Keith in early 1921. They visited Nice, which they had admired from the air a year before.[7] In February they went to Paris, where the French Aero Club hosted a reception attended by a number of Europe's most prominent aviators and aviation industrialists. The club's president declared the England-to-Australia flight was the greatest feat in the history of aviation.[8]

The brothers were feted in London, where they arrived on 18 February. The Air Ministry, the Overseas Club, the Royal Aero Club and the Imperial Air Fleet Committee all hosted lunches or dinners to acclaim Ross and Keith's achievement. They met King George V at Buckingham Palace during the investiture of Keith's knighthood (the Prince of Wales having conferred Ross's back in Australia). The brothers also visited the Vickers factory at Weybridge, where G-EAOU had been fitted out for the flight to Australia. The workers, whose number had declined with the post-war slump in aviation orders, gave them a rousing reception filmed by a cameraman from Pathé News.[9] Ross told them, 'If it had not been for the good workmanship in the machine we should never have got through.'[10] Afterwards, Ross and Keith inspected one of the company's new designs, an amphibious flying boat Vickers had dubbed the 'Viking'. Ross had apparently already started discussions with Vickers about his aspirations to fly around the world. Perhaps he was already thinking about using an aeroplane that could operate from both land and water.

The Ross Smith Flight from London to Australia opened at the Philharmonic Hall in London on 7 March. Keith replaced Hurley on stage and the brothers presented a shorter two-hour feature. At first, audiences were slow to fill the performances. Without Hurley's involvement, the advertising and promotion were far more subdued. Some additional newspaper coverage helped ticket sales to pick up later in March and sustained the Philharmonic season for three and a half months, finishing on 19 June. Later in the summer, Ross would appear at a handful of dates in British holiday towns, but otherwise he was done with show business—and probably glad of it too.

Ross and Keith spent the summer of 1921 with Andrew and Jessie, who travelled from Australia to see their boys. The family visited Scotland in June.[11] They must have relished the time together away from the demands of Ross and Keith's celebrity.[12] The holiday was brief, however; at the beginning of July, Ross had to return to London at the request of the Australian Prime Minister, William Morris Hughes.

Hughes had come to London for the 1921 Imperial Conference, a forum of British government and dominion representatives held every four years to discuss strategic, economic and political matters of significance to the empire. With aviation on the agenda, Hughes wanted Ross's advice. In some handwritten notes for the prime minister, he discussed the prospect of establishing a commercial air service between Britain and Australia. Despite having no experience with them personally, Ross had come to favour airships for the route, predicting that, with existing technology and some additional infrastructure, the trip from London to Australia, via Cape Town, could be made in ten days. Aeroplanes would take longer to cover the distance and numerous aerodromes needed to be built between Calcutta and Australia's major cities.[13] On 16 July, Ross and Hughes inspected the new continental flying service base at Croydon airport and Ross went for an eight-hour cruise in the British airship *R33*.[14] This experience apparently confirmed Ross's belief in the dirigible for long-range flights. Later in July, as the Australian representative on an Imperial Air Communications Committee appointed by the conference to investigate the viability of an empire-wide air service, Ross joined the other members in recommending that British and dominion parliaments consider investing in a passenger-carrying airship fleet serviced by bases across the imperial world. Ultimately, the cost of this scheme—estimated by Ross and his colleagues at £8.3 million over five years—would prove prohibitive and the scheme was aborted.[15] On 21 August, Ross and Keith were among those who farewelled Hughes at Victoria Station for his return to Australia.

All the while, throughout 1921, work quietly continued on plans for a round-the-world flight. For as long as possible, Ross and Keith kept this a closely guarded secret, believing that as soon as news of it broke they would be inundated by distractions—'the usual bombardment of mascots and stupid letters', as Ross anticipated in a letter to a friend.[16]

By May 1921, negotiations with Vickers were apparently underway. While Ross lectured in the Philharmonic, Peter Acland, the aviation branch manager who had been Ross's principal benefactor for the England–Australia flight, made inquiries to obtain navigational charts of China, Japan, Korea, Alaska and Canada—regions that Ross planned to traverse after following 'the usual route to Calcutta'.[17] After flying across Canada, Ross and Keith, who had also secured Jim Bennett for their crew, would then complete the global circuit with a trans-Atlantic flight, via either the Azores or directly, from Newfoundland to Ireland, as Alcock and Brown had in 1919. 'With a certain amount of luck,' wrote Ross, 'I think we can do it easily in 3 months.'[18]

With a route marked out, in July Ross began corresponding with engine manufacturers to find out about the performance of their latest designs.[19]

Word of the project leaked in September, when somebody at the Canadian Air Board let slip that Ross had requested permission to fly there as part of a round-the-world flight. When newspapers in Australia and Britain broke the story, Keith made a statement confirming it but giving away few details—only that they had been planning the flight for the past eighteen months.[20]

Indeed, organising such an endeavour was proving incredibly complex. Ross found it difficult, even with his celebrity, to secure firm commitments. It took until December 1921 to convince Vickers that the scheme had a reasonable chance of success. The company offered Ross the latest version of its Viking flying boat, along with spare parts, to a maximum value of £4000.[21] The brothers were in Madrid at the time, on holidays with the Bortons, so they had to cut their trip short and hurry back to London.[22] Within a week, the British engine manufacturer D. Napier and Son offered Ross three of its 450-horsepower Lion engines, one to start with and the other two to ship ahead to Japan and Canada in case replacements were required. Once again, Shell and Wakefield backed Ross, offering to provide petrol and oil to the 47 stops that the brothers had mapped out across Europe, the Middle East, Asia and North America.[23] Additional expenses would be covered by a partnership between Sydney's *Sun* and London's *Daily Mail* to the tune of £15,000. In return, Ross would supply them with exclusive reports.[24]

By mid-January 1922, Ross was reporting to a friend that the flight was 'all fixed up now'; the Viking that Vickers had promised was under construction at the Weybridge plant and fuel was being delivered at landing sites around the globe. 'It is a great relief to know that it is settled,' he admitted, 'more especially as at first everyone told me either that I was mad or that I could never get the backing.'[25]

Ross wrote to the Air Ministry on 21 January, outlining his plans for the world flight. He had, in an unofficial capacity, already canvassed the flight with representatives of some of the countries over which he planned to fly.

Now he asked the Air Ministry to secure permission for him officially. 'It is unnecessary to point out the advantages and prestige that will be gained for British Aviation if we are successful,' he added, 'and in addition we should obtain much valuable aeronautical data.'[26] To journalists who wanted to portray Ross and Keith as daredevils who were flying around for the adventure of it, the brothers emphasised that the flight was about demonstrating the potential of aviation. 'It is just a commercial undertaking,' they said in a statement:

> We believe that in aviation lies the future of the world, and we aspire to show that if one can go round the earth in an aeroplane, there is no reason why the aeroplane should not be the vehicle of commerce. And when that has come to pass, the material progress of humanity will have reached a point which now no mortal dreams . . .[27]

Yet in a response to the *Sun*'s correspondent in London a few months later, the restlessness and wanderlust that had always compelled Ross was also again apparent. 'Frankly I've often wondered why myself,' he responded when asked why he was going to try to fly around the globe. 'The idea has been in my mind ever since I landed in Australia. Anyhow we want to see the British Empire and be the first round the world by air.'[28] Adventure, business and empire nationalism, it seems, all compelled Ross towards this next great adventure.

Vickers had developed its first amphibious aeroplane, the aptly named Viking, shortly after the Great War by integrating elements of maritime and aviation design. 'The machine is a boat construction surmounted by a biplane,' said the *Daily Telegraph*'s aviation correspondent. 'Its 450 hp Napier engine is mounted high up between the wings, driving a propeller behind the wings.'[29] The hull was constructed of double-ply mahogany and polished, making the aircraft resemble a 'cigar box with wings'; it could accommodate a crew of four in two cockpits, both positioned forward of the engine and wings.[30] Nine coats of dope and fabric sealed the timber wings and an aluminium-coloured finish was applied to keep them cool in tropical climates.

The Mark IV Viking that Vickers offered to Ross featured state-of-the-art technology. It had a retractable landing gear and an inflatable tail-skid that doubled as a rudder, allowing it to operate from land or water, as Ross planned to do where no aerodromes existed, such as in Hong Kong.[31] The cockpit had a wireless set, through which Keith would be able to receive direction-finding signals from navigational beacons. A light-up 'control indicator' on the instrument panel assisted its pilot to keep the aircraft on course in cloud and fog. The Viking's cockpit even included a specially designed cigarette holder, modelled on a miner's safety lamp, so the crew could safely smoke in the air.

Ross's Viking could carry 1500 litres of fuel, giving it, when cruising at 135 kilometres per hour, a range of nearly 2900 kilometres—nearly double the maximum range of G-EAOU during the England-to-Australia flight. Ross anticipated the Atlantic crossing would take twenty hours, although most other stages would be considerably shorter.[32]

The additional fuel capacity with which Vickers had equipped the Viking allowed little room for cargo. 'We shall just have the suits we stand up in,' explained Ross to reporters. 'Our luggage will consist of one clean shirt, one set of underclothes, two pairs of socks, one pair of stockings, a blanket, shaving kit, soap, and a few odds and ends of toilet articles . . . We shall take a fishing line and a few hooks, and a sporting gun.' Ross and Keith would each carry a pistol in case they were stranded among unfriendly natives 'or amongst the Bolsheviks'.[33]

The Viking's unique design made it an idiosyncratic machine to fly and at the time—as Vickers had only produced a few of them—there were not many pilots with experience in handling them. The hull's solid timber construction made the aircraft heavy; it required a long take-off run, climbed very slowly and could easily stall at slow speeds. Compared with the Vimy, which had relatively unresponsive and sluggish controls, the Viking required a far more nuanced touch; it was a less forgiving aircraft to fly. Perhaps Ross learned this on 4 April when he went up in one for the first time with one of Vickers' test pilots. In two and a half hours of dual instruction, they made four water landings together.[34] Ross would no doubt have been aware that Sir John Alcock had been killed flying the Viking prototype in December 1919, six months after his successful flight across the Atlantic.

With the Viking ready and his plans nearly complete, in early April Ross announced that he, Keith and Bennett would start on Anzac Day, 25 April 1922.[35] There were rumours that they would take off in spectacular style from the River Thames at Westminster. Two weeks before the start date, Vickers invited the press to the Weybridge factory to see the aeroplane and interview the crew. Reporters watched as the Australian airmen and the factory's engineers made final adjustments to the Viking and demonstrated some of its novel features. Ross impressed journalists by switching on the navigational wireless set and picking up signals transmitted by a direction-finding beacon in Paris.[36]

The new aircraft clearly delighted Ross and Keith. 'The way in which the brothers fondled it affectionately and patted it on the back, while examining every bolt and wire suggested that it was an animate and sentient being,' wrote one reporter.[37] As he discussed the upcoming journey, Ross exuded confidence and paid tribute to Viking's builders, most of whom had worked on G-EAOU. 'They are all taking the greatest interest in it, and regard it as something very special,' he said.[38]

Such was Ross's confidence that, in front of reporters, he shrugged off a warning by the aeroplane's designer, Rex Pierson, that it did not have the fuel capacity to cross the Atlantic in one stage. Even if they jettisoned the heavy landing gear, they would be 270 kilometres short. He urged Ross to take the central Atlantic route and stop over in the Azores. Ross was adamant, though: he wanted to make a 'daring finish'. The *Sun*'s correspondent quoted him as replying, 'We'll be 20 hours in the air if the wind blows at 10 miles an hour; and we ought to make Ireland.'[39] It was an incredibly risky proposition—but then again, so was this whole endeavour. And Ross had not yet even flown the Viking by himself.

39

VALHALLA

The conditions on 13 April 1922 were ideal for the first test flight of Vickers Viking G-EBBZ. It was a warm and sunny spring day—a welcome relief after a long, cold winter. A mild westerly breeze swept across Brooklands aerodrome and the adjacent aircraft factory of Vickers Limited.[1] By mid-morning, hundreds of people had gathered to witness the aircraft's first flight. Alongside the factory's workers, who came out to watch, were journalists and many others associated with the aviation industry. Racing enthusiasts had also come to Brooklands that morning to see motorcyclists practise on the banking oval track that surrounded the airfield.

As the Viking was wheeled out from the hangars, a reporter from the Press Association chatted with Ross. The Australian airman seemed 'completely absorbed' with the round-the-world flight he planned to begin in less than a fortnight: 'He looked forward to it as a first-class adventure in the delightful care-free spirit of a schoolboy.' When the journalist tried to turn the conversation back to the flight to Australia in 1919, Ross 'spoke almost unwillingly about it' and 'appeared quite unimpressed by the magnitude of what he had already done and the great task he was to attempt'.[2]

Around 11 a.m., the Viking was ready. Keith was coming from London but had not yet arrived; he was running late. Apparently eager to get started, Ross decided not to wait. He, Bennett and Vickers' chief test pilot, Stan Cockerell, would take the Viking up for its test flight. Cockerell took the controls with Ross alongside him; Bennett sat in the rear cockpit.

Taking off, the Viking climbed to 2000 feet and began flying circuits of the aerodrome. Cockerell found the machine to be in excellent flying trim; it handled beautifully as he put it through various manoeuvres.[3] Evidently chafing to get his own hands on the controls, after half an hour Ross suggested they land so he could take the Viking up himself.[4]

Cockerell landed and climbed out of the cockpit without switching off the engine. Sliding across, Ross took the controls; there were no safety belts to fasten. He looked to the crowd for Keith, but still could not see him. Shouting 'Cheerio!', Ross pushed the throttle lever forward.[5] It was about 12.20 p.m.[6]

After gathering enough speed on Brooklands' grass runway, Ross pulled the Viking away from the ground. The spectators cheered and Ross waved as the aeroplane gained altitude, 'soaring perfectly' in Cockerell's assessment—although some thought Ross was climbing rather steeply.[7] Once at 500 feet, Ross turned right, beginning a wide circuit of the airfield while still climbing.[8] At about this moment, Keith arrived on the tarmac; it must have disappointed him to see that he was only just too late to join his brother on this historic first test of the aeroplane that would soon circle the globe.[9]

Within five minutes or so, Ross had completed his first circuit. At 1500 feet above the race track on the aerodrome's southern boundary, he put the Viking into a tight, almost vertically banked, right turn back towards the aerodrome. The few spectators who knew the aeroplane well watched with concern: at low speeds, the aircraft became tail heavy, requiring careful handling.[10] Others assumed that Ross was just doing some 'stunt flying'.[11] Some thought they heard the engine throttle down before the turn; perhaps Ross intended to land.[12] Part-way through the 180-degree turn, the Viking's upward-pointing wing rolled over and the aircraft tumbled into a spinning nosedive.

Keith and the other spectators watched, 'spell-bound with horror', as the Viking fell 'like a whirling leaf towards the earth'.[13] Ross promptly did as all pilots were trained to do in such situations: throttle down and—somewhat counter-intuitively—push the stick forward to pitch the aircraft into an even steeper dive. It worked; for a moment, the aeroplane stopped spinning but then started again when Ross opened the throttles—too prematurely, according to some witnesses.[14] Repeating the procedure, he once again had the aeroplane under control.

But it was too late.

Still in a near-vertical dive, the Viking plunged into the heavily wooded top of the speedway's Byfleet Banking. 'It dashed to the ground with terrific force,' wrote one observer.[15] The aeroplane crashed through the trees and ploughed nose-first into the ground beside the steeply angled concrete racing track.

First on the scene was motorcyclist Claude Temple, who had been rounding the bend when the Viking came down.[16] He found the aeroplane 'smashed to pieces', its engine torn off and lying several metres away, and the wings 'reduced to matchwood'.[17] The forward section of the hull, including the cockpits, had been obliterated and the undercarriage thrust up through the plywood fuselage. Fuel belched from the ruptured tank; fortunately no fire had started.

A few metres from the wreck, Bennett lay among the fir trees. Temple thought he saw him move, but could tell immediately that his body had been horribly mangled; he was obviously beyond any help.[18] Clearing the wreckage away, some of the motorcyclists and others who were arriving on the scene discovered Ross, pinned beneath the pulverised remains of the hull and also obviously dead. He had a large gash down the right side of his face, 'as if caused by an axe', said one. His body was 'awfully shattered and crushed'.[19] There was nothing they could do but tear some sheets of fabric from the wings to cover the two airmen's broken bodies.[20]

At the moment of the crash, the onlookers were momentarily stunned. 'Then,' according to one, 'there was a rush by hundreds of men, headed by Sir Keith Smith, who gave a broken cry as the horrible possibilities flashed upon him.'[21] When Keith arrived at the crash site, he collapsed at Ross's side and wept.[22] One account claimed that he 'was overcome with grief and flung himself across his brother's body, and was only removed with difficulty'.[23]

It was a profoundly sad moment, one that other witnesses later recalled too.[24] Soon an ambulance from Weybridge arrived to collect Ross and Bennett and take them to the local mortuary. Sir Trevor Dawson, the Managing Director of Vickers Limited, led Keith from the terrible scene and accompanied him back to London. Shortly after the accident, the bright skies above Brooklands turned overcast. Rain fell heavily during the afternoon.[25]

Everybody was stunned. What had begun just minutes before as the triumphant first act of an epoch-making adventure had finished in the most abrupt and shockingly tragic manner imaginable. Sir Ross Macpherson Smith, 29 years old and the world's most highly regarded airman, had been accidentally killed in an instant. The tragic irony that he lost his life flying in the place where he had first laid eyes upon an aeroplane, twelve years earlier, would be missed by the many journalists who wrote about the disaster in the coming days.

40

NOW HE BELONGS TO THE EMPIRE

Shortly before his fatal test flight, Ross is reported to have told Keith that, if anything went wrong, nobody else should be held accountable. 'Australians never sequel,' he said.[1]

Nevertheless, there were two official inquiries into the accident: a coronial inquest in Weybridge, two days after the crash, then, during the following month, an investigation on behalf of the Air Council, the governing body of the RAF.[2]

To the relief of the management at Vickers Limited, both inquiries absolved the company of any responsibility as far as mechanical failure was concerned.[3] The testimony of Vickers' test pilot, Stan Cockerell, who flew the Viking for half an hour before handing over the controls to Ross, indicated that the aircraft performed exactly as it should. In their examination of the wreckage, the Air Council's accident investigators found no evidence of mechanical defects either.

Both the coroner and the Air Council noted the Viking's peculiar handling characteristics, especially when flying at low speeds. The Air Council also observed that, while Ross had over a thousand hours' experience, he had done little flying in the year before the accident. In fact, in the *two years* since Ross delivered the Vimy to the Australian Government at Point Cook, there are only three recorded occasions on which he piloted an aeroplane: one exhibition flight in Brisbane and two in Sydney during the lecture film tour. It had, perhaps, been eighteen months since Ross had been at the controls of an aeroplane. In the fortnight before the accident, he had received two lessons of dual instruction on the Viking but he had never flown it by himself before taking over from Cockerell, immediately before the accident.[4]

Ross's lack of flying experience in the months leading up to the accident is indeed significant. But so too is the nature of the flying he had done before that. The Vimy, on which Ross logged nearly 200 hours, was a comparatively easy aeroplane to fly. He had become accustomed to piloting a machine that, he thought, 'answers to her controls wonderfully, even at slow speeds'. Importantly, as Ross himself noted, the Vimy 'stalls very slowly', giving the pilot plenty of warning and 'time to think what he is going to do'.[5] The Viking was a very different aeroplane—unforgiving if handled incorrectly and particularly dangerous if turned at slow speeds.

The coroner ruled that Ross and Bennett had died 'by misadventure'. He deemed that Ross had been killed after falling into a spin at a low altitude; although he did not think mechanical failure had contributed, he could not determine what had caused the spin. The Air Council went further, attributing the accident to 'an error of judgement' that resulted from Ross's inexperience on the Viking. This conclusion seems reasonable, given our knowledge of what happened on the day of the accident and of Ross's flying experience in the months preceding it. Yet there was another factor noted by neither the coroner nor the Air Council.

Ross had approached his flight around the world with impatience and confidence. They were both lifelong characteristics of his personality, which often served him well; in this instance, though, they worked together with fatal consequences. Planning the round-the-world flight took eighteen months—an exasperatingly long period from Ross's perspective, given the four weeks it took to arrange the flight to Australia in 1919. There are hints in his few surviving letters from this period that Ross found this delay frustrating—especially the time it took him to convince those who thought the idea preposterous.[6] More broadly, Ross found the gradual pace of civil aviation's development in Britain vexing.[7] Perhaps in reaction to this, he exuded confidence and optimism about his plans to fly around the world; he was impatient to get started.[8] His disregard of a warning from the Viking's designer that the aircraft lacked the range to cross the northern Atlantic is telling.[9] Though a risk-taker, Ross Smith had not frequently been reckless; prudence usually figured in his daring. In his final days, though, he became impetuous and over-confident—just the sort of pilot who might insist on taking the controls of an unfamiliar and difficult-to-fly aircraft without waiting for his brother to join him as planned.

Keith cabled his parents with the terrible news immediately after the accident. To beat the newspapers, he sent the cable via two routes. Perhaps sensing the urgency of the message it contained, telegraphists across the globe pushed it through as a priority; it arrived at Aviemore only a few hours after the accident—in what must have been almost record time. It was late Thursday evening in Adelaide and Andrew, who had been out of town, had only just arrived home to spend the Easter weekend. Though undoubtedly shaken with grief and shock, it fell to him to convey the heartbreaking news to Jessie.[10]

Adelaide's newspaper offices also received word via cable late that night. The following morning, Good Friday, the newspapers carried reports of the accident and Ross's death. On the Lord Mayor's instructions, the bells of the city's Town Hall rung out during the morning—just as they had, some recalled, when Ross flew the Vimy over Adelaide two years earlier. 'Although it was a sacred holiday,' observed one reporter, 'a few of the public buildings shook out their sad bunting, and while the flags drooped at half-mast, the bells tolled their sorrowful tidings to little bunches of excursionists as they hurried to their trains and trams.'[11]

In the following days, Jessie and Andrew wanted to be alone to grieve privately but, as hundreds of letters and telegrams arrived, bringing condolences and tributes from all over the world, they began to realise the extent to which their sorrow was shared by many others: Ross's death was not only a loss to their family but a loss to the nation and to the British Empire.

Accordingly, on 19 April, Andrew and Jessie permitted a journalist from *The Register* into their home to share some of what they felt—and their gratitude—with those in the outside world who mourned for their son too.

The reporter found the family's dining table piled with letters and cables. Among them were messages from heads of state, generals and the famous—as well as ordinary strangers who simply admired Ross and his achievements. Some of the most affecting, thought *The Register*'s correspondent, were those from the opera singer Dame Nellie Melba ('My heart bleeds for you, but how proud you must be'); the Secretary of Harris Scarfe ('The esteem and affection which we all had for Ross was extraordinary'), the Adelaide Rowing Club ('He was, as you know, one of our most illustrious and esteemed members') and the Brisbane Aero Club, which considered Ross's death 'the greatest loss ever sustained by the cause of aviation'. Reflecting on such sentiments, Jessie said she felt 'most deeply' the kindness that had been shown by Ross's many friends and admirers. 'Before Ross died,' she concluded, 'he belonged to us, but now he belongs to the empire.'[12]

That same day, the Commonwealth Government announced that it would repatriate Ross's and Bennett's remains and give them a state funeral. Prime Minister Hughes instructed the Australian High Commissioner in London to make arrangements with Keith to bring both airmen back to Australia. The government offered the Smith family a state funeral in Melbourne and there was a suggestion that Ross could then be buried in Canberra. But Andrew and Jessie wanted Ross returned to Adelaide; they chose North Road Cemetery, just ten minutes' walk from the family home on Stephen Terrace, in Gilberton. For the long journey across the seas, Ross's and Bennett's bodies would be embalmed and encased in lead-lined caskets, made of English oak.

Keith accompanied the two airmen home aboard the new government-owned steamer SS *Largs Bay*. The caskets were carried in the ship's forward hold, separate from the cargo and under the direct responsibility of the ship's officers. During the voyage, the passengers held a memorial service and donated money to purchase a wreath.

The *Largs Bay* docked in Port Adelaide early on 14 June 1922. Many had gathered and, as the ship's crane lowered Ross's coffin, draped in an Australian flag, all heads were bowed. 'Perfect silence prevailed as it was lowered to the wharf,' described one witness. 'Flags on all the vessels and buildings at the harbour were at half-mast, and as the cortege moved off the siren of the *Largs Bay* sounded a final salute to South Australia's hero.' Bennett's casket remained on board for the voyage to Melbourne and burial in his hometown.[13]

A horse-drawn hearse carried Ross's casket to St Peter's Cathedral where it was to lay in state for 24 hours before the funeral. Mounted on a catafalque in the cathedral's chancel and draped with the Union Jack, the coffin was flanked by three tall candles on each side and topped with two black cushions: one holding Ross's flying goggles, cap and gloves and the other his medals. Four airmen, wearing the distinct blue uniform of the recently established Royal Australian Air Force (RAAF), served as the catafalque party; two stood at the head of the casket and the other two at its foot, heads bowed and arms reversed.

After a private viewing for the family, the cathedral opened its doors to a procession of public mourners. All afternoon, the people of Adelaide—Ross's friends, neighbours and colleagues; people who did not know him personally but admired him all the same—filed past the catafalque in silence. 'The proceedings were conducted with due decorum and solemnity,' reported one visitor. 'Under the influence of cloud-covered skies the light during the afternoon was dim and the Cathedral empty, silent, and still, save for the mournful procession of people.'[14]

Mourners continued filing through the cathedral until ten o'clock that night before resuming early the following day. 'Throughout the city during the cold, grey morning there was an atmosphere of sorrow and depression, and people were waiting in hushed expectancy for the beginning of the solemn funeral march,' reported the *Chronicle*'s correspondent. Around noon, the sun came out—a fitting reminder, thought this journalist, of Ross's well-known and much-admired warmth and his cheery demeanour.[15]

Another journalist, riding a tram filled with school students and commuters from the suburbs that morning, observed how a 'settled gravity and seriousness' prevailed among the people of Adelaide:

> Quite plainly this was no mere excitement over a pageant—it was something poignantly actual. Low-voiced question and answer about plans—or the flowers 'the office' was sending that was all. In the streets there was the same settled expression—as if now, as never before, the people were thinking quietly, seriously as one.[16]

Shops, offices and hotels closed at 2 p.m. and half an hour later the funeral service commenced with the singing of hymns. Admission to the cathedral was by invitation only but, by one estimate, 10,000 people waited outside.[17] The Reverend Julian Bickersteth, headmaster of St Peter's College, delivered the address. He began by reminding those present that they 'represented a great multitude . . . throughout the whole empire' who likewise mourned Ross and that, 'Following the splendid example of his parents, we cannot claim him alone for ourselves, for he belongs to his whole generation.' Nevertheless, Ross was an 'Adelaide boy'—and the people of South Australia should, he reasoned, 'be pardoned a little local pride'.

Bickersteth then eulogised Ross by recounting his life in Adelaide—his upbringing in 'a Christian home', school days at Queen's, successes on the sporting field and employment before the war at 'a well-known business firm'. Ross had distinguished himself at war, but also lived long enough to demonstrate that 'courage, unselfishness, and high endeavour . . . belong no less to the days of peace'. Ross had led an admirable life, concluded Bickersteth, 'spent full of strenuous effort to increase man's mastery over nature and to make the rough places smooth for those who come after them'.[18] As the eulogy made clear, Ross embodied the towering ideals among which he had been raised. He was, by the standards of his time, masculine, modern, martial and a martyr to the progress of British civilisation—a true hero of the age.

At the conclusion of the 45-minute service, the casket was mounted onto an aircraft trailer for its journey to the internment at North Road Cemetery. Troopers of the light horse, riding white chargers, led the procession, followed by a firing party of 50 airmen from the RAAF and a marching band of returned servicemen. A dozen carriages conveyed the chief mourners and behind them followed hundreds of ex-servicemen in uniform. Overhead, four aircraft of the RAAF circled. The procession extended along much of the 4-kilometre route from the cathedral to North Road Cemetery. 'There were probably 30,000 or 40,000 people within a few hundred yards of the cathedral,' reported the press. 'It is impossible to compute the number of the crowd on the route and at the cemetery. The road was lined by dense crowds on either side all the way.'[19]

Several thousand people, many having waited since early that morning, along with 4000 ticket holders, gathered around the small plot of green lawn beside the cemetery chapel, which had been chosen as Ross's final resting place. The grave was prepared carefully so that 'not a particle of earth' would be visible to the mourners; 'palm leaves, entwined with flowers and autumn leaves' lined and surrounded the neatly dug pit.[20] Great heaps of wreaths and floral tributes had been arranged around the plot by the time Andrew, Jessie and Keith arrived at the head of the funeral cortege.

Eight Air Force pallbearers carried the casket to the graveside as the St Peter's boys' choir sang hymns. Andrew, Jessie and Keith stood together, silently, beside the grave and at the epicentre of a city's grief and its pride. As the coffin was lowered into the ground, the dean of the cathedral committed Ross to eternity with a benediction. A band of highland pipers droned through a lament and the chief mourners cast handfuls of soil into the grave—some had come from Jessie's birthplace in Scotland. The Air Force firing party then shattered the winter afternoon's stillness with three volleys of rifle fire. A bugler played the last post. Keith saluted his brother.

As the family left the graveside, noticed a journalist, 'the crowd surged forward to take a final glance at the coffin'.[21] Perhaps people could not believe that the world's greatest aviator had been forever consigned to the earth. The incredulity of it all resonated in the verses that a South Australian poet, Beatrice Bevan, would pen later on that sombre afternoon. 'Is the young knight lying dead?' she wondered. 'Can earth hold a spirit fled?'[22]

EPILOGUE

Andrew Smith joined his two youngest sons in death just two years later. In November 1924, he returned to the city from Mutoooroo feeling unwell; he died at home within a few days. He was 73 years old. Shortly before Ross's death, Andrew had been appointed to the Mutooroo Pastoral Company's Board of Directors. He was, at the time of his passing, 'one of the best-known figures in the pastoral world of South Australia'.[1] When Ross and Keith made it to Australia in the Vimy in 1919, his boss had remarked that he was not surprised: 'they are sons of Andrew'.[2]

Jessie lived alone at Aviemore for another 23 years before her death in December 1947 at 87 years of age. She remained active in the community, opening the family home for garden parties to fundraise for various civic causes. Jessie seems to have lived comfortably, travelling frequently to visit friends and family. In 1927 she spent nine months travelling around Europe with a friend. They toured the old battlefields of the Western Front and she visited Colin's grave at Lijssenthoek in Belgium. Yet, despite Jessie's continued involvement in public life, she avoided attending services held in Adelaide to mark the anniversaries of the England-to-Australia flight.[3] She would send apologies and express her gratitude.

Keith spent the month following Ross's funeral at Mutooroo, 'miles from anywhere, having a holiday'. He still desired to undertake the round-the-world flight himself and, with Andrew and Jessie's blessing, wrote to Vickers that he planned to return to Britain via Asia and North America to gather at 'first hand' information about the route.[4] Peter Acland, the aviation manager at Vickers, however, talked him out of it. He now doubted the value of such a flight, reasoning that pioneering aviators such as Keith were 'more useful if devoted to organising and running commercial services'.[5] It went unsaid, but he and his colleagues perhaps also doubted whether the company's reputation could sustain another famous airman being killed in one of its aeroplanes.

Accordingly, Vickers appointed Keith its agent for Australia—a position he would occupy for the rest of his life. In 1924, while in London, Keith became engaged to Anita Crawford, an old friend from Adelaide. They returned to Australia later that year and married. Much to Keith's frustration, little of his work would involve aeroplanes: the civil aviation industry in Australia developed gradually between the wars and Vickers proved unwilling to invest in the local manufacture of aircraft. Keith's work mostly involved the sale of products from other parts of Vickers' vast industrial enterprise—mainly machinery for Australia's manufacturing industry. It wasn't until 1954 that Keith managed to sell any Vickers aircraft in Australia. That year, Trans-Australian Airlines purchased six of the company's Viscount airliners. They completed the journey from Britain to Australia in 45 hours over the course of seven days—a fraction of the time in which Keith had done the journey with Ross in 1919; the trip was also considerably more comfortable—and safer.

Keith and Anita travelled extensively on behalf of the company. During the Second World War, he served as vice-chairman of the RAAF's recruiting drive committee and in 1946 he joined the board of directors of British Commonwealth Pacific Airlines. He also served on the boards of a number of other Australian companies, including Qantas Empire Airways.

In 1955, Keith became ill with cancer; he died in Sydney on 19 December—a day before his 65th birthday. He and Anita had no children. Keith had become a moderately wealthy man, his estate being valued at £33,700. In 1986, Lady Anita Smith bequeathed the family's estate to establish the Sir Ross and Sir Keith Smith Fund to support the study of science and aeronautics in South Australia. Keith was buried in

Adelaide, at North Road Cemetery, alongside Andrew, Jessie, Ross and a plaque commemorating Colin.

After the flight, Wally Shiers and his wife Helena settled in Sydney. He opened a garage at Bondi Junction and was associated with a few different aviation companies established around the burgeoning airfield at Mascot during the 1920s. In 1929, Shiers qualified for his pilot's licence and the following year attempted to fly to Britain with a twenty-year-old aviator, Dave Smith. Flying Smith's Ryan monoplane (a similar design to Lindbergh's *Spirit of St Louis*), the pair had a forced landing in Western Australia and then crashed in Siam, where they abandoned the flight. During the 1930s, Shiers worked for New England Airways and he oversaw the manufacture of parachutes for the Air Force during the Second World War. Shiers returned to Adelaide in 1965; he died there three years later.

Many of Ross's wartime comrades went on to play important roles in the development of civil and military aviation in Australia and throughout the empire.

Richard Williams became the founding Chief of Air Staff of the RAAF, a position he occupied at various times until 1939; today he is regarded as the 'Father of the RAAF'. After the war, Williams spent nearly a decade as Director-General of the Department of Civil Aviation. He died in 1980.

Within a year of surveying the route across Queensland and the Northern Territory for Ross and the other competitors of the 1919 England-to-Australia air race, Hudson Fysh and Paul McGinness established Queensland and Northern Territory Aerial Services—better known as QANTAS, and nowadays Australia's national airline.

Several other airmen from No. 1 Squadron, including Frank McNamara, Adrian Cole, Peter Drummond, Allan Murray Jones, Lawrence Wackett and Ernest Mustard served in either the RAF or the RAAF during the inter-war decades. All rose to senior ranks and some, such as Murray Jones, Wackett and Mustard, afterwards had careers in civil aviation too.

Les Sutherland also joined the Air Force but, while learning to fly in 1926, broke his neck in an air crash. He survived to be medically discharged and afterwards worked as Vacuum Oil Company's aviation representative. During the Depression, Sutherland became secretary of the New Guard, an anti-communist paramilitary organisation that attracted many ex-soldiers. In 1935 his colourful war memoir, *Aces and Kings,* featured a chapter devoted to Ross. 'I have no illusions about myself,' he wrote. 'But now, nineteen years later, it is my proudest memory that for eighteen months I was tent-mates with "Hadji", and that I war-flew with him.' Sutherland lived in Mosman; he died in 1967.[6]

Biffy Borton remained in the RAF until 1933, retiring as an Air Vice Marshal. He married and turned his hand to business but proved, according to his grandson, 'more adept at losing money than making it'. In 1963 Biffy was forced to sell the family estate, Cheveney, where Ross and the Vimy crew had enjoyed such fine hospitality in 1919. Corresponding with Archibald Grenfell Price, Ross's first biographer, in the mid-1960s, Borton fondly recalled his adventures with Ross, reflecting on how the young Australian had been one of his dearest friends.[7] Borton died in 1969 at 82 years of age. His last words were reportedly to a nurse, fussing at his bedside, 'Nurse would you kindly stop talking balls?' The lively sense of humour and irreverence that Ross had appreciated five decades earlier evidently endured throughout Biffy's long life.[8]

In these careers, we glimpse something of the possibilities that life might have held for Ross had he lived. 'Who knows what Ross Smith would have accomplished with his great organizing ability and charm, in addition to his high qualifications as a pilot?' wondered Hudson Fysh in his autobiography, *Qantas Rising.*[9] Even so, it is difficult to imagine Ross settling down, marrying and being content with life in either the corporate or service worlds. Had he done so, it is almost certain that he would have continued to find the gradual pace of aviation's evolution confoundingly slow, and would have restlessly continued to push the boundaries.

Indeed, despite the acclaim that Ross's great flight attracted in 1919, and the promise it seemed to auger for aviation in the post-war world, trans-continental services developed slowly. The imperial airship routes in which

Ross saw so much promise came to naught. After Parer and McIntosh's epic 208-day journey, it took another six years for anyone to successfully fly the England-to-Australia route again. In mid-1926, the British aviator Alan Cobham flew a De Havilland DH50 biplane from London to Darwin in 32 days—three days slower than Ross and his crew in 1919. Cobham chose a seaplane for the route as there were still few aerodromes between India and Australia. It would be 1935 before the establishment of an airmail and passenger service between London and Darwin. Even then, the journey would take ten days and cost the equivalent of A$23,000 per fare. British Air Ministry officials were not being cynical when they described Ross's feat in 1919 as 'exceptional', and warned that 'many hundreds of thousands of pounds must be spent before the route is commercially opened up'.[10]

It is easy to say—as many undoubtedly will during the air race's centenary in 2019—that Ross Smith and his great flight have been 'forgotten'. If true now, though, this has not always been the case. In the aftermath of his death, Ross loomed large in the popular memory of his countrymen and women, particularly in his home state of South Australia. Six months after the funeral, a committee chaired by Adelaide's Lord Mayor appealed to the public for funds to erect a memorial to Ross in the city. It collected nearly £2500 in donations in a little over a month and would eventually secure nearly double this amount.[11] The British sculptor Frederick Brook Hitch won the tender to produce a bronze statue of Ross in his flying gear, to be mounted on a granite plinth in Creswell Gardens, beside Adelaide Oval. South Australia's Lieutenant-Governor unveiled the Ross Smith Memorial on 10 December 1927—the eighth anniversary of the Vimy's arrival in Darwin. In an editorial, *The Advertiser* claimed that, although others had made record-breaking flights that 'eclipsed' Ross's achievement, his feat remained 'as fresh in memory as ever it was'. The Smith brothers had 'blazed the trail' and 'struck the popular imagination as no other flight has done'.[12]

Ross's statue in Creswell Gardens became the location for memorial services held each December by the Queen's Old Boys and Air Force

Associations to mark the anniversary of the England-to-Australia air race. These continued for nearly three decades, but attendance appears to have declined over time. The last memorial service was reported by Adelaide's press in 1954; for the flight's 40th anniversary five years later, the newspapers mention no commemorative events at all. This is perhaps surprising given the move of the Vickers Vimy G-EAOU from Canberra to Adelaide the year before, for permanent display in a memorial building at Adelaide Airport. Paid for by public subscription, the Vimy memorial's opening ceremony in April 1958 was attended by 40,000 people. Richard Williams opened the memorial and both Lady Anita Smith and Wally Shiers attended.

Popular memory of Ross and the 1919 England-to-Australia air race experienced a revival at the end of the following decade—the flight's 50th anniversary. In 1969, Archibald Grenfell Price published his biography of Ross and Keith, *The Skies Remember*, and philatelist Nelson Eustice wrote a history of the air race.[13] The Postmaster-General's Department also issued a set of anniversary stamps. The major commemorative event for the year, however, was a re-enactment of the air race, sponsored by British Petroleum and a number of other companies. The offer of a $25,000 prize attracted nearly 200 applications, from which 76 aircraft started and 56 made it to Sydney. Competitors had to follow the route flown by Ross and his crew in 1919. The race attracted press coverage in the thirteen countries from which competitors hailed and thousands of people came to see the aircraft at their various stops along the way; 30,000 turned out at Mascot Airport in Sydney, to witness the race's conclusion.

The efforts of Peter McMillan and Lang Kidby, who flew a replica of the Vimy from Britain to Australia in 1994, brought the flight back into the public's consciousness for its 75th anniversary. The flight garnered international press coverage and resulted in both the publication of a book by McMillan (which included an account of the historical flight by aviation historian Terry Gwynn-Jones) and a film by *National Geographic*. Interest in the flight's history was apparently sufficient to warrant a new edition of Eustis's book and the issuing of yet more commemorative postage stamps.

The centenary of the Great War has once again brought Ross's life into focus. The State Library of South Australia included Ross's letters and diaries in its program to digitise and transcribe its manuscripts relating to the service of First World War soldiers. In June 2018, the RAAF held a service at Ross's grave 'as part of the Centenary of Anzac and in the lead up to the Centenary of the Epic Flight (2019)'.[14] A program of events coordinated by the History Trust of South Australia was being planned for 2019 to promote public awareness of 'the men, the plane and the centenary of a journey as awe-inspiring as the moon landing 50 years later'.[15]

While no longer the household name he once was, Sir Ross Macpherson Smith has, therefore, never quite been forgotten. As with all those who achieve great things, there is a point at which their significance slips from memory into history. For Ross, this occurred in the 1950s—the point at which his contemporaries began retiring from public life and passing away. The absence of any children born to Ross or Keith perhaps hastened his and the flight's transformation from lived experience into artefacts of history.

Furthermore, Ross died at the beginning of the era of long-distance aviation exploration. The great flights by Charles Lindbergh, Kingsford Smith and Ulm, Bert Hinkler, Alan Cobham, Jean Batten and Amelia Earhart followed, weaving a larger and more complex narrative around the pioneering trans-continental flights that the Smiths (and Alcock and Brown) made in 1919. Even had Ross lived and been successful in his circumnavigation of the Northern Hemisphere in 1922, it seems unlikely that this, in itself, would have made much difference to the prominence of his legacy. The team of US Army Air Service aviators who, in four aircraft, first flew around the world in 1924 are hardly well known today either.

Ironically, to be properly understood and appreciated, Ross's life and achievements need the context that subsequently obscured them. Flying an aeroplane from Britain to Australia in 1919 represented a truly extraordinary achievement. Although still many years away from being a reality for ordinary people, by travelling halfway around the globe by air in 28 days, Ross and his crew showed the world how far and how rapidly aviation had evolved during the Great War and provided a glimpse of what might be possible in the future. Their flight set the challenge for those who followed as well as an example of what might be achieved when courage, resilience and resourcefulness are applied to push the existing technology out beyond the boundaries of what its designers intended.

The spectacle of Ross's achievement also made a singularly important contribution to the development of air-mindedness in Australia. Before 1919, few Australians had seen an aeroplane; aviation was to most a remote phenomenon—a technological fad confined to Europe and the United States. The Vimy's tour of Australian towns and cities and the subsequent lecture film helped bring the air age to ordinary Australians. For most, the Vimy was the first aeroplane they had ever seen up close and Sir Ross Smith was the first aviator they ever knew—and, indeed, idolised.

The details of his life may have faded, but the notion that aviation holds profound significance and extraordinary potential for humankind resounds.

ACKNOWLEDGEMENTS

I accrued many debts during the four years it took to research and write *Anzac & Aviator*.

I was able to research this book in archives throughout Australia and overseas with a grant generously provided by the History Trust of South Australia' SA History Fund. The Trust's willingness to fund professionally trained researchers working outside the academy has great merit and should continue. I hope this book will make a useful contribution to the Trust's efforts to interpret Ross Smith's life and the air race during the centenary in 2019.

Much of my research occurred at the State Library of South Australia, where Carolyn Spooner provided invaluable support and shared her deep knowledge of the Smith papers and related collections. Carolyn has assisted my many inquiries over the past four years and helped me to make the most of my visits to Adelaide. She has my deepest gratitude.

At numerous other archives and museums, staff have likewise gone out of their way to assist me in tracking down obscure documents; I thank them all: Nadine Bjelic (Records Management, SACE Board); Richard Dunley (formerly National Archives, UK); Erica Johnson (Ewart Library, Dumfries); Andrea McKinnon-Matthews (archives of St Peter's College Adelaide); Mike Milln (South Australian Aviation Museum); Mike Nelmes (Narromine Aviation Museum); Lyn O'Grady (Walkerville Historical Society); Gabrielle Sexton (National Railway Museum in Port Adelaide); Ashley Ekins (Australian War Memorial); and Ross Mahoney (formerly

RAF Museum, Hendon). Lainie Anderson, who is writing her own account of the 1919 England-to-Australia air race, also generously shared some of her sources while her husband Max kindly showed me around some of Adelaide's sites relating to Ross's life.

Peter Stanley, my colleague at University of New South Wales, Canberra, enthusiastically encouraged this project as he has with all my previous books. Peter also kindly assisted me with researching in Indian archives, a new experience for me. Jeff Grey, who supervised my doctoral thesis at UNSW also encouraged this project and provided some important early advice but, sadly, did not live to see its completion. He once told me every serious historian should attempt a biography at some point in his career: I hope, with this book, I've risen to the challenge.

I thank those who have given me permission to consult privately held or curated papers: Ann Price and her son James for permission to consult the Sir Archibald Grenfell Price Papers at the State Library of South Australia; Ashley Ekins, who shared family papers relating to his grandfather (a friend of Ross's); Andrew Winter who, several years ago, provided me with an enlightening letter from Ross to his grandfather, Stanley Winter Irving; and David Baker, whose family holds the papers of Sir Geoffrey Salmond in the United Kingdom. I appreciate the time that Adam Lomman and Kirsty Lee, current managers of Mutooroo, took to correspond with me. Several researchers helped me obtain records when I was unable to travel myself: Adam Sutch, Brett Holman, William Westerman and Lee Richards at the National Archives in London; Arka Chowdhury in Kolkata and Alissa Gorrie in Canberra. My good friend and colleague Jonathon Dallimore, of the History Teachers' Association of New South Wales, provided hours of stimulating conversation about the theory and method of historical biography. Translations by Mirjam Kawalla gave me, an ashamedly monolinguist, access to Dutch sources.

Early in this project—my first biography—I approached Kristen Alexander for advice. Her books on Australian aviators have established her reputation as one of Australia's leading historians in the field. From its beginnings, she enthusiastically and generously supported this project—not the least by reading the manuscript at various stages and offering incisive criticism. Her contribution to this book has been considerable and her friendship invaluable; I thank her for both and hope to see her next one on the shelves soon.

At Allen & Unwin, Rebecca Kaiser has been a strong (and patient) advocate of this project; I am grateful for her support and encouragement. Thanks also to Tom Bailey-Smith and Sue Jarvis who edited the text.

I am greatly honoured by Andy Thomas's foreword. I could think of nobody more appropriate—a South Australian, a pioneer of aviator of his own era and a lifelong admirer of Ross Smith—to introduce the story of Ross's life. I thank him for his generosity and support.

Finally, to my family: my wife Melissa and children, Harriet (six) and Edmund (Ted—four). This book has taken me away from you sometimes but also provided us some exciting adventures as a family (a sweltering summer in Adelaide where you played in that city's beautiful parks while I played in the archives comes to mind). I hope it has all been worth it and that, in years to come, you will understand why I felt this was such an important story to tell.

NOTE ON SOURCES

From Ross Smith's life, a rich archive of primary source material remains for historians to draw upon. It is my hope that, far from being the last word on the subject, this book might stimulate further research into him and his historic flights.

The least-thoroughly documented part of Ross's life is his youth. Reconstructing his childhood and adolescent years requires the careful synthesis of a range of sources and the speculative use of 'soft', or circumstantial, evidence. Genealogical records provide the basic outline of the family's history, but prove challenging to use given the commonality of the surnames 'Smith' and 'Macpherson' in the record. Unfortunately, both of Ross's schools are now closed and records for the period during which he attended them do not survive. The State Library of South Australia (SLSA) holds the papers of a teacher from Queen's who worked there in the decade before Ross attended (Lewis B. Cross, PRG 763), providing some clues to the type of education he had. The only accounts of Ross as a youngster were composed in hindsight: a letter that his friend, Jack Howard, wrote to Dr A.A. Lendon in July 1927 (SLSA PRG 18/24) and an interview with Andrew and Jessie Smith in *The Observer*, published on 13 December 1919. Ross wrote almost nothing about his time in the cadets and militia; fortunately, his friend Clifford Browne kept a diary of the world tour that mentions Ross several times (SLVIC MS 8036). Finally, newspapers provide an essential means of outlining Ross's activities between the time he left school in 1909 and his enlistment in 1914. The social pages, in particular, allow us to identify what he did for recreation and the circle of friends he formed during this period. The digitisation of newspapers provides the means to search enormous volumes of newsprint for mentions of Ross and the Smith family.

We first hear Ross's voice in the historical record in a letter he wrote to his mother from a troopship in October 1914. He would continue writing letters on an almost-weekly basis to Jessie throughout the war. Many of these (though unfortunately not Jessie Smith's responses) are preserved in the Smith family papers at the SLSA. A large number of the original, handwritten letters are in PRG 18/17. Another file, PRG 18/24, contains an unpublished manuscript prepared by Dr A.A. Lendon on behalf of the family during the 1920s. It includes transcriptions of most of the letters in PRG 18/24 as well as others, not preserved there. Lendon also transcribed some of Ross's letters to Keith and to a few other friends. The originals of many of these letters have apparently not survived but, where comparison is possible, it seems that Lendon omitted some details (evidenced by his use of ellipses). Inexplicably, there is a gap in the letters (both in the surviving originals and Lendon's transcriptions) extending from August 1917 to March 1918. Fortunately, some of this period is covered by a surviving diary in which Ross made daily entries between November 1916 and January 1918. Some passages suggest that Ross may have written these entries retrospectively; it is detailed but not particularly reflective.

Official records created by Australian and British military authorities also provide important evidence regarding Ross's wartime activities. His time in the 3rd Australian Light Horse, 1st Machine Gun Squadron and No. 1 Squadron AFC is documented by the war diaries these units maintained and which have been preserved by the Australian War Memorial (AWM) in AWM 4. As the AFC operated within the British RFC (and, after April 1918, RAF), many pertinent operational records remain in Britain at the National Archives (NAUK). Particularly useful are Ross's combat and reconnaissance reports during 1916–17, which are appended to the war diary of 5th Wing RFC in the NAUK's AIR 1 series.

Supplementing the official records, many of Ross's comrades also wrote about their wartime experiences, providing useful (if, in some cases, retrospective) context and insight into his personality. The relative paucity of Ross's letters from Gallipoli made it necessary for me to look at a dozen or so collections of private records and memoirs by men in his unit, held by the AWM. Several of his comrades in No. 1 Squadron also produced memoirs—those by Richard Williams, Hudson Fysh, Eric Roberts, Lawrence Wackett and Leslie Sutherland all discuss Ross, as do Mark Lax's edited diaries of Joe Bull, who worked as Ross's mechanic, which are also valuable.

Besides a few letters written to his mother, Ross and Borton's survey of aerodromes in Asia is thoroughly documented in a file of official correspondence and reports kept by the Air Ministry (NAUK AVIA 2/1783). Borton wrote many of these but there are some under Ross's signature too. Ross also kept a notebook during the voyage, which includes notes on aerodromes, local contacts and sketch maps (SLSA PRG 18/31).

The period in which Ross prepared for the England-to-Australia flight is one of the more poorly documented parts of his life. What we can apparently know is revealed in files from Vickers (copies of which the National Library of Australia holds: MS 6093) and the Smith family papers (SLSA PRG 18/26). The Air Ministry's file on the competition also contributes some useful background (NAUK AVIA 2/1795).

There are five contemporary, first-hand records of the flight itself: Keith Smith's diary (SLSA PRG 18/31); some letters that the brothers wrote to their parents during the journey (SLSA PRG 18/28); the Vimy's log book (SLSA PRG 18/29); the maps Keith used (and annotated) during the flight (State Library of New South Wales [SLNSW] M Z/MT3 118gmof/1919/1); and the cables Ross sent to the newspapers from their various stops (printed in various newspapers but also preserved at the SLNSW A1633). The next most contemporary sources are a fourteen-page letter that Ross wrote to Vickers in January 1920 (SLSA PRG 18/28) and a report he wrote for the company in April 1920 (NAUK AIR1/2193/244/2). These reveal the mechanical difficulties Ross kept from the press to protect the company's reputation.

Immediately after the flight, newspapers in Britain and Australia published an account by Ross (e.g. *The Sun,* 12 December 1919). During 1920, Ross and Frank Hurley wrote a longer 35,000-word narrative that was serialised in Australia's *Life* magazine and published in full in the March 1921 edition of *National Geographic* in the United States. This version was published again, shortly after Ross's death, as *14,000 Miles Through the Air.* Although Ross presumably authorised this account, its epic style and the preservation of a draft manuscript, written in Hurley's handwriting, at the NLA (MS 883) suggests that the famous photographer played a considerable role in its production. Indeed, given the paucity of time that Ross had, he probably ghost-wrote it. For this reason, I limited my use of this account, relying instead upon the contemporary sources where possible.

The final stage of Ross's life is another for which the archival record contains some gaps. A few letters that Ross wrote to Borton and their mutual friend, Janette Verney, survive, providing a useful insight into how he privately responded to his celebrity (SLSA PRG 1067/2 and 18/63). Ross and Keith did their best to keep the round-the-world flight a secret for as long as possible, so few details about the planning appeared in the press before early 1922. A Vickers file, however, copied and deposited at the NLA, contains some useful material (Mfm M2587-2590), as does some correspondence between Ross and Vickers (SLSA PRG 18/35). The fatal accident at Brooklands was covered extensively in the press, though—as might be expected—the accounts need to be compared carefully as the newspapers carried some conflicting details. The Air Council's official report on the accident is in NAUK AVIA 2/125.

Despite the richness of the sources that document Ross's life, they represent only a fraction of his lived experience. Even after reading what I believe to be the vast majority of everything that Ross ever wrote or said that survives, besides most of what anyone ever wrote about him, some conspicuous gaps, silences and mysteries remain. Much more might yet be said about his youth, particularly his experiences at school and the five years in which he worked for Harris, Scarfe & Co.—an aspect of his life about which I could say little.

Ross's romantic life remained elusive too, with the documents raising more questions on this point than they provided answers. Details remain to be confirmed regarding his entry into the England-to-Australia air race—a competition he apparently did not plan to join until only a few weeks before he and his crew started. And our knowledge of the final year of his life, spent in Britain, remains patchy. It will be for future scholars to evaluate what I have provided and do their best to provide answers to these questions.

BIBLIOGRAPHY

Archival sources

Australian War Memorial, Canberra (AWM)

Private records

Adrian Cole PR88/154
Harry Stanley Conigrave PR04498
Tom Nesbit Crase MSS1071
Archie Dick 2DRL/0337
Roy J. Dunk 3DRL/7268
Charles Douglas Garden PR04616
Francis Lister Godlee PR01507
John R. Harris PR84/003
Arthur S. Hutton 3DRL/3371
Humphrey Courtenay Gilbert Kempe PR05493
Cecil Clyde Lord PR01690
Jack Morton Playne PR83/067
Joseph Marmion Ranford 1DRL/0551
Frank Milton Rowell 3DRL/6763B
Ross Macpherson Smith 1DRL/0655
Alexander Surplice PR03276

Official records

Australian Imperial Force unit war diaries, 1914–18 War AWM4
Australian Imperial Force Headquarters (Egypt), Central registry files AWM22
Australian Red Cross Wounded and Missing Inquiry Bureau 1DRL/0428
Recommendation files for honours and awards, AIF, 1914–18 War AWM28
Unit embarkation rolls 1914–18 War AWM8
Unit manuscript histories AWM224
Written records, 1914–18 War AWM25

Bayerisches Hauptstaatsarchiv, Abteilung IV: Kreigsarchiv, Munich (BHStA IV)

Bavarian Flying Squadron 304, Flug und Luftschiffe, file 54

British Pathé

Weybridge World Fliers, 1921, 228.45

National Archives of Australia, Canberra and Melbourne (NAA)

Australian Imperial Force personnel dossiers 1914–1920 B2455

Air Services Branch: Correspondence files A705

Department of Defence: Correspondence files MP84/1

Department of Defence: Courts-martial files A471

Department of Defence: General correspondence files MP367/1

Reports of the United Kingdom Air Ministry Accident Investigation Branch MP187/7

National Archives of the United Kingdom, Kew (NAUK)

Air Ministry: Air Historical Branch: Papers (Series 1) AIR 1

Air Ministry and Ministry of Defence: Registered files AIR 2

Air Ministry and predecessor and successors: Civil Aviation, Registered Files AVIA 2

National Library of Australia, Canberra (NLA)

William Morris Hughes MS 1538

Frank Hurley MS 883

Ross Macpherson Smith MS 1725

Eric Roberts NLA TRC 536

Walter Shiers MS 8627

Richard Williams NLA TRC 121/50

The Sir Ross Smith flight official souvenir JAFp GEN SIR

Vickers Limited MS 6093

Vickers PLC MS 2587-2590

Privately held papers

Ashley Ekins (Ashley Ekins, Canberra)

Sir Geoffrey Salmond (David Baker, Salisbury)

Stanley Winter Irving (Andrew Winter Irving, Nagambe)

Royal Archives, Windsor Castle (RA)

Cables sent during England–Australia flight RA PS/PSO/GV/PS/MAIN/26654/14-23a

Royal Australian Air Force Museum, Point Cook (RAAFM)

Albert Victor Tonkin

State Library of New South Wales, Sydney (SLNSW)

Maps used on the England to Australia flight M Z/MT3 118gmof/1919/1

Ross Smith, telegrams to *The Sun*, SLNSW A1633.

State Library of South Australia, Adelaide (SLSA)

Amyas Borton PRG 1067

Lewis B. Cross PRG 763

A.S. Hutton D4975

Alfred Austin Lendon PRG 128

A. Grenfell Price PRG 7

Ross Macpherson Smith PRG 18

Ross Smith Memorial Committee SRG 787

State Library of Victoria, Melbourne (SLVIC)

Clifford Harding Browne MS 8036

State Records Office of Western Australia (SRO WA)

Will of Donald Macpherson, 4 May 1872, Series 34, Cons3403, Item 1887–854.

Published sources

Anon, *Travel in India or city, shrine and sea beach: Antiquities, health resorts and places of interest on the Bengal–Nagpur railway, The Bombay Times* Press, Bombay, 1916.

Anne Baker, *From biplane to Spitfire: The life of Air Chief Marshal Sir Geoffrey Salmond KCB KCMG DSO*, Leo Cooper, Barnsley, 2003.

Alan Barcan, *A history of Australian education*, Oxford University Press, Melbourne, 1980.

C.E.W. Bean, *Official history of Australia in the war of 1914–1918 – volume II: The story of Anzac*, Angus & Robertson, Sydney, 1938 (1924).

—— *Here my son: An account of the independent and other corporate boys' schools of Australia*, Angus & Robertson, Sydney, 1950.

Joan Beaumont, *Broken nation: Australians in the Great War*, Allen & Unwin, Sydney, 2013.

Frank M. Blackwell, *The story of 3rd Australian Light Horse Regiment*, Third Light Horse Regimental Club, Adelaide, 1950.

Malcolm Booker, *The great professional: A study of W.M. Hughes*, McGraw Hill, Sydney, 1980.

Arthur Close Borton and Guy Slater (eds), *My warrior sons: The Borton family diary, 1914–1918*, P. Davies, London, 1973.

J.M. Bruce, *British aeroplanes 1914–18*, Putnam, London, 1957.

Craig Campbell and Helen Proctor, *A history of Australian schooling*, Allen & Unwin, Sydney, 2014.

Fred T. Clark, 'Squadron commander', *Cross and Cockade US*, vol. 11, no. 2, 1970, 146–54.

F. Clune, *D'air devil: the story of Pard Mustar, Australian air ace*, Angus & Robertson, Sydney, 1941.

Chris Coulthard-Clark, *McNamara VC: A hero's dilemma*, Air Power Development Centre, Canberra, 1996.

F.M. Cutlack, *Official history of Australia in the war of 1914–1918 – volume VIII: The Australian Flying Corps in the western and eastern theatres of war, 1914–1918* (12th ed), Angus & Robertson, Sydney, 1942.

Rhys Crawley, *Climax at Gallipoli: The failure of the August offensive*, University of Oklahoma Press, Norman, OK, 2014.

Martin Crotty, *Making the Australian male: Middle-class masculinity 1870–1920*, Melbourne University Press, Melbourne, 2001.

Robert Dixon, *Photography, early cinema and colonial modernity: Frank Hurley's synchronized lecture entertainments*, Anthem Press, London, 2011.

Edward Erickson, *Ottoman Army effectiveness in World War I: A comparative study*, Routledge, Abingdon, 2007.

—— *Palestine: The Ottoman campaigns of 1914–1918*, Pen & Sword Military, Barnsley, 2016.

Nelson Eustis, *The greatest air race: England–Australia 1919*, Rigby, Adelaide, 1969.

William Findlay, *The Mutooroo Pastoral Company Limited after fifty years*, The Advertiser Printing Office, Adelaide, 1951.

Hudson Fysh, *Qantas rising: The autobiography of the flying Fysh*, Angus & Robertson, Sydney, 1965.

Jeffrey Grey, *The war with the Ottoman Empire*, Oxford University Press, Melbourne, 2015.

Frederick William Haig, *Airman oilman: Frederick William Haig autobiography*, Frederick Publishing, Los Angeles, 1996.

Meredith Hooper, *God 'elp all of us: Three great flights*, Methuen, Sydney, 1986.

D.C. Howell-Price, *The Light Horse pocket book*, Angus & Robertson, Sydney, 1913.

Matthew Hughes, *Allenby and British strategy in the Middle East 1917–1919*, Frank Cass, Oxford, 1999.

H.A. Jones, *The war in the air: Being the story of the part played in the Great War by the Royal Air Force: volume 5*, Oxford University Press, Oxford, 1935.

—— *The war in the air: Being the story of the part played in the Great War by the Royal Air Force: volume 6*, Clarendon Press, Oxford, 1937.

Phillip E. Jones, *Education in Australia*, Nelson, Melbourne, 1974.

Humphrey Kempe, *Participation*, Hawthorne Press, Melbourne, 1973.

Colin Kerr, *Archie: the biography of Sir Archibald Grenfell Price*, Macmillan, Melbourne, 1983.

Rob Langham, *Bloody Paralyser: The giant Handley Page bombers of the First World War*, Fonthill, London, 2014.

Thomas Edward Lawrence, *The seven pillars of wisdom: A triumph*, Oxford University Press, Delhi, 1955.

Mark Lax, *One airman's war: Aircraft mechanic Joe Bull's personal diaries 1916–1919*, Banner Books, Maryborough, 1997.

Peter Maiden, *The sky racers: The 1919 air race from London to Australia*, Central Queensland University Press, Rockhampton, 2010.

J.P. McCoy and K. Keohane, 'Interview with G.N. Mills former observer with the Australian Flying Corps', *The 14–18 Journal*, 1968.

Alasdair McGregor, *Frank Hurley: A photographer's life*, Viking, Melbourne, 2004.

Peter McMillan, *Vimy: The flying machine that moved humanity*, Alicat, Melbourne, 2011.

Michael Molkentin, *Fire in the sky: The Australian Flying Corps in the First World War*, Allen & Unwin, Sydney, 2010.

—— *Australia and the war in the air*, Oxford University Press, Melbourne, 2014.

Gareth Morgan, 'Australian Flying Corps Roll of Honour 1915–1921: Part Three', *The 14–18 Journal*, 2010.

Paula Nagel, *North Adelaide, 1837–1901, a social history of North Adelaide*, Austaprint, London, 1974.

R.M. Playfair and A.C. Robinson, *A biological survey of the North Olary Plains South Australia 1995–1997*, Biological Survey and Research Natural Resources Group, Department of Environment and Natural Resources, Adelaide, 1997.

A. Grenfell Price, *The skies remember: The story of Ross and Keith Smith*, Angus & Robertson, Sydney, 1969.

Robin Prior, *Gallipoli: The end of the myth*, UNSW Press, Sydney, 2009.

Eric Roberts, *Box kites and beyond*, Hawthorne Press, Melbourne, 1976.

Chas Schaedel, *South Australian airmen of the Great War*, South Australian Aviation Museum History Group and Avonmore Books, Adelaide, 2015.

Clive Semple, *Airway to the East 1918–1920 and the collapse of No. 1 Aerial Route Royal Air Force*, Pen & Sword, Barnsley, 2012.

Lynsey Shaw Cobden, The nervous flyer: Nerves, flying and the First World War, *The British Journal for Military History*, vol. 4, no. 2, 2018, 121–42.

Christopher Shores, Norman Franks and Russell Guest, *Above the trenches: A complete record of the fighter aces and units of the British Empire air forces 1915–1920*, Grub Street, London, 1990.

Ross Smith, 'From London to Australia by aeroplane: A personal narrative of the first aerial voyage half around the world', *National Geographic* (Washington), vol. XXXIX, no. 3, 1921, 229–339.

—— *14,000 miles through the air*, Macmillan, London, 1922.

Neil C. Smith, *The Third Australian Light Horse Regiment, 1914–18: A short history and listing of those who served*, Mostly Unsung Military History and Research Publications, Gardenvale, 1993.

Peter Stanley, *Quinn's Post, Anzac, Gallipoli*, Allen & Unwin, Sydney, 2005.

—— *Bad characters: Sex, crime, mutiny, murder and the Australian Imperial Force*, Pier 9, Sydney, 2010.

—— *Digger Smith and Australia's Great War: Ordinary name—extraordinary stories*, Pier 9, Sydney, 2011.

Craig Stockings and John Connor (eds), *Before the Anzac Dawn: A military history of Australia to 1915*. NewSouth Publishing, Sydney, 2013.

L.W. Sutherland and Norman Ellison, *Aces and kings*, John Hamilton, London, 1935.

University of Adelaide, *University of Adelaide Public Examinations Board Manual 1909–1911*.

Craig Wilcox, *For hearths and homes: Citizen soldiering in Australia 1854–1945*, Allen & Unwin, Sydney, 1998.

Richard Williams, *These are facts: The autobiography of Air Marshall Sir Richard Williams, KBE, CB, DSO*, Australian War Memorial and AGPS, Canberra, 1977.

V. M. Yeates, *Winged victory*, Jonathon Cape, London, 1972.

Unpublished/self-published sources

Michael Maton, *The Distinguished Flying Cross to Australians*, self-published, 2000.

Brian Edward O'Connor, 'History of Queen's College North Adelaide 1883–1949', Master of Education thesis, University of Adelaide, 2002.

Online sources

Geoffrey H. Manning, *A compendium of the place names of South Australia*, State Library of South Australia, Adelaide, 2012. Retrieved from <www.slsa.sa.gov.au/digitalpubs/placenamesofsouthaustralia>.

NOTES

1 Mutooroo

1 Geoffrey H. Manning, *A compendium of the place names of South Australia*, State Library of South Australia, Adelaide, 2012, <www.slsa.sa.gov.au/digitalpubs/placenamesofsouthaustralia>, accessed 8 August 2016.

2 R.M. Playfair and A.C. Robinson, *A biological survey of the North Olary Plains South Australia 1995–1997*, Biological Survey and Research Natural Resources Group, Department of Environment and Natural Resources, South Australia, 1997, p. 35.

3 'The parents of the heroes', *The Observer* (Adelaide), 13 December 1919, p. 35.

4 Janet (no surname) to A. Grenfell Price, 26 January c. 1967, SLSA PRG7/2/51.

5 'Glentromie', *The Inquirer and Commercial News* (Perth), 20 April 1887, p. 2.

6 'News of the week', *The Inquirer and Commercial News* (Perth), 29 February 1888, p. 3.

7 Will of Donald Macpherson, 4 May 1872, SRO WA, Series 34, Cons3403, Item 1887-854.

8 A.A. Lendon, 'Sir Ross Smith', *Queen's College Magazine*, SLSA PRG 18/24.

9 'Found dead', *Adelaide Observer*, 28 July 1900, p. 30.

10 William Findlay, *The Mutooroo Pastoral Company Limited after fifty years*, The Advertiser Printing Office, Adelaide, 1951, p. 10.

11 'Mutooroo water service', *Daily Herald* (Adelaide), 3 December 1912, p. 8.

12 'The late Andrew Smith', *The Register* (Adelaide), 20 November 1924, p. 9.

13 'Family notices', *Barrier Miner* (Broken Hill), 26 November 1924, p. 2.

14 Findlay, *The Mutooroo Pastoral Company*, p. 26.

15 'Sir Ross Smith KBE: A memorial lecture by Dr A.A. Lendon at Queen's College, c. 1922', SLSA PRG 128/16.

16 'Obituary', *The Register* (Adelaide), 19 November 1924, p. 13.

17 'The parents of the heroes', *The Observer* (Adelaide), 13 December 1919, p. 35.

18 Paula Nagel, *North Adelaide, 1837–1901: A social history of North Adelaide—a*

study of the evolution of a suburb and its community during its first sixty-four years, showing the emergence of distinctly separate classes and the consequences that these distinctions brought, Austaprint, Adelaide, 1974, p. 66.

2 Froggy

1 Paula Nagel, *North Adelaide*, 1837–1901, p. 65.

2 Queen's School Prospectus, 1893, SLSA PRG 763/6/3.

3 Brendan E. O'Connor, 'History of Queen's College North Adelaide 1883–1949', MEd thesis, University of Adelaide, 2002, p. 55.

4 Annotations on the back of a photograph of Queen's students, c. 1902, SLSA B 29751. Ross and Keith are pictured among students in this image.

5 O'Connor, 'History of Queen's College North Adelaide', p. 56.

6 Ross to Miss Benda, 5 November 1916, SLSA PRG 18/24.

7 'Airmen go to races', *The Herald* (Melbourne), 28 February 1920, p. 7.

8 A. Grenfell Price, *The skies remember: The story of Ross and Keith Smith*, Angus & Robertson, Sydney, 1969, p. 5.

9 'School speech days', *The Advertiser* (Adelaide), 20 December 1904, p. 6.

10 'Personal careers', *The Observer* (Adelaide), 13 December 1919, p. 35.

11 J.G. Howard to A.A. Lendon, 14 July 1927, SLSA PRG 18/24; Grenfell Price, *The skies remember*, p. 5.

12 'Sir Ross Smith mother's pride', *The Argus* (Melbourne), 20 April 1922, p. 7.

13 'The parents of the heroes', *The Observer*, 13 December 1919, p. 35.

14 Ross to Jessie Smith, 9 May 1915 and 13 June 1915, SLSA PRG 18/24.

15 'Mother's tribute', *The Register* (Adelaide), 20 April 1922, p. 7. Ross also refers to his love of heights in a letter he wrote to his mother shortly after he began training with the Australian Flying Corps: Ross to Jessie Smith, 7 November 1916, SLSA PRG 18/24.

16 Ross to Jessie Smith, 20 February 1917, SLSA PRG 18/24.

17 'The ace of aircraft', *The Sun* (Sydney), 6 December 1919, p. 1; A.A. Lendon, 'Sir Ross Smith', *Queen's College Magazine*, SLSA PRG 18/24; Ian McIntosh, 'Weather totally unfit for flying', *The Rolls-Royce Magazine*, September–November 1979, pp. 23–7.

18 Janet to Grenfell Price, 26 January c. 1965, SLSA PRG7/2/51. This was also reported in the press following the 1919 air race: 'Set the world agog', *The Sun* (Sydney), 15 February 1920, p. 2.

19 *University of Adelaide Public Examinations Board Manual 1909–1911*, University of Adelaide, 1911, pp. 50–9.

20 'The parents of the heroes', *The Observer* (Adelaide), 13 December 1919, p. 35.
21 Ross to Jessie Smith, 20 February 1917, SLSA PRG 18/24.

3 A little more *éclat*

1 Craig Stockings, 'Australia's boy soldiers: The army cadet movement', in Craig Stockings and John Connor (eds), *Before the Anzac dawn: A military history of Australia to 1915*, NewSouth Publishing, Sydney, 2013, pp. 174–6.
2 'Mounted cadets wanted', *The Express and Telegraph* (Adelaide), 13 January 1908, p. 4.
3 A.W. Cleaveland to the Secretary, Department of Defence, 16 May 1910, NAA MP84/1 1832/17/24.
4 'Australian cadets to start on world tour', *The Evening Standard* (Washington DC), 6 June 1910, p. 10.
5 Clifford Harding Browne, diary, 2 and 13 June 1910, SLVIC MS8036 Envelope 12.
6 'Australian cadets', *Daily Herald* (Adelaide), 15 October 1910, p. 14.
7 'Australian cadets', *Daily Herald* (Adelaide), 15 October 1910, p. 14.
8 'Memorial hall', *Sydney Morning Herald*, 23 August 1920, p. 8.
9 'Australian cadets', *Daily Herald* (Adelaide), 15 October 1910, p. 14.
10 Browne, diary, 13 July 1910, SLVIC MS8036 Envelope 12.
11 Browne, diary, 13 July 1910, SLVIC MS8036 Envelope 12.
12 *Flight*, 6 August 1910, p. 624.
13 Browne, diary, 22, 23 and 26 August 1910, SLVIC MS8036 Envelope 12.

4 Aviemore

1 Craig Wilcox, *For hearths and homes: Citizen soldiering in Australia 1854–1945*, Allen & Unwin, Sydney, 1998, pp. 65–71.
2 'Grime of working', *The Register* (Adelaide), 18 May 1911, p. 5.
3 J.G. Howard to A.A. Lendon, 14 July 1927, SLSA PRG 18/24.
4 'An interesting interview', *Brisbane Courier*, 3 January 1920, p. 7.
5 The tattoo is noted on Ross's AIF attestation form under 'distinctive marks'. This document also indicates he had an appendicitis scar: AIF dossier, Ross Macpherson Smith, NAA B2455.
6 'Electric tattooing: A modern application of art', *The Advertiser*, 7 July 1911, p. 7.
7 Ross to Jessie Smith, 18 November 1916, SLSA PRG 18/24.
8 See, for example, Ross to Keith Smith, 6 May 1915, SLSA PRG 18/24.

9 J.G. Howard to A.A. Lendon, 14 July 1927, SLSA PRG 18/24.
10 J.G. Howard to A.A. Lendon, 14 July 1927, SLSA PRG 18/24.
11 'The realm of women', *The Mail* (Adelaide), 25 April 1914, p. 2.
12 'Society news and events', *The Mail* (Adelaide), 13 December 1919, p. 12.
13 J.G. Howard to A.A. Lendon, 14 July 1927, SLSA PRG 18/24.
14 Ross to Jessie, 26 February 1915, SLSA PRG 18/24.

5 The Great War

1 'Expeditionary Force camp at Morphettville', *Port Pirie Recorder and North Western Mail*, 13 August 1914, p. 3.
2 J.G. Howard to A.A. Lendon, 14 July 1927, SLSA PRG 18/24.
3 'Boyhood days', *The Herald* (Melbourne), 24 February 1920, p. 1.
4 3rd Light Horse Regiment embarkation roll, 22 October 1914, AWM8 10/8/1.
5 D.C. Howell-Price, *The Light Horse pocket book*, Angus & Robertson, Sydney, 1913, pp. 38–9.
6 Ross to Jessie Smith, 24 November 1914, SLSA PRG 18/24.
7 'Agreement for employees engaged during shearing', *The Herald* (Adelaide), 20 October 1900, p. 5.
8 Frank M. Blackwell, *The story of 3rd Australian Light Horse regiment*, Third Light Horse Regimental Club, Adelaide, 1950, p. 4.
9 Blackwell, *The story of 3rd Australian Light Horse regiment*, p. 134.
10 'The Morphettville camp', *The Register* (Adelaide), 31 August 1914, p. 11.
11 Invitation to Adelaide Rowing Club Smoke Social, 4 September 1914, provided by Ashley Ekins.
12 'Adelaide Rowing Club', *The Mail* (Adelaide), 11 November 1914, p. 2.
13 'The Soldiers' Farewell', *The Observer* (Adelaide), 26 September 1914, p. 44.
14 'The Morphettville camp', *The Express and Telegraph* (Adelaide), 6 October 1914, p. 4.
15 'At the camp night bivouacs', *Daily Herald* (Adelaide), 17 October 1914, p. 5.
16 Ross to Keith Smith, 6 May 1915, SLSA PRG 18/24.
17 Ross to Jessie Smith, 12 March 1918, SLSA PRG 18/24.

6 Six-bob-a-day tourists

1 Ross to Jessie Smith, 29 October 1914, SLSA PRG 18/24.
2 Ross to Jessie Smith, 24 November 1914, SLSA PRG 18/24.
3 Ross to Jessie Smith, undated, SLSA PRG 18/24.
4 Ross to Jessie Smith, 7 December 1914, SLSA PRG 18/24.

5 'Our boys in Egypt', *The Laura Standard*, 29 January 1915, p. 3.
6 Ross to Jessie Smith, 7 December 1914, SLSA PRG 18/24.
7 Ross to Jessie Smith, 15 December 1914, SLSA PRG 18/24.
8 'Wonderful Egypt', *The Register* (Adelaide), 22 January 1915, p. 6.
9 Ross to Jessie Smith, 10 January 1915, SLSA PRG 18/24.
10 Ross to Jessie Smith, 13 April 1915, SLSA PRG 18/24.
11 Ross to Jessie Smith, 13 April 1915, SLSA PRG 18/24.
12 Ross to Jessie Smith, 24 April 1915, SLSA PRG 18/24.
13 Ross to Jessie Smith, 15 December 1914, SLSA PRG 18/24.
14 Ross to Jessie Smith, 29 December 1914, SLSA PRG 18/24.
15 Ross to Jessie Smith, 1 April 1915, SLSA PRG 18/24.
16 Ross to Jessie Smith, 1 April 1915, SLSA PRG 18/24.
17 Ross to Jessie Smith, 7 May 1915, SLSA PRG 18/24.
18 Ross to Jessie Smith, 10 January 1915, SLSA PRG 18/24.
19 John Barnett, court martial proceedings, December 1914, NAA A471 17850.
20 Ross to Jessie Smith, 26 February 1915, SLSA PRG 18/24.
21 Peter Stanley, *Bad characters: Sex, crime, mutiny, murder and the Australian Imperial Force*, Pier 9, Sydney, 2010, p. 36.
22 Ross to Jessie Smith, 29 December 1915, SLSA PRG 18/24.
23 William Vincent Rule, court martial proceedings, 6 March 1915, NAA A471 18096.
24 Ross to Jessie Smith, 21 January 1915, SLSA PRG 18/24
25 John Howard to Archibald Grenfell Price, 3 February 1967, SLSA PRG 7/2/51.
26 Ross to Jessie Smith, 20 March 1915, SLSA PRG 18/24.
27 See, for example, 'Turkey's doom approaching', *The Mail* (Adelaide), 6 March 1915, p. 8.
28 Ross to Jessie Smith, 1 April 1915, SLSA PRG 18/24.
29 Ross to Jessie Smith, 27 March 1915, SLSA PRG 18/24.
30 Ross to Jessie Smith, 15 December 1914, SLSA PRG 18/24.
31 Ross to Jessie Smith, 29 December 1914, SLSA PRG 18/24.
32 Ross to Jessie Smith, 8 May 1915, SLSA PRG 18/24.
33 Ross to Jessie Smith, 29 April 1915, SLSA PRG 18/24. 'White' was actually Thomas Anderson Whyte.
34 Ross to Keith Smith, 6 May 1915, SLSA PRG 18/24.
35 J.M. Ranford, diary, 9 May 1915, AWM 1DRL/551.
36 Ross to Jessie Smith, 9 May 1915, SLSA PRG 18/24.
37 H.S. Conigrave, diary, 9 May 1915, AWM PR04498.

7 Anzac

1 Humphrey Kempe, *Participation*, Hawthorne Press, Melbourne, 1973, p. 30.
2 Ross to Jessie Smith, 31 October 1915, SLSA PRG 18/24.
3 Ross to Jessie Smith, 31 October 1915, SLSA PRG 18/24.
4 Ross to Jessie Smith, 31 October 1915, SLSA PRG 18/24.
5 Kempe, *Participation*, p. 31; Ross to Jessie Smith, 31 October 1915, SLSA PRG 18/24.
6 A.S. Hutton, diary 14 and 22 May 1915, SLSA D4975; F.L. Godlee, diary, 22 May 1915, AWM PR01507.
7 Ross to Jessie Smith, 31 October 1915, SLSA PRG 18/24.
8 Kempe, *Participation*, p. 33.
9 A. Surplice, diary, 16 May 1915, AWM PR03276.
10 Ross to Jessie Smith, 31 October 1915, SLSA PRG 18/24.
11 Ross to Jessie Smith, 31 October 1915, SLSA PRG 18/24.
12 Kempe, *Participation*, p. 36.
13 Surplice, diary, 16 May 1915, AWM PR03276.
14 Kempe, *Participation*, p. 36.

8 Life in the trenches

1 Conigrave, diary, 18 May 1915, AWM PR04498.
2 Ross to Jessie Smith, 24 July 1915, SLSA PRG 18/24.
3 Ross to Jessie Smith, 31 October 1915, SLSA PRG 18/24.
4 Kempe, *Participation*, p. 47.
5 Ranford, diary, 24 May 1915, AWM 1DRL551.
6 Ross to Jessie Smith, 31 October 1915.
7 Ross to Jessie Smith, 13 June 1915, SLSA PRG 18/24.
8 Ross to Jessie Smith, 31 October 1915.
9 Ross to Jessie Smith, 31 October 1915, SLSA PRG 18/24; Ross to Keith Smith, 4 August 1915, SLSA PRG 18/24.
10 Ross to Jessie Smith, 1 February 1916, SLSA PRG 18/24.
11 Ross to Keith Smith, 30 July 1915, SLSA PRG 18/24.
12 Ross to Keith Smith, 4 August 1915, SLSA PRG 18/24.
13 Ross to Jessie Smith, 10 July 1915, SLSA PRG 18/24.
14 Ross to Jessie Smith, 3 July 1915, SLSA PRG 18/24.
15 Ross to Jessie Smith, 21 March 1916, SLSA PRG 18/24.
16 Hutton, diary, 20 May, 29 May and 2 June 1915, SLSA D4975.
17 Ross to Jessie Smith, 10 September 1915, SLSA PRG 18/24.

18 Ross to Jessie Smith, 3 July 1915, SLSA PRG 18/24.
19 Ross to Jessie Smith, 31 October 1915, SLSA PRG 18/24.
20 Ross to Jessie Smith, 31 October 1915, SLSA PRG 18/24.
21 Ross to Keith Smith, 30 July 1915, SLSA PRG 18/24.
22 Ross to Jessie Smith, 30 May 1915, SLSA PRG 18/24.
23 Ross to Jessie Smith, 27 October 1915, SLSA PRG 18/24.
24 Ross to Jessie Smith, 20 June 1915, SLSA PRG 18/24.
25 Ross to Jessie Smith, 16 July 1915, SLSA PRG 18/24.
26 Ross to Jessie Smith, 26 August 1915, SLSA PRG 18/24.
27 Ross to Jessie Smith, 30 July 1915, SLSA PRG 18/24.
28 Ross to Jessie Smith, 20 June 1915, SLSA PRG 18/24.
29 Blackwell, *The story of the 3rd Australian Light Horse Regiment*, p. 38.
30 Ross to Jessie Smith, 31 October 1915, SLSA PRG 18/24.

9 The August offensive

1 Ross to Jessie Smith, 31 October 1915, SLSA PRG 18/24.
2 Kempe, *Participation*, p. 55.
3 Ross to Jessie Smith, 31 October 1915, SLSA PRG 18/24; Conigrave, diary, 27 August 1915, AWM PR04498; F.L. Godlee, diary, 8 August 1915, AWM PR01507.
4 Conigrave, diary, 27 August 1915, AWM PR04498.
5 Ross to Jessie Smith, 31 October 1915, SLSA PRG 18/24.
6 Conigrave, diary, 10 August 1915, AWM PR04498; Surplice, diary, 14 August 1915, AWM PR03276.
7 Ross to Jessie Smith, 3 May 1916, SLSA PRG 18/24.

10 Quinn's Post

1 Ross to Jessie Smith, 31 October 1915, SLSA PRG 18/24.
2 Conigrave, diary, 10 August 1915, AWM PR04498.
3 Surplice, diary, 14 August 1915, AWM PR03276.
4 Conigrave, diary, 18 August 1915, AWM PR04498.
5 Ranford, diary, 16 August 1915, AWM 1DRL551; Surplice, diary, 15 August 1915, AWM PR03276.
6 Ross to Jessie Smith, 12 March 1916, SLSA PRG 18/24.
7 Hutton, diary, 16, 17, 22 and 29 August 1915, SLSA D 4975.
8 3rd Light Horse Regiment, war diary, August and September 1915, AWM4 10/8/9 and 10/8/10.

9 Conigrave, diary, 10 September 1915, AWM PR04498.
10 Ross to Jessie Smith, 10 September 1915, SLSA PRG 18/24.
11 Kempe, *Participation*, p. 59.
12 Ross to Jessie Smith, 31 October 1915, SLSA PRG 18/24.
13 Ross to Jessie Smith, 18 October 1915, SLSA PRG 18/24.
14 Ross to Jessie Smith, 31 October 1915, SLSA PRG 18/24.
15 Ross to Jessie Smith, 28 December 1915, SLSA PRG 18/24.
16 Ross to Jessie Smith, 7 March 1916, SLSA PRG 18/24.
17 See, for example, Robin Prior, *Gallipoli: The end of the myth*, UNSW Press, Sydney, 2009; Rhys Crawley, *Climax at Gallipoli: The failure of the August offensive*, University of Oklahoma Press, Norman, OK, 2014; Jeffrey Grey, *The war with the Ottoman Empire*, Oxford University Press, Melbourne, 2015.

11 Cutting some ice

1 Ross to Jessie Smith, 13 October 1915, SLSA PRG 18/24.
2 Ross to Jessie Smith, 13 October 1915, SLSA PRG 18/24.
3 Ross to Jessie Smith, 18 October 1915, SLSA PRG 18/24.
4 Ross to Jessie Smith, 27 October 1915, SLSA PRG 18/24.
5 Ross to Jessie Smith, 13 February 1915, SLSA PRG 18/24.
6 Ross to Jessie Smith, 4 November 1915, SLSA PRG 18/24.
7 Ross to Jessie Smith, 17 November 1915, SLSA PRG 18/24.
8 Ross to Jessie Smith, 22 November 1915, SLSA PRG 18/24.
9 Ross to Jessie Smith, 28 November 1915, SLSA PRG 18/24.
10 Ross to Jessie Smith, 14 December 1915, SLSA PRG 18/24.
11 Ross to Jessie Smith, 20 January 1916, SLSA PRG 18/24.
12 Ross to Jessie Smith, 14 December 1915, SLSA PRG 18/24.
13 Ross to Jessie Smith, 13 January 1916, SLSA PRG 18/24
14 Ross to Jessie Smith, 20 January 1916 and 2 June 1916, SLSA PRG 18/24.
15 Ross to Jessie Smith, 28 November 1915, SLSA PRG 18/24.
16 Ross to Jessie Smith, 28 December 1915, SLSA PRG 18/24.
17 Ross to Jessie Smith, 15 January 1916, SLSA PRG 18/24.
18 Ross to Jessie Smith, 7 February 1916, SLSA PRG 18/24.
19 Ross to Jessie Smith, 14 February 1916, SLSA PRG 18/24.
20 Ross to Jessie Smith, 1 March 1916, SLSA PRG 18/24
21 Ross to Jessie Smith, 12 March 1916, SLSA PRG 18/24.
22 Ross to Jessie Smith, 21 March 1916, SLSA PRG 18/24.
23 Ross to Jessie Smith, 4 April 1916, SLSA PRG 18/24.

12 Once more out in the desert

1 Ross to Jessie Smith, 8 April 1916, SLSA PRG 18/24.
2 Ross to Jessie Smith, 16 April 1916, SLSA PRG 18/24.
3 Ross to Jessie Smith, 23 April 1916, SLSA PRG 18/24.
4 Ross to Jessie Smith, 3 May 1916, SLSA PRG 18/24
5 Ross to Jessie Smith, 5 May 1916, SLSA PRG 18/24.
6 Ross to Jessie Smith, 20 May 1916, SLSA PRG 18/24.
7 Ross to Jessie Smith, 25 May 1916, SLSA PRG 18/24.
8 Ross Smith, 'The battle of Romani', 15 August 1916, SLSA PRG 18/23.
9 1st Light Horse Brigade HQ to HQ Anzac Mounted Division, 1 June 1916, AWM4 10/1/23.
10 Ross to Jessie Smith, 10 June 1916, SLSA PRG 18/24.
11 Ross to Jessie Smith, 24 June 1916, SLSA PRG 18/24.
12 Ross to Jessie Smith, 18 June 1916, SLSA PRG 18/24.
13 'The Battle of Romani', 15 August 1916, SLSA PRG 18/24.
14 Ross to Jessie Smith, 18 June 1916, SLSA PRG 18/24.
15 'Ross to Jessie Smith, 15 July 1916, SLSA PRG 18/24.
16 'The battle of Romani', 15 August 1916, SLSA PRG 18/23; Ross to Jessie Smith, 1 July 1916, SLSA PRG 18/24.
17 Ross to Jessie Smith, 24 June 1916, SLSA PRG 18/24.
18 Ross to Jessie Smith, 24 June 1916, SLSA PRG 18/24.
19 Ross to Jessie Smith, 29 July 1916, SLSA PRG 18/24.
20 Ross to Jessie Smith, 15 July 1916, SLSA PRG 18/24.
21 Ross to Jessie Smith, 1 July 1916, SLSA PRG 18/24.

13 The savage satisfaction of seeing them drop

1 Ross to Jessie Smith, 18 June 1916, SLSA PRG 18/24.
2 'The battle of Romani', 15 August 1916, SLSA PRG 18/24.
3 Ross to Jessie Smith, 29 July 1916, SLSA PRG 18/24.
4 'The battle of Romani', 15 August 1916, SLSA PRG 18/24.
5 Kempe, *Participation*, p. 73.
6 'The battle of Romani', 15 August 1916, SLSA PRG 18/24. All of Ross's following quotes relating to the battles of Romani and Bir-el-Abd come from this account he wrote to Jessie, unless otherwise noted.
7 Kempe, *Participation*, p. 74.
8 Ross to Jessie Smith, 10 September 1916, SLSA PRG 18/24.
9 Ross to Jessie Smith, 17 August 1916, SLSA PRG 18/24.

10 Ross to Jessie Smith, 9 November 1916, SLSA PRG 18/24.
11 'The fight at Romani', *The Advertiser*, 6 October 1916, p. 8.
12 Hudson Fysh, *Qantas rising: The autobiography of the flying Fysh*, Angus & Robertson, Sydney, 1965, p. 40.
13 1st Australian Machine Gun Squadron, war diary, 9 August 1916, AWM4 24/30/1.
14 Kempe, *Participation*, p. 78.
15 1st Australian Machine Gun Squadron, war diary, 14–21 August 1916, AWM4 24/30/1.
16 Edward Erickson, *Palestine: The Ottoman campaigns of 1914–1918*, Pen and Sword, Barnsley, 2016, p. 69.
17 Ross to Jessie Smith, 6 August 1916, SLSA PRG 18/24.
18 Ross to Jessie Smith, 17 August 1916, SLSA PRG 18/24.
19 Ross to Jessie Smith, 26 August 1916, SLSA PRG 18/24.
20 Ross to Jessie Smith, 17 August 1916, SLSA PRG 18/24.
21 Ross to Jessie Smith, 22 August 1916, SLSA PRG 18/24.
22 Ross to Jessie Smith, 10 September 1916, SLSA PRG 18/24.
23 Ross to Jessie Smith, 17 August 1916, SLSA PRG 18/24.
24 Ross to Jessie Smith, 17 August 1916, SLSA PRG 18/24.
25 Ross to Jessie Smith, 22 August 1916, SLSA PRG 18/24.
26 Ross to Jessie Smith, 25 September 1916, SLSA PRG 18/24.
27 Ross to Jessie Smith, 17 August 1916, SLSA PRG 18/24.
28 Ross to Jessie Smith, 8 February 1917, SLSA PRG 18/24.
29 Ross to Jessie Smith, 26 August 1916, SLSA PRG 18/24.

14 The coming thing

1 Ross to Jessie Smith, 22 August 1916, SLSA PRG 18/24.
2 Ross to Jessie Smith, 1 September 1916, SLSA PRG 18/24.
3 Ross to Jessie Smith, 17 April 1916, SLSA PRG 18/24.
4 Ross to Jessie Smith, 25 September 1916, SLSA PRG 18/24.
5 'Mr Jones' story: cup full of petrol would have saved him', *The Chronicle* (Adelaide), 10 January 1914, p. 18.
6 Data from TROVE Newspapers, <http://trove.nla.gov.au/newspaper>, based on a search of articles with aviation-themed terms on 30 October 2017.
7 'Australian Flying Corps', *The Register* (Adelaide), 15 January 1913, p. 15.
8 'Aircraft', *The Register*, 25 April 1914, p. 13.
9 Ross to Jessie Smith, 25 September 1916, SLSA PRG 18/24.
10 Ross to Jessie Smith, 4 October 1916, SLSA PRG 18/24.

11 Ross to Jessie Smith, 23 October 1916, SLSA PRG 18/24.

12 Ross to Jessie Smith, 13 October 1916, SLSA PRG 18/24.

13 Michael Molkentin, *Australia and the war in the air*, Oxford University Press, Melbourne, 2014, pp. 48–53.

14 Ross to Jessie Smith, 27 October 1916, SLSA PRG 18/24.

15 Ross to Keith Smith, 5 November 1916, SLSA PRG 18/24.

16 J.M. Bruce, *British aeroplanes 1914–18*, Putnam, London, 1957, p. 368.

17 Ross to Keith Smith, 5 November 1916, SLSA PRG 18/24.

18 Ross to Keith Smith, 5 November 1916, SLSA PRG 18/24; Ross to Jessie Smith, 22 November 1916, SLSA PRG 18/24.

19 Ross to Jessie Smith, 29 March 1917, SLSA PRG 18/24.

20 Ross Smith, diary, 1 November 1916, SLSA PRG 18/19/1.

21 Ross to Jessie Smith, 18 November 1916, SLSA PRG 18/24.

22 Frederick William Haig, *Airman oilman: Frederick William Haig autobiography*, Frederick Publishing, Los Angeles, 1996, p. 17; Eric Roberts, *Box kites and beyond*, Hawthorne Press, Melbourne, 1976, p. 17.

23 Fred T. Clark, 'Squadron Commander', *Cross and Cockade US*, vol. 11, no. 2, 1970, pp. 146–54.

24 Ross Smith, reconnaissance report, 4 November 1916, NAUK AIR1/1756/204/141/20.

25 Ross Smith, diary, 4 November 1916, SLSA PRG PRG/18/19/1.

26 Ross to Jessie Smith, 27 October 1916, SLSA PRG 18/24.

27 Ross to Jessie Smith, 7 November 1916, SLSA PRG 18/24.

28 Ross to Jessie Smith, 9 November 1916, SLSA PRG 18/24.

29 Ross to Jessie Smith, 18 November 1916, SLSA PRG 18/24.

30 For the social character of the Australian Flying Corps' personnel, see Michael Molkentin, *Fire in the sky: The Australian Flying Corps in the First World War*, Allen & Unwin, Sydney, 2010, pp. 29–31 and 48–53.

31 Ross to Jessie Smith, 18 November 1916, SLSA PRG 18/24.

32 Ross to Jessie Smith, 7 November 1916, SLSA PRG 18/24.

33 Ross to Jessie Smith, 6 December 1916, SLSA PRG 18/24.

34 Ross to Jessie Smith, 28 November 1916, SLSA PRG 18/24.

15 Hadji

1 Mark Lax, *One airman's war: Aircraft mechanic Joe Bull's personal diaries 1916–1919*, Banner Books, Maryborough, 1997, pp. 12–13; Adrian Cole, 'Merry old souls', unpublished manuscript memoir, AWM PR88/154, p. 13.

2 Ross Smith, diary, 9 December 1916, SLSA PRG PRG/18/19/1; Chris Coulthard-Clark, McNamara VC: *A hero's dilemma*, Air Power Development Centre, Canberra, 1996, pp. 28–9.

3 Ross to Jessie Smith,18 November 1916, SLSA PRG 18/24; Ross to Jessie Smith, 28 January 1917, SLSA PRG 18/24.

4 Cole, 'Merry old souls', p. 13.

5 Ross Smith, diary, 21 December 1916, SLSA PRG PRG/18/19/1.

6 Ross Smith, diary, 23 December 1916, SLSA PRG PRG/18/19/1; Roberts, *Box kites and beyond*, p. 25.

7 Ross to Jessie Smith, 22 December 1916, SLSA PRG 18/24; Ross to Keith Smith, 26 December 1916, SLSA PRG 18/24.

8 Ross to Jessie Smith, 1 January 1917, SLSA PRG 18/24.

9 Ross to Keith Smith, 26 December 1916, SLSA PRG 18/24.

10 Ross to Jessie Smith, 12 January 1917, SLSA PRG 18/24.

11 Ross to Jessie Smith, 12 January 1917, SLSA PRG 18/24.

12 Ross to Jessie Smith, 12 January 1917, SLSA PRG 18/24.

13 Ross to Jessie Smith, 14 December 1916 and 12 January 1917, SLSA PRG 18/24.

14 Cole, 'Merry old souls', p. 15; Roberts, *Box kites and beyond*, p. 31.

15 Ross to Jessie Smith, 14 December 1916, SLSA PRG 18/24.

16 Ross to Jessie Smith, 28 January 1917, SLSA PRG 18/24.

17 Ross to Jessie Smith, 20 January 1917, SLSA PRG 18/24. See also Roberts, *Box kites and beyond*, p. 28; Eric Roberts interviewed by Fred Morton, NLA TRC 536.

18 Cole, 'Merry old souls', p. 15

19 Ross Smith, diary, 12 February 1917, SLSA PRG 18/19.

20 Ross to Jessie Smith, 20 February 1917, SLSA PRG 18/24.

21 Ross Smith, diary, 18 February 1917, SLSA PRG 18/19/1.

22 Ross to Jessie Smith, 1 March 1917, SLSA PRG 18/24.

16 Gaza

1 'History of the Royal Flying Corps in Palestine, 1917', NAUK AIR1/2415/303/28.

2 Ross Smith, diary, 17 March 1917, SLSA PRG PRG/18/19/1.

3 Ross Smith, diary, 12 January 1917, SLSA PRG PRG/18/19/1.

4 Ross to Jessie Smith, 17 March 1917, SLSA PRG 18/24.

5 J.P. McCoy and K. Keohane, 'Interview with G.N. Mills former Observer with the Australian Flying Corps', *The 14–18 Journal*, p. 79.

6 Molkentin, *Fire in the sky*, p. 83.

7 Jessie Smith to Australian Imperial Force Base Records, 14 March 1917, Ross Macpherson Smith's Australian Imperial Force dossier, NAA B2455 SMITH R P.

8 Ross to Jessie Smith, 28 January 1917, SLSA PRG 18/24.

9 Ross Smith, reconnaissance report, 5 March 1917, NAUK AIR1/1757/204/141/26.

10 Ross Smith, diary, 7 March 1917, SLSA PRG 18/19/1.

11 'Despatch dealing with operations of the 5th Wing Royal Flying Corps . . . March 1917', NAUK AIR1/1757/204/141/26; 'Appreciation of the situation on the eastern front of Egypt on 9/3/17', AWM4 1/6/12 Part 1.

12 EEF GHQ Intelligence Branch War Diary, 11 March 1917, AWM4 1/8/11.

13 'Lieut. R.M. Smith M.C.', *The Register* (Adelaide), 17 May 1917, p. 8; 'Narrative of operations of the 19/3/17 of 5th Wing, Royal Flying Corps', NAUK AIR1/1757/204/141/26.

14 Ross to Jessie Smith, 25 March 1917, SLSA PRG 18/24.

15 Ross to Jessie Smith, 29 March 1917, SLSA PRG 18/24.

16 Borton, 'Signals to be used in case of forced landing in the desert', 9 March 1917, TNA AIR1/1757/204/141/26. Earlier examples of AFC pilots landing to rescue each other in the Middle East include Lieutenant Percy Snell's rescue of Lieutenant John Tunbridge on 7 March 1917 and Snell's attempt to rescue Lieutenant Leonard Heathcote two days later, which he had to abandon due to the proximity of Turkish troops.

17 Ross Smith, diary, 20–21 March 1917, SLSA PRG/18/19/1.

18 Eastern Force Order No. 33, 24 March 1917, NAUK AIR1/1757/204/141/26.

19 Ross Smith, diary, 24 March 1917, SLSA PRG PRG/18/19/1.

20 Grey, *The war with the Ottoman Empire*, pp. 116–17.

21 Ross to Jessie Smith, 29 March 1917, SLSA PRG 18/24.

22 Ross Smith, diary, 27 March 1917, SLSA PRG PRG/18/19/1.

23 Ross Smith, diary, 26 March 1917, SLSA PRG PRG/18/19/1.

24 Ross to Jessie Smith, 29 March 1917, SLSA PRG 18/24.

25 Ross Smith, diary, 27 March 1917, SLSA PRG PRG/18/19/1. Reports of the sorties Ross flew during the battle are filed in 5th Wing Royal Flying Corps war diary, March 1917, NAUK AIR1/1757/204/141/26.

26 'Personal careers', *The Observer* (Adelaide), 13 December 1919, p. 35.

27 Ross Smith, diary, 5 April 1917, SLSA PRG PRG/18/19/1.

28 'The flight to Australia', *Flight*, 6 November 1919, p. 1447.

29 Ross to Jessie Smith, 23 May 1917, SLSA PRG 18/24.

30 Ross to Jessie Smith, 16 April 1917, SLSA PRG 18/24.

31 Report on Combat in the Air, Captain Williams and Lieutenant Ross Smith, 15 April 1917, NAUK AIR1/1757/204/141/28.
32 Ross to Jessie Smith, 16 April 1917, SLSA PRG 18/24.
33 Ross to Jessie Smith, 11 March 1917, SLSA PRG 18/24.
34 Molkentin, *Fire in the sky*, pp. 101–5.
35 Ross to Jessie Smith, 11 March 1917, SLSA PRG 18/24.
36 Ross Smith, diary, 19 April 1917, SLSA PRG PRG/18/19/1.
37 Grey, *The war with the Ottoman Empire*, p. 123.
38 Ross to Jessie Smith, 23 April 1917, SLSA PRG 18/24.
39 Ross to Jessie Smith, 23 May 1917, SLSA PRG 18/24.

17 Quite an airman now

1 Richard Williams, *These are facts: The autobiography of Air Marshal Sir Richard Williams KBE CB DSO*, Australian War Memorial and AGPS, Canberra, 1977, p. 57.
2 Ross to Jessie Smith, 1 January 1917, SLSA PRG 18/24.
3 Brigadier General L.E.O. Charlton to GOC Middle East Brigade, 13 April 1917, NAUK AIR1/130/15/40/214.
4 Brigadier General Geoffrey Salmond to the Director of Air Organisation, 7 May 1917, NAUK AIR1/130/15/40/214.
5 Major Rutledge to the Commandant, Australian Imperial Force HQ Egypt, 14 April 1917, AWM22 31/4/2000.
6 Ross to Jessie Smith, 4 May 1917, SLSA PRG 18/24.
7 Ross to Jessie Smith, 23 May 1917, SLSA PRG 18/24.
8 Ross to Jessie Smith, 30 June 1917, SLSA PRG 18/24.
9 V.M. Yeates, *Winged victory*, Jonathon Cape, London, 1972, p. 83.
10 Ross Smith, diary, 2 June 1917, SLSA PRG 18/19/1.
11 Ross Smith, diary, 7 June 1917, SLSA PRG 18/19/1.
12 Ross to Jessie Smith, 30 June 1917, SLSA PRG 18/24.
13 Ross to Jessie Smith, 21 June 1917, SLSA PRG 18/24.
14 Ross to Jessie Smith, 7 July 1917, SLSA PRG 18/24.
15 Chas Schaedel, *South Australian airmen of the Great War*, South Australian Aviation Museum, Adelaide, 2005, p. 131.
16 Molkentin, *Australia and the war in the air*, p. 54.
17 Gareth Morgan, 'Australian Flying Corps Roll of Honour 1915–1921: Part Three', *The 14–18 Journal*, 2010, 60.
18 Ross to Jessie Smith, 30 June 1917, SLSA PRG 18/24.
19 Ross to Jessie Smith, 23 May 1917, SLSA PRG 18/24.

20 No. 1 Squadron manuscript history, AWM224 MSS514.

21 Others in the British Army and government did not share the prime minister's strategic perspective. See Matthew Hughes, *Allenby and British strategy in the Middle East 1917–1919*, Frank Cass, Oxford, 1999, pp. 23–42.

22 Hughes, *Allenby and British strategy*, p. 15.

23 Ross to Jessie Smith, 12 June 1917, SLSA PRG 18/24.

24 Ross to Jessie Smith, 30 June 1917, SLSA PRG 18/24.

25 Ross to Jessie Smith, 31 March 1918, SLSA PRG 18/24.

26 Les Sutherland and Norman Ellison, *Aces and kings*, John Hamilton, London, 1935, p. 34.

27 See, for example, Ross to Jessie Smith, 10 January 1915, 20 January 1916 and 25 June 1918, SLSA PRG 18/24.

28 Ross to Jessie Smith, 29 May 1918, SLSA PRG 18/24; Ross to Keith Smith, 25 December 1918, SLSA PRG 18/24.

29 Ross Smith, diary, 17 July 1917, SLSA PRG 18/19/1.

30 Richard Williams, *These are facts*, p. 75.

31 Ross Smith, diary, 22 July 1917, SLSA PRG 18/19/1.

32 Ross to Jessie Smith, 25 August 1917, SLSA PRG 18/24.

33 Ross to Jessie Smith, 7 October 1918, SLSA PRG 18/24; Lax, *One airman's war*, p. 74.

34 'Photographic work of the Royal Flying Corps in Sinai and Palestine during 1917', NAUK AIR1/2415/303/28; See lists of photographs taken 5th Wing War diaries for June [NAUK AIR1/1757/204/141/31], July [NAUK AIR1/1758/204/141/33] and August [NAUK AIR1/1758/204/141/35].

35 Ross Smith, diary, 4 August 1917, SLSA PRG 18/19/1; Ross Smith, Combat in the air report, 4 August 1917, NAUK AIR1/1758/204/141/35.

36 Lax, *One airman's war*, p. 64.

37 Ross Smith, Combat in the air report, 1 September 1917, NAUK AIR1/1758/204/141/37; Ross Smith, diary, 1 September 1917, SLSA PRG 18/19/1.

38 Ross Smith, diary, 25 September 1917, SLSA PRG 18/19/1.

39 Ross to Keith Smith, 6 October 1917, SLSA PRG 18/24.

40 The photograph is reproduced in Sutherland and Ellison, *Aces and kings*, facing p. 41.

41 Ross to Jessie Smith, 15 June 1918 and 11 August 1918, SLSA PRG 18/24.

42 F.M. Cutlack, *The official history of Australia in the war of 1914–1918, vol. 8, The Australian Flying Corps in the Western and Eastern theatres of war, 1914–1918*, University of Queensland Press, Brisbane, 1984 [1923], p. 75.

43 'Sir Ross Smith', *The Sun* (Sydney), 10 January 1920, p. 5.

44 Ross's impressions of this significant development are lost; the letters he wrote to his mother during the latter part of 1917 do not appear to have survived.

45 Ross to Keith Smith, 6 October 1917, SLSA PRG 18/24.

18 Vengeance is only poor consolation

1 10th Battalion War Diary, 6 October 1917, AWM4 23/27/24; Lieutenant Colin Macpherson Smith 10th Battalion, Australian Red Cross Society Wounded and Missing Enquiry Bureau files, 1914–18 War, AWM 1DRL/0428.

2 Family Notices, *The Chronicle* (Adelaide), 20 October 1917, p. 27.

3 Ross to Jessie Smith, 23 May 1917, SLSA PRG 18/24.

4 Ross to Jessie Smith, 20 July 1918, SLSA PRG 18/24

5 Ross to Jessie Smith, 15 June 1918, SLSA PRG 18/24

6 Ross Smith, diary, 31 October 1917, SLSA PRG 18/19/1.

7 Ross Smith, diary, 2 November 1917, SLSA PRG 18/19/1.

8 Ross Smith, diary, 2 November 1917, SLSA PRG 18/19/1; Ross to Keith Smith, 19 November 1917, SLSA PRG 18/24.

9 Williams, *These are facts*, p. 61; Cole, 'Merry old souls', p. 75.

10 Ross Smith, diary, 7 November 1917, SLSA PRG 18/19/1.

11 'Bavarian Flying Squadron 304: Extracts from report on the evacuation of the aerodrome at Arak el Manshije', BHStA IV, Flug und Luftschiffe, file 54.

12 Ross Smith, diary, 8 November 1917, SLSA PRG 18/19/1.

13 'Bavarian Flying Squadron 304: Extracts from report on the evacuation of the aerodrome at Arak el Manshije', BHStA IV, Flug und Luftschiffe, file 54.

14 Ross Smith, diary, 9 November 1917, SLSA PRG 18/19/1.

15 H.A. Jones, *The war in the air: Being the story of the part played in the Great War by the Royal Air Force, volume 5*, Oxford University Press, Oxford, 1935, pp. 243–4.

16 Ross Smith, diary, 10 November 1917, SLSA PRG 18/19/1.

17 Ross Smith, diary, 10 and 12 November 1917, SLSA PRG 18/19/1.

18 Ross to Keith Smith, 19 November 1917, SLSA PRG 18/24.

19 Ross to Keith Smith, 13 November 1917, SLSA PRG 18/24.

20 Molkentin, *Australia and the war in the air*, p. 154.

21 Ross Smith, diary, 15 November 1917, SLSA PRG 18/19/1; Molkentin, *Australia and the war in the air*, p. 155.

22 Ross Smith, diary, 27 November 1917, SLSA PRG 18/19/1.

23 Ross Smith, diary, 29 November 1917, SLSA PRG 18/19/1.

24 Ross Smith, diary, 5 and 16 December 1917, SLSA PRG 18/19/1.
25 Ross Smith, diary, 9 December 1917, SLSA PRG 18/19/1.
26 Ross to Keith Smith, 19 November 1917, SLSA PRG 18/24.
27 Ross to Keith Smith, 28 December 1917, SLSA PRG 18/24.
28 Ross Smith, Recommendation for Bar to Military Cross, n.d., AWM28 2/116.
29 Ross to Keith Smith, 28 December 1917, SLSA PRG 18/24.
30 Ross Smith to Stanley Winter-Irving, 24 January 1918, private collection of Andrew Winter-Irving.
31 See Martin Crotty, *Making the Australian male: Middle-class masculinity 1870–1920*, Melbourne University Press, Melbourne, 2001.
32 Captain John Harris, diary, 25 June 1918, AWM PR84/003.
33 Harris, diary, 22 January 1918, AWM PR84/003.
34 Ross Smith to Stanley Winter-Irving, 24 January 1918, private collection of Andrew Winter-Irving.
35 Captain John Harris, letter to wife, 23 December 1917, AWM PR84/003; Fysh, *Qantas rising*, p. 49.
36 Ross Smith to Stanley Winter-Irving, 24 January 1918, private collection of Andrew Winter-Irving.

19 Brisfits and baggage

1 Ross to Keith Smith, 19 November 1917, SLSA PRG 18/24.
2 Bruce, *British aeroplanes 1914–18*, pp. 128–30.
3 Ross Smith, diary, 31 December 1917, SLSA PRG 18/19/1.
4 Ross Smith to Stanley Winter-Irving, 24 January 1918, private collection of Andrew Winter-Irving; Ross to Jessie Smith, 12 March 1918, SLSA PRG 18/24.
5 Ross Smith to Stanley Winter-Irving, 24 January 1918, private collection of Andrew Winter-Irving.
6 Ross Smith, diary, 16 January 1918, SLSA PRG 18/19/1.
7 Cutlack, *The Official History of Australia in the War of 1914–18*, vol. 8, p. 95.
8 Ross to Jessie Smith, 15 June 1918, SLSA PRG 18/24.
9 H. Hamshaw Thomas, 'Geographical reconnaissance by aeroplane photograph, with special reference to the work done on the Palestine front', *The Geographical Journal*, vol. 55, no. 5, 1920, 352.
10 Ross Smith, diary, 30 January 1918, SLSA PRG 18/19/1.
11 Ross to Jessie Smith, 12 March 1918, SLSA PRG 18/24.
12 Lynsey Shaw Cobden, 'The nervous flyer: Nerves, flying and the First World War', *The British Journal for Military History*, vol. 4, no. 2, 2018, 138.

13 Frank Hurley, diary, 16 February 1918, NLA MS883.

14 'Observer, pilot, and Bristol Fighter F2B aircraft, Serial B1146, of No. 1 Squadron, Australian . . .', AWM P03631.013.

15 Hurley, diary, 25 February 1918, NLA MS883.

16 Ross to Jessie Smith, 20 February 1917, SLSA PRG 18/24.

17 Borton to Jessie Smith, 15 April 1922, PRG 18/24.

18 'The Sun's aviator in action', *The Sun* (Sydney), 8 December 1919, p. 1.

19 Ross to Jessie Smith, 25 June 1918, SLSA PRG 18/24.

20 Ross to Jessie Smith, 7 July 1918, SLSA PRG 18/24.

21 Ross to Jessie Smith, 12 March 1918, SLSA PRG 18/24.

22 Ross to Jessie Smith, 25 June 1918, SLSA PRG 18/24.

23 Capt. R.M. Smith, 'Combats in the air', 7 May 1918, AWM4 8/4/5 Part 1.

24 Ross to Jessie Smith, 17 May 1918, SLSA PRG 18/24.

25 Ross to Jessie Smith, 17 May 1918, SLSA PRG 18/24.

26 Sutherland and Ellison, *Aces and kings*, p. 130.

27 Sutherland and Ellison, *Aces and kings*, pp. 130–8.

28 Capt. R.M. Smith, 'Combats in the air', 22 May 1918, AWM4 8/4/5 Part 1; Ross to Jessie Smith, 29 May 1918, SLSA PRG 18/24.

29 Ross to Jessie Smith, 25 June 1918, SLSA PRG 18/24.

30 Ross to Jessie Smith, 31 March 1918, SLSA PRG 18/24.

31 Ross to Jessie Smith, 15 June 1918, SLSA PRG 18/24.

32 Capt. R.M. Smith, 'Combats in the air', AWM4 8/4/6 Part 1; Ross to Jessie Smith, 25 June 1918, SLSA PRG 18/24.

33 Christopher Shores, Norman Franks and Russell Guest, *Above the trenches: A complete record of the fighter aces and units of the British Empire air forces 1915–1920*, Grub Street, London, 1990, pp. 6–10.

34 For the Royal Flying Corps' official position on publicising the exploits of individual pilots, see Major General Sir Hugh Trenchard to CIGS (and attached undated memorandum), 5 October 1917, NAUK AIR1/522/16/12/5.

35 Anonymous, 'Interview with Captain Eric Rupert Dibbs formerly of the Australian Flying Corps', *The 14–18 Journal*, 1967, 91.

36 C. Alma Baker (ed.), *Souvenir of ninety-four gift battleplanes which helped us to victory*, August 4th, 1914 to November 11th, 1918, Field Press, London, c. 1920, p. 3.

37 Ross to Jessie Smith, 7 October 1918, SLSA PRG 18/24.

38 Haig, *Airman oilman*, p. 17; Roberts, *Box kites and beyond*, p. 17; John Harris to wife, 10 March 1918, AWM PR84/003.

39 Ross mentioned Williams' stringency in Ross Smith to Stanley Winter-Irving, 24 January 1918, private collection of Andrew Winter-Irving.

40 'Sir Ross Smith', *The Sun* (Sydney), 10 January 1920, p. 5.

41 Williams, *These are facts*, p. 194.

42 The details of Addison's service come from papers in his Australian Imperial Force dossier: Capt. Sydney Addison, NAA B2455, ADDISON S W.

43 Ross to Jessie Smith, 5 May 1918, SLSA PRG 18/24.

44 Medical Case Sheet 15304, Capt. Sydney Addison, NAA B2455, ADDISON S W.

20 Biffy and the Bloody Paralyser

1 Ross to Jessie Smith, 12 March 1918, SLSA PRG 18/24.

2 Ross to Jessie Smith, 25 June 1918, SLSA PRG 18/24.

3 Lt Col C.A. Burnett to CO 40th Wing Royal Air Force, 22 June 1918, PRG 18/24. Borton was on leave in the United Kingdom at the time so Burnett, the acting OC Palestine Brigade, responded.

4 Brigadier General Amyas Borton to Major General John Salmond, 20 November 1918, NAUK AIR1/2415/303/28.

5 Sutherland and Ellison, *Aces and kings*, pp. 24–5.

6 Ross to Jessie Smith, 20 July 1918, SLSA PRG 18/24.

7 Ross to Jessie Smith, 20 July 1918, SLSA PRG 18/24.

8 Ross to Jessie Smith, 20 July 1918, SLSA PRG 18/24.

9 Ross to Jessie Smith, 20 July 1918, SLSA PRG 18/24.

10 Lax, *One airman's war*, p. 122.

11 *Commonwealth of Australia Gazette*, 23 May 1919, no. 61, p. 901.

12 Ross to Jessie Smith, 30 July 1918, SLSA PRG 18/24.

13 Ross to Jessie Smith, 22 August 1918, SLSA PRG 18/24.

14 For Borton's account of this flight, see SLSA PRG 1067/7/2.

15 See Rob Langham, *Bloody Paralyser: The giant Handley Page bombers of the First World War*, Fonthill, London, 2014.

16 For an account of this flight, see Clive Semple, *Airway to the East 1918–1920 and the collapse of No. 1 Aerial Route Royal Air Force*, Pen & Sword, Barnsley, 2012, pp. 35–62.

17 Ross to Jessie Smith, 11 August 1918, SLSA PRG 18/24.

18 Williams, *These are facts*, p. 92

19 Ross to Jessie Smith, 22 August 1918, SLSA PRG 18/24.

20 Ross to Jessie Smith, 22 August 1918, SLSA PRG 18/24.

21 Ross to Mrs King, 15 September 1918, PRG 18/24.

22 Ross to Jessie Smith, 22 August 1918, SLSA PRG 18/24.

23 Ross to Constance Jean Warren, 4 September 1918, SLSA PRG 18/62.

24 Ross to Jessie Smith, 10 September 1918, SLSA PRG 18/24.

25 Ross to Jessie Smith, 10 September 1918, SLSA PRG 18/24.

21 Armageddon

1 Force Order No. 68, 9 September 1918, AWM4 1/6/29 1/6/29 Part 3.

2 H.A. Jones, *The war in the air: Being the story of the part played in the Great War by the Royal Air Force*, volume 6, Clarendon Press, Oxford, 1937, p. 210; Geoffrey Salmond, 'The work of the Royal Air Force in the final offensive in Palestine', n.d., NAUK AIR1/498/15/321/1.

3 Captain R.M. Smith, 'Report on bomb dropping', 19 September 1918, No. 1 Squadron War diary, Appendix 3, AWM 8/4/9 Part 2; Captain R.M. Smith and Lieutenant M.D. Lees, 'Report on attack on troops by aircraft', 19 September 1918, No. 1 Squadron War diary, Appendix 4, AWM 8/4/9 Part 2.

4 Ross to Jessie Smith, 20 September 1918, SLSA PRG 18/24.

5 Borton to Salmond, 20 November 1918, NAUK AIR1/2415/303/28; 'Diary of work of Royal Air Force during operations from 17/9/18 to 24/9/18', NAUK AIR1/2393/244/2.

6 Edward Erickson, *Ottoman Army effectiveness in World War I: A comparative study*, Routledge, Abingdon, 2007, p. 153.

7 Resume of operations of the 40th Wing, Royal Air Force, 13.9.18 to 19.9.18, AWM4 8/4/9 Part 1.

8 Ross to Jessie Smith, 20 September 1918, SLSA PRG 18/24.

9 Capt. R.M. Smith, 'Report on bomb dropping', 19 September 1918 War diary, Appendix 3, AWM4 8/4/9 Part 2; Ross to Jessie Smith, 20 September 1918, SLSA PRG 18/24.

10 Ross to Jessie Smith, 24 September 1918, SLSA PRG 18/24.

11 Grey, *The war with the Ottoman Empire*, pp. 168–9.

12 Sutherland and Ellison, *Aces and kings*, pp. 255–6.

13 No. 1 Squadron Australian Flying Corps War Diary, September 1918, Summary of events and information for 20-21.9.18, AMW4 8/4/9 Part 1.

14 Ross to Jessie Smith, 20 September 1918, SLSA PRG 18/24.

15 Thomas Edward Lawrence, *The seven pillars of wisdom: A triumph*, Oxford University Press, Delhi, 1955, p. 633.

16 No. 1 Squadron war diary, 16 May 1918, AWM4 8/4/5 Part 1.

17 Lawrence, *The seven pillars of wisdom*, p. 638.

18 Capt. R.M. Smith, 'Combats in the air', 22 September 1918, AWM4 8/4/9 Part 2.

19 F. Clune, *D'air devil: The story of Pard Mustar, Australian air ace*, Angus & Robertson, Sydney, 1941, p. 94.

20 Ross to Jessie Smith, 24 September 1918, SLSA PRG 18/24.

21 Lawrence, *The seven pillars of wisdom*, p. 640.

22 Capt. R.M. Smith, 'Combats in the air', 22 September 1918, AWM4 8/4/9 Part 2.

23 Ross to Constance Jean Warren, 27 September 1918, SLSA PRG 18/62.

24 Ross to Jessie Smith, 24 September 1918, SLSA PRG 18/24.

25 Albert Victor Tonkin, 'Description of incidents with Lawrence of Arabia', Tonkin papers, RAAFM.

26 Lawrence, *The seven pillars of wisdom*, p. 640.

27 Capt. R.M. Smith, 'Report on bomb dropping', 23 September 1918, AWM4 8/4/9 Part 2.

28 Sutherland and Ellison, *Aces and kings*, pp. 260–1.

29 Ross to Jessie Smith, 24 September 1918, SLSA PRG 18/24.

30 Ross to Jessie Smith, 7 October 1918, SLSA PRG 18/24.

31 Sutherland and Ellison, *Aces and kings*, pp. 37–47. Although Sutherland's account seems exaggerated, Richard Williams also mentioned the cave of champagne in an interview he gave in 1972. Richard Williams, interview with Mel Pratt, NLA TRC 121/50.

32 Michael Maton, *The Distinguished Flying Cross to Australians*, self-published, 2000.

33 Ross to Jessie Smith, 7 October 1918, SLSA PRG 18/24.

34 Ross to Jessie Smith, 24 October 1918, SLSA PRG 18/24.

35 Ross to Keith Smith, 26 October 1918, SLSA PRG 18/24. Ross later heard that a British armoured car patrol picked up the two German airmen.

36 Capt. R.M. Smith, 'Combats in the air', 19 October 1918, AWM4 8/3/10 Part 1.

37 Ross to Jessie Smith, 24 October 1918, SLSA PRG 18/24.

38 Ross Macpherson Smith recommendation for Bar to DFC, 22 October 1918, AWM28 2/116.

39 Ross to Jessie Smith, 24 October 1918, SLSA PRG 18/24.

40 Major Addison, reconnaissance report, 23 October 1918, AWM4 8/4/10 Part 1.

41 Ross to Keith Smith, 25 December 1918, SLSA PRG 18/24.

42 Ross to Jessie Smith, 24 October 1918, SLSA PRG 18/24.

43 Ross to Keith Smith, 26 October 1918, SLSA PRG 18/24.

22 Preaching the gospel of the RAF

1 Joan Beaumont, *Broken nation: Australians in the Great War*, Allen & Unwin, Sydney, 2013, pp. 515–17.
2 Ross to Jessie Smith, 12 November 1918, SLSA PRG 18/17.
3 Ross to Jessie Smith, 12 November 1918, SLSA PRG 18/17.
4 Ross to Jessie Smith, 12 November 1918, SLSA PRG 18/17.
5 Ross Smith, 'From London to Australia by aeroplane: A personal narrative of the first aerial voyage halfway around the world', *National Geographic* (Washington), vol. 39, no. 3, 1921, 229. This anecdote was also published in the Australian press: 'Suggested in jest', *Daily Mail* (Brisbane), 20 May 1920, p. 3.
6 Borton to his father, 8 October 1918, quoted in Arthur Close Borton and Guy Slater, *My warrior sons: the Borton family diary, 1914–1918*, P. Davies, London, 1973, p. 202.
7 Letter from Borton to his father, 27 November 1918, quoted in Borton and Slater, *My warrior sons*, p. 215.
8 J.P. McCoy and K. Keohane, 'Interview with G.N. Mills former observer with the Australian Flying Corps, *The 14-18 Journal*, 1968, p. 77.
9 Ross to Jessie Smith, 29 December 1918, SLSA PRG 18/17.
10 Ross to Jessie Smith, 28 November 1918, SLSA PRG 18/17.
11 Ross to Jessie Smith, 28 December 1918, SLSA PRG 18/17.
12 Ross to Jessie Smith, 28 November 1918, SLSA PRG 18/17.
13 Borton to Grenfell Price, 11 January 1968, SLSA PRG7/2/51; Ross to Keith Smith, 25 December 1918, SLSA PRG 18/24.
14 Ross to Jessie Smith, 2 December 1918, SLSA PRG 18/17.
15 Anne Baker, *From biplane to spitfire: The life of Air Chief Marshal Sir Geoffrey Salmond KCB KCMG DSO*, Leo Cooper, Barnsley, 2003, pp. 147–8.
16 'Egypt, Syria, Mesopotamia in three days', *Chicago Daily Tribune*, 4 December 1918, p. 2.
17 Ross to Keith Smith, 25 December 1918, SLSA PRG 18/24.
18 Ross to Jessie Smith, 29 December 1918, SLSA PRG 18/17.
19 Ross to Jessie Smith, 29 December 1918, SLSA PRG 18/17.
20 'By air to India', *The Times of India*, 17 December 1918, p. 8.
21 Ross to Jessie Smith, 29 December 1918, SLSA PRG 18/17.
22 Ross to Jessie Smith, 29 December 1918, SLSA PRG 18/17.
23 'Stop press—the first aeroplane from Europe to India', *The Indian Daily News*, 11 December 1918, p. 1.

24 'Arrival at Karachi', *The Times of India*, 4 December 1918, p. 7.

25 'Cairo to India by aeroplane', *Flight*, 19 December 1918, p. 1431. Measuring the journey on Google Earth using direct routes between the stops indicates a total distance, from Cairo to Karachi, of 2389 miles (3844 kilometres)—similar to what the press reported.

26 Ross to Jessie Smith, 29 December 1918, SLSA PRG 18/17.

27 Borton and Slater, *My warrior sons*, p. 215.

28 Ross to Jessie Smith, 29 December 1918, SLSA PRG 18/17.

29 Ross to Jessie Smith, 29 December 1918, SLSA PRG 18/17.

30 Ross to Jessie Smith, 29 December 1918, SLSA PRG 18/17.

31 Ross to Jessie Smith, 29 December 1918, SLSA PRG 18/17.

32 'The military aeroplane', *The Times of India*, 17 December 1918, p. 8.

33 Reminiscences of Walter Henry Shiers, 29 October 1966, SLSA PRG 7/2/55.

34 Ross to Keith Smith, 25 December 1918, SLSA PRG 18/24.

35 'Aeroplane in Calcutta', *The Bengalee* (Calcutta), 18 December 1918, p. 4.

36 'General Salmond's tour', *The Times of India*, 19 December 1918, p. 10.

37 'The flying generals', *Indian Daily News*, 18 December 1918, p. 2.

38 'The flying generals', *Indian Daily News*, 18 December 1918, p. 2.

39 Ross to Jessie Smith, 29 December 1918, SLSA PRG 18/17.

40 BFI, 'From England to India by Air (1917 [sic])', Youtube, 10 August 2017, https://www.youtube.com/watch?v=pGeBmDjKxJk.

41 See, for example: 'Great British Air Flights to India', *The Christian Science Monitor* (Boston), 20 December 1918, p. 2; 'Aero ends 3950 mile trip', *The Washington Post*, 20 December 1918, p. 1; 'The new age', *The North China Herald* (Shanghai), 28 December 1918, p. 776; 'The flight to India', *The Manchester Guardian*, 28 December 1918, p. 7.

42 Handwritten notes on flight Cairo–Calcutta, n.d., SLSA PRG 18/25. Ross noted these same figures in his letter to Jessie on 29 December 1918.

43 'Gen. Salmond's flight', *The Indian Daily*, 20 December 1918, p. 1.

44 'Future of aviation', *The Times of India*, 19 December 1918, p. 10.

45 'Conquest of the air', *World* (Hobart), 20 December 1918, p. 5.

46 'Cairo to Delhi', *The Advertiser* (Adelaide), 16 December 1918, p. 8; 'To India by air', *The Journal* (Adelaide), 20 December 1918, p. 1; 'Intrepid South Australian aviator', *The Observer* (Adelaide), 21 December 1918, p. 28; 'Cairo to Delhi', *The Chronicle* (Adelaide), 21 December 1918, p. 20; 'Intrepid South Australian aviator', *The Register* (Adelaide), 17 December 1918, p. 4; 'Purely personal', *Southern Cross* (Adelaide), 20 December 1918, p. 12.

47 'Intrepid South Australian aviator', *The Register* (Adelaide), Tuesday 17 December 1918, p. 4.

48 'The Australian Captain Ball', *The Sun* (Sydney), 13 July 1919, p. 13.

49 'Flight to Australia', *Colac Herald*, 20 December 1918, p. 1.

50 'School speech days', *The Register*, 17 December 1918, p. 6.

23 An awfully good time

1 Anon, *Travel in India or city, shrine and sea beach: Antiquities, health resorts and places of interest on the Bengal–Nagpur railway*, The Bombay Times Press, 1916, p. 16.

2 Ross to Keith Smith, 25 December 1918, SLSA PRG 18/24.

3 Ross to Jessie Smith, 29 December 1918, SLSA PRG 18/17.

4 Ross to Jessie Smith, 29 December 1918, SLSA PRG 18/17.

5 Air Ministry to Aeronautics Delhi (Royal Air Force HQ India), 26 December 1918, NAUK AVIA2/1783.

6 'Handley Page aeroplane', *The Times of India*, 18 December 1918, p. 9.

7 Ross to Keith Smith, 7 February 1919, SLSA PRG 18/24.

8 Salmond to Air Ministry, 14 December 1918, NAUK AVIA2/1783.

9 CAS minute, 18 December 1918, NAUK AVIA2/1783; DFO, minute, 8 January 1919, NAUK AVIA2/1783.

10 Minute number 8, 27 January 1919, NAUK AVIA2/1783. Two days later Treasury increased this to £10,000.

11 Air Ministry to Aeronautics Delhi (Royal Air Force HQ India), 26 December 1918, NAUK AVIA2/1783.

12 GOC Royal Air Force Middle East to the Air Ministry Personal for Gen. Salmond, 25 March 1919, NAUK AVIA2/1783.

13 Ross to Keith Smith, 7 February 1919, SLSA PRG 18/24.

24 South Asian survey

1 Ross to Keith Smith, 18 February 1919, SLSA PRG 18/24.

2 Ross to Jessie Smith, 15 March 1919, SLSA PRG 18/17.

3 Ross to Jessie Smith, 15 March 1919, SLSA PRG 18/17.

4 Ross to Borton, 10 May 1920, SLSA PRG 106/7/3

5 Ross to Keith Smith, 18 February 1919, SLSA PRG 18/24.

6 Borton to Director of Flying Operations, 10 March 1919, NAUK AVIA2/1783; 'Calcutta Letter', *The Times of India*, 2 August 1919, p. 10.

7 Ross to Keith Smith, 10 March 1919, SLSA PRG 18/24.

8 Ross to Keith Smith, 10 March 1919, SLSA PRG 18/24.

9 Ross Smith, notes on aerodromes in south Asia, March–June 1919, SLSA PRG 18/31.

10 Ross to Jessie Smith, 15 March 1919 (note added 21 March 1919), SLSA PRG 18/17.

11 Borton, 'Report on aerodrome site selected at Akyab', 14 March 1919, NAUK AVIA2/1783.

12 Borton, 'Report on aerodrome sites at Rangoon and Thayetmyo', 24 March 1919, NAUK AVIA2/1783; Ross Smith, notes written at Rangoon, 17 March 1919, SLSA PRG 18/31.

13 Ross to Jessie Smith, 15 March 1919 (note added 21 March 1919), SLSA PRG 18/17.

14 Borton, 'Report on suggested aerodrome site at Megui', 27 March 1919, NAUK AVIA2/1783.

15 Ross to Jessie Smith, 15 March 1919 (note added 21 March 1919), SLSA PRG 18/17.

16 Borton, 'Report on Victoria Point', 30 March 1919, NAUK AVIA2/1783; Ross Smith, notes written at Victoria Point, 29 March 1919, SLSA PRG 18/31.

17 Borton, Report on sites at Penang and vicinity, 5 April 1919, NAUK AVIA2/1783.

18 Ross to Jessie Smith, 15 March 1919 (note added 21 March 1919), SLSA PRG 18/17.

19 Ross to Jessie Smith, 15 March 1919, SLSA PRG 18/17.

20 Ross to Keith Smith, 29 April 1919, SLSA PRG 18/24.

21 Borton, 'Action taken at Singapore on return from Borneo', 23 June 1919, NAUK AVIA 2/1783.

22 Ross Smith, notes written at Singapore, 6 April 1919 to 11 April 1919, SLSA PRG 18/31.

23 Ross to Keith Smith, 29 April 1919, SLSA PRG 18/24.

24 Borton, 'Report on action taken in Netherlands East Indies', NAUK AVIA 2/1783.

25 Ross to Keith Smith, 29 April 1919, SLSA PRG 18/24.

26 Ross Smith, notes written at Muntok, 18 May 1919, SLSA PRG 18/31.

27 GOC Singapore to War Office, 10 April 1919, NAUK AVIA 2/1783.

28 'Report on suggested aerodrome site at Mergui', 27 March 1919, NAUK AVIA2/1783.

29 Ross Smith to Brigadier General A.E. Borton, 7 June 1919, NAUK AVIA2/1783.

30 Ross Smith to Colonial Secretary, Straits Settlements, 7 June 1919, NAUK AVIA2/1783.

31 Borton to the Director of Flying Operations, 23 June 1919, NAUK AVIA2/1783.

25 The great race

1 Lt. Col. (name illegible) to CGCA, 27 June 1919, NAUK AVIA2/1783.

2 Ross Smith, 'From London to Australia by aeroplane: A personal narrative of the first aerial voyage halfway around the world', *National Geographic* (Washington), vol. 39, no. 3, 1921, 231.

3 Ross Smith, 'From London to Australia by aeroplane', 231. In 1922 this was published as *14,000 miles through the air*.

4 Reminiscences by W.H. Shiers on the flight, 1967, SLSA PRG 7/2/55.

5 Borton to Dickson, 29 May 1967, SLSA PRG 7/2/51.

6 'By air', *Sydney Morning Herald*, 20 March 1919, p. 6.

7 Ross to Keith Smith, 29 April 1919, SLSA PRG 18/24.

8 Borton to Jessie Smith, 17 August 1919, SLSA PRG 18/24.

9 Borton to Jessie Smith, 17 August 1919, SLSA PRG 18/24.

10 Borton to Dickson, 29 May 1967, SLSA PRG 7/2/51.

11 Ross to Keith Smith, 29 April 1919 (text added 17 May 1919), SLSA PRG 18/24.

12 Australian Imperial Force personnel dossier for Walter Shiers, NAA B2455, SHIERS WALTER HENRY; Australian Imperial Force personnel dossier for James Bennett, NAA B2455, BENNETT J M.

13 Australian Imperial Force personnel dossier, NAA B2455, SMITH R M; Borton to Jessie Smith, 17 August 1919, SLSA PRG 18/24.

14 Reminiscences by W.H. Shiers on the flight, 1967, SLSA PRG 7/2/55.

15 Reminiscences by W.H. Shiers on the flight, 1967, SLSA PRG 7/2/55.

16 Reminiscences by W.H. Shiers on the flight, 1967, SLSA PRG 7/2/55.

17 Williams, *These are facts*, pp. 112–13.

18 Richard Williams, memorandum, 16 September 1920, SLSA PRG 7/2/46. Writing a year later, Williams recalled that Ross had called him on about 12 September 1919.

19 CGCS to CAS, n.d., 1919, NAUK AVIA2/1783.

20 Minutes of meeting at Air Ministry, 19 September 1919, NAUK AVIA2/1783.

26 God 'elp all of us

1 Richard Williams to CGCA, 20 September 1919, NAUK AVIA2/1795. The pilots of the crews who remained at this time were Captain E.C. Howell

(Martinsyde), Captain G.C. Matthews (Sopwith), Lieutenant R.M. Douglas (Alliance), Lieutenant V. Rendle (Blackburn).

2 G.C. Matthews to Ross Smith, 9 September 1920, SLSA PRG 7/2/46.

3 Richard Williams, memorandum, 16 September 1920, SLSA PRG 7/2/46; Cable, Air Ministry to Simlasub, 8 October 1919, NAUK AVIA2/1783; C.D. Coulthard-Clark, *The third brother: The Royal Australian Air Force 1921–39*, Allen & Unwin, Sydney, 1991, pp. 14–15.

4 A year later, Williams would recall that Ross submitted an entry to the competition on 17 September 1919—that is, a couple of days before the briefing at Adastral House (Richard Williams, memorandum, 16 September 1920, SLSA PRG 7/2/46.). A list of competitors, written on 20 September, however, does not include Ross's name (Richard Williams to CGCA, 20 September 1919, NAUK AVIA2/1795). A news cable dated 10 October reported that he was currently 'negotiating' with an aviation company to use one of their aeroplanes and the Royal Aero Club (which administered entries) did not register Ross's entry with the Air Ministry until 18 October (Secretary, Royal Aero Club to The Controller of Information, Department of Civil Aviation, 18 October 1919, NAUK AVIA2/1795). If he did mention anything about entering the race to Williams in mid-September, it was therefore speculative and informal—not a firm entry.

5 CAS to CGCA, 12 August 1919, NAUK AVIA2/1783.

6 Archibald Grenfell Price, *The skies remember: The story of Ross and Keith Smith*, Angus & Robertson, Sydney, 1969, pp. 79–80; Caddell to Pierson, 4 June 1919, NLA MS 6093; 'Sir Ross Smith', *The Sun* (Sydney), 10 January 1920, p. 5.

7 Borton to Grenfell Price, 16 May 1968, PRG 7/2/51.

8 Ross Smith, *14,000 miles through the air*, Macmillan, New York, 1922, p. 5; Ross to Borton, 25 January 1920, SLSA PRG 106/7/2. In her biography of her father, Air Marshal Sir Geoffrey Salmond, Anne Baker quotes a letter that, she claims, Ross wrote to Vickers at Salmond's prompting. In it Ross describes the route he proposes to take and argues for the flight's potential to generate business for Vickers in Australia. He also makes some strangely inaccurate and ostentatiously out-of-character statements about his wartime flying record, including that he had flown in England and France (he had not) and that his only two accidents were due to enemy action (neither was). In 2012 Mrs Baker kindly permitted me to examine the two suitcases she had of Sir Geoffrey's papers at her home in Salisbury. Although I found many useful letters by her father and his contemporaries in the collection, I did not

come across this particular letter, purported to be by Ross. As a consequence of this, and given the strange aspects of its contents, I have decided not to employ it in my account of how Ross and Vickers came to an agreement to enter the race. (Anne Baker, *From biplane to spitfire: the life of Air Chief Marshal Sir Geoffrey Salmond KCB KCMG DSO*, Leo Cooper, Barnsley, 2003, pp. 159–60.)

9 Peter McMillan, *The greatest flight*, Turner Publishing, Atlanta, GA, 1995, p. 253.

10 Bruce, *British aeroplanes 1914–18*, p. 703.

11 Smith, *14,000 miles through the air*, pp. 8–9.

12 'Australian flight', n.d., SLSA PRG 18/26.

13 W.A.C. Caddell to Ross Smith, 28 October 1919, SLSA PRG 18/26.

14 Keith Murdoch to Seymour Darlington, 25 October 1919, SLSA PRG 18/26.

15 'Instructions for despatch of telegrams and cablegrams', nd, SLSA PRG 18/27; Keith Murdoch to Seymour Darlington, 25 October 1919, SLSA PRG 18/26.

16 Secretary, Royal Aero Club to The Controller of Information, Department of Civil Aviation, 18 October 1919, NAUK AVIA2/1795.

17 Peter Maiden, *The sky racers: The 1919 air race from London to Australia*, Central Queensland University Press, Rockhampton, 2010, p. 82.

18 Williams, *These are facts*, p. 114.

19 Air Ministry to Airoute St Raphael, 17 October 1919, NAUK AVIA2/1795; 'Australians Flight', *Daily Herald* (Adelaide), 18 October 1919, p. 5.

20 It has been suggested that Ross initially planned to take Lieutenant Ernest Mustard, his wartime observer, as navigator and co-pilot. It seems that Shiers was the source of this claim in his 1967 oral history (SLSA PRG7/2/55). This is not, however, substantiated in any other private or official documents and seems unlikely, given that Mustard had at the time returned to Australia for demobilisation.

21 'Flight to Australia', *World* (Hobart), 14 June 1919, p. 5.

22 Reminiscences by W.H. Shiers, 1967, SLSA PRG 7/2/55.

23 Certificate of service in the Royal Flying Corps, SLSA PRG 18/22; 'The flight to Australia', *Flight*, 6 November 1919, p. 1447.

24 Keith Smith, log book, SLSA PRG 18/20

25 W.A.C. Caddell to Ross Smith, 28 October 1919, SLSA PRG 18/26.

26 'Proposed timetable stopping places and distances for Vickers Vimy flight to Australia', n.d., SLSA PRG 18/26.

27 Competition conditions issued by the Royal Aero Club, 22 May 1919, NAUK AVIA2/1795.

28 'Proposed timetable stopping places and distances for Vickers Vimy flight to Australia', n.d., SLSA PRG 18/26.

29 'The Australian government flight competition', *Flight*, 23 October 1919, p. 1396.

30 Ross Smith to Governor-General of the Dutch East Indies, 14 October 1919, SLSA PRG 18/26.

31 Borton to Captain van Mourik, 23 October 1919, SLSA PRG 18/26.

32 Acting General Secretary Welter to Ross Smith, 24 October 1919, SLSA PRG 18/26.

33 Smith, *14,000 miles through the air*, pp. 8–9.

34 Vickers Limited to Dutch East Indies GG, 31 October 1919, PRG 18/26. This two-week delay to wait for the preparation of the Dutch airfields was also later reported by Keith Murdoch's cable service: 'Flying light', *Sun* (Sydney), 8 December 1919, p. 1.

35 Smith, *14,000 miles through the air*, p. 10.

36 Smith, *14,000 miles through the air*, p. 10.

37 Reminiscences by W.H. Shiers, 1967, SLSA PRG 7/2/55.

38 Vickers Vimy G-EAOU log book, SLSA PRG 18/29.

39 Smith, *14 000 miles through the air*, p. 11.

40 Smith, *14 000 miles through the air*, p. 9; 'Proposed timetable stopping places and distances for Vickers Vimy flight to Australia', n.d., SLSA PRG 18/26.

41 'The great flight', *Northern Territory Times and Gazette*, 13 December 1919, p. 5.

42 Ross Smith to Vickers Limited (Sydney), 2 January 1920, SLSA PRG 18/28.

43 List of spares carried by the Vimy on the flight to Australia, n.d., NLA MS6093.

44 'Pisa reached', *The Sun* (Sydney), 15 November 1919, p. 1.

45 Smith, *14,000 miles through the air*, p. 82.

46 'Nothing to smoke in the air', *Evening Telegraph*, 2 May 1921, p. 11.

47 'Pisa reached', *The Sun* (Sydney), 15 November 1919, p. 1; 'Capt. Ross Smith's flight', *The Straits Times* (Singapore), 1 December 1919, p. 8.

48 'The Australian government flight competition', *Flight*, 23 October 1919, p. 1396.

49 Reminiscences by W.H. Shiers, 1967, SLSA PRG 7/2/55.

50 These maps are preserved in the State Library of New South Wales' manuscript collection: SLNSW M Z/MT3 118gmof/1919/1.

51 Smith, *14,000 miles through the air*, p. 13.

52 Smith, *14,000 miles through the air*, pp. 11–12.

53 Copy of cable from Vickers to A. Peeley, 15 October 1919, SLSA PRG 18/26.

54 Vickers Vimy G-EAOU log book, SLSA PRG 18/29; Airworthiness Certificate No. 253, SLSA PRG 18/28/2.

55 Ross Smith, *14,000 miles through the air*, p. 14.

56 'Sir Ross Smith', *Daily News* (Perth), 23 July 1920, p. 7.

57 After Ross lost his flying log book in the fire aboard the RIMS *Sphinx*, he apparently did not replace it so there is no primary record that survives recording that Ross was indeed on this test flight. Keith's log book, however, does survive (SLSA PRG 18/20) and indicates that he went on it—and that it was his first ever flight on the Vimy. The Vimy's log book (SLSA PRG 18/29) also records this flight, though only vaguely records the passengers as 'several' (i.e. it records no passengers' names). It seems reasonable, however, to assume that Ross was on this test flight too and that, given no mention of any earlier flight by him in the Vimy, it was his first.

58 Smith, *14,000 miles through the air*, p. 15.

59 Shiers to Archibald Grenfell Price, n.d., PRG 7/2/51.

60 Ross to Borton, 26 November 1919, SLSA PRG 106/7/1.

27 Class 5—unfit for flying

1 Smith, *14,000 miles through the air*, p. 15.

2 Smith, *14,000 miles through the air*, p. 15.

3 Richard Williams, memorandum, 16 September 1920, SLSA PRG 7/2/46.

4 Keith Smith to Jessie Smith, 12 November 1919, SLSA PRG 18/28/3. A copy of this meteorological report, marked 0730 12 November 1918, is in the Smith papers: SLSA PRG 18/30/9. It predicted 'Clouds 800 to 1000 feet, Thick ground mist, wind 4 to 12 mph' over Lympne and the Channel.

5 Keith Smith, diary, 12 November 1919, SLSA PRG 18/31; 'Shy Australian Flyers', *The Register* (Adelaide), 5 April 1921, p. 4.

6 'Pisa reached', *The Sun* (Sydney), 15 November 1919, p. 1.

7 Reminiscences by W.H. Shiers, 1967, SLSA PRG 7/2/55.

8 Borton and Slater, *My warrior sons*, p. 219.

9 Smith, *14,000 miles through the air*, pp. 19–20.

10 Ross Smith, telegrams to *The Sun* (Sydney), SLNSW A1633.

11 Reminiscences by W.H. Shiers, 1967, SLSA PRG 7/2/55.

12 Ross Smith, *14,000 miles through the air*, p. 24.

13 Ross to Borton, 26 November 1919, SLSA PRG 106/7/1.

14 Keith Smith, diary, 12 November 1919, SLSA PRG 18/31.

15 Ross Smith, 'England to Australia flight' (report to Vickers Limited), 18 April 1920, NAUK AIR1/2193/244/2.

16 Keith Smith to Jessie Smith, 12 November 1919, PRG 18/28/3.

17 Smith, 'England to Australia flight' (report to Vickers Limited), 18 April 1920, NAUK AIR1/2193/244/2.

18 Keith Smith, diary, 12 November 1919, SLSA PRG 18/31.

28 Crossing the Mediterranean

1 Smith, *14,000 miles through the air*, p. 30.

2 Ross to Borton, 26 November 1919, SLSA PRG 106/7/1.

3 Keith Smith, diary, 13 November 1919, SLSA PRG 18/31.

4 Ross to Jessie Smith, 13 November 1919, SLSA PRG 18/28.

5 'Greatest story of the air', *The Sun* (Sydney), 12 December 1919, p. 1.

6 Ross Smith, 'England to Australia flight' (report to Vickers Limited), 18 April 1920, NAUK AIR1/2193/244/2.

7 Undated note in pocket notebook, SLSA PRG 18/30.

8 Smith, 'England to Australia flight' (report to Vickers Limited), 18 April 1920, NAUK AIR1/2193/244/2.

9 Smith, *14,000 miles through the air*, p. 33.

10 Vickers Vimy G-EAOU log book, SLSA PRG 18/29; Keith Smith, diary, 13 November 1919, SLSA PRG 18/31.

11 Ross Smith to Vickers Limited (Sydney), 2 January 1920, SLSA PRG 18/20.

12 Ross Smith, telegrams to *The Sun*, SLNSW A1633.

13 Keith Smith, diary, 14 November 1919, SLSA PRG 18/31.

14 'Aerial voyage', *Daily Herald* (Adelaide), 19 November 1919, p. 5.

15 Ross Smith, telegrams to *The Sun*, SLNSW A1633.

16 Ross Smith, 'England to Australia flight' (report to Vickers Limited), 18 April 1920, NAUK AIR1/2193/244/2.

17 'Bogged at Pisa', *The Sun*, 19 November 1919, p. 1.

18 Keith Smith, diary, 15 November 1919, SLSA PRG 18/31.

19 'Airmen killed', *The Times* (London), 19 May 1919, p. 12.

20 Keith Smith, diary, 15 November 1919, SLSA PRG 18/31.

21 Smith, 'England to Australia flight', 18 April 1920, NAUK AIR1/2193/244/2.

22 'Chasing Poulet', *The Sun*, 20 November 1919, p. 1.

23 Keith Smith, diary, 16 November 1919, SLSA PRG 18/31.

24 Smith, *14,000 miles through the air*, p. 40.

25 Ross Smith, telegrams to *The Sun*, SLNSW A1633.

26 Ross Smith, telegrams to *The Sun*, SLNSW A1633.

27 Smith, 'England to Australia flight' (report to Vickers Limited), 18 April 1920, NAUK AIR1/2193/244/2.

28 Ross Smith, telegrams to *The Sun*, SLNSW A1633.

29 Smith, *14,000 miles through the air*, p. 43.

30 Semple, *Airway to the East 1918–1920*, pp. 41–2.

31 Smith, *14,000 miles through the air*, pp. 43–4.

32 Smith, *14,000 miles through the air*, p. 46.

33 Reminiscences by W.H. Shiers, 1967, SLSA PRG 7/2/55.

34 Ross to Borton, 26 November 1919, SLSA PRG 106/7/1.

35 Smith, *14,000 miles through the air*, p. 49; Keith to Jessie Smith, 19 November 1919, PRG 18/28.

36 Semple, *Airway to the East 1918–1920*, p. 160.

29 Do your best but do nothing foolhardy

1 'Proposed timetable stopping places and distances for Vickers Vimy flight to Australia', n.d., SLSA PRG 18/26

2 Smith, *14,000 miles through the air*, p. 52.

3 'Aerial voyage', *Daily Herald* (Adelaide), 20 November 1919, p. 5.

4 'Aerial voyage', *Daily Herald* (Adelaide), 20 November 1919, p. 5.

5 'Nothing foolhardy', *The Sun* (Sydney), 18 November 1919, p. 7.

6 'The moving picture show', *The Sun*, 21 November 1919, p. 4.

7 'Hughes' message', *The World* (Hobart), 30 October 1919, p. 5.

8 Ross Smith, telegrams to *The Sun*, SLNSW A1633.

9 'Greatest story of the air', *The Sun* (Sydney), 12 December 1919, p. 1.

10 Keith to Jessie Smith, 22 November 1919, SLSA PRG 18/24.

11 Smith, *14,000 miles through the air*, p. 54.

12 Smith, 'England to Australia flight', 18 April 1920, NAUK AIR1/2193/244/2.

13 Ross to Borton, 26 November 1919, SLSA PRG 106/7/1.

14 Smith, 'England to Australia flight', 18 April 1920, NAUK AIR1/2193/244/2.

15 Keith Smith, diary, 20 November 1919, SLSA PRG 18/31.

16 Keith Smith, diary, 23 November 1919, SLSA PRG 18/31.

17 Smith, *14,000 miles through the air*, p. 62.

18 Smith, 'England to Australia flight', (report to Vickers Limited) 18 April 1920, NAUK AIR1/2193/244/2.

19 Keith to Jessie Smith, 22 November 1919, SLSA PRG 18/24.

20 Smith, 'England to Australia flight', (report to Vickers Limited) 18 April 1920, NAUK AIR1/2193/244/2.

21 Ross to Jessie Smith, 22 November 1919, SLSA PRG 18/28.

30 Chasing Poulet

1 Keith Smith, diary, 23 November 1919, SLSA PRG 18/31.

2 Keith to Andrew Smith, 24 November 1919, SLSA PRG 18/28.

3 Smith, *14,000 miles through the air*, pp. 73–4.

4 Smith, *14,000 miles through the air*, pp. 65–9.

5 Smith, *14,000 miles through the air*, pp. 68.

6 Keith Smith, diary, 25 November 1919, SLSA PRG 18/31.

7 Smith, *14,000 miles through the air*, p. 76.

8 Keith to Andrew Smith, 25 November 1919, SLSA PRG 18/28.

9 Smith, *14,000 miles through the air*, p. 76.

10 Smith, *14,000 miles through the air*, p. 76.

11 Smith, *14,000 miles through the air*, p. 76.

12 'Australian flight', *The Times of India* (Bombay), 27 November 1919, p. 9.

13 Smith, 'England to Australia flight' (report to Vickers Limited), 18 April 1920, NAUK AIR1/2193/244/2.

14 Ross to Borton, 25 January 1920, SLSA PRG 1067/1/2.

15 Smith, *14,000 miles through the air*, p. 78.

16 Keith Smith, diary, 26 November 1919, SLSA PRG 18/31.

17 Smith, 'England to Australia flight' (report to Vickers Limited), 18 April 1920, NAUK AIR1/2193/244/2.

18 Smith, *14,000 miles through the air*, p. 78.

19 Keith to Jessie Smith, 27 November 1919, SLSA PRG 18/28.

20 Smith, *14,000 miles through the air*, p. 80.

21 'Flight to Australia', *The Express and Telegraph* (Adelaide), 28 November 1919, p. 1.

22 Smith, 'England to Australia flight' (report to Vickers Limited), 18 April 1920, NAUK AIR1/2193/244/2; Keith Smith, diary, 28 November 1919, SLSA PRG 18/31.

23 'Australian flight', *The Times of India*, 29 November 1919, p. 11.

24 'Australian flight', *The Times of India*, 29 November 1919, p. 11.

25 'Captain Ross Smith in Calcutta—a brilliant reception', *The Bengalee* (Calcutta), 29 November 1919, p. 6.

26 'Calcutta letter', *The Times of India*, 5 December 1919, p. 8.

27 'To Australia by air', *The Times of India*, 26 November 1919, p. 9.

28 'Australian flight', *The Times of India*, 29 November 1919, p. 11.

29 'Captain Ross Smith in Calcutta—a brilliant reception', *The Bengalee*, 29 November 1919, p. 6.

30 Smith, *14,000 miles through the air*, p. 81.

31 'Captain Ross Smith's departure—farewell at the Maidan', *The Bengalee*, 30 November 1919, p. 4.

32 'Captain Ross Smith's departure—farewell at the Maidan', *The Bengalee*, 30 November 1919, p. 4.

33 Ross to Borton, 25 January 1920, SLSA PRG 1067/1/2.

34 Smith, *14,000 miles through the air*, p. 82.

35 Smith, *14,000 miles through the air*, p. 82; Smith, 'England to Australia flight' (report to Vickers Limited), 18 April 1920, NAUK AIR1/2193/244/2.

36 Smith, *14,000 miles through the air*, p. 82.

31 The Far East

1 Smith, *14,000 miles through the air*, pp. 73–4.

2 Keith Smith, diary, 30 November 1919, SLSA PRG 18/31.

3 Smith, *14,000 miles through the air*, p. 85.

4 Smith, *14,000 miles through the air*, p. 85.

5 'Flight to Australia', *The Maitland Daily Mercury*, 1 December 1919, p. 2.

6 Keith Smith, diary, 30 November 1919, SLSA PRG 18/31.

7 Smith, *14,000 miles through the air*, p. 88.

8 Smith, *14,000 miles through the air*, p. 88.

9 Different sources provide different maximum altitudes for the day. Keith claims that it was 8000 feet in his diary (the most contemporaneous source). Ross stated in his report to Vickers that they had to climb to 9000 feet. In *14,000 miles through the air* he says that they went to 11,000 feet. The Vickers Vimy, equipped with Rolls-Royce Eagle VIII engines, had a service ceiling of 7000 feet and an absolute ceiling of 10,500 feet.

10 Smith, *14,000 miles through the air*, p. 90.

11 Smith, *14,000 miles through the air*, pp. 92–3.

12 Smith, *14,000 miles through the air*, pp. 92–3.

13 Smith, *14,000 miles through the air*, pp. 92–3.

14 Smith, *14,000 miles through the air*, pp. 93–4.

15 Keith Smith, diary, 2 December 1919, SLSA PRG 18/31.

16 Smith, 'England to Australia flight' (report to Vickers Limited), 18 April 1920, NAUK AIR1/2193/244/2.

17 Ross Smith to Vickers Limited (Sydney), 2 January 1920, SLSA PRG 18/28.

18 Smith, 'England to Australia flight' (report to Vickers Limited), 18 April 1920, NAUK AIR1/2193/244/2.

19 Smith, 'England to Australia flight' (report to Vickers Limited), 18 April 1920, NAUK AIR1/2193/244/2.

20 Smith, *14,000 miles through the air*, pp. 98–9.

21 Smith, *14,000 miles through the air*, pp. 98–9.

22 Keith Smith, diary, 2 December 1919, SLSA PRG 18/31.

23 'The England to Australia flight', *Flight*, 18 December 1919, p. 1621.

24 'Greatest story of the air', *The Sun* (Sydney), 12 December 1919, p. 1.

25 Smith, 'England to Australia flight' (report to Vickers Limited), 18 April 1920, NAUK AIR1/2193/244/2.

26 Smith, 'England to Australia flight' (report to Vickers Limited), 18 April 1920, NAUK AIR1/2193/244/2.

27 Keith Smith, diary, 3 December 1919, SLSA PRG 18/31.

28 Keith Smith, diary, 3 December 1919, SLSA PRG 18/31; Smith, *14,000 miles through the air*, p. 101.

29 Smith, *14,000 miles through the air*, p. 101.

30 'Greatest story of the air', *The Sun* (Sydney), 12 December 1919, p. 1.

31 Smith, 'England to Australia flight', 18 April 1920, NAUK AIR1/2193/244/2.

32 Keith Smith, diary, 4 December 1919, SLSA PRG 18/31.

33 Smith, 'England to Australia flight', 18 April 1920, NAUK AIR1/2193/244/2.

34 Smith, 'England to Australia flight', 18 April 1920, NAUK AIR1/2193/244/2.

35 'The course', *The Singapore Free Press and Mercantile Advertiser*, 5 December 1919, p. 6.

36 'Singapore and Aviation, *Malaya Tribune* (Singapore), 4 December 1919, p. 4.

37 'The airman arrives', *Malaya Tribune*, 5 December 1919, p. 5.

38 'The airman arrives', *Malaya Tribune*, 5 December 1919, p. 5.

39 'St Andrew's School', *The Singapore Free Press and Mercantile Advertiser*, 5 December 1919, p. 12.

40 Smith, 'England to Australia flight' (report to Vickers Limited), 18 April 1920, NAUK AIR1/2193/244/2.

41 'Aviators arrive', *The Straits Times* (Singapore), 5 December 1919, p. 9.

42 'Flight to Australia', *The Singapore Free Press and Mercantile Advertiser*, 5 December 1919, p. 6.

43 'Aviators arrive', *The Straits Times*, 5 December 1919, p. 9.

44 'Aviators arrive', *The Straits Times*, 5 December 1919, p. 9; 'Vimy's flight', *The Beaudesert Times*, 13 February 1920, p. 4.

45 'The course', *The Singapore Free Press and Mercantile Advertiser*, 5 December 1919, p. 6.
46 'Airmen entertained', *Malaya Tribune*, 5 December 1919, p. 4.
47 'ASD Entertainment', *The Straits Times*, 5 December 1919, p. 10.
48 'Airmen entertained', *Malaya Tribune*, 5 December 1919, p. 4.

32 The bamboo runway

1 'The airman arrives', *Malaya Tribune* (Singapore), 5 December 1919, p. 5.
2 Secretary of the Governor-General (Dutch East Indies) to the Consulate-General of the Netherlands in Singapore, 29 November 1919, SLSA PRG 18/28.
3 Smith, 'England to Australia Flight' (report to Vickers Limited), 18 April 1920, NAUK AIR1/2193/244/2.
4 Smith, *14,000 miles through the air*, p. 107.
5 Smith, *14,000 miles through the air*, p. 108.
6 Smith, 'England to Australia flight' (report to Vickers Limited), 18 April 1920, NAUK AIR1/2193/244/2.
7 'The airmen depart', *Malaya Tribune* (Singapore), 6 December 1919, p. 4.
8 Smith, *14,000 miles through the air*, p. 108.
9 'The airmen depart', *Malaya Tribune*, 6 December 1919, p. 4.
10 Ross and Keith Smith notebook, SLSA PRG 18/30.
11 Smith, *14,000 miles through the air*, p. 108.
12 Ross and Keith Smith notebook, SLSA PRG 18/30.
13 Smith, 'England to Australia flight' (report to Vickers Limited), 18 April 1920, NAUK AIR1/2193/244/2.
14 Keith Smith, diary, 6 December 1919, SLSA PRG 18/31.
15 Ross and Keith Smith notebook, SLSA PRG 18/30.
16 Smith, 'England to Australia flight', 18 April 1920, NAUK AIR1/2193/244/2; Smith, *14,000 miles through the air*, p. 111.
17 'Ter onvangst van den Australie-vlieger', *Bataviaasch Nieuwsblad*, 6 December 1919 (second edition), p. 1.
18 'De vlucht van Ross Smyth', *Bataviaasch Nieuwsblad*, 8 December 1919 (first edition), p. 1.
19 'Ross Smith's own story of flight from London to Darwin', *The Herald* (Melbourne), 12 December 1919, p. 1.
20 Smith, 'England to Australia flight' (report to Vickers Limited), 18 April 1920, NAUK AIR1/2193/244/2.
21 Smith, *14,000 miles through the air*, p. 114.

22 Smith, *14,000 miles through the air*, p. 116.
23 Smith, *14,000 miles through the air*, p. 117.
24 Ross Smith's own story of flight from London to Darwin', *The Herald* (Melbourne), 12 December 1919, p. 1.
25 Reminiscences by W.H. Shiers on flight, 1967, SLSA PRG 7/2/55 p. 37.
26 Smith, *14,000 miles through the air*, p. 118.
27 Keith Smith, diary, 8 December 1919, SLSA PRG 18/31.
28 'De vlucht Europa-Australië', *Het nieuws van den dag voor Nederlandsch-Indië*, 8 December 1919, p. 5.
29 Smith, 'England to Australia flight' (report to Vickers Limited), 18 April 1920, NAUK AIR1/2193/244/2.
30 Notes on Sheet 49, SLNSW M Z/MT3 118gmof/1919/1.
31 Keith Smith, diary, 8 December 1919, SLSA PRG 18/31.
32 Smith, *14,000 miles through the air*, p. 120.
33 Secretary of the Governor-General (Dutch East Indies) to the Consulate-General of the Netherlands in Singapore, 29 November 1919, SLSA PRG 18/28.
34 Notes on Sheet 54, SLNSW M Z/MT3 118gmof/1919/1.
35 'Ross Smith's own story of flight from London to Darwin', *The Herald* (Melbourne), 12 December 1919, p. 1.
36 Notes on Sheet 54, SLNSW M Z/MT3 118gmof/1919/1.
37 Notes on Sheet 54, SLNSW M Z/MT3 118gmof/1919/1.
38 Ross to Borton, 25 January 1920, SLSA PRG 106/7/2.
39 'Ross Smith's own story of flight from London to Darwin', *The Herald* (Melbourne), 12 December 1919, p. 1.
40 Smith, *14,000 miles through the air*, p. 120.

33 The supreme hour of our lives

1 'The great flight', *Northern Territory Times and Gazette* (Darwin), 13 December 1919, p. 5.
2 Keith Smith, diary, 10 December 1919, SLSA PRG 18/31; Smith, 'England to Australia flight', 18 April 1920, NAUK AIR1/2193/244/2.
3 Smith, 'England to Australia flight', 18 April 1920, NAUK AIR1/2193/244/2.
4 Smith, *14,000 miles through the air*, p. 128.
5 Keith Smith, diary, 10 December 1919, SLSA PRG 18/31.
6 Notes on Sheet 54, SLNSW M Z/MT3 118gmof/1919/1.
7 Keith Smith, diary, 11 December 1919, SLSA PRG 18/31.

8 Bottle containing a message, which was dropped from the plane by Ross Smith and party on the first flight from England to Australia, and picked up by HMAS *Sydney*, 1919; with typescript statement by Capt. Cayley of HMAS *Sydney*, 1922, SLNSW R 109.

9 'The great flight', *Northern Territory Times and Gazette*, 13 December 1919, p. 5.

10 That Ross felt regret that Borton could not join them during the flight is evident in Ross to Borton, 26 November 1919, SLSA PRG 106/7/1.

11 Smith, *14,000 miles through the air*, p. 125.

12 'Journey's end', *The Sun*, 11 December 1919, p. 1.

13 'The great flight', *Northern Territory Times and Gazette*, 13 December 1919, p. 5.

14 'Journey's end', *The Sun*, 11 December 1919, p. 1.

15 'The great flight', *Northern Territory Times and Gazette*, 13 December 1919, p. 5.

16 Smith, *14,000 miles through the air*, p. 125.

17 Fysh, *Qantas rising*, p. 88.

18 'The great flight', *Northern Territory Times and Gazette*, 13 December 1919, p. 5.

19 'The great flight', *Northern Territory Times and Gazette*, 13 December 1919, p. 5.

20 Smith, *14,000 miles through the air*, p. 126.

21 'The great flight', *Northern Territory Times and Gazette*, 13 December 1919, p. 5.

22 'Dinner to the aviators', *Northern Territory Times and Gazette*, 20 December 1919, p. 11.

23 'The great flight', *Northern Territory Times and Gazette*, 13 December 1919, p. 5.

24 The great flight', *Northern Territory Times and Gazette*, 13 December 1919, p. 5.

34 Everyone has gone quite mad

1 'Most wonderful flight', *The Sun*, 13 December 1919, p. 1.

2 'Captain Smith's triumph', *New York Times*, 11 December 1919, p. 12.

3 Ross Smith to Vickers Limited (Sydney), 2 January 1920, SLSA PRG 18/28.

4 'Ross Smith flight', *Daily Examiner* (Grafton), 4 June 1920, p. 3.

5 'The call at Sydney demand', *The Sun*, 14 December 1919, p. 1.

6 'The great flight', *Northern Territory Times and Gazette*, 13 December 1919, p. 5.

7 Smith, 'England to Australia flight' (report to Vickers Limited), 18 April 1920, NAUK AIR1/2193/244/2.
8 Smith, 'England to Australia flight' (report to Vickers Limited), 18 April 1920, NAUK AIR1/2193/244/2.
9 Smith, *14,000 miles through the air*, pp. 129–30.
10 Smith, *14,000 miles through the air*, p. 181.
11 Ross Smith to Vickers (Sydney), 2 January 1920, SLSA PRG 18/28.
12 Barton Adams to Vickers Limited, 12 January 1920, NLA MS6093.
13 Smith, 'England to Australia flight', 18 April 1920, NAUK AIR1/2193/244/2.
14 Smith, *14,000 miles through the air*, p. 183.
15 'Ross Smith', *Northern Territory Times and Gazette*, 20 December 1919, p. 15.
16 'Ross Smith safe', *The Australasian*, 20 December 1918, p. 37.
17 Ross Smith to Vickers Limited (Sydney), 21 December 1919, NLA MS 6093.
18 Ross Smith to Vickers Limited (Sydney), 2 January 1920, SLSA PRG 18/28.
19 'Captain Sir Ross Smith, his brother also knighted', *Brisbane Courier*, 24 December 1919, p. 7.
20 'What will mother say?', *The Observer* (Adelaide), 3 January 1920, p. 33.
21 Controller-General of Civil Aviation to Secretary of State, minute sheet, 12 December 1919, NAUK AIR2/119.
22 Ross Smith to Amyas Borton, 25 January 1920, SLSA PRG 1067/2.
23 See correspondence on this within the Air Ministry in NAUK AIR2/119.
24 *Commonwealth of Australia Parliamentary Debates, Hansard*, House of Representatives, 26 February 1920, no. 9 1920.
25 'Ross Smith's engine fails', *Geelong Advertiser*, 27 December 1919, p. 3.
26 Reminiscences by W.H. Shiers, 1967, SLSA PRG 7/2/55.
27 Ross Smith to Vickers Limited (Sydney), 2 January 1920, SLSA PRG 18/28.
28 Ross Smith to Borton, 25 January 1920, SLSA PRG 1067/2.
29 'Ross Smith', *Northern Star* (Lismore), 1 January 1920, p. 5.
30 Keith Smith, diary, 25 December 1919, SLSA PRG 18/31.
31 Ross Smith to Vickers Limited (Sydney), 25 December 1919, NLA MS 6093.
32 Ross Smith to Vickers Limited (Sydney), 8 January 1920, NLA MS 6093.
33 Ross Smith to Vickers Limited (Sydney), 27 December 1919, NLA MS 6093.
34 Ross Smith to Vickers Limited (Sydney), 2 January 1920, SLSA PRG 18/28.
35 'Our flying knights', *Daily Mail* (Brisbane), 3 January 1919, p. 7.
36 'Message to his mother', *The Sun*, 7 January 1920, p. 3.
37 Ross Smith to Borton, 25 January 1919, SLSA PRG 1067/2.
38 'Our flying knights', *Daily Mail*, 3 January 1920, p. 7.

39 'An interesting interview', *Brisbane Courier*, 3 January 1920, p. 7.

40 'Air prize', *The Mail* (Brisbane), 3 January 1920, p. 2.

41 Alasdair McGregor, *Frank Hurley: A photographer's life*, Viking, 2004, p. 216.

35 Fame and fortune

1 'Australia from above—Captain Hurley's story', *The Sun* (Sydney), 15 February 1920, p. 1.

2 'Bells ring at Bathurst', *The Sun*, 14 February 1920, p. 5.

3 Smith, *14,000 miles through the air*, p. 185.

4 'Australia from above—Captain Hurley's story', *The Sun*, 15 February 1920, p. 1.

5 'The arrival', *The Sun*, 15 February 1920, p. 2.

6 Vickers to Ross Smith (cable), 13 December 1919, NLA MS 6093.

7 'The landing', *Sydney Morning Herald*, 16 February 1920, p. 7.

8 'Hounslow to the heads', *Daily Telegraph*, 16 February 1920, p. 5.

9 This photograph was published on the front page of the *Sunday Times* (Sydney), 15 February 1920, p. 1.

10 'The landing', *Sydney Morning Herald*, 16 February 1920, p. 7.

11 'A memorable day', *Sydney Morning Herald*, 16 February 1920, p. 7.

12 'Civic welcome', *Sydney Morning Herald*, 16 February 1920, p. 7.

13 'A memorable day', *Sydney Morning Herald*, 16 February 1920, p. 7.

14 Ross Smith to Amyas Borton, 10 May 1920, SLSA PRG1067/2.

15 'Hero worship', *The Sun*, 18 February 1920, p. 5.

16 'Marriage proposals made to flyers', *Riverine Herald* (Echuca), 28 February 1920, p. 2.

17 'Hero worship', *The Sun*, 18 February 1920, p. 5.

18 Ross Smith to Borton, 10 May 1920, SLSA PRG1067/2.

19 'The gallery voice', *The Sun*, 19 February 1920, p. 9; 'Voice in the gallery', *The Sun*, 23 February 1920, p. 4.

20 'The Vicars-Vimy' (sic), *The Wyalong Advocate and Mining, Agricultural and Pastoral Gazette*, 24 February 1920, p. 2.

21 'Captain Ross Smith', *The Age* (Melbourne), 17 February 1920, p. 8.

22 Ross Smith to Borton, 10 May 1920, SLSA PRG1067/1.

23 'Last night at Henty', *The Herald*, 25 February 1920, p. 1.

24 Secretary of the Prime Minister's Department to the Secretary of the Department of Defence, 22 March 1920, NAA MP367/1 415/1/1767.

25 'Sir Ross Smith goes shopping', *The Herald*, 26 February 1919, p. 1.

26 'Aerial mail carried', *The Herald*, 1 March 1920, p. 1.

27 'Airmen to lecture', *The Herald*, 1 March 1920, p. 1.

28 'Marriage proposals made to flyers', *Riverine Herald* (Echuca), 28 February 1920, p. 2.

36 Leaving an old and trusty friend

1 Ross to Jessie Smith, 28 November 1916, SLSA PRG 18/24.

2 'Ross Smith reaches Australia', *Daily Telegraph*, 11 December 1919, p. 5; 'Hope to fly to Adelaide', *Brisbane Courier*, 3 January 1920, p. 7.

3 Ross Smith to the Directors, Vickers Limited, London, 14 April 1920, SLSA PRG 18/28.

4 Ross Smith to the Directors, Vickers Limited, London, 14 April 1920, SLSA PRG 18/28.

5 Ross had made these arrangements and spoken to the press the previous day, 18 March 1920, but went to Parliament House for the official handover the following day: 'Adelaide flight sanctioned', *The Herald* (Melbourne), 18 March 1920, p. 1.

6 'Vickers-Vimy flies to Adelaide', *The Herald* (Melbourne), 23 March 1920, p. 1.

7 Ross Smith to the Directors, Vickers Limited, London, 14 April 1920, SLSA PRG 18/28.

8 'Wonderful trip across', *The Register* (Adelaide), 24 March 1920, p. 12.

9 'The engine lovers', *The Register*, 24 March 1920, p. 12.

10 'Wonderful trip across', *The Register*, 24 March 1920, p. 12.

11 'The landing', *The Advertiser* (Adelaide), 24 March 1920, p. 7.

12 'Sir Ross Smith's views', *The Sun*, 19 April 1920, p. 1.

13 'Historic flight concluded famous aviators welcomed home', *Daily Herald* (Adelaide), 24 March 1920, p. 2.

14 'The landing', *The Advertiser*, 24 March 1920, p. 7.

15 'The landing', *The Advertiser*, 24 March 1920, p. 7.

16 'Ross Smith's return', *The Herald*, 27 March 1920, p. 1.

17 Ross to the Directors, Vickers Limited, London, 14 April 1920, SLSA PRG 18/28; 'The Vickers Vimy', *The Register*, 1 April 1920, p. 6.

18 Ross Smith to Borton, 10 May 1920, SLSA PRG 1067/1.

19 Ross Smith to Borton, 10 May 1920, SLSA PRG 1067/1; John Howard to A. Grenfell Price, 3 February 1967, SLSA PRG 7/2/51.

20 'Flying', *Daily Herald*, 8 April 1920, p. 3.

21 'Flying', *Daily Herald*, 8 April 1920, p. 3.

37 The aristocracy of achievement

1 'Two words to the foot', *The Sun* (Sydney), 26 April 1920, p. 4.

2 'Ross Smith flight', *Daily Mail* (Brisbane), 25 May 1920, p. 3.

3 It appears that a full-length assembly of the two-and-a-half-hour film that Hurley and Ross toured has not survived. A 45-minute cut, with intertitles, that appears to be a complete and stand-alone feature (and hence may have been screened after the lecture tour as a re-run), survives in the collection of the National Film and Sound Archive of Australia, Item 1535.

4 McGregor, *Frank Hurley: A photographer's life*, p. 218.

5 Robert Dixon, *Photography, early cinema and colonial modernity: Frank Hurley's synchronized lecture entertainments*, Anthem Press, London, 2012, p. 162.

6 Frank Hurley, 'The Ross Smith flight from London to Australia', NFSA, 1535; Dixon, *Photography, early cinema and colonial modernity*, p. 159.

7 Frank Hurley, 'Ross Smith as I knew him', *Life* (Melbourne), pp. 520–2.

8 Ross Smith to Amyas Borton, 10 May 1920, SLSA PRG 1067/1.

9 'Advertising', *The Register* (Adelaide), 1 May 1920, p. 10.

10 'Ross Smith flight', *Daily Mail*, 25 May 1920, p. 3.

11 'Advertising', *The Advertiser* (Adelaide), 11 May 1920, p. 8.

12 'The moving row of magic and shadow shapes', *The Sun*, 13 June 1920, p. 16.

13 'Ross Smith flight film', *Evening News* (Sydney), 16 June 1920, p. 11.

14 'Aviators to lecture', *The Herald* (Melbourne), 2 March 1920, p. 1.

15 'Late Sir Ross Smith', *The Telegraph* (Brisbane), 12 December 1923, p. 2.

16 'England to Australia', *Daily Herald* (Adelaide), 4 May 1920, p. 3.

17 'The great flight', *The Telegraph* (Brisbane), 26 May 1920, p. 3.

18 'The Ross Smith films', *Sunday Times* (Sydney), 13 June 1920, p. 3.

19 'The moving row of magic shadow shapes', *The Sun*, 13 June 1920, p. 16.

20 'A woman's Melbourne letter', *Western Mail* (Perth), 15 July 1920, p. 29.

21 'Sir Ross Smith', *National Advocate* (Bathurst), 1 July 1920, p. 3.

22 Ross to Borton, 10 May 1920, SLSA PRG 1067/1.

23 'Sir Ross Smith', *Sydney Morning Herald*, 11 June 1920, p. 10.

24 'Commercial aviation', *The Sun*, 11 June 1920, p. 4.

25 See, for example, 'Ross Smith coming west', *Call* (Perth), 16 July 1920, p. 2.

26 Ross to Borton, 10 May 1920, SLSA PRG 1067/1.

27 'Sir Ross Smith's plans', *The Herald* (Melbourne), 21 August 1920, p. 1.

28 Keith Isaacs, 'Parer, Raymond John Paul (1894–1967)', *Australian Dictionary of Biography*, National Centre of Biography, Australian National University,

<http://adb.anu.edu.au/biography/parer-raymond-john-paul-7951/text13841>, published first in hardcopy 1988, accessed 3 December 2018.

29 'Parer's flight', *The Australasian* (Melbourne), 28 August 1920, p. 40; 'Wonderful stunt', *The Sun*, 23 August 1920, p. 5.

30 'Reception arranged at Flemington race course on 24th February 1920 for the arrival of the winners of the England/Australia aeroplane flight competition', n.d., NAA MP367/1 415/1/1767.

31 *The last flight of the late Capt. C.E. Howell DSO, MC, DFC, Royal Air Force and his mysterious death at Corfu: An appeal*, self-published, Melbourne, 1920, pp. 4–5. A copy of this pamphlet is in the papers of Sir Archibald Grenfell Price, SLSA PRG 7/2/54.

32 Ross Smith to George Pearce, 10 September 1920, SLSA PRG 7/2/46.

33 G.C. Matthews to Ross Smith, 9 September 1920, SLSA PRG 7/2/46.

34 'Flying light', *The Sun*, 8 December 1919, p. 1.

35 Six of the seven issues featuring Ross's serialised story are held at *Life: A record for busy folk*, May–October 1920, SLNSW Q059/L.

36 Ross Smith, 'From London to Australia by aeroplane: A personal narrative of the first aerial voyage halfway around the world', *National Geographic* (Washington), vol. 39, no. 3, 1921, 229–39.

37 Dixon, *Photography, early cinema and colonial modernity*, p. 155.

38 Smith, *14,000 miles through the air*, pp. v–vi.

39 'Greatest story of the air', *The Sun*, 12 December 1919, p. 1.

40 'The first aerial voyage from London to Australia', NLA MS 883, Series 1, Item 14.

38 Viking

1 Hurley, 'Ross Smith as I knew him', p. 521. The timing of this is corroborated by Keith's claim, in September 1921, that plans had been underway for a round-the-world flight for eighteen months: 'Air race round world', *Daily Mail* (London), 29 September 1921, p. 5.

2 'Imperial and foreign news items', *The Times* (London), 21 August 1920, p. 9; 'Foreign news', *Aerial Age Weekly* (New York), 20 September 1920, vol. 12, no. 2, p. 54.

3 'World flight', *Daily Herald* (Adelaide), 21 August 1920, p. 4.

4 'Personal', *The West Australian* (Perth), 27 October 1920, p. 6; 'Mainly about people', *Daily News* (Perth), 28 October 1920, p. 3; 'Happenings in two hemispheres: What the world is doing and saying', *Sunday Times* (Perth), 31 October 1928, p. 10.

5 'Australia and aviation', *The Times of India* (Mumbai), 8 November 1920, p. 12.

6 Ross Smith to Janette Verney, 25 October 1920, SLSA PRG 18/63.

7 'Australia's pilots', *Daily Herald* (Adelaide), 5 February 1921, p. 5.

8 'The greatest flight', *Daily Herald*, 21 February 1921, p. 5.

9 *Weybridge World Fliers 1921*, British Pathé film archive, 228.45.

10 'Australian airmen at Weybridge', *The Times*, 23 February 1921, p. 9.

11 Ross Smith to Janette Verney, n.d. ['1922' is annotated on this letter but its content suggests c. June 1921], SLSA PRG 18/63.

12 'Boyhood days', *The Herald* (Melbourne), 24 February 1924, p. 1.

13 Ross Smith, manuscript notes on England to Australia air service, 7 July 1921, NLA MS 1538 Series 25 Folder 18.

14 'Up in the air', *The Sun* (Sydney), 18 July 1921, p. 1.

15 'Conference of Prime Ministers and Representatives of the United Kingdom, the Dominions, and India (Summary of Proceedings and Documents of the), Held in June, July, and August, 1921, at London', Appendix to the Journals of the House of Representatives, New Zealand, 1921 Session I-II, A-04.

16 Ross Smith to Janette Verney, 13 January 1922, SLSA PRG 18/63.

17 Ross Smith to Vickers Limited, 17 January 1922, SLSA PRG 18/35.

18 Ross Smith to Janette Verney, 13 January 1922, SLSA PRG 18/63.

19 'Vickers Vimy useful loads at various distances', 18 July 1921, NLA M2587-2590.

20 'Air race round world', *Daily Mail*, 29 September 1921, p. 5.

21 Memorandum to the chairman, Vickers Limited, 8 December 1921, NLA M2587-2590.

22 Ross Smith to Janette Verney, 9 December 1921, SLSA PRG 18/63.

23 Lt Col Whiston A. Bristow, Director, Ogilvie and Partners Limited to Captain Acland, 14 December 1921, NLA M2587-2590.

24 'The Sun aids flight', *The Sun*, 12 March 1922, p. 2.

25 Ross to Janette Verney, 13 January 1922, SLSA PRG 18/63.

26 Ross Smith to Air Ministry, 21 January 1922, NLA M2587-2590.

27 Translation of Tomas Borras, 'On aerial roads: round the world in an aeroplane—the brothers Ross and Keith Smith', *El Sol*, 10 December 1921, NLA M2587-2590.

28 'World flight', *The Sun*, 6 April 1922, p. 1.

29 'World flight', *Daily Telegraph* (London), 13 April 1922, p. 11.

30 Peter Pigott, *On Canadian wings: A century of flight*, Hounslow, Toronto, 2005, p. 54.

31 Ross Smith to Vickers Limited, 17 January 1922, SLSA PRG 18/35.

32 'Statement on accident to Vickers Viking IV G-EBBZ at Brooklands on 13th April 1922', 17 May 1922, NAUK AVIA 2125; 'It's a pearl', *The Sun*, 12 April 1922, p. 1.
33 'Intending world fliers killed', *Evening Telegraph*, 13 April 1922, p. 1.
34 Vickers Limited to Major A.T. Cooper, Air Ministry, 3 May 1922, NLA M2587-2590.
35 'World flight', *The Sun*, 6 April 1922, p. 1.
36 'Sir Ross Smith's Flight', *The Times*, 13 April 1922, p. 9.
37 'It's a pearl', *The Sun*, 12 April 1922, p. 1.
38 'Sir Ross Smith's Flight', *The Times*, 13 April 1922, p. 9.
39 'It's a pearl', *The Sun*, 12 April 1922, p. 1.

39 Valhalla

1 'Statement on accident to Vickers Viking IV G-EBBZ at Brooklands on 13th April 1922', 17 May 1922, NAUK AVIA 2125; 'Flight disaster', *Daily Telegraph* (London), 15 April 1922, p. 9.
2 'Lost pioneers', *Aberdeen Journal*, 15 April 1922, p. 5.
3 'Brooklands', *Exeter and Plymouth Gazette*, 17 April 1922, p. 6.
4 'Sir Ross Smith's death', *The Times* (London), 17 April 1922, p. 17.
5 'Flight disaster', *Daily Telegraph*, 15 April 1922, p. 9.
6 'Sir Ross Smith killed', *Aberdeen Journal*, 14 April 1922, p. 5.
7 'Flight disaster', *Daily Telegraph*, 15 April 1922, p. 9; 'Statement on accident to Vickers Viking IV G-EBBZ at Brooklands on 13th April 1922', 17 May 1922, NAUK AVIA 2125.
8 'Statement on accident', 17 May 1922, NAUK AVIA 2125.
9 'Sir Ross Smith killed', *The Times*, 15 April 1922, p. 12.
10 'Statement on accident', 17 May 1922, NAUK AVIA 2125.
11 'Sir Ross Smith killed', *The Times*, 15 April 1922, p. 12.
12 'Statement on accident', 17 May 1922, NAUK AVIA 2125. The motorcyclist Claude Temple, who was perhaps closest to the aircraft when it went into a spin, also reported that he heard the engine stop before the aircraft started spinning: 'Sir Ross Smith's death', *The Times*, 17 April 1922, p. 17. Another witness, not named but described as an experienced pilot, claimed the engine was 'running full' when the turn was made: 'Flight disaster', *Daily Telegraph*, 15 April 1922, p. 9.
13 'Sir Ross Smith killed', *Aberdeen Journal*, 14 April 1922, p. 5.
14 'Airman's fatal pause', *Aberdeen Journal*, 17 April 1922, p. 5.
15 'Sir Ross Smith killed', *The Times*, 15 April 1922, p. 12.

16 'Sir Ross Smith's death', *The Times*, 17 April 1922, p. 17.
17 'Sir Ross Smith killed', *The Times*, 15 April 1922, p. 12.
18 'Sir Ross Smith's death', *The Times*, 17 April 1922, p. 17.
19 'Flight disaster', *Daily Telegraph*, 15 April 1922, p. 9.
20 'Sir Ross Smith killed', *The Times*, 15 April 1922, p. 12.
21 'Ross Smith's death', *The Argus* (Melbourne), 19 May 1922, p. 7.
22 'Cheerio!', *The Register* (Adelaide), 17 April 1922, p. 5.
23 'Sir Ross Smith killed', *Aberdeen Journal*, 14 April 1922, p. 5.
24 'Flight disaster', *Daily Telegraph*, 15 April 1922, p. 9; 'Sir Ross Smith killed', *The Times*, 15 April 1922, p. 12; 'Cheerio!', *The Register* (Adelaide), 17 April 1922, p. 5.
25 'Flight disaster', *Daily Telegraph*, 15 April 1922, p. 9.

40 Now he belongs to the empire

1 'Sir Ross Smith killed', *The Times* (London), 15 April 1922, p. 12.
2 'Brooklands', *Exeter and Plymouth Gazette*, 17 April 1922, p. 6; 'Statement on accident to Vickers Viking IV G-EBBZ at Brooklands on 13th April 1922', 17 May 1922, NAUK AVIA 2/125.
3 Walter Caddell to The Secretary, Air Ministry, 25 May 1922, NAUK AVIA 2/125.
4 Vickers Limited to Major A.T. Cooper, Air Ministry, 3 May 1922, NLA M2587-2590.
5 Smith, 'England to Australia flight', 18 April 1920, NAUK AIR1/2193/244/2.
6 Ross to Janette Verney, 13 January 1922, SLSA PRG 18/63; 'Air girdle round world', *The Sun*, 12 March 1922, p. 2; 'Late cable news Sir Ross Smith's flight', *Sydney Morning Herald*, 20 March 1922, p. 9.
7 'Machine of the future', *The Sun* (Sydney), 20 February 1921, p. 1; 'Threat of paralysis', *The Sun*, 25 February 1921, p. 1.
8 'Preparations for trip', *The Register* (Adelaide), 17 April 1922, p. 5; 'Sir Ross Smith's flight', *The Times*, 13 April 1922, p. 9; 'Lost pioneers', *Aberdeen Journal*, 15 April 1922, p. 5.
9 'It's a pearl', *The Sun*, 12 April 1922, p. 1.
10 'News from Sir Keith Smith', *The Register* (Adelaide), 15 April 1922, p. 7.
11 'Adelaide shocked', *The Sun*, 16 April 1922, p. 2.
12 'Mother's tribute', *The Register*, 20 April 1922, p. 7.
13 'Ross Smith', *The Chronicle* (Adelaide), 17 June 1922, p. 37.
14 'Ross Smith', *The Chronicle*, 17 June 1922, p. 37.
15 'Ross Smith', *The Chronicle*, 17 June 1922, p. 37.
16 'The concourse of mourners', *The Journal* (Adelaide), 15 June 1922, p. 1.

17 'A national hero mourned', *The Advertiser* (Adelaide), 16 June 1922, p. 9.
18 'A true knight', *The Journal*, 15 June 1922, p. 1.
19 'A national hero mourned', *The Advertiser*, 16 June 1922, p. 9.
20 'Gallant airman's grave', *The Register*, 15 June 1922, p. 7.
21 'A national hero mourned', *The Advertiser*, 16 June 1922, p. 9.
22 'Death and life', *The Express and Telegraph* (Adelaide), 16 June 1922, p. 2.

Epilogue

1 'Obituary', *The Chronicle* (Adelaide), 22 November 1924, p. 44.
2 'The late Andrew Smith', *The Observer* (Adelaide), 22 November 1924, p. 38.
3 'Queen's College hero', *The Advertiser* (Adelaide), 12 December 1932, p. 10; 'First plane flight to Australia', *The Advertiser*, 11 December 1939, p. 14; 'Epic flight recalled', *The Advertiser*, 11 December 1944, p. 4.
4 Keith Smith to Peter Acland, 15 July 1922, NLA M2587-2590.
5 Acland to Keith Smith, 27 July 1922, NLA M2587-2590.
6 Sutherland and Ellison, *Aces and kings*, p. 34.
7 Borton to Dickson, 29 May 1967, SLSA PRG 7/2/51.
8 Borton and Slater, *My warrior sons*, p. 220.
9 Fysh, *Qantas rising*, p. 268.
10 'Ross Smith diary', *The Sun* (Sydney), 13 December 1919, p. 1.
11 Minutes of the Sir Ross Smith Fund Executive Committee, 23 November 1922, SLSA SRG 787/1.
12 'The Ross Smith Memorial', *The Advertiser*, 10 December 1919, p. 12.
13 A. Grenfell Price, *The skies remember: The story of Ross and Keith Smith*, Angus & Robertson, Sydney, 1969; Nelson Eustis, *The greatest air race: England–Australia 1919*, Rigby, Adelaide, 1969.
14 Royal Australian Air Force, 'Sir Ross Smith commemoration service', <www.airforce.gov.au/news-and-events/events/general/sir-ross-smith-commemoration-service consulted 16 January 2019>, accessed 16 January 2019.
15 South Australian History Trust, 'Epic flight centenary', <https://history.sa.gov.au/events/centenary-of-epic-flight>, accessed 16 January 2019.

INDEX